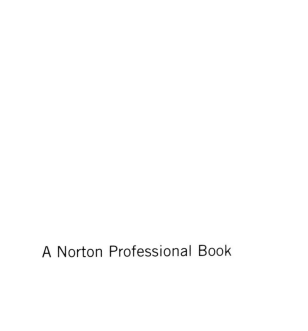

A Norton Professional Book

EMDR SOLUTIONS II

*For Depression, Eating Disorders,
Performance, and More*

Robin Shapiro, Editor

W. W. Norton & Company
New York • London

For information about permission to
reproduce selections from this book, write to
Permissions, W. W. Norton & Company, Inc.,
500 Fifth Avenue, New York, NY 10110

For information about special discounts for bulk
purchases, please contact W. W. Norton
Special Sales at specialsales@wwnorton.com or 800-233-4830

Manufacturing by Courier Westford
Book design by Bytheway Publishing Services
Production manager: Leeann Graham

Library of Congress Cataloging-in-Publication Data

EMDR solutions II : for depression, eating disorders, performance and
  more / Robin Shapiro, editor. — 1st ed.
       p.   cm.
   Includes bibliographical references and index.
   ISBN 978-0-393-70588-1 (hardcover)
   1. Eye movement desensitization and reprocessing.   2. Psychic
trauma—Treatment.   3. Depression, Mental—Treatment.   4. Eating
disorders—Treatment.   I. Shapiro, Robin.
   RC489.E98E468 2005
   616.85′2—dc22   2009004494

   ISBN: 978-0-393-70588-1

W. W. Norton & Company, Inc., 500 Fifth Avenue, New York, N.Y. 10110
www.wwnorton.com

W. W. Norton & Company Ltd., Castle House, 75/76 Wells St., London W1T 3QT

1   2   3   4   5   6   7   8   9   0

To Doug Plummer, my beloved, for all that you are

To the EMDR HAP staff and volunteers,
for your generous good works

Contents

Contributors

Cheryl Clayton, L.C.S.W., is in private practice in Virginia. She has specialized in the treatment of adolescent and adult sexual offenders and their families since 1994. She has published articles and presented at state and national conferences on the use of EMDR with sexual offenders.

Linda J. Cooke, L.C.S.W., B.C.D., is in private practice in Kennebunk, Maine, and is a lecturer at Boston College in Chestnut Hill, Massachusetts. She is certified in EMDR and is an EMDR consultant. Ms. Cooke has over 15 years of clinical, supervision, and consultation experience and works with adolescents, adults, and families. She specializes in the treatment of individuals with eating disorders, complex trauma, and dissociation.

Katherine Davis is a social worker in private practice in New Haven, CT and an EMDR trainer for the EMDR Humanitarian Assistance Programs. She was the clinical director of Hamden Mental Health Center and is the coauthor of Connecticut's first child-abuse law and two EMDR HAP specialty workshops, and an article in F. Shapiro, F. W. Kaslow, and L. Maxfield (eds.), 2007 *Handbook of EMDR and Family Therapy Processes.*

DaLene Forester, Ph.D., L.M.F.T., is the clinical director of New Directions to Hope, a nonprofit counseling center in Redding, California, and the director and trainer with Advanced Education Institute, a provider of continuing education for psychotherapists, also in Redding, California. DaLene specializes in the treatment of eating disorders and posttraumatic stress disorder (PTSD). She is an EMDRIA-Approved Consultant and Trainer.

Celia Grand, L.C.S.W., B.C.D., is a psychotherapist in private practice in Cape Elizabeth, Maine, specializing in trauma treatment of adults and couples. Trained in Sensorimotor Psychotherapy, EMDR, and Psychosynthesis, she is on the faculty of the Sensorimotor Psychotherapy Institute, an EMDR facilitator and consultant, and served on the EMDR International Association board.

David Grand, Ph.D., is an EMDR Institute Facilitator and EMDRIA-Approved Consultant and Trainer. He is the author of *Emotional Healing at Warp Speed: The Power of EMDR* (Random House, 2001). Dr. Grand is a national and international lecturer on the topic of EMDR and performance and creativity enhancement. He is in practice in New York City and has appeared on *NBC Nightly News,* CNN, the Discovery Channel, and in articles in the *New York Times, O, The Oprah Magazine,* and *Newsday.* Dr Grand is the developer of BioLateral Sound CDs for EMDR, which have sold over 50,000 units worldwide.

The Reverend Martha S. Jacobi, M.Div., L.C.S.W., is a pastoral psychotherapist in private practice in New York City. She is a pastor of the Evangelical Lutheran Church in America and an EMDRIA-Approved Consultant. Her practice specializations include trauma and spirituality, bereavement, and consultation with clergy.

Jim Knipe, Ph.D., has been a psychologist in independent practice since 1994. He is currently the Colorado Springs regional coordinator for EMDRIA, and an instructor at the Colorado School of Professional Psychology. Since 1995, he has been involved in humanitarian EMDR training projects in Oklahoma City, Turkey, Indonesia, and the Middle East and is currently the international coordinator for EMDR's Humanitarian Assistance Program. He has written on the use of EMDR with complex cases, including a chapter in *EMDR Solutions: Pathways to Healing.*

Dr. Ulrich Lanius is a psychologist in private practice in Vancouver, British Columbia, specializing in the treatment of traumatic stress syndromes. He is a facilitator for the EMDR Institute and an EMDRIA-Approved Consultant. He has presented nationally and internationally on the neurobiology of attachment and dissociation, as well as on the use of EMDR in populations with dissociative disorders. His chapter on EMDR, dissociative clients, and the adjunctive use of opioid antagonists was in *EMDR Solutions: Pathways to Healing.*

Catherine Lidov, M.S.W., L.C.S.W., is an EMDRIA-Certified therapist with a private psychotherapy practice in Durham, North Carolina. She works with adolescents and adults, and she frequently presents on psychotherapy with suicidal and self-injuring adolescents.

Judy Lightstone, Ph.D., M.A., M.S., a New Zealand registered psychologist, is an EMDRIA-Approved Provider of Continuing Education, California Licensed, and an Approved CME provider. She is founder of the PychoSomatic Integration (PSI) Institute and is in private practice in Auckland. She offers online training and consultation specializing in the treatment of eating disorders, trauma, and dissociation at www.psychotherapist.org, and has provided clinical training and consultation throughout the United States and New Zealand for 22 years.

Elizabeth (Liz) Massiah , M.S.W., R.S.W., Reg. Psychologist, works primarily with trauma. She shares her work time with clients both at the Canadian Forces army base in Edmonton, Alberta, and her own practice. She has been a CUSO (Canadian University Students Overseas) volunteer teaching English literature in East Malaysia and a legal rights advocate for the lesbian and gay community.

Janet McGee, L.C.S.W., maintains a private psychotherapy practice for adults and children in New York. Her approach enhances the natural ability of the mind/body to heal from trauma and addictions. Janet has presented on issues of teenage development, addiction, eating disorders, and trauma. She is part of a surgical-medical team working with children in Honduras.

Ann Marie McKelvey, L.P.C.C., P.C.C., EMDR Consultant, Transitions Coach, MentorCoach International Trainer, and psychotherapist creates psychologically spacious environments for her clients utilizing EMDR and Positive Psychology applications. She facilitates Creative Aging Playshops and Retreats in Santa Fe, New Mexico and is currently in the Chaplaincy Program at Upaya Zen Center. Her Web site is www.AnnMarieMcKelvey.com.

Katie O'Shea, M.S., L.M.H.C., provides clinical, consultation, and training services in Spokane, Washington. She has worked extensively with child abuse and neglect (emotional, physical, and sexual) with victims and offenders of all ages, including the development of a therapeutic foster care program for sexualized children, domestic violence laws and services, addictions (inpatient and outpatient evaluation and treatment/drugs, alcohol, and sexual), somatic disorders, and war trauma. As an EMDR Institute Facilitator since 1994, Katie teaches the Children's Specialty. Since 2003, she has presented a 2-day workshop, the Early Trauma Protocol.

Dr. Sandra Paulsen has spoken, written, trained, and consulted on the power, benefits, and risks of the combination of EMDR and ego state therapy to treat trauma and dissociation since 1992 and is an EMDRIA Certified Consultant. She moderates an EMDR forum for Dr. Francine Shapiro at www.behavior.net. She published an illustrated guide to EMDR and ego state therapy, *Looking Through the Eyes,* and cofounded the Bainbridge Institute for Integrative Psychology in Bainbridge Island, Washington, integrating EMDR and somatic psychotherapies with healing practices from indigenous cultures.

Ronald J. Ricci, Ph.D., serves as the clinical ddministrator for Sex Offender Services for Resources For Human Development, Inc., in Philadelphia. He is a licensed Marriage and Family Therapist, VA Certified Sex Offender Treatment Provider, and PA Sex Offender Assessment Board Approved Provider for Sexually Violent Predators. His primary research focus since 1999 has been use of EMDR with sex offenders.

Janie Scholom, B.S.N., L.C.S.W., has been a psychotherapist in private practice with children, adolescents, and adults, in the Washington, D.C., metropolitan area since 1984, specializing in treating eating disorders and trauma. Janie is a facilitator for the EMDR Institute and an EMDRIA-Approved Consultant. She has presented on integrating EMDR with eating disorders as well as general presentations on EMDR.

Andrew Seubert, L.P.C., N.C.C., is the codirector of ClearPath Healing Arts Center in Corning, New York. He is a licensed psychotherapist and a trained music therapist and has extensive training in Gestalt therapy. He works with couples, trauma, eating disorders, dually diagnosed (MH/MR) adults, and the integration of spirituality and psychotherapy. He has written several articles about therapeutic approaches with MH/MR people, including a chapter in *EMDR Solutions*.

Robin Shapiro, L.I.C.S.W., an EMDRIA-Approved Consultant, maintains a private therapy and consultation practice in Seattle, Washington. She has presented at regional and international EMDRIA conferences, trained EMDR practitioners, and is on the board of directors of the EMDR Humanitarian Assistance Program. She is the editor of and a contributor to *EMDR Solutions: Pathways to Healing*, a contributor to O'Donohue and Levensky's *Promoting Treatment Adherence*, a medical textbook, and the author of a therapy-oriented blog at www .traumatherapy.typepad.com.

Acknowledgments

Thank you to the writers, who contributed your expertise, creativity, and enthusiasm for this healing work, while enduring my revisions, nagging, and not-so-subtle suggestions. You can be proud of yourselves for the suffering you will help to alleviate in thousands of clients.

Thanks to the clients, our true teachers, who have cocreated every innovation in our chapters. A special thank you to the clients who allowed their stories to be told in case examples throughout the book.

We owe a huge debt to Francine Shapiro for her brilliant invention and ongoing cultivation of EMDR. Twenty years ago, could you have imagined that more than 40,000 clinicians all over the world would be using your process to relieve so much trauma?

To Elly Welt, my mother, who taught me to read, write, and edit; who raised me; and who continues to support me. She insisted on editing most of this book, after swearing that she wouldn't take the time from her own writing project. Thanks again, Mom.

Thanks to Deborah Malmud at Norton Professional Books for backing another unasked-for edited book and to Andrea Costella and Kristen Holt-Browning for gracefully guiding the writers, *Solutions II,* and me through the publishing process. Thanks to Sheryl Rowe and Muriel Jorgensen for editing, including 115 comments on one chapter.

Thanks to Andrew Seubert, who initiated the eating disorders special interest group (EMDR EDSIG) writing the "Eating Disorders" unit. Thanks to the EDSIG writers. You have contributed an important and unprecedented body of work to the EMDR canon.

I blame this book on Mary Ann Herzing. If she had not invited me to Boise to speak about EMDR and depression, I wouldn't have found out that I had so much to say about it and wouldn't have begun the laborious process of writing, organizing writers, editing, re-editing, and re-editing that has eaten up my year.

Thanks again to David Calof and the rest of our dissociation study group, Helen Hopper, Doug McLemore, and Becky Durocher. As trained professionals, they could tolerate my whining about missed deadlines, recalcitrant writers, and the blow-by-blow accounts of the book in progress. Thanks to my colleagues and friends for their enthusiasm and support during this process.

Apologies to the loyal readers of my blog, www.traumatherapy .typepad.com; I promise to start posting again as soon as I send in this book and the next.

When I apologetically told my husband, Doug, that I seemed to be writing another book, he said, "I support you one hundred percent!" And he has.

EMDR Solutions II

Introduction

Robin Shapiro

THE REAL NAME OF THIS BOOK WON'T FIT ON THE COVER. IT IS EMDR Solutions II for Depression, Eating Disorders, Performance, Coaching, Dissociation, Attachment Issues, Complex Trauma, Somatic Therapy, Early Trauma, Medically Based Trauma, Sex Offenders, and Spiritual Issues. As EMDR (Eye Movement Desensitization and Reprocessing) matures, its clinicians are targeting the trauma at the heart of, or secondary to, nearly every emotional or behavioral malady. As clinical research shows us the confluence of temperament, attachment history, affect, and trauma in every complex client (Schore, 2003; Siegel, 1999; and many more), clinicians have found new ways to direct the EMDR's Standard Protocol toward their healing. This book contains a broad sample of creative solutions to many clinical conundrums.

In the beginning, I imagined a "Treating Depression" unit, David Grand's chapter "EMDR and Performance," and a mixture of unrelated chapters. I put the word out, contacting the writers from *EMDR Solutions: Pathways to Healing*, online communities, and people whose work I knew about and admired. As the chapters came in, most fell into natural units.

UNIT I: TREATING DEPRESSION

In the last decade, I've spent many hours explaining the signs of endogenous, trauma-based, and attachment-based depression to consultees. When I was invited to Boise to do a 4-hour training about EMDR in the treatment of depression, the material was right on the top of my brain. I couldn't go wrong quoting the results of Bessel van der Kolk's groundbreaking study of the effect of EMDR on trauma-based depression (van der Kolk et al., 2007) or using Stephen Porges's polyvagal theory (Porges, 2001) as a starting point. When I brought in my own clinical experience, I had a unit. Jim Knipe offered a chapter on shame-based depression, and I knew that this master clinician would bring a great new perspective to EMDR treatment. He did. When Katherine Davis sent me her chapter, I thought it would be about postpartum depression. Instead, it was about postpartum posttraumatic stress disorder (PTSD) (often disguised as depression) and it moved to the unit "Treating Bodily and Medically Based Trauma."

UNIT II: TREATING EATING DISORDERS

Andrew Seubert wondered if he could invite the eating disorders special interest group (EDSIG) to contribute overlapping chapters. A unit was born. When I read through the eating disorder (ED) chapters, I saw that they had applications for any disorders of desire, compulsivity, anxiety, affect dysregulation and affect avoidance, and dissociation. I hope that all of you take in these chapters. Any of them will improve your clinical skills, even if you never plan to work with ED clients. The unit includes DaLene Forester's clear and elegant overlays of EMDR's Standard Protocol to treat specific eating/body disorders for her two chapters on bulimia and body dysmorphia. Other chapters deal with diverse pieces of the ED puzzle. Andrew Seubert gives a survey of the etiology of EDs. Janis Scholom addresses early phases of the EMDR Protocol. Linda J. Cooke and Celia Grand dig into the neurobiology of EDs. They give an illuminating tour of the research showing the physical and neurological bases of the disorders and how to use that knowledge to help clients regulate their affect. Janet McGee writes about how to future-pace and contain the inevitable relapses in ED treatment. Catherine Lidov illuminates the nature of desire and what to do when it goes awry. Andrew Seubert and Judy Lightstone wrote separate sections of the ego state and ED chapter. They contrast their creative and useful approaches.

UNIT III: PERFORMANCE, COACHING, AND POSITIVE PSYCHOLOGY

I admired David Grand's performance work for years and was delighted when he agreed to contribute a chapter. His 15 guidelines will help you guide athletes, performers, and others through the blocks that keep them from doing their best. Ann Marie McKelvey had written a rave review of *EMDR Solutions: Pathways to Healing* in the second issue of the *EMDR Journal of Practice and Research*. At the end, she complained that there were no chapters about coaching or positive psychology. So I asked her for one. She gave me two. I paired them with the performance chapter since all emphasize positive function rather than dysfunction. I placed this positive unit between the ED and complex trauma units in order to give you readers a break from deep, dissociative trauma. Ann Marie became the cheerleader of the entire project. I hope that her enthusiasm infects you, too.

UNIT IV: SOLUTIONS FOR
COMPLEX TRAUMA

I asked Katie O'Shea if she would contribute her early trauma protocol. As she began to write, she realized that she had two different chapters, the early trauma chapter and one on preparation techniques, including a thorough and understandable explanation of the EMDR process, affect "containers," and emotional resetting. Sandra Paulsen and Ulrich Lanius each wanted to write a chapter on somatic therapy and ego states. I had them talk to each other and they decided to collaborate. Sandra is one of the "big names" in ego state/dissociation work in EMDR. Ulrich is a master of translating obscure brain research into EMDR-friendly methodology. They are both master clinicians. Their chapter is a brilliant synthesis of research, somatic therapy, and treatment of dissociation. Elizabeth Massiah works with Canadian soldiers. She shows us how to work with clients who suffer extremely intrusive images. And I write about treating obsessive-compulsive personality disorder, a disorder of affect tolerance and avoidance. If I had seen the chapters on preparation techniques and the embodied self/somatic and ego state interventions earlier in editing process, I would have put them at the beginning of the book. I suggest that you read them first, since many of the other chapters refer to "containers" (preparation) or "ego states" (embodied self).

UNIT V: TREATING BODILY AND
MEDICALLY BASED TRAUMA

Bodies get sick, get injured, and sometimes have babies. EMDR can clear the PTSD that arises from illness, developmental body processes,

giving birth, injuries, and the medical treatment for them. I wrote a
chapter about treating a variety of medical traumas. Katherine Davis
contributed one about clearing traumatic stress from the birth process.
And I present a protocol for using EMDR to treat multiple chemical
sensitivity. It's amazing what EMDR can undo!

UNIT VI: MORE EMDR SOLUTIONS

Ronald J. Ricci and Cheryl Clayton share their experience and advice
about working with sex offenders. If you don't plan to work with this
population, read it anyway. You will learn even more about affect tolerance, denial, and working with other clinicians and systems.
Martha S. Jacobi's chapter about religious and spiritually attuned
clients shows us how to elegantly navigate through issues of belief
and spiritual community. It takes a broad topic and gives us precise
interventions.

USING *SOLUTIONS II*

This book is a manual for doing EMDR with diverse client populations. If you took both parts of the EMDR training and have experience and knowledge of a specified client population, you should be
able to use the procedures with few problems. If you aren't schooled
in EMDR (the basic training is at least 50 hours long), get the training before you mess up your clients with this powerful psychotherapy! If you know what you're doing, know your clients well, and
remember that the therapeutic relationship must be strong before
you try any technique, you will find uses for many of the solutions
in this book.
    You might think about reading about your specialties and skip-
ping the rest of the chapters. Yet, I hope you read them all. There are
gems in every chapter. Even if you don't work with eating disorders,
you can use many of the techniques in that unit with other addicted,
dissociated, or complex clients. If you don't work with offenders,
Ricci and Clayton's chapter speaks to trauma treatment in complex
cases, impulse control, and other issues that are germane to many
clients.

RESEARCH CONSIDERATIONS

EMDR's Standard Protocol has stood the test of peer-reviewed research and hundreds of thousands of individual clinical experiences. EMDR's full protocol is empirically validated when used on PTSD. Most chapters in *EMDR Solutions II* focus on trauma targets and thus conform to the research. Some of the uses in this book must be labeled "experimental." When the writers point EMDR toward a nontrauma target, it may work very well or even be the most efficacious use of EMDR in a specific circumstance. Any readers who would like to do research on any of the topics should talk to the writers.

CASE HISTORIES

Every case history in *EMDR Solutions II* is either a composite or is here with the client's permission. All names and life circumstances are changed in order to preserve anonymity.

CHAPTER CONVENTIONS

What the therapist says or should say to a client is in *italics,* with or without quotation marks. Occasionally, italics are used for other emphases, and I'll leave it to you to know the difference. Common EMDR terms are capitalized, especially those referring to a step of the Standard Protocol. If you've forgotten some of the terms, there's a glossary near the end of this book.

ATTRIBUTION

Francine Shapiro created and named EMDR, the Standard Protocol, and most of the common EMDR terms (for which we are forever grateful). Assume attribution to her and her invention in every chapter. Her definitive guide to EMDR is *Eye Movement Desensitization and Reprocessing: Basic Principles, Protocols, and Procedures* (2nd ed.) (F. Shapiro, 2001). If you are an EMDR clinician and you haven't read it, go get it now!

REFERENCES

Porges, S. W. (2001). The polyvagal theory: Phylogenetic substrates of a social nervous system. *Physiology and Behavior, 79*, 503–513.

Schore, A. (2003). *Affect regulation and disorders of the self.* New York: Norton.

Shapiro, F. (2001). *Eye movement desensitization and reprocessing: Basic principles, protocols, and procedures* (2nd ed.). New York: Guilford Press.

Siegel, D. (1999). *The developing mind.* New York: Guilford Press.

van der Kolk, B. A., Spinazzola, J., Blaustein, M. E., Hopper, J. W., Hopper, E. K., Korn, D. L., et al. (2007, January). A randomized clinical trial of eye movement desensitization and reprocessing (EMDR), fluoxetine, and pill placebo in the treatment of posttraumatic stress disorder: Treatment effects and long-term maintenance. *Journal of Clinical Psychiatry, 68*(1), 37–46.

TREATING DEPRESSION

Chapter 1

Introduction to Assessment and Treatment of Depression with EMDR

Robin Shapiro

DEPRESSION IS PROFOUNDLY PHYSICAL. IT AFFECTS COGNITION, EMOTION, and nearly every system in the body. Depressed people feel fatigued, sometimes immobile. They eat and/or sleep too much, or not enough. In an attempt to raise their moods, they may take in more sugars, carbohydrates, fats, caffeine, alcohol, illicit drugs, or nicotine than in their pre-depression lives. Their moods can swing from sadness to extreme irritation, from anxiety to hopelessness to flat inertia. Their cognitions can run from "I'm worthless" (shame) to "the world is screwed up, and always will be" (hopelessness). Depressed people report anhedonia (loss of pleasure in ordinarily pleasurable activities) and often forget that there ever was pleasure, connection, and meaning in their lives. They are likely to contemplate suicide, and the most likely to carry it out. Their bodies may hurt, develop heart disease or diabetes, and be unresilient when ill.

According to centuries of experts depression is caused by:

- Too much black bile (Hippocrates of Cos, ca. 460–380 BCE). Cure: bloodletting.
- An invasion or possession by a nasty spirit (numerous cultures for the last 10,000 years).
- A mind and body's response to "learned helplessness" from being unable to act efficaciously (Seligman 1991).
- Repression of aggressive urges caused by interpsychic conflict. Repression of any motion, notion, or emotion (Negri, 1982).

- A chemical imbalance, often consisting of too little serotonin, dopamine, or other neuroreceptors (medicine) or a lack of the building blocks of serotonin, dopamine, and other neuroreceptors (naturopathy).
- Not enough light stimulating the pineal gland at the right time or, relatedly, a lack of Vitamin D.
- Lack of social engagement (Porges, 2005).
- Bad thoughts that cause bad feelings (Burns, 1992).
- Attachment injury causing extreme shame (Chapter 4) or "hunkering down" (Chapter 5).
- A bodily response to the triggering of an ego state (van der Hart et al., 2006).
- A disturbance in the homeostasis of the body, originating in the peripheral nervous system, with too much "braking" coming from the parasympathetic side.
- Or more specifically, a dorsal vagal response, slowing or shutting down (braking) many body/brain functions in order to conserve energy, often in response to a hyperaroused (accelerated) unmyelinated ventral vagal reaction to trauma, emotional or physical stress, or anxiety (Porges, 1995, 2001, 2005).

Successful treatment for depression aids clients to stop unnecessary "braking" and to be able to "accelerate" at a functional pace, thereby being capable of social engagement, enjoyment, function, and normal responsive moods. EMDR, a multimodal therapy, brings together client history, the therapeutic relationship, cognitions, emotions, and attention to the body sensation. EMDR can heal trauma-based depression, whether based in posttraumatic stress disorder (PTSD) or smaller *t* relational trauma. It can facilitate the healing and management of biologically based depression.

Of the many lenses through which to view depression, the polyvagal theory is an umbrella containing the others. It's a simple and comprehensive well-researched explanation for a complex phenomenon. And it's easy for me to pick interventions when I look through its lens. Here, it is in a nutshell:

There are two major nerves that run between brain and body, the dorsal vagus and the ventral vagus. Engagement of the ventral vagus turns us "on." When the evolutionary older unmyelinated part of the ventral vagus is engaged, we are in a state of high alert. It is often "on" in response to threat or perceived threat. The "newer" myelinated part of the ventral vagus, a mammalian/human innovation, is "on" when we are socially or intellectually engaged. It brings on a state of pleasant, not overwhelming arousal, seemingly tied to the "affect of interest" and definitely tied (in numerous research studies) to social engagement in infants, children, and adults. The phylogentically oldest nerve, the dorsal vagus, damps down the nervous system and is tied to recuperative states (think of the last time you had a 104 degree temperature), shock, submission, and playing dead. Depression is its chronic manifestation. At our best, we experience constant shifting between the turning on (ventral vagal) and braking (dorsal vagal) mechanisms in our bodies that regulate digestion, heart rate coherence, and many other physical phenomena, including mood and attentiveness. The research on the far-ranging manifestations and implications of these two vagal nerves has resulted in new body-based and relational-based treatments for anxiety disorders, major depression, autism, and others (MayoClinic.com, 2006; Ogden, Minton, & Pain, 2006; Servan-Schreiber, 2004). When distressed or shut-down people become truly socially engaged, they shift to a myelinated ventral vagal state with an increase of heart rate coherence, an engagement of more parts of their thinking brain, and many other effects. (What an elegant explanation for the good effects and affects of a connected therapeutic relationship!) Some people with formerly intractable depression are being treated with implanted stimulators that supply small electric pulses directly to vagal nerves. In many of these patients, the depressed mood and other symptoms shift appreciably (MayoClinic.com, 2006).

Think about someone with PTSD. External and internal triggers put her into hyperarousal—afraid and ready to take flight or start a fight. Her amygdala is on fire. unmyelinated ventral vagus is on, until after hours, days, months, or years, her body can't handle its red alert status. The dorsal vagal response takes over. The body slows. In some cases it can barely respond, much less go into alert status. The heart rate slows, the digestion shuts down; our client just wants to sleep or play video games or drink. It's hard for her to connect with others or remember other states (happiness, connectedness, efficacy). Her body, her brain, her thoughts, her responses are all depressed. She may stay in this shut-down state, or alternate between hyperarousal (anxiety) and hypoarousal (depression).

Depression seems to coincide with the turning on of the dorsal vagus nerve that suppresses the ventral vagus nerve, thus inhibiting both watchful or aggressive states and socially engaged and learning states. It has many causes, from strictly biochemical (lack of light and nutrients; and/or genetics, as in bipolar and unipolar disorders) to strictly a response to trauma or physical or emotional stress or loss or a response to (often small *t*) attachment injuries that caused an inhibition of social engagement (a myelinated ventral vagal function), causing a dorsal vagal reaction. Of course many depressions include more than one etiology. Chronic depression, whatever the original etiology, can stem from many overlapping causes. And chronic or repeated depression can forge broad neural pathways to cognitive and physical states with millions of connections, making them even harder to transform.

In treating depression, you can utilize many techniques to "flip" the vagal switch. Your clients can start with easy physical interventions: exercise, more light in the winter, and omega-3 supplements. If there are big "T" traumas, or big or small *t* attachment disruptions, we can clear them with EMDR. Some clients need medication to shift their hormonal balance, stabilize moods, or change their serotonin levels.

HOW CAN EMDR HELP?

If the depression is clearly trauma-based, EMDR clears the trauma and the depression goes away. Van der Kolk, et al. (2007) did a groundbreaking study about the effects of EMDR treatment versus Prozac versus a control group on traumatized depressed people. Here's what they found:

> Eighty-eight PTSD subjects diagnosed according to DSM-IV criteria were randomly assigned to EMDR, fluoxetine, or pill placebo. They received 8 weeks of treatment and were assessed by blind raters posttreatment and at 6-month follow-up. The primary outcome measure was the Clinician-Administered PTSD Scale, DSM-IV version, and the secondary outcome measure was the Beck Depression Inventory-II. The study ran from July 2000 through July 2003. RESULTS: The psychotherapy intervention was more successful than pharmacotherapy in achieving sustained reductions in PTSD and depression symptoms, but this benefit accrued primarily for adult-onset trauma survivors. At 6-month follow-up, 75.0% of adult-onset versus 33.3% of child-onset trauma subjects receiving EMDR achieved asymptomatic end-state functioning compared with none in the fluoxetine group. (van der Kolk et al., 2007, pp. 37–46)

What does this mean? In only eight sessions of the purest "on-proto-col" EMDR, 75% of adult-onset trauma survivors were freed of PTSD *and* depression. Only 33% of the child-onset trauma survivors completely cleared their symptoms. Some had partial clearing. Many of the EMDR group continued to test better on each follow-up test, despite no new therapeutic intervention. The clinicians in the study thought they could have cleared the symptoms of most of the child-onset group if they had had more than eight sessions. Clearly, EMDR can clear trauma-based depression.

EMDR's Adaptive Information Processing model (AIP) suggests that "there appears to be a neurological balance in a distinct physiological system that allows information to be processed to an 'adaptive resolution.' . . . (C)onnections to appropriate associations are made and the experience is used constructively by the individual and is integrated into a positive emotional and cognitive schema. Essentially, what is useful is learned and stored with the appropriate affect and is available for future use" (F. Shapiro, 2001, p. 16). The Assessment Phase of EMDR induces a physical and emotional state—the client's reaction to the trauma/target. The next stages, Desensitization, Installation, and Body Scan, bring the client to an adaptive resolution, capable of social engagement, connection with the prefrontal orbital cortex (Siegel, 1999), and, I believe, a myelinated ventral vagal state.

Both the AIP and the polyvagal system speak of the body/brain's ability to come to a state of homeostasis. When we clear traumatized and other dysregulated states with EMDR, it is easier for the body to regulate itself, for social engagement and affects of interest to occur, and for people to stay out of deeply distressed (unmyelinated ventral) and depressed (dorsal vagal) states. The very structure of the Desensitization Phase (focus on the distressing event, and then a break to socially engage the therapist) may create its own balance between different vagal states.

Onetime events are the easiest to clear. Attachment difficulties tied to overt abuse and neglect are easy to spot and easy to target, though not always quick to clear. Some trauma is subtle. Many attachment traumas are small *t* repetitive incidents of, for instance, a mother's head turning away when a baby tries to engage her, a good response when the child takes care of her (forsaking himself), or a "hunkering down" in response to a chronically, but vaguely, threatening situation or subtle shaming. You'll read two different chapters about using EMDR with attachment-related depression.

Some depression is innate, either inherited or caused by some chronic or episodic dysfunction in the body. EMDR can help keep clients on track with the many useful modalities for lessening and sometimes eradicating the symptoms of endogenous depression.

CLIENT HISTORY

In order to treat depression, you need to know its etiology in each client. Unless you are faced with the (nearly mythical) perfectly attached, well-supported, low trauma client with one discrete distressing incident, and depression ever since, it may take you a while to understand your client's depression and its antecedents. I do most intakes using Maureen Kitchur's Strategic Developmental Model (SDM) (2005). The SDM is anchored by a genogram (family tree) and an extensive client and family history. Among its "nosy, snoopy questions" are queries about depression, alcoholism, and other disorders in the family. I usually highlight the representations of depressed family members on the family tree with a colored marking pen. If there is a family history of depression, it becomes graphically obvious to both my client and me. Clients often say something like, "Oh, it's not just me!" The intake procedure, and especially the genogram, can give them a context for their malady.

It's not enough to determine the presence of familial depression. Keep asking questions that explain the context of depression in the family. If there are four generations of bipolar disorder, the diagnosis may seem straightforward. But keep in mind that your client's depression may arise from the big "T" and small "t" traumas of being parented by an impaired caregiver, not her genetics. A family of Holocaust survivors may hand down nongenetic depression from the effects of generational trauma (R. Shapiro, 2005). Here are some other questions to ask your clients, whether or not there is a family history of depression:

- *What kind of parent was your mother's mother? Her father? Your father's parents?*
- Note the disruptions of attachment that can come with premature birth, illness, military service, birth of other children, and separations. *Were your parents or siblings hospitalized when you were young? Were you? Were either of your parents gone from home for more than a few days? Were you? What happened?*

- What stressors faced the parents and grandparents? Were they broke? Immigrants from a war-torn country? Living in a dangerous neighborhood? Soldiers? Living in a rigid, unforgiving community?
- *What kinds of abuse happened in each generation?*
- *Who used alcohol or drugs? Any alcoholics/addicts?*
- *Who has been to therapy? Do you know why?*
- *Do you know if anyone in your family is taking antidepressants? Other psychotropic meds?*
- *Has anybody been hospitalized for depression? Other emotional reasons?*
- *What kinds of illnesses run in your family?*
- *What is your health history?*

This last question is extremely important in diagnosing depression. Joseph McCreery (2007), a Seattle psychiatrist, allowed me to print his good advice on my blog, www.traumatherapy.typepad.com:

> Any moderately or severely depressed, anxious or chronically fatigued patient should have a medical lab screen (if not obtained within the last year) to include: complete blood count, thyroid functions, and a chemistry panel including electrolytes, BUN, creatinine and liver function tests. Sleep apnea is another physical disorder that contributes to fatigue, depression, and anxiety (and increased risk of cardiovascular problems). Any patient with snoring—periods of about 10 seconds of apnea (no breathing) followed by a deep snoring or snorting inhalation, and accompanied by daytime sleepiness—should be sent for a sleep evaluation. Medical abnormalities such as these, when screened for and treated, can do much to improve patients' well-being and improve therapy outcomes. These tests can easily be done by a primary care provider at a therapist's request.

I've sent depressed clients to physicians who found thyroid dysregulation, chronic fatigue syndrome, or blood pressure problems. When the physical problems were treated, the depressive symptoms went away. (See Chapter 3.)

Assessing Depression

After you've learned their histories, you need to know your clients' present situations.

- *What do you do for work? What do you like/hate about your job/school/ household/status?*
- What kind of social connections do they have? (Isolation is depressing and depression causes isolation.) *Tell me about your connections with friends. With coworkers. With family.*
- What are their current life stressors? Ask about finances, relationships, family, roommates, commute, and so on.
- What are their current joys, interests, obsessions?
- Are there any recent losses of people, pets, or status? Are there any changes? Moves? Job changes? Graduation?

Once you have the context of their lives, you can zero in on the symptoms of their depression. You may buy Beck's famous, often-revised inventory (Beck, Ward, Mendelson, Mock, & Erbaugh, 1961) with its 21 questions. You can download the 10-question MDI, the Major Depression Inventory from the World Health Organization (http://www.who-5.org/). Or you can embed your questions into your intake, leaving room for explanations and digressions.

You can start with these and use your clinical curiosity and your heartfelt human response to follow up on each answer:

- *How long have you felt like this?*
- *Did something in particular happen to bring it on?*
- *How soon after the baby was born did this depression start?*
- *Does it come and go, or is it constant?*
- *What does it feel like inside of you when you're depressed? How bad is it right now?*
- *What other physical symptoms do you have?*
- *How is your sleep? Too much? Not enough? Any early waking?*
- *How is your eating? Do you have an appetite? Are you craving sugar and caffeine? Are you eating too much? Bingeing? Tell me about it.*
- *What's your concentration like? Do you have trouble reading? Paying attention?*
- *Are you tired much of the time? Tell me more.*
- *How is your motivation to get things done?*
- *Are you avoiding doing what you need to do? How badly are you beating yourself up for that?*
- *Some people get isolated when they feel low. What's happening to your social life?*

- *Some people get low when they get isolated. What kind of relationships do you have?*
- *What's your enjoyment level? Can you remember enjoying things more before this depression grabbed you? Do you have any sex drive? Do you still like food? Is there anything that still gives you joy?*
- *Do you get nervous?* If so, *What's that like? Do you have worried thoughts, over and over?*
- *Are you feeling guilty a lot of the time? Are you blaming yourself for things you really aren't in control of?*
- *Do you feel irritable a lot of the time? How is your patience?*
- *What are you doing to avoid this depression? Drinking? Eating? Gambling? Overworking? Computer games? TV?*
- *Do you have any feelings of hopelessness?* (With some younger clients I ask, *Does everything suck? Do you suck? Do you think you or it will always suck?*)
- *Do you ever feel that life isn't worth it?*
- *Are you having any suicidal thoughts? How strong? Any plans? What keeps you alive? What do you think could push you over the edge? Is it that you want to be dead, or that you want this bad feeling to stop?*
- *Is there a cycle to your depression, not tied to what's happening to you?*
- *Do you ever get too speedy?*

The answers to these questions will give you a rough idea of your clients' experience. The next step is to decide on your plan of attack.

Treatment Planning

Sometimes it's easy. You spot the symptoms of low thyroid function (hair loss, fatigue, weight gain, and cold hands and feet), send them to their doctor or an endocrinologist and do supportive therapy until the drugs kick in and patient feels back to normal. You notice that depression kicked in a month after last year's car accident and you clear the trauma with EMDR and your grateful and newly buoyant client smiles as he waves good-bye. Or spotting the family history of bipolar disorder/postpartum depression/major depression and seeing all the symptoms in your client, you send them to a psychiatrist or ARNP (nurse practitioner) for medication (and they actually go and actually take their medications) and then follow the suggestions in Chapter 3.

Other cases are more complex, harder to figure out, or take longer to resolve. Your client's depression may be secondary to a dissociative disorder, Axis II disorder, or unavoidable stressful life circumstance. While continuing to explore the cause of the depressed state (sending the client to your most savvy diagnostician/medicator; asking more questions; doing some resource intervention [Kiessling, 2005]), you can move ahead with interventions that help most depressed people, whatever the etiology of their depression. Nearly any kind of regular exercise, an increase in omega-3 (fish oil) supplements, guided exercises that increased heart rate coherence, and social engagement help the body rise from the depths (Servan-Schreiber, 2004). If clients are immobilized by depression, medical intervention is your first step. If they have enough mobilization to allow their friends to drag them out for a daily walk, get to the store for fish oil, and connect with you, you might see improvement in the first few weeks.

It's helpful to explain what's happening in physical terms. I find that it's less shaming than other explanations. *"Your body has three main nerves that connect to your brain. One turns on to put you in red alert, fight-or-flight mode. One turns on when you're socially or pleasantly engaged. And one is the dimmer switch, slowing down the body's and brain's responses. It sounds like your dimmer switch has been stuck for a long time, causing your depression. We're going to work together to turn the light back to full on."*

You can add whatever further explanation makes sense:

- *After that surgery/long illness/loss/stressful time at work/getting through the divorce your body turned down the dimmer switch to force you to rest. We've got some work to do to get your energy turned back on.*
- *Your whole life, you've been using that dimmer switch to turn off your true self to try to please the people around you. You haven't done it on purpose; it's a reflex that happened in childhood and then automatically kept going. Your official diagnosis is Depression. Our working diagnosis is "Hunkered Down" and our treatment plan is "dehunkering" to turn that energy switch back on* (Chapter 5). (I've had several clients say words to the effect of "You really get me!" after this diagnosis.)
- *When we did that family tree, we saw how depression has colonized your mother's family. Some of what you're experiencing is the effect of having a depressed mom. When she couldn't respond to you when you were a baby, your dimmer switch went on and stayed partially on for much of your life. We can clear that part of your depression with EMDR and other therapy. It seems that you may have inherited some of the physically based depression and anxiety, too. We're going to work on some management skills to*

help you turn up the dimmer switch and turn down the mobilization/anx-iety switch so that you can feel more balanced. If we can't turn down the switch quickly, I want you to meet with my nurse practitioner/psychiatrist colleague who may prescribe some medications that can get you up and functioning so that our other therapies have a chance to work. (See more discussion of medications in Chapter 3.)

Notice that I used "we" in each example. Depression is daunting. Clients need to know that you are joined with them against their symptoms. Be transparent about what you think is the cause. If you can't figure it out, you can say that, and keep looking for the causes. Use general practitioners, neurologists, psychiatrists, and your most invasive curiosity until it makes sense to you and your client. In the meantime, use your best management skills to help them. I've run into four cases that made no sense to me. It turned out that two were based in head injuries that hadn't turned up on the genogram. Now I always ask, *Did you ever get hit in the head or fall on your head?"* in my nosy, snoopy intake. Another woman had a rare metabolic disorder that lowers dopamine, exacerbated by a constant bombardment of neuro-toxins from her mold-infested rental house. She became less dopey and more focused when she got out of the moldy house. It took an in-ternist, a psychiatric nurse practitioner, and me two years of befuddle-ment before we understood the clinical picture.

REFERENCES

Beck, A. T., Rush, A. J., Shaw, B. F., & Emery, D. (1979). *Cognitive therapy of depression.* New York: Guilford Press.

Beck, A. T., Ward, C. H., Mendelson, M., Mock, J., & Erbaugh, J. (1961). An inventory for measuring depression. *Archives of General Psychiatry, 4,* 561–571.

Burns, D. (1992). *Feeling good: The new mood therapy.* New York: Morrow/Avon Press.

Kiessling, R. (2005). Integrating resource development strategies into your EMDR practice. In R. Shapiro (Ed.), *EMDR solutions: Pathways to healing* (pp. 57–87). New York: Norton.

Kitchur, M. (2005). The strategic developmental model for EMDR. In R. Shapiro (Ed.), *EMDR solutions: Pathways to healing* (pp. 8–56). New York: Norton.

Mayo Clinic staff. (2006). Vagus nerve stimulation. www.mayoclinic.com/health/vagus-nerve-stimulation/MY00183/UPDATEAPP.

McCreery, J. (2007, October 28). "Thyroid disease and other differential diagnoses." Message posted to http://traumatherapy.typepad.com/attachment _therapy/medicine_and_psychology/

Negri, T. (1982). Transformational movement. Class presented by the Institute for Movement Therapy. Seattle, WA.

Ogden, P., Minton, K., & Pain, C. (2006). *Trauma and the body*. New York: Norton.

Porges, S. W. (1995). Orienting in a defensive world: Mammalian modifications of our evolutionary heritage. A polyvagal theory. *Psychophysiology, 32*(4), 301–318.

Porges, S. W. (2001). The polyvagal theory: Phylogenetic substrates of a social nervous system. *Physiology and Behavior, 79*, 503–513.

Porges, S. W. (2005). The role of social engagement in attachment and bonding: A phylogenetic perspective. In C. S. Carter, L. Ahnert, K. E. Grossmann, S. B. Hardy, M. E. Lamb, S. W. Porges, et al. (Eds.), *Attachment and bonding: A new synthesis* (pp. 33–54). Cambridge, MA: MIT Press.

Seligman, M. E. P. (1991). *Helplessness: On depression, development, and death* (2nd ed.). New York: Freeman.

Servan-Schreiber, D. (2004). *The instinct to heal*. New York: Rodale Press.

Shapiro, F. (2001). *Eye movement desensitization and reprocessing: Basic principles, protocols, and procedures* (2nd ed.). New York: Guilford Press.

Shapiro, R. (2005). EMDR with cultural and generational introjects. In R. Shapiro (Ed.), *EMDR solutions: Pathways to healing* (pp. 228–240). New York: Norton.

Siegel, D. (1999). *The developing mind*. New York: Guilford Press.

Van der Hart, O., Nijenhuis, E., & Steele, K. (2006) *The haunted self*. New York: Norton

van der Kolk, B. A., Spinazzola, J., Blaustein, M. E., Hopper, J. W., Hopper, E. K., Korn, D. L., et al. (2007, January). A randomized clinical trial of eye movement desensitization and reprocessing (EMDR), fluoxetine, and pill placebo in the treatment of posttraumatic stress disorder: Treatment effects and long-term maintenance. *Journal of Clinical Psychiatry, 68*(1), 37–46.

Chapter 2

Trauma-Based Depression

Robin Shapiro

GO BACK AND READ CHAPTER 1, "INTRODUCTION TO ASSESSMENT AND Treatment of Depression with EMDR," if you haven't. Good. Now you know that van der Kolk et al. (2007) have shown that most trauma-based depression goes away or is greatly lessened by EMDR treatment and that the treatment effects last and continue to build, long past treatment termination. I believe that when we attack traumatic depression with EMDR, we help flip the polyvagal switch from dorsal braking to myelinated ventral vagal life engagement.

SIMPLE TRAUMA

Depression may have multiple etiologies. Check for attachment injuries, biological propensities, and trauma in your intake. If your client has simple adult-onset posttraumatic stress disorder (PTSD) with depression, the depression may disappear with the trauma clearing. Here's a composite case:

Maggie

Maggie is 27 years old and works in the Seattle software industry. Last year, due to a reorganization in her workplace, her good, supportive manager was replaced with an autocratic jerk. Maggie, who had been the golden girl on her previous team, became the scapegoat on her current team. She was undercut at every turn, and then, after 6 months, precipitously laid off. She came to therapy with moderate to severe depression, unsure of herself for the first time she remembers, and highly avoidant of a finding another job. She denied a family history of depression, significant childhood trauma, or much trauma outside of work. Her symptoms included lethargy, anhedonia, social isolation, low self-esteem, negative self talk, too much sleep, leaking tears at odd times, and lack of motivation. She denied ever having "felt this way before."

On the second session we easily installed a Safe Place and the circle of everyone who loves her and had a little difficulty in installing a memory of when she was most proud (Leeds, 1999). I validated the grief she was feeling after the loss of her good boss, job, and coworkers. I explained trauma, depression, and how her body's dimmer switch came on when she had too much anxiety, stress, and grief from her job. After I described EMDR, we picked EMDR targets. One of the strongest was a visual of her boss's face with his lip curled in contempt. On the third session, we went after that image. Negative Cognition (NC): "Something's wrong with me." Positive Cognition (PC): "I'm competent and acceptable." Subjective Units of Disturbance (SUD): 9—anxiety and shame in body core. On an initial float-back attempt, she found no past connections. She processed easily. Her affect went from anxiety to anger as we continued through humiliating event after humiliating event. She recounted how her boss had separated her from her team, given her no-win jobs, and failed to listen or respond to her. At the end of the first session, the SUD was 4 and the affect was angry and much less shut down. I got a promise from her that she would walk around Greenlake at least three times in the next week. During the week, while walking, she remembered an experience with a fourth-grade teacher that reminded her of her job. We processed through that (SUD 8, down to 0) and went back to the original target. The SUD was 2. Three sessions later we'd processed through the whole work debacle, including the layoff and ensuing paralysis. Maggie reported feeling more energized and ready to start looking for work. We met three more times, using Future Templates of job-hunting strategies and new work situations. Imagine yourself running into a manager like the last one. He's using the same tactics. Before we could get through the Assessment Phase Maggie said, "If I get one like him, I'm so out of there! I don't deserve to be treated like a non-human. I'm a great worker and I don't work for jerks!" We installed that and went back to job strategizing. At the last session, Maggie was back to her vital, clear self. She called a month later with news that she had landed a good job, on a good team, with a good boss.

COMPLEX TRAUMA

Maggie was a "best case scenario." Often, the trauma is more complex and deep-seated. In case after case, I've seen clients' depressions lift when EMDR cleared the PTSD from war trauma, complex grief, childhood abuse, sexual assault, and years of abusive relationships. In most of those cases, we acknowledged but did not treat the depressive symptoms with anything besides EMDR's Standard Protocol for trauma.

CONCLUSION

The Standard Protocol of EMDR is effective in clearing both trauma and trauma-based depression.

REFERENCES

Leeds, A. (1999). Strengthening the Self: Creating successful treatment outcomes for adult survivors of abuse and neglect. Workshop, Seattle, WA.

van der Kolk, B. A., Spinazzola, J., Blaustein, M. E., Hopper, J. W., Hopper, E. K., Korn, D. L., et al. (2007, January). A randomized clinical trial of eye movement desensitization and reprocessing (EMDR), fluoxetine, and pill placebo in the treatment of posttraumatic stress disorder: Treatment effects and long-term maintenance. *Journal of Clinical Psychiatry*, 68(1), 37–46.

Chapter 3

Endogenous Depression and Mood Disorders

Robin Shapiro

DEPRESSION IS PHYSICAL. IT AFFECTS ALL BODILY FUNCTIONS. WHETHER depression is caused by a response to trauma or stress, a dysfunctional relationship, a malfunctioning thyroid, the flu, painkillers, or genetic disorders, it makes us feel down. Respiration and movement can be "retarded." Mood is "low." People feel heavy. This chapter deals with depression that arises from bodily dysfunctions.

During illness, our bodies slow down (going into dorsal vagal states) to put energies toward healing, taking energy away from concentration and motivation. After recuperation, some enjoy the return of energy and enjoyment, while others can't seem to flip the "on" switch and continue to stay slow, low, and depressed. The chronic, low-grade stress of poverty, a bad job, or a sick child can keep us on "alert status" (unmyelinated vagal state) until our exhausted bodies creep or dive into dorsal vagal braking and depression. Imbalanced hormones can depress us, whether they are gender-related (testosterone, estrogen/ progesterone), thyroid, or others. Some people are on an inherited roller coaster of changing moods. In those so prone, the manifestations of bipolar disorder or "unipolar" depression can be triggered by external stress, a few sleeplessness nights, medications, a bad social interaction, or other disruption in attachment, recreational drugs, the change of seasons, or internal processes. Others inherited a propensity for dragged-out, unchanging low-grade depression: dysthymia. People who have been depressed for years, even if the etiology was attachment or trauma-related, develop the neural pathways and unbalanced chemistry of an endogenous depression. Their bodies have adjusted to living in that neural, hormonal, dorsal vagal "groove." You may need to help them boost their energy before you can use EMDR or other methods to clear the traumatic or attachment-based cause. If the physical causes are fixable and fixed, you may still need to use EMDR to help them out of their reflexive bodily, cognitive, and behavioral ruts.

TREATMENT

You've done the intake. You've sent your client to the doctor or the specialized psychiatric practitioner. You know what you're dealing with, or you don't yet. You can't find a trauma trigger, except the trauma of being depressed. You've empathized with your client's misery. What do you do now? You can start with supporting your client's body to come to equilibrium. Move on to physical interventions.

PHYSICAL INTERVENTIONS

- Three grams of omega-3 fish oil, each day, makes a big difference for many people (McManamy, 2004; Servan-Schreiber, 2004). I give out a sheet of the best-rated brands and the cheapest places to get them, along with links to research about it.
- Exercising at least three times each week has been shown to help lift depression in a large percentage of people; five to seven times is even better. Exercise helps ease most depression, whatever the cause. Aerobic exercise is good, but research shows that almost any kind of exercise can improve mood (Servan-Schreiber, 2004).
- Reducing "depressants": Many people "self-treat" with alcohol, drugs, caffeine, sugar, and fatty and high-carbohydrate foods. They may feel an initial boost from the substance, then a drift (or dive) into an even lower mood, necessitating more substance use. Most people see an improvement in their moods when they reduce their intake of these substances.

  ○ Alcohol and marijuana are depressants. I explain that using these drugs is like taking pills to make your depression worse. Substance abuse may be causing the depression, masking depression, or an attempt to cure the problem. An exploration of substance abuse may lead to a treatment program, then back to therapy to deal with the underlying issues, including major depression.

- Ecstasy and amphetamines actually deplete the brain of neurotransmitters, especially serotonin. Research shows that some people must take antidepressants after extensive use of these drugs, even if they weren't depressed before they started using.
- For people who are eating sugars and fats to boost their mood, sometimes it helps to explain that more protein all day long, starting at breakfast, can cut down the need for sugars and carbohydrates and help them get off the carbohydrate-induced roller coaster, and on the road to feeling better.
- Caffeine can cause its own roller-coaster effect. The more coffee people use to bring them up, the harder they crash down. People who are prone to agitated depression with disturbed sleep find that some of their symptoms lessen considerably if they let go of their 10 daily lattes. Garden-variety depression also lessens.

- Light regulation. Those of us who live in the North (especially the cloudy Northwest, as I do) see many cases of seasonal affective disorder (SAD). I send about 10 people each winter for light boxes or dawn simulators. Light boxes must have at least 10,000 lumens or luxes of light to be optimally helpful. If people sit in front of them for 20 to 60 minutes each day, especially at the beginning of each day, it can make a huge difference in their moods and energy levels. (If you suspect your client is bipolar, beware of light boxes. They have been known, on occasion, to precipitate manic episodes.) Dawn simulators don't need to be as bright. They start a simulated sunrise in your bedroom at the right time for your body clock to wake you up. Both kinds of light get us out of our states of hibernation. Vitamin D supplements (at least 2,000 IUs) can also help us Northern dwellers, since we aren't absorbing the weak winter sun through our layers of coats and clouds.
- Heart rate coherence exercises (Servan-Schreiber, 2004) or mindfulness meditation can help "reset" the body. Most depressed people don't breathe very deeply. More oxygen and the "dual attention" focus of meditation can help lift many moods.
- Refer to a medical provider who will look for underlying physical

causes: low thyroid, hormones, genetic propensity for depression, heart disease or other major disease.

How does EMDR fit into these simple physical interventions? Sometimes, it doesn't. If your clients diligently run out of your office to get the fish oil and light boxes, cut down on the alcohol and caffeine, up their protein intake, go see their doctors, and hop onto the nearest treadmill every day, you don't need EMDR to get them going. If, like many depressed people, they feel too overwhelmed to make even minute changes in their routine, you can start with inducing a "state change" (F. Shapiro, 2001) with Resource Installation, and then move them to a small "trait change" with some mild Future Templates. Once you can do full-blown EMDR trauma processing, here are some common targets that are caused by the depression itself.

EMDR TARGETS

- Losses of and grief over fun, sex drive, ability to think quickly or make decisions or engage people or to look or feel attractive; and after a long, destructive depression: lost jobs, lost relationships, and lost opportunities.
- Fear of the depression staying or, if lessened, fear of recurrence.
- Identity issues—"Who am I? What kind of person am I if I have depression?"
- Responses of other people. "Hey, lighten up!" "How come you never want to do anything?" "You're a black hole." "I'm done."
- Distressing affect. Whatever the etiology, depressed people often reflexively suppress the distressing feelings of anger, loneliness, grief, or even hope, thus deepening their depression. You can target fear of a particular feeling or ask *What emotion is sitting under your depression right now?*
- The feeling of depression itself.
- Cognitions:

Negative Cognitions (NCs)	Positive Cognitions (PCs)
• It's my fault.	It's a disease. *or* It's physical.
• I'm lazy.	I'm depressed.
• I'm defective.	I'm acceptable and right now I'm depressed.

- I'm unlovable.
- I can't do anything until I'm not depressed.
- I can't do anything.

I'm lovable even when depressed.
I'm not waiting until
I feel better.
I'm doing something right now.
I'm doing a little at a time.

PCs don't fix everything. They are a fix for cognitive distortions. Don't be afraid to go into the darkness with your clients. Validate how rotten they feel. Denying distress is a breach of the therapeutic relationship. Your clients are dealing with something horrible. Their friends are telling them to "buck up" and they physically can't. They need to come to acceptance of this paralyzing disease, even as you help alleviate its symptoms.

CASE EXAMPLE

Moderate Depression

Janet (a composite example) is 44 years old, slightly unkempt, functional, but just hanging on. She looks tired, moves slowly, and has fairly flat affect, even when her eyes fill with tears. On her mother's side of the family, there are generations of depression. There's no history of manic episodes in her family or in herself. Her life was "okay," except for the depression: a sweet husband, friends, good kids, a job that she used to like, only garden-variety trauma. She reports irritability and lack of patience ("Like I'm PMS-ing all the time") and sadness, fatigue, poor concentration ("I can't read anymore"), and eating more carbs and sugar than before. She's gained 10 pounds. She's sleeping too much. She denies hair loss and feeling cold (low thyroid symptoms). She's more isolated because she's not calling her friends to do anything. Janet's not feeling suicidal, just overwhelmed and "slowed down." She's felt this way for 3 months.

After the genogram, Kitchur's (2005) nosy, snoopy questions, a symptom list, and an explanation of EMDR, we set the agenda.

RS: *It seems you have a moderate depression. Given your history and your gender, it could come from different kinds of physical causes. I'm wondering about a perimenopausal cause, straight old inherited depression, some combination of both, or some other physical cause. It's winter in Seattle, if you hadn't noticed, and many people with the biological potential for de-pression find that it kicks in in the dark. Do you have a good doctor? It's time to give her some blood so that she can find out if your hormones are doing it to you or if it's something else. I'll write down some things she may want to check and I'm sure she'll think of more things* (thyroid and female hormones, vitamin D levels). *In the meantime, there are things you can do and we can do that help most kinds of depression. If your de-pression doesn't start lifting with these interventions, then your doctor or I might send you to a specialist to look at a need for antidepressants.* (The threat, or possibly the stigma, of antidepressants is often quite moti-vating for people to try other tactics.)

Are you taking any vitamins or supplements? No? There's a lot of re-search that says that fish oil is helpful for raising people out of depression. The researchers recommend 3 grams a day, which is one at each meal. Do you have it in you to go to the Coop or the supplement store to pick them up and then take them? You think you can? Great. Exercise is another well-researched technique. Getting aerobic is good, but just about anything you do that's regular will help. What kind of exercise are you getting now? Walking? How much? Once every 2 weeks won't help much. Do you think you could bump it up? When I asked you that, you look defeated. You've al-ready been trying and you can't? Let's see if we can get you going.

(Resource Installation [Kiessling, 2005; Leeds, 1998].) *I want you to think of a time, before this depression, when you had motivation and power and accomplished something that was hard to do. You got it? What thoughts went with that? . . . When you think about it, where do you feel it in your body? Focus on those thoughts and feelings and watch my fingers.* (10 count Bilateral Stimulation [BLS].) *How was that? Good? Stay with that.* (Three more sets.) *Feeling even stronger? Great! Could you put your body in a posture that goes with feeling strong?* (J. sits up and pushes out her chest, with head held high.) *Go with that!* (BLS.) *You're looking good! Think about exercising, now. Could you do it. Go with that.* (BLS.) *Right now, can you think of people who could help you get your body moving?*

Janet: My husband could take me for walks after dinner and on the weekends. My coworker would probably walk with me at lunchtime.

RS: *Go with that!* (BLS.) *Can you imagine asking your husband tonight? Yes? Go with that.* (BLS.) *How would that go? Good! Go with that.* (BLS.) *How about your coworker? No? What stands in the way?*

Janet: I haven't told her that I'm depressed. And I don't want to admit it to her or myself.

RS: *What's it mean about you if you're depressed?*

Janet: I'm a loser. (Notice there may be a great target here that may speak to her feelings about the depressed people in her family and society's aspersions on people who aren't "happy, happy, happy." But I'm leaving it alone until later. For now, we're trying to get her moving.)

RS: *What would you rather think about yourself?*

Janet: I don't know. . .

RS: *How about "I'm a regular okay person whose body has turned on her, and I'm acceptable anyway"* (a new narrative and a PC in one).

Janet: That would work.

RS: *Let's shorten it for your unconscious mind. How about, "I'm acceptable, even when I'm depressed"?*

Janet: Yeah, though I don't feel it.

RS: *You don't have to, yet. When you think about telling your coworker and asking for her help, how true does it feel that you're acceptable, even though you're depressed, on a 1 to 7 scale, 7 feeling totally true, and 1 not at all true?*

Janet: 2.

RS: *And what emotion do you get when you imagine asking her?*

Janet: Like guilty . . . no, shame.

RS: *How big is that shame, when you think about asking her and think you're a loser and are feeling that shame. 0 to 10, 10 being the strongest it could be?*

Janet: 7.

RS: *And where are you feeling that in your body?*

Janet: Shoulders and chest and stomach.

RS: *Okay. Go with that. And remember you can ask for a break anytime.* (BLS.)

We process through her grief about being depressed. It goes to some feelings about her depressed mom. They clear. She gets angry and mobilized about being depressed. (Yay! That's a great sign, because the depression was working to weigh that feeling down, in my opinion. And when people who are depressed feel angry about it, they often stop blaming themselves for their depression.) Then, about 20 minutes after we started, she becomes calmer, more present, and reports that the shame feeling has gone away. We go back to target.

RS: *So think about telling your friend at work and asking her to walk with you. 0 to 10, how distressed do you feel when you imagine that?*

Janet: It's gone. It's 0. And besides that, I realize I can tell her or not tell her why, though I'd probably tell her.

RS: *When you think about telling her, how true does it feel, 1 to 7, that you're acceptable, even if you're depressed.*

Janet: Pretty true, a 5.5.

RS: *What stops it from being a 7?*

Janet: That it may not be acceptable in the culture at work. In fact, I know it isn't. I don't want word to get around because it will affect my work situation.

RS: *Is it true inside you that you're acceptable, even if you're depressed?*

Janet: Yes. That's a 7.

RS: *Think about asking your friend to walk with you at lunch, without explaining why. And hold the idea that you're acceptable. Go through asking her to walk with you. (BLS) What do you get now?*

Janet: I'm going to tell her tomorrow at work that I want to get in shape and ask her to walk with me.

RS: *Think about doing that, and scan your body for any discomfort or sensation.*

Janet: I feel pretty good. In fact, I feel a little better than I did before we started doing this. I guess some of what I've been feeling is depressed and mad about being depressed, and that part isn't there so much.

RS: *Go with that!*

Janet: This stuff is cool.

RS: *Yeah, I know! So you're going to ask your husband to "walk the wife" on the weekends, and your coworker to walk during the week at lunch. This is good in two other ways. First, if you're walking at noon, you're going to get maximum light exposure, even through the clouds. Light often helps to lift depression. Second, there's a guy named Stephen Porges (2001, 2005), a researcher who found out that positive social engagement actually flips the depression switch inside many people. It isn't a total cure, but it helps. So if you're talking and making eye contact and feeling connected, you're fighting depression. You have to try it with people who actually can connect. Do your husband and your coworker have the ability to connect with people? With you? Yeah? Great! Are there friends to whom you can tell the whole story? Plan some time with them, too.*

Let's look at what you're doing tomorrow. You're going to call your doctor for a screening. You're talking to your husband and the woman at work. You're getting omega-3 supplements on the way home. Where at? Great that it's on your way home. I'm going to ask you to do one more thing: No-

tice if any thoughts like "loser" come up this week. In fact, we just did a piece of work. Notice if there are any leftovers from the work we did—old memories, old feelings—and notice if any new feelings or thoughts come up. If it's old bad stuff, bring it in and we'll clear it. If it's new good stuff, we'll reinforce it.

Notice that we left the session on a "we" note; that we went after the nearly inevitable shame of depression; that I brought in social engagement, her support network, and most of what is shown to work with moderately depressed clients. We're already moving forward while we're looking for the cause.

In the next session we targeted her eating patterns, which brought up more shame, which cleared. She leaves with a plan to add more protein to each meal and have some healthier snacks at regular intervals. She's "come out" to her close friends, who have volunteered to walk with her on the weekends and to keep in closer touch. Her mood is beginning to lift and she's feeling hopeful about future improvements.

Later, when Janet's doctor finds that her estrogen and progesterone hormones are out of whack, and gives her a prescription, Janet is already feeling about one-third better. She's getting regular exercise and light (walking at lunch gives her maximum daylight in our dark city), is eating more protein and less sugar, taking her omega-3's and vitamin D's, and feeling less shame and hopelessness about being depressed. A month after starting birth control pills to help with her perimenopausal depression, she's feeling back to normal. On the last of our 10 weekly sessions, we targeted her fear that depression would return and what she would do if that happened. We discussed that she may have a biological predisposition for depression, which could be impacted by stress, other hormones, trauma, or the aging process. We talked about the possibility, in the future, that she may need antidepressant medication or to come back to therapy. We also discussed that she may be just fine on the regimen that she's already doing.

RS: *How would you know if the depression was coming back?*

Janet: I'd be slow and stupid and wanting to eat all the time.

RS: *What would you do?*

Janet: First, I'd start exercising. Then I'd make sure I had people around. I'd look at my supplements and make sure I was taking the omega's.

RS: *Great. Can I wave at you, while you imagine doing that?*

Janet: Sure. (BLS.)

RS: *Got it? Great! What if those things aren't enough?*

Janet: I'd make an appointment with my doctor and maybe with you.

RS: *Go with that.* (BLS.)

Janet: I'm glad that you're both around. But it's scary to think that it could come back.

RS: *Any thoughts about yourself that go with that fear?*

Janet: Not so much. I don't feel ashamed anymore, just scared. . . . Maybe that I won't be able to deal with it.

RS: *How true does it feel that you can deal with the depression if it comes back? 1 to 7. A 3? And when you think about it coming back, and that sense you can't deal with it, how big is the fear? 0 to 10. 6? And where are you feeling that fear? Go with that.* (BLS.)

We do six rounds. The fear moves through, then some sadness about having been depressed. Her cognition changes near the end to "I'm not alone. I've got my husband, my friends, my doctor, and you to help me get through this, if it happens again."

RS: *Go with that!* (2 rounds BLS.) *Imagine the depression coming back and fighting it with all of us on your team.* (2 more rounds BLS.)

Janet: It's good. I know what to do and I can deal with it.

RS: *Go with that.*

Chronic Severe Depression

EMDR can be penicillin. A patient is "infected" with posttraumatic stress disorder (PTSD) after a traumatic event and the wound festers until the medication (trauma processing) is applied. The infection/ trauma goes away and the body/brain goes back to its normal homeostasis. The patient is cured and goes home whole. EMDR often becomes part of insulin, a chronic treatment for a chronic condition, when it's used in treating genetic bipolar disorder and chronic major depression. It's not a cure for the disease, but it helps keep the client functional and coming back, over and over, to homeostasis. The ingredients of my "insulin" for severely depressed and bipolar clients are:

1.   the containment of the therapeutic relationship
2.   using the social engagement of the relationship in session to "reset" the client's biology

3.   affect tolerance training
4.   psychotropic medications
5.   the EMDR protocol and related techniques for state change, then
      trait change.

Megan

Megan, another composite, is 58 and has been depressed, in varying
degrees, since she was a child. Her genogram is full of depressed or
alcoholic relatives and shows three suicides in her mother's and maternal grandmother's generations. Half of her siblings are on antidepressants. Megan has been hospitalized many times and had shock therapy
(electroconvulsive therapy [ECT]) as a young woman. She's been hospitalized once in the 8 years of our relationship. She's taking two antidepressants prescribed by a skilled psychiatrist. She's been on nearly
every antidepressant and mood stabilizer on the market. Despite that,
her moods range from nearly okay to agitated/anxious to totally shut
down. (Her psychiatrist and I wonder about a Bipolar II diagnosis, but
mood stabilizers, including lithium, don't do anything for her, so
we've shelved that idea.) She is intelligent, with a wry, but understandably black, sense of humor. She's been suicidal on and off since her
teen years, but with few serious attempts. She has a sensitive, overreac-
tive nervous system. She's an introvert and, like many depressives, one
of Elaine Aron's (1996) "highly sensitive people." She seems to have a
natural mood swing between dysthymia and all-out major depression.
Her depression is physical, but also reactive. Small things knock her
into illness or depression. Despite everything, she manages to get to
work on most days. This isn't one of them. She called saying that she
couldn't get out of bed. The session started on the phone and resumed,
3 hours later, in my office.
    On the phone:

RS: *Oh no! The bed monster has you again! That so sucks! Have you even
       been up to pee? You* are *depressed.* (Using the relationship, matching,
       empathizing, acknowledging, and externalizing the problem.)
Megan: Yeah, it's really terrible this morning. I'm so lazy. I shouldn't
       be alive. I want to be dead.
RS: *The bravest woman I know, battling the worst depression,* lazy?! *That
       depression thinking has grabbed you, too.* (Reframe of cognition and ig-
       noring the suicidal thinking for now, historically it goes away with

the state shift.) *I think you are too depressed to remember to breathe. Is that so? So let's do some breathing. Take two deep breaths. Make that belly move. Now don't force the breath anymore, but keep letting it move your belly. At the end of every exhale, take a little break, and notice when your body picks up the breath again for the inhale. You're probably going to start feeling more soon, as the energy moves through your body.* (She does, applying the Butterfly Hug, tapping herself while hugging herself [Boel, 1999] and, after a few minutes, starts crying gently.) *Can you tap and breathe your way through those tears.* (She does. She cries for about 3 minutes.) *How are you doing?*

Megan: Not as paralyzed.

RS: *Great! We've won one battle against the forces of depression! How about getting up and turning on the shower water before you hang up on me?*

Megan: I can do that now.

RS: *Great! Do you need a dose of therapy today, or do you want to go to work and check in on the phone? I could see you or phone you at 1:30.*

Megan: I don't want to, but I better come in.

RS: *Good choice. I look forward to seeing you. Are you ready for the shower? And then some fuel?*

Megan: I haven't really been eating much.

RS: *How about meds?*

Megan: I didn't eat or take meds last night. I went straight to bed. (No surprise to me!)

RS: *Can you do both before you come? I want you to have some energy for the therapy.*

Megan: (Sighs) I will.

Later, in person, she's lost the boost from our phone interaction, is not making eye contact, and is sitting inertly with a crumpled posture. I'm thinking about Porges, and about how when someone is in a dorsal vagal (shut-down) state, social engagement can activate a myelinated ventral vagal (present and connected) state. I attempt to join with her.

RS: *Really bad weather running through you today.*

Megan: Yeah.

RS: *I'm so sorry!*

Megan: Yeah, but it doesn't help.

It's time to bring out the big guns.

RS:　*First, let's get some breathing going. Two deep breaths into your belly, then regularly, but deeply. Pauses after the exhale.* (She does for a few minutes, and straightens her posture, as color comes back into her face.) *I want you to imagine connecting to your neighbor's little dog.* (Dogs are easier than humans for her.) *His tail is wagging, and he's jumping up and down when he sees you. . . . What do you notice in your body right now? A little warmth in your chest? Can you hold the tappers?* (Three short sets of BLS, as she gains more color and more light in her eyes.) *Can you look into my eyes now? Great! What's that like?*

Megan:　I see you and I like you better than when I came in.

RS:　*Where do you feel that liking? Chest?* (BLS.) *It's stronger? I feel it too. Keep going.* (BLS.) *Think of three other people that you connect with when you're connectable.* (More BLS.)

She's more in the room, and almost smiling. Over the years, I've noticed that most of this fragile woman's depressions are triggered by some external event, often a social one. We're ready to see if there was a trigger for her current depressed state.)

RS:　*Did anything happen before you went down the tubes this time?*

Megan:　Everything happened. (Typical depressed globalization. I'm not biting.)

RS:　*Could you pick the first bad thing or the worst one?*

Megan:　My boss hates me. (We parse out exactly what happened and find a target.)

RS:　*Before we do the setup for EMDR, I want to be sure we don't blow you back into shutdown. I want you to do three things through the processing. No matter what you're feeling, keep sitting up straight and keep breathing deeply.* (Otherwise, she'll depress herself in order to keep those feelings down.) *Second, keep connected with me. It's hard to go down the tubes when you're socially engaged. I'll coach you on these things. Third, keep in mind that you get a break anytime. We want to defuse the depression, not add to it. Agreed? Let's go.*

She starts out with a typical cognition, "I'm horrible," but I have another idea to try out.

RS:　*Let's go underneath the depression a little. Could you possibly be mad at your boss? Yes? What do you say to yourself when you're angry?*

Megan:　I don't deserve to be angry.

Flipped to a PC: "I can have my feelings." VOC (Validity of Cognition Scale) 2 and "I can tolerate my feelings." VOC 1½. She feels mad, a 9 SUDS (Subjective Units of Disturbance Scale). And it's everywhere. She stays locked on my eyes, glaring as we process. I remind her to breathe between sets, and the anger dissipates. By the end, we can do a complete installation of "I can have my feelings."

Megan: I can tolerate my feelings is stuck at a 5.
RS: *What stops it?*
Megan: History. When I don't feel, I end up in bed, for days. I don't tolerate my feelings.
RS: *How true is it, right now in your gut, that you are learning to tolerate your feelings?*
Megan: A 7.

We run that through with the experience with the boss. It stays true and we install it. We go on to the target.

RS: *Think about if your boss treats you that way today when you go to work.* It cleared. And then, *How would you like to deal with both the boss and the feelings you have after this.*
Megan: I want to stand up for myself and keep breathing and be mad if I'm mad.
RS: *What do you say to yourself about yourself when you think of doing that.*
Megan: I'm about halfway between that and "It's too scary."
RS: *What's the flip side?*
Megan: I can stand up for myself, and keep breathing, and feel, even if I'm scared.
RS: *Think about standing up and breathing and being mad, if you're mad. And "It's too scary." How scary is it, 0 to 10?*
Megan: About a 5. In my gut.
RS: *Keep breathing and go for it.* (BLS.)

About four rounds later, the fear comes down, her chin comes up, and she's ready to roll. We install, "I can stand up for myself" and future pace appropriate responses, including saying nothing, but continuing to breathe and feel when dealing with her slightly unreasonable boss. We tap through each situation. She looks stronger.

A final question:

RS: *What was your level of depression when you were stuck in bed this morning?*

Megan: About a 9.

RS: *What is it now?*

Megan: I still feel it, but it's about a 4. I can function with a 4. (A 4 is reasonably good for this client.)

RS: *What are you going to do until our appointment next week?*

Megan: Eat. Take my meds and my omega 3's. Breathe. Try to walk to work. Remember looking into your eyes. Remember who I love. And play with Buddy (the neighbor's dog).

RS: *Visualize doing that every single day. Go with that.* (BLS.) *Got it?*

Megan: Got it!

I'd like our therapy to be penicillin. And I know that it's insulin. We've been chipping away at her depression for years with every skill at my disposal. We've processed every trauma and attachment target with EMDR. We've done ego-state work with the depressed states and all parts. In the meantime she has an arsenal of skills that she can often, but not always, use. She's more resilient. She's less reactive. She uses many less sick days and vacation days on her depression. She hasn't been in the hospital in 6 years. The therapeutic relationship sustains her and it gave her the support, 3 years into therapy, to start trauma processing with EMDR. Clearing trauma was helpful. She's less triggered and triggered less often though EMDR couldn't fix her body's propensity to take a dive. As with my bipolar clients, she has a variable therapy schedule. When the depression is low, her resilience is high, and she's able to meet her social engagement needs outside therapy, she comes in once or twice each month. When the depression is upon her, she may come in weekly, and occasionally twice weekly. As her fragility increases with her aging process, I fear that her good psychiatrist, her tight therapeutic relationship, her medications, and all that we all know may not be enough to sustain her.

Bipolar Disorder

True bipolar disorder is genetic. Some bipolar processes are trauma based. Complex PTSD and dissociative identity disorder (DID) are often misdiagnosed as bipolar disordered. Traumatized people may swing from an activated (red alert!) unmyelinated ventral vagal state to an all-systems inhibited (depressed) dorsal vagal state (Porges, 2001) for which EMDR *is* penicillin. Clear the trauma, and you stop the mood swings (van der Kolk et al., 2007). People with extreme trauma and poor attachment may experience these mood states as ego states, for which EMDR tied with ego state therapy is the "magic pill." I've "cured" nearly 20 cases of misdiagnosed bipolar disorder with EMDR and ego state therapy. Make sure your "bipolar" clients are truly bipolar. And if they are, remember that they will still have trauma separate from or caused by their bipolar disease.

Containment in the therapeutic relationship is key when working with bipolar clients. When clients are unstable, or hanging out in the extreme ups or downs, I schedule more sessions, have check-in phone calls, and keep in close contact with medicators, and sometimes the clients' families or other support people (with written permission, of course). The first time therapy ends, I make sure that bipolar clients know that they can come back for another round anytime their "weather" starts acting up. *First call Diane to straighten out the meds. Then call me. If you're not sure about the meds and you just feel weird, call me first and we'll figure it out.* I have often called or had clients call their medicator from my office during a session. With a few people I've developed a changeable schedule. Monthly visits when the internal weather is reasonably clear, with more available as needed. This schedule has circumvented several potential hospitalizations, with some people for whom no combination of medications has been adequate.

Human beings regulate each other's biology and moods (Porges, 2001, 2005; Schore, 1994; Siegel, 1999). People at nearly every point on the bipolar roller coaster can be reached and partially regulated by social interaction. Use yourself to match the intensity, but not the content, of the despair, rage, self-hatred, or overbuoyancy in the client in front of you. Connect. Engage. Respond. If you can do this while holding on to yourself and some degree of grounding, you can usually enact some "state change" in your clients, no matter how intensely "up" or "down" the client was when walking in the door.

Affect tolerance and regulation skills are vital. Teach every tool that helps clients take a step back from their states. Mindfulness meditation allows clients to watch their thoughts and emotions (dual attention) while regulating the underlying energy levels. Teach them every skill that allows control over mood, energy level, or thoughts. David Servan-Schreiber (2004) quoted research on the efficacy of heart rate coherence training. EMDR can be directed at the content of mood swings, and more. BLS can help settle anxiety, speediness, agitation, and some depression. Strenuous exercise helps balance out depressed and manic states. Social engagement does, too. Self-talk (or self-argument) can be helpful: For different states, one creative client developed, "Slow down, I'm manic today!" and "I'm not lazy, I'm just crazy." They worked for her.

Here is my favorite bipolar metaphor/installation:

It's helpful to think of your moods as weather blowing through your body. There's not much we can do about weather. But we can mitigate its effects. A house or the right clothes can keep the worse effects outside of you. But they don't do everything. Imagine that you are a house. Can you do that? A big storm is blowing through the windows. The wind blows some papers off the table and brings in some dust. But you're still standing. You can stand firmly and watch those high and low moods blow through you. They'll affect you, but they don't have to blow you down. Medications can be like storm shutters: They keep the worst winds out. What we do in this office can shore up the house and quiet some of the storms. Feel your strong body. Feel the structure of your house. It has stood through all the storms and it will get stronger and stronger.

Do you know how to drive in the snow? Do you remember the first time how scary it was when the car slipped? Think of how it is now. You have to pay conscious attention to your driving on ice. You have to do it enough times that you start automatically turning into the skids, with your feet off the brake. Remember the last time you drove through that snowy pass, and what you did to stay on the road. Can you feel that sense of sliding while you have the sense of control in your body? Where? Focus on that. (BLS.)

EMDR with Bipolar Disorder

Warning: With a truly bipolar disordered person, it may be dangerous to use EMDR to clear activating material if your client isn't well medicated and stable. How can EMDR be dangerous? Trauma processing may bring on stress or sleeplessness or distressing affect that may activate manic states or a spiral down to depression. A post-processing missed night's sleep for a regular trauma client is distressing, but easily handled. That same sleepless night could precipitate a manic state and a hospitalization for a bipolar client. EMDR's Assessment Phase bundles cognitions, emotions, and body feelings to enhance the target for processing. The Desensitization Phase can intensify affect and sometimes bring on abreactions. Many bipolar clients can tolerate this kind of activation. Some don't. Be careful! To do EMDR, or any therapy with a bipolar client, know your client well and cultivate a good relationship with your client's medicator. Get the necessary releases, and talk to the doctor or ARNP about how you can best support your client. Discuss the risks of doing EMDR with the medicators to see what they think.

The first processing target is often the client's distress about having the diagnosis. Cognitions are key, both at the beginning of therapy and throughout.

When you think about having bipolar disorder, what does that say about you? Here are some NCs, and possible PCs.

Negative Cognitions	Positive Cognitions
• It's my fault.	I have a disease.
• I can't do anything until I'm not depressed/manic.	I'm not waiting until I feel better.
• I'm a hopeless case.	I'm learning to manage this disease.
• I'm crazy.	So what! I can have a good life. (My favorite.)
• I'll always feel this way.	My feelings change.
• I won't be able to keep this feeling.	I'll get it back.
• I'll never have a normal life.	I'll have a good life.
	I'll be better than I am now.
	I'm adequate to deal with this.
	I'm getting my life back.
	I have a controllable disease, and I'm dealing with it.

The emotions that arise in processing are often shame, going to anger about having this disease, going to grief, going to acceptance. You may process any or all of these feelings more than once. Sometimes I think that bipolar states are like ego states: Things learned in an up state or a "normal" state may not translate when the person is depressed. You many find yourself processing similar material through different states.

Medications

If bipolar or severely depressed clients don't want to do meds, I do what I call "creative enabling." They don't have to take medications to stay in therapy, but the subject has to stay on the therapeutic table. I use Motivational Interviewing techniques (Miller & Rollnick, 2002) to help clarify what clients feel about medication and, usually, to get them ready to try a trial of them. With EMDR, we target their biggest fears about taking medications: what it means about them ("crazy people take meds"), mind control, taking away their creativity or energy, and so on. After that I often use the Two-Hand Interweave (R. Shapiro, 2005) to help them with their choice: *In one hand hold all your resistance to trying medications. In the other hand hold the possible benefits.* (BLS.) Or I might try, *In one hand, hold all the people who've tried to get you to take meds. In the other, hold what you most want to do for yourself.* (BLS.) I've seen people let go of resistance with this one. It seems to seat the responsibility for the good idea in themselves, rather than me, their doctor, their parents, or their friends.

With some clients, I've done processing of their fears about the first session with the psychiatrist. Many have had traumatic interactions with unskillful medicators, inpatient programs, or other institutions. Often these past traumas must be cleared before the client can consider meeting a new doctor. I sometimes offer to go with them to the first appointment with the medicator. And living in a city, I have been able to ferret out several good psychiatrists and nurse practitioners, so that I can vouch for their competence and humanity before that first appointment. *No, I don't think Diane would ever see anyone as a "sick bug"; she's got too much heart for that. Did you have that experience before? That sounds awful. Tell me about it, and then let's clear it out.* Most general practitioners don't have the background to deal with a complex bipolar client or severe depression. If possible, get your client a referral to a good psychiatrist or psychiatric ARNP.

People with bipolar disorder are notorious for stopping their medications in order to experience the highs that can go with manic states; to avoid the side effects of their meds (often weight gain, a sense of dullness, or dry mouth); or because they forget what happens when they aren't on medications. Remember that bipolar states act like ego states. Clients may not remember what they learned when in a different mood or mode. I've used Jim Knipe's Level of Urge to Avoid protocol (Knipe, 2005) with some "forgetting" bipolar clients. It goes like this: *How good does it feel, on a scale of 0 to 10, 10 being the best possible feeling, when you think about stopping your meds? A 9? Where do you feel that great feeling? Go with that.* (BLS.) Keep going rounds, especially if the client's brain begins to remind them of the past peccadilloes, bankruptcies, and lost relationships resulting from manic sprees or the hospitalizations from their deep, deep depression. If the Level of Urge doesn't come down on its own, you can throw in a Two-Hand Interweave to bring some reality to the situation: *In one hand, hold how good it would feel to quit your meds. In the other hand, hold the past consequences of quitting your meds. Go with that.* (BLS.). . . . *Oh, you're starting to feel antsy about it. Keep going.* (BLS.) *You're still paying off bills from that time? Go with that.* (BLS.) *You don't want to go there again? Stay with that!* (BLS.)

Clients have sworn at me after this intervention, usually while laughing. They say, "You've taken all the fun out of it!" And I say, *I let your brain consider the real consequences and then I got out the way. You're the one that came to the realization about the consequences.* I like this because I get to stay out of "nag" role and let the clients' brains come up with both the plusses and the consequences of a course of action. With some people, I get to do this exercise over and over again, depending on where they are in their "forgetting" disease process.

On two occasions, with acutely manic, going on psychotic, clients, I got on my knees, with my head on the floor, and pleaded with them to take medications to forestall another hospitalization. The intervention was successful in both cases. Sometimes you need to be dramatic with people who are experiencing dramatic symptoms.

Mania

With bipolar, you get to deal with the ups along with the downs. The best medications can't contain all swinging moods. Mania can manifest as a high mood with grandiose features; anxiety with obsessive-compulsive features; or irritability that may explode into rage. I generally don't do trauma processing with clients who are experiencing mania. But I do EMDR with floridly manic clients when the mania has triggered a past trauma to the point of abreaction. At that point, we run quickly through the Assessment Phase and start processing, because the cognitions, affect, and body awareness are already painfully on the surface. At these times, content can sometimes blaze through, quickly and intensely, never to bother the client again. Alas, in true bipolar disorder, clearing trauma can lessen but not eradicate the symptoms of the disease.

Pieces of EMDR can be useful to corral run-away thoughts and emotions. BLS alone can calm people down (Wilson, Silver, Covi, & Foster, S., 1996). I've had floridly manic people tap on themselves to slow the thoughts and calm the affect. It's never completely vanquished the agitation, but it has worked to bring it down from a 10 (or "500") SUDS score to a more manageable 3 to 5 and sometimes less. Resource Installation of a Healing Place or of a calm or patient past state can be useful. The Two-Hand Interweave can help grandiose people find a little reality in their brains. Here is a typical interaction with a manic person.

RS: *Wow! That weather is really blowing through you today.*

Client (with pressured speech):   I'm so fast that everything else is in slow motion. People talk too slow. Traffic drives me crazy. And I want to do everything, right now, all at once.

RS: *How about some tapping to see if we can slow you down a little?*

Client: I forgot I could do that. I'll tap on myself, because it would be too much to get it from the outside right now. (Does continual butterfly hug, tapping self over heart.) Every time I do it, it calms me down. It's working already.

RS: *Would it be too intense to look into my eyes for a while?*

Client: I think I could. (Looks.) There you are! I get so in my head I kind of forget.

RS: *Just feel the tapping and notice what it feels like to be in contact.*

Client: (Sighs and drops shoulders.) I know what you're doing. I remember that article about that Porges guy (2005). It says that when you're socially connected you can't be too revved or too depressed. You're doing that to me, aren't you?

RS: *You got it. It looks like it's working.*

Client: It is. I'm starting to relax. I kept going around and around today about my mom. What if something happens to her? I'm worried that she'll get bird flu and die. (Relaxing allows the obsessive thoughts to rise to the surface.)

RS: *We know these thoughts. Let's do two things with this. First, I'll remind you.*

Client: For the ten thousandth time.

RS: *Yep. That your body is full of energy and anxiety and your brain is trying to come up with a good reason for it. While you're tapping, feel that revved-up place in your body that's holding all that anxiety. . . . Think about your mom. . . . Go back to your gut.*

Client: Maybe it is in my body. It's moving a little, but I'm worried about this bird flu thing.

RS: *Go with that.*

Client: My stomach is less buzzy, but I don't know if it's safe not to be worried.

RS: *Try this. In one hand, put that your mom is going to die someday, hopefully in bed at 102 years old. In the other, put that it's going to be bird flu, this week, despite the fact that she doesn't work on a chicken farm in China. Focus on those taps you're doing, and just notice.*

Client: Well, they both suck, but bird flu isn't very likely. I don't know about 102, maybe 90. I'll be 65 and could handle it by then.

RS: *What do you notice now?*

Client: Calmer by half, not thinking about Mom, thinking about lunch.

RS: *Keep tapping and take yourself to that beach on Kauai.* (This client's Safe Place.) *See if you can get yourself a few points calmer.*

Client: All I want to do is jump up and play beach volleyball. (She's manic, even in her safe place.)

RS: *Imagine that. Make 1 minute in this office be an hour of volleyball, during which time you win, and then lie back down on the beach for a while.*

Client: (90 seconds later) That was great. I'm at a 4 now. I'm ready to go, and I will call the doc about checking my lithium levels as soon as I get outta here. Will you call the doctor, too, and tell her what a nut I am? Great. Thanks.

RS: *Wait! So, about 5,000 times this week, notice your body when you get scary thoughts about anything. Remember to tap on yourself. Right now, can you imagine scary thoughts coming in . . . and remembering to tap?* (BLS.) *Good! Go with that.* (BLS.) *Now imagine another scary thought situation . . . and tapping. . . .* (BLS.) *Good! So see you next week, and don't forget to call me if you get too squirrelly.* (A little future pacing imbedded in a Future Template.)

In my experience, if you practice a helpful new behavior in the office, people are more likely to do it outside the office. Notice the enhanced containment at the end: *Call me, I'm available.*

RELATIONSHIPS

Some mood disordered people have been impacted since childhood. Bipolar children can display attention deficit disorder (ADD) symptoms and be extremely emotionally reactive and hard to regulate with regular parenting skills (Papolus & Papolus, 1999). Their exasperated parents may discipline them harshly or avoid them. Depressed, unresponsive children may not be able to elicit loving interactions from their parents. As these children go out into the world, they may be subject to everything from harsh discipline in school, to shunning, teasing, or harassment by peers, to being forgotten or ignored by people around them. There may be many EMDR targets pertaining to the impact of past relationships on self-esteem, identity, and interpersonal skills.

Mood disorders inevitably affect current relationships. Bipolar people may lose the trust of their families and friends because of their sometimes erratic behavior. Depressed people may not reach out or respond well to others. In American culture, we believe that people should have control over their moods. Others around your depressed clients may confuse depression with momentary bad moods and will be telling your clients to "just get over it," "buck up," "stop taking those awful meds," or, my favorite, "If you loved me, you wouldn't be in this mood." If your clients have had awful experiences with their families, friends, recovery groups, or coworkers about their depressions and medications, go after those experiences with the Standard Protocol. Use the whole three prongs. Clear what happened (who said what), what if it happened again right now, and inoculate against future occurrences. (Sister saying again to a manic client, "You just do this for attention.") Have them practice what they'd say or do in those situations. In Future Template mode, you can also have them clear resistance to telling people. "I really have to exercise, or I get depressed." "I'm sorry, but I'm too depressed. If I can climb out of the hole, maybe next week." "Yes, I do need an accommodation at work. It's a diagnosed disease and it can be debilitating." And, "Maybe you don't need to take these drugs, but I do. I'm sorry you don't believe me. You should read Kay Redfield Jamison's book *An Unquiet Mind* (Jamison, 1995) and tell me what you think when you're done. Until then, I don't want to hear about it."

SUMMARY

EMDR doesn't fix mood disorders. But it can help clients to manage their states, affect, and thoughts brought on by mood disorders. We can use EMDR to create resources in clients; calm runaway affect, practice coping, and create Future Templates for manageable futures. And, of course, to clear the traumas that trigger depressive or manic processes and the traumas that arise from living with these diseases.

REFERENCES

Aron, E. (1996). *The highly sensitive person.* New York: Broadway Books.

Boel, J. (1999). The butterfly hug. *EMDRIA Newsletter, 4*(4), 11–13.

Jamison, K. R. (1995). *An unquiet mind.* New York: Knopf.

Kiessling, R. (2005). Integrating resource development strategies into your EMDR practice. In R. Shapiro (Ed.), *EMDR Solutions: Pathways to healing* (pp. 57–87). New York: Norton.

Kitchur, M. (2005). The strategic developmental model for EMDR. In R. Shapiro (Ed.), *EMDR solutions: Pathways to healing* (pp. 8–56). New York: Norton.

Knipe, J. (2005). Targeting positive affect to clear the pain of unrequited love, codependence, avoidance, and procrastination. In R. Shapiro (Ed.), *EMDR solutions: Pathways to healing* (pp. 189–212). New York: Norton.

Leeds, A. (1998). Lifting the therapeutic burden of shame: Using EMDR resource installation to resolve a therapeutic impasse. In Philip Manfield (Ed.), *Extending EMDR: A casebook of innovative applications.* Renamed *EMDR casebook* (pp. 256–282). New York: Norton.

McManamy, J. (2004). Omega-3 for depression and bipolar disorder. Retrieved from McMan's Depression and Bipolar Web http://www.mcmanweb.com/omega3.html. Accessed November 1, 2008.

Miller, W., & Rollnick, S. (2002). *Motivational interviewing.* New York: Guilford Press.

Papolus, D. F., & Papolus, J. (1999). *The bipolar child: The definitive and reassuring guide to childhood's most misunderstood disorder.* New York: Broadway Books.

Porges, S. W. (2001). The polyvagal theory: Phylogenetic substrates of a social nervous system. *Physiology and Behavior, 79,* 503–513.

Porges, S. W. (2005). The role of social engagement in attachment and bonding: A phylogenetic perspective. In C. S. Carter, L. Ahnert, K. E. Grossmann, S. B. Hardy, M. E. Lamb, S. W. Porges, et al. (Eds.), *Attachment and bonding a new synthesis* (pp. 33–54). Cambridge, MA: MIT Press.

Schore, A. (1994). *Affect regulation and the origin of the self: The neurobiology of emotional development.* Hillsdale, N.J.: Erlbaum.

Servan-Schreiber, D. (2004). *The instinct to heal.* New York: Rodale Press.

Shapiro, F. (2001). *Eye movement desensitization and reprocessing: Basic principles, protocols, and procedures* (2nd ed.). New York: Guilford Press.

Shapiro, R. (2005). The two-hand interweave. In R. Shapiro (Ed.), *EMDR solutions: Pathways to healing.* New York: Norton.

Siegel, D. (1999). *The developing mind: Toward a neurobiology of interpersonal experience.* New York: Guilford Press.

van der Kolk, B. A., Spinazzola, J., Blaustein, M. E., Hopper, J. W., Hopper, E. K., Korn, D. L., et al. (2007, January). A randomized clinical trial of eye movement desensitization and reprocessing (EMDR), fluoxetine, and pill placebo in the treatment of posttraumatic stress disorder: Treatment effects and long-term maintenance. *Journal of Clinical Psychiatry, 68*(1), 37–46.

Wilson, D., Silver, S. M, Covi, W., & Foster, S. (1996). Eye movement desensitization and reprocessing: Effectiveness and autonomic correlates. *Journal of Behavior Therapy and Experimental Psychiatry, 27*, 219–229.

Chapter 4

"Shame Is My Safe Place"

Adaptive Information Processing Methods of Resolving Chronic Shame-Based Depression

Jim Knipe

SOME CLIENTS ARE CHRONICALLY DEPRESSED DUE TO LIFELONG CONVICtions of their own unworthiness and "badness." The cases in this chapter illustrate how EMDR-related methods can help clients who have learned to shame themselves as a way to maintain an idealized image of a valued parent and/or defend against the reality and pain of childhood abuse. At the beginning of therapy, for each of these clients, the traumatic origins of their shame feelings were dissociated and not available to the adult ego state. Consequently, each client experienced a self-definition of profound defectiveness and moral badness. This negative identity was driven by both sensory information (a feeling of shamefulness) and intellectual conviction. As Damasio (1999) pointed out, what we "know" about self is based largely on what "feels true" about self. Body sensations are a major determinant of the sense of knowing what is real, what is true, what is happening, or what has happened in the past. Thus, for each of the cases described here, comprehensive therapy involved processing negative identity and self-referencing Negative Cognitions (NCs), and specific and detailed focus on the deeply entrenched feelings and sensations that were intrinsic parts of shamefulness.

The formation of a core identity is one of the tasks of childhood.

This task can go awry in many ways for a child living in a dysfunctional environment. For such children, it's logical to say, "It is better to be a bad child with good parents than a good child with bad parents." It seems true, both intuitively and from clinical practice, that for an abused child, a sense of "badness" about self may be less horrible than an awareness of the full reality and implications of abuse—the shock, the betrayal, the confusion, the vulnerability of being little in a world of uncaring big adults. If you are a "bad" child with good parents, you still have good parents, at least in your mind. You then have hope, because you could someday learn to be a perfect child, and maybe your parents would finally give you the love, acceptance, and guidance you need. Of course, there are many possible reasons why parents might be "bad" or deficient in their caretaking role—illness, their own mental disturbance, fear of parenting responsibilities, narcissism, addictions—to name a few. Parents who are frightened or immature will often project their own doubts and fears onto their children with shaming words (e.g., "You are a crybaby," "You are a brat," "What's wrong with you!!? You are too . . . noisy, angry, needy, quiet, anxious," etc.). Whatever the cause, for many children attempting to make sense of a dysfunctional family situation, a self-definition of "badness" is an adaptive and compelling option. We could use psychodynamic language and say that the identity of shame serves as a psychological defense, protecting the child in such circumstances from the full impact of traumatic loss and emotional abandonment.

Thirty years later, this shamed-child-now-grown-up may find themself in a therapist's office, seeking help for lifelong chronic depression, inappropriate self-blame, and low self-esteem. John Bradshaw (2005) has written extensively about the ways that "toxic shame" is both a cause and an effect of addictive disorders, and is often a way of covering feelings of childhood abandonment. Tomkins, described in Nathanson (1992), describes the emotion of shame as an experience that can be either part of healthy functioning or maladaptive and irrational. Within Tomkins's definition, shame is an automatic, neurologically programmed response that occurs when the person is activating interest or excitement that is unwise, inappropriate, or not supported by the person's environment. Subjectively, the emotion of shame is experienced by an individual as an unpleasant flattening of all affect. For example, a person waves to an old friend and then, too late, realizes that the person who was greeted so warmly is actually a total stranger. A shame feeling may follow, with a strong sense of disorientation, a felt diminishing of physical energy, perhaps a lowered head, accompanied by cognitions of self-blame. The person's previously positive affects of interest and excitement are immediately squelched. Shame often occurs in a person who "gets caught" doing something that violates personal or societal rules of morality, but, as we see with many clients in therapy, shame feelings can be activated when there is no fault or moral transgression. For example, victims of assault or robbery will often experience disorientation, a wide-ranging flattening of interest and excitement, along with highly irrational self-criticism (e.g.,"I shouldn't have been walking in that park," "I should have had better locks for my front door"). For both children and adults, the disturbing emotion of shame can be a way of maintaining an illusion of living in a controllable, predictable world, and denying the fact that in life horrible events can occur randomly, outside of one's control.

The standard EMDR procedures (F. Shapiro, 2001) will usually be effective for most clients with this type of history, in helping them resolve feelings of shame and intrinsic "badness." Present-day, negative self-referencing cognitions of unworthiness and shamefulness can provide a bridge to identification of the traumatic events in the past that were the origins of feelings of inappropriate responsibility, and the memories of those events can then be processed using the standard eight-phase EMDR model.

However, many clients who have a deep sense of defectiveness are not fully aware of how those feelings began. An abused child may dissociate information about the trauma as an adaptive response to an "impossible" situation, that is, since intrinsic needs for self-protection and escape from harm may be in direct conflict with needs to seek attachment and comfort from the only caretakers available (Liotti, 2004, 2006). As this child grows up, the public, "apparently normal" part of the personality (van der Hart, Nijenhuis, & Steele, 2006) may continue to have a vague, yet pervasive sense of "badness" that is maintained both internally ("I know I *am* bad because I *feel* like a bad person all the time, and I can't ever snap out of it!") or externally, through a distorted interpretation of present-day frustrations and stresses ("These bad things happen to me because I deserve it."). A person may only partially dissociate the original trauma—the "normal" part of the personality may have a vague recollection of the abuse, but minimize its importance—or the person may have ongoing, chronic feelings of anxiety and shame, but not be aware of the origin of these feelings in childhood events.

Because of this dissociative disconnect, in therapy these individuals may be highly illogical when describing themselves or their families of origin. For example, a client may say, "My daddy was the best daddy anyone could ever have!" even while it is clear from other sources of information that the father behaved very inappropriately. Or, a client might argue, like a lawyer in court, about his or her own pervasive defectiveness as a human being. A client may report being in a constant state of intense self-criticism. Or another client with a similar history may have a shaky sense of being "okay" but be vulnerable to the intrusion of a dissociated, ashamed state of mind in which the client is unable to see or accept any positive feedback or compliment. Frequently, I have pointed out to a client that we are in a *"funny argument"*—I am listing the client's positive qualities, while the client is countering my view, vehemently presenting alleged evidence of their own defectiveness or inadequacy. In these instances, it is as though the feeling of shame is intractable, resistant to all rational discussion. This is a debate that should be within the client, not between the client and the therapist. But the needed inner dialogue may be oddly prevented by an emotional investment in maintaining an identity of "badness," even while suffering from the ongoing feelings of shame. Somehow (to quote one of the clients in the transcripts, below), "It is better to be bad."

THEORETICAL FOUNDATIONS

Psychological defenses, including the defense of self-shaming, can often be treated and resolved with EMDR-based interventions. The term *psychological defense* is being used very broadly here, as any mental or behavioral process that functions to block or prevent the conscious emergence of disturbing (usually posttraumatic) information or affect. With standard EMDR, focused on trauma, we target the negatives: negative posttraumatic images, cognitions, emotions, and physical sensations. The client, aware of the safety of the therapist's office, is asked to access elements of the unresolved trauma memory, and through sets of Bilateral Stimulation (BLS), the trauma memory is transformed into a normal memory, now integrated into the person's larger sense of self, with an increase in client self-esteem, as measured by the Validity of Cognition (VOC) Scale. This is the situation that we, as EMDR therapists, always want to help the client get to—simultaneous awareness of both the safe present and the traumatic past—so that

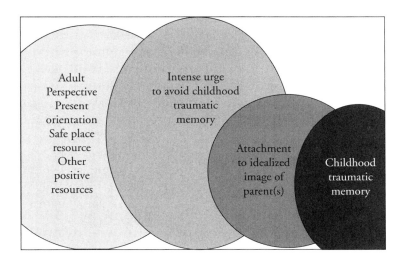

Figure 4.1 An avoidance defense and an idealization defense block the emergence of intrusive traumatic memory material. These defenses enable the person to continue to function in present reality, but access to and healing of the trauma is prevented.

therapeutic processing can be initiated. However, for clients who have significant psychological defenses or dissociative fragmentation, the achievement of simultaneous dual attention—present and traumatic past—can be impaired. Reflexive defense prevents direct connection with the posttraumatic disturbance. Figure 4.1 illustrates a disordered ego state structure in which avoidance and idealization defenses prevent direct conscious access of the dissociated part holding the trauma memories. The defensive ego states, in contrast to the traumatic memory states, tend to hold *positive* affect—for example, the relief of avoidance, the positive feelings of narcissistic entitlement, or the highly valued feelings of connection with an idealized caretaker.

A basic premise of the approach described in this chapter is that if a client with this type of defensive structure is willing and able to hold in mind the *relatively positive* affective aspects of their psychological defense, and then engage in sets of BLS (either Eye Movements [EMs], or alternating right-left hand Taps or Auditory tones), the defense will tend to weaken in intensity and importance, revealing the underlying posttraumatic disturbance, which can then be directly processed using standard EMDR procedures.

A. J. Popky (1994, 2005) pioneered the use of BLS information processing with addictive urges, which often serve a defensive function.
For the past 15 years, I have adapted Popky's protocol to the targeting
of various forms of psychological and behavioral avoidance (Knipe,
2002, 2005, 2007). For example, a woman in her 20s had successfully
used standard EMDR to resolve her feelings of loss and grief regarding
the death of a close friend. Following this work, she came into a subsequent session and told me that she would like to attempt to work on
something else. She had a strong sense that she had been sexually
abused as a child. For years, she had had a lingering sense of shame
about herself, which seemed to her to be linked to the possibility of
abuse. She said, "I don't know who it was. But I am sure it happened. I
don't want to know, but I *do* want to know." As we discussed the situation further, she said, "It is true I don't want to know, but even more
strongly, I want to get over this." With her informed consent regarding
where processing might lead, I began by asking a question that is useful in targeting an avoidance defense: *"What's good about not knowing?"*
This question is intended to bring to the center of her awareness the
feelings of relief and containment associated with the avoidance. Her
answer to this question was, "If I knew, I don't think I could stand it!" I
replied, *"Stay with that,"* and initiated a set of EMs. Then, she said, "Actually, I think I do know who it was, but don't have any memory pictures of it." Again, I said, *"Stay with that,"* and began another set of
EMs. Processing continued in this way for approximately 30 minutes,
with increasingly clear information emerging about how her cherished
uncle had initially showed affection and then abused her when she
was 8 years old. She also remembered that she had closed her eyes
during the actual abuse, so she wouldn't have to be so aware of what
was happening. In this session, and in three subsequent sessions, she
was able to see and understand how her idealized attachment to her
uncle had stood in the way of her being able to remember what had
happened. She was able in these sessions to focus on, process, and
largely resolve the abuse incidents. She reported, following these sessions, that her sense of "defectiveness" and "badness" simply was no
longer present, and instead she was enjoying significantly increased
feelings of self-worth.

This form of question (*"What's good about_____?"*) can be used to
initiate targeting with a wide variety of psychological defenses—defenses that would otherwise block effective EMDR processing. In the
case above, the avoidance defense was targeted by asking, *"What is
good about . . . (the avoidant thought or action)?"* The targeted avoidance

may be of a feared childhood memory, or of a present-day action (e.g., *"What's good about . . . not admitting that you were wrong in that argument with your friend . . . not talking to your spouse about your sex life . . . not talking to your boss about a raise . . . putting off paying your bills,"* etc.). If a therapist uses this intervention, it is important that the client be asked this question in a way that is clearly free of any judgmental attitude or shaming.

An alternative way of targeting avoidance is to use the 0–10 scale. The therapist says to the client, *"Right now, when you realize we could be using this session to talk about that very difficult old memory, how much, 0 to 10, do you* not want to? *How much would you rather talk about anything else?"* Then, *"Where do you feel that (number) in your physical sensations?"* To begin targeting, the therapist says, *"Think of that wish or impulse to* not talk about it, *and where that is in your body, and follow my fingers."* With the client's permission, sets of BLS are then initiated, and information processing can proceed. Typically, the numbers—the Level of Urge to Avoid (LOUA) score—will go down just like a Subjective Units of Disturbance Scale (SUDS) score with continuing sets of BLS. After several sets, the therapist can go back to target with questions like, *"How intense,* right now, *is that urge or wish to not talk about it?"* In this way, the client is able to keep the protection of the avoidance defense while actually processing information related to the underlying trauma. Usually, when the LOUA score goes down to about a 3 or 4, the client will be able to directly access and begin to process the traumatic incident. The standard EMDR procedures can then be used without the interference of the avoidance defense.

Elsewhere, I have described ways of targeting other types of psychological defenses, such as a narcissistic false self (Knipe, 2002), codependent caretaking, procrastination, and the inappropriate idealization of a former lover (Knipe, 2005). In each of these examples, entrenched defenses were weakened through combining BLS with the positive affect contained within the defense, allowing direct processing of posttraumatic disturbance.

TARGETING THE PSYCHOLOGICAL
DEFENSE OF SHAME

The two clients described below are representative of a larger group of approximately 20 clients who initially presented with shame-based depression. These two individuals differ from the larger group only in that they were asked, and very generously agreed, to allow me to videotape their sessions for use in consultation, in training programs, and in this chapter. The transcripts from their sessions are presented verbatim, except for minor editing for clarity. The first transcribed session for each of these two clients shows a progression from "I know I am a very bad person" to "I can know, objectively and intellectually, that I am an adequate and good person, but I still have intense shame feelings, especially when I think of events in my childhood." We could think of this as progress from "I am shame" to "I have shame." Then, during the second transcribed session for each client, the therapeutic focus is on freeing these clients from the remaining visceral aspects of their shame identities.

Shame Originating in Specific, Dissociated Childhood Trauma

"Whitney" was a 57-year-old woman in a long-established marriage, with children and grandchildren, referred for EMDR by her non-EMDR woman therapist, for treatment of the identified traumas of a rape at age 13 and sexual abuse by a previous male therapist 10 years prior to the referral. During initial history-taking, the client reported that throughout her life, she had suffered from what she described as "angst"—a word intended to convey not only chronic anxiety but also her depression and sense of being somehow deeply flawed. She described her family of origin as "very loving." Father was a respected minister; mother was a highly admired "pillar of the community." Within her childhood home, Whitney was given affection and caring, "99.9% of the time." However, she also stated that this positive growing-up world was sometimes disrupted by unexpected and extremely shaming verbal attacks by one or both parents. She stated that the memory of these incidents was even more troubling to her than the remembered sexual abuse, so our initial EMDR targets were selected moments of parents' rage.

During the EMDR Preparation Phase, Whitney had trouble identifying a soothing "Safe Place," but after several weeks of sessions, she said she felt clear acceptance and safety in my office, and it was not difficult for her to turn her attention to that safety when asked to do so. She then appeared ready for the trauma work. When one of the highly disturbing incidents with parents was targeted, her NC was "I am terrible; I am evil, like Hitler." She had trouble identifying a corresponding Positive Cognition (PC), and so I suggested the words, "I am okay," but when I asked her VOC score with this PC, she said, "Not even '1.' " When I asked further questions to get at a PC that would be more plausible to her (e.g., *"What would you rather think about yourself?"*), she became visibly anxious and reported feeling "spacy." I took this as a red flag, indicating the presence of possible dissociative elements to her clinical picture. This impression was confirmed when I suggested that we "pause in this EMDR work and take things a little more slowly." She took my statement as evidence that EMDR could never work for her because she was so "horrible and evil," and went into a trancelike state of being unable to concentrate and unable to give a clear report of what she was experiencing. It was helpful for her when I suggested some interventions to help her become reoriented (tossing a pillow back and forth, having a drink of water), and she reported that she was tuned in once again to the safety of my office, but this exchange demonstrated the likely presence of highly disturbing dissociated memory material.

In the weeks that followed, I tried to keep our interaction "lighter" while we explored additional aspects of her presenting problems. It became increasingly clear that her depressed affect was directly associated with feelings of intense shame that were "always there" and were "the air that I breathe." She could give no clear reasons for this negative assessment of herself, but these statements were consistent with other aspects of the way she interacted. Both in therapy, and in relationships in general, she would frequently, and almost compulsively, apologize for imagined insensitivities on her part. When she did this in our therapy sessions, I would point out to her that she had done absolutely nothing wrong, and in fact had many positive qualities (such as kindness, generosity, and a wide-ranging empathy for others). But these reassuring statements from me appeared to have no effect. It seemed that her negative ego state was a core identity, unaffected by logic or facts. She said that she felt more understood by me when I listened, without debate, to the depths of her self-loathing.

As sessions continued, she was able to give more information about her history, while still remaining "present." As we were discussing the rape at age 13, she suddenly got a disturbing memory picture of the perpetrator, which then shifted to a picture of her father's face, and a previously dissociated, entire memory of a very early incident of sexual abuse, when she still was in diapers. She said, "This feels real. This is important. We have to talk about this." In spite of her obvious fear, she was determined to continue. In this memory, her father was "doing something inappropriate," when her mother unexpectedly walked in and asked, with some anger, "What's going on here?" She remembers her father answering, "Nothing." The client was adamant in describing this memory, that she *had caused* her father to be sexually abusive to her. She spontaneously said that this incident was somehow the origin of the visceral feeling, later put to words, of "I am shameful and bad. I am evil." She even said, "That is when I first knew, I am a whore." The transcript of this session, from my written notes, continues as follows. Whereever "EMs" occurs in the transcript, that is a moment when I said, "Stay with that" or "Think of that," followed by a set of EMs.

JK: *Do you really think that a little baby could be to blame? How could you have made your father do something like that?*

Whitney: I just know that I made him do it.

JK: *If you heard about this happening to a little child, or if it happened to a child you loved—your own children when they were little, or your grandchildren, would you blame the child?*

Whitney: I would never blame a child for that. But when I think of myself in that situation, I know that I am completely to blame.

JK: *So the rules for you, when you were a baby, are just different from all other babies?*

Whitney: Yes. I guess so. I feel so scared right now—I can hardly talk. (long pause) You know, that feeling about myself—that I am evil, that's my only safe place. I can't give that up. I know that sounds strange, but I just can't give that up.

Her way of expressing this contradiction indicated that she was not only disturbed and confused by her paradoxical feelings, but also motivated to explore the contradiction. Why did she *need to keep* a problem that she had wanted so long to eliminate from her life? In saying this, she did not have the vacant, dissociated look on her face, and her clarity of mind indicated to me that we had sufficient emotional safety to continue to explore this issue.

JK: *On a scale of 0 to 10, how strong is that need to never give up that idea, that you are a whore, that you are evil, that you are despicable?*

Whitney: It's a 10.

JK: *Where is that "10" in your physical sensations?*

Whitney: My chest and my abdomen.

JK: *Just hold that in mind, when your mother walks in, and are you able to be both here and there, right now?*

Whitney: Yes.

JK: *Stay with that and follow my fingers.* (EMs.)

This question was intended to access and target the positive emotional investment in what appeared to be a shame defense. In the dialogue that follows, the client is clearly going back and forth between shame, attachment-related idealization of parents, and direct awareness of the fear and abandonment feelings of the trauma.

Whitney: (After the first set of EMs) But they had their crap too. (EMs.) The world changed right at that moment. It was just as bad for them as it was for me. (EMs.) Something got set in motion and it was never the same after that. (EMs.) I have to think that my dad was just having a bad day and a weak moment. I want you to know, he really was a good man. (EMs.) But I didn't have any advocate; I needed an advocate. (EMs.) It seems like just a little more of a picture now, not so real. (EMs.)

It seemed that we had reached the end of a channel of information, and so I asked the client to go back to the original target image.

JK: *Think again of when your mother said, "What is going on here?" What do you get now?*

Whitney: I can't believe my mother just let it go. I know she saw what he did. (EMs.) My mother was so sweet, such a good person. You wouldn't believe how kind she was. (EMs.) It must have been terrible for her. (EMs.) I think it was harder for her than it was for my dad. But I needed for her to stand up for me and she didn't. I can't stand to keep that thought. (EMs.) I am feeling the loss of both my parents. I can't stand it. (EMs.) Do you know how this feels? It really feels like I just found out that someone died. (EMs.) It's like, I am me and I'm looking at that baby. (EMs.) The baby is a whore. (EMs.) If I weren't a whore, my mother would have done something. (EMs.) If it were one of my children, I can't imagine what my gut reaction would have been. I would have gone ballistic. (EMs.) When I look I see that child had no value. That child did not have any value at that moment. One time my husband was picking on our daughter, really meanly, and I was so mad, I just lunged at him. I made it clear; there would be none of that. Mom should have reacted that way. (EMs.) But there had to be something wrong with me. But then I remember that she was molested.

JK: *Do you think that made a difference in how she reacted when she saw what was happening to you?*

Whitney: He is just wearing a mask when he says, "Nothing." She puts on a mask because she doesn't know what else to do. I feel so sad, I don't think I can stand it.

JK: *Is this too hard for you to be able to continue?*

Whitney: No, I can. I want to. I have to understand this.

Whitney's determination, and her continued clarity in talking about this incident, told me that she was not in danger of sinking into a dissociative abreaction, so I asked her to go back again to the original image.

JK: *Think again of when your mother said, "What is going on here?" What do you get now?*

Whitney: That's when I put on a mask, too, so that no one can see— that I am a whore. (EMs.)

JK: *Right now, on a scale of 0 to 10, how much do you still need to hang on to that belief about yourself, that you are evil, you are bad, you are despicable, you are a whore?*

Whitney: Right now, not at all. I just feel so sad. I see what happened as like what you read about sometimes, where someone is cleaning a gun and it just goes off and kills them. I don't want to blame my mother and father. But I see now, my father had a weakness. And my mother didn't know what to do.

JK: *So when you think of the moment of your mother coming into the room and saying, "What is going on here?" when you think of that again right now, what do you get?*

Whitney: It's very, very sad, but it is different than before. I think I just want to feel sad about that for a while.

Because of the intensity of this session, I suggested that the client come back 2 days later. During the intervening time, she became aware of another, separate incident of sexual abuse by her father, one in which the abusive behavior went farther. The realization that this happened more than once was extremely troubling to her, and was experi-

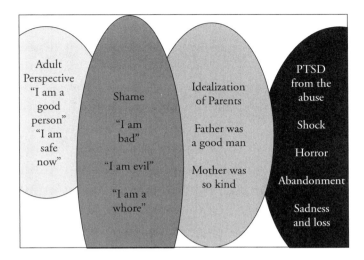

Figure 4.2 "Whitney"—Structure of dissociated parts of personality before the initial transcripted session

enced as a severe loss, since it meant she could no longer maintain her cherished, idealized image of her father. She reported, over a period of several subsequent weeks, that her feelings of shame, but also her sense of the specialness and goodness of her parents, were each significantly diminished.

Visual representations of Whitney's apparent personality structure, before the session described above, and after, are shown in Figures 4.2 and 4.3, with the relative size of different ovals representative of the relative importance of different ego states within her overall personality.

Three weeks after this session, after several additional sessions focused on less emotionally charged topics, we targeted the images of the second, more difficult memory of abuse. During the intervening weeks, Whitney had achieved an ability to see that her intense feelings of "badness" were connected, not with her present life or behavior, but with her images and memories of abuse. Still, she felt a high level of disturbance, and so to provide an extra measure of containment, we used a variation of Fraiser's (2003) Dissociative Table method. In her session, I drew a picture similar to Figure 4.4, and we used the picture as part of our discussion.

As I drew the picture, the taped session continued as follows. My questions are guided by the structure of the EMDR Assessment Phase

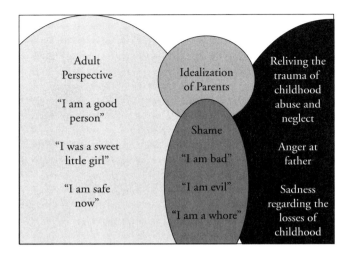

Figure 4.3 "Whitney"—Structure of parts of personality at the start of the second transcripted session

procedural steps, with different questions answered by either the adult or the child "parts."

JK: *I am going to put two imaginary chairs here, in front of a big imaginary television screen. Okay? In this chair here* (JK points to larger chair), *how about putting the part of you that is here right now? Like, the part of*

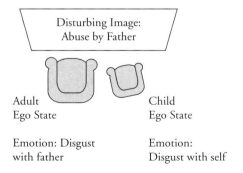

Figure 4.4 Modified Dissociative Table Method (Fraiser, 2003)

you that knows you are okay, and that you understand some things now. The part of you that is, perhaps, sadder, but wiser, in an objective, adult sense. How would you . . . what is the word for that part of you, like, "adult self" . . . what would you say?

Whitney: Umm . . . my adult self, my *emerging* adult self.

JK: *Okay. Good. You're on your way. Strictly speaking, from the point of view of your emerging adult self, are you okay?*

Whitney: Right now?

JK: *Yes.*

Whitney: Yes. I think I am beginning to see that.

JK: *Now, let's have the other part in this chair* (JK points to smaller chair)—*the part of you that feels like a child and still at times has that feeling of "angst." When you look through the eyes of* this *part* (JK points to "adult" chair), *life looks different than when you look through* these *eyes* (JK points to "child" chair). *Right?*

Whitney: Yes.

JK: *Can you go back right now and put on the imaginary TV screen, a picture of what you got in touch with 3 weeks ago? What is the image that comes into your mind, when you think of that right now?*

Whitney: It is that whole visual image of what he is doing to me. It is gross. It is so gross.

JK: *You, the adult, can look at this. You, the adult, have feelings and emotions about it. What emotion do you have about it right now? What is the name of the emotion that you have right now, when you look at this, as an adult?*

Whitney: I am pretty disgusted with my dad. I have been [disgusted] just recently.

JK: *Yes.*

Whitney: And that is kind of new for me, you know.

JK: *I do know. Now, can you shift over, and look through the eyes of this child, at this same exact picture? And what is the emotion you feel right now?*

Whitney: Disgust for myself. Yes. (Increased physical agitation)

JK: *Is it the "I'm a whore" feeling?*

Whitney: (Sigh) Yes.

JK: *I am going to ask some questions, and they may be hard questions, but just answer whatever feels true.*

Whitney: Okay.

JK: *From your adult perspective today, again, looking at this, what is your answer, as an adult, to this child, who says, "I'm a whore"? What do you know about that, that is different from what the child is saying?*

Whitney: I know that she was a victim. And she wasn't a whore.

JK: *So you know you were a victim.*

Whitney: I do know that. Children are not to blame for what is done to them.

JK: *And as a child, you were not a whore?*

Whitney: Right.

JK: *Put that in words that don't have a negative. In other words, state it positively. "I was* not *a whore. I was a victim." How would you put that positively?*

Whitney: I was . . . I was just a sweet, innocent child that got abused.

JK: *Yes. When the child in you looks at this picture, of your dad and what he is doing, how true does that feel to her? What is* her *reaction to those words, right now: "I was a sweet, innocent child"?*

Whitney: I *don't feel* that yet! I feel *so* responsible! That image just makes me furious at myself! It doesn't make sense, I know.

JK: *Right now, you the adult, can you look at this child? Where does she feel that shame, in* her *body, right now?*

Whitney: In her pelvis.

The therapy method of the two chairs, in front of a screen displaying a trauma image, sets up the conditions of dual attention stimulation—that is, simultaneous awareness of the safe present along with the traumatic past. Before beginning EMs, however, I ask the "adult part" to simply look at the "child part." This is more than just accessing a traumatic memory. This is asking the client to reverse the dissociative process that has for so long provided protection from the overwhelming affect contained in this memory material. With the structure of the dissociative table, along with a sufficiently strong sense of present orientation and safety, the "adult part" is able to maintain a visual image of the child in the trauma. BLS is then initiated in a way that maintains the therapeutic balance between past and present, and trauma processing begins to occur.

JK: *Can you, the adult, just see this child, while it is happening? There she is. Yes. Can you just look at her, and see whatever you see? Can you just look at her, and see her shock? I am going to move my fingers, and just look at her, and see whatever you see. (EMs.) And now look again, and whatever happens to catch your attention right now, when you look at her. What do you see right now?*

Whitney: For some reason, I have the image that I am trying not to cry. You know, how kids do that, when they [Whitney makes hesitant breathing sounds]. I don't know why. That is an image that I am having right now.

JK: *And just keep looking at her.* (EMs.)

Whitney: I just have an image of being trapped on this table. (EMs.) I think I just reached a point where I couldn't . . . I couldn't take it, and that is when I must have started fighting it, in some fashion, and that kind of creeps me out, because my dad was such a control freak! But I think I maxed out . . . it was too much. I think originally I just lay there, and let it happen. (EMs.)

JK: *Look at the child again. And what do you get now, when you look at her?*

Whitney: I get this feeling that *she's gone!* I get this feeling that she *is* gone! I get the feeling that she is now a whore, a full-fledged whore! I really get that feeling right now. (EMs.)

One advantage of this structure of two chairs is that the adult part can be the source of interweaves that are useful to the child part.

JK: *What do you, the adult, have to say about that?*

Whitney: She's *not!* But I became that, just at that moment. (EMs.)

This remembered moment is when Whitney's irrational shame identity began, and in order to fully process and resolve this problem, we need to focus on the exact details of what she experienced, and how she, as a child, interpreted this event.

JK: *Notice what it means when you say, "I became that, at that moment." Like, was it some kind of decision, or some kind of shift, in this child? What, exactly, was the shift?*

Whitney: Well, because I wouldn't have known what a whore was . . . it was just a shift of . . . a knowing . . . a knowing of the *evilness* of you . . . a feeling like that. Ahh!

JK: *So, a shift in terms of "I'm evil"? Like "I wanted to be good, but I have to forget that. I have to abandon that idea. I can't ever be a good person." Something like that?*

Whitney: I just *became* it, in that moment. In that moment, it just feels like . . . there are no words for it. It just happened inside of me. That is who I was now.

Because of the importance of this remembered moment, we focus precisely on it, and add the BLS.

JK: *So go back, right now, and* as an adult, observe the child *right at this moment when the shift happens and she becomes a whore, so you can watch exactly what is happening. Because if you can watch what is happening, all of your understandings and all of your life experience and all the things you know that this little baby doesn't know, can be brought to solve this problem. Because the truth is, she came to a conclusion that wasn't true. It is absurd to think that a baby is a whore.*

Whitney: Right.

JK: *Can you see that?*

Whitney: Yes. (EMs.)

JK: *So just look right at her, right at the moment that this shift is taking place. Just* see what you can see. *Just see whatever you see, when that shift is taking place.*

Whitney: Oh, God. It is so hard to describe it. I can *feel* it. I can so feel that moment.

It seems, from everything Whitney has said, that her "whore" feeling is serving a defensive purpose, and so I ask her, as an interweave, to focus on the positive affect associated with her sense of shame.

JK: *Here is a thought. For the baby,* what is good *about her shifting from the shock and the terror to "I'm a whore"? What's good about that?*

Whitney: Because she *accepts* it then! It changes the trauma of it all, somehow. (EMs.)

JK: *You said, a few weeks ago, that the thought "I'm a whore" has been your safe place.*

Whitney: Yes . . . It became my safe place then, didn't it? (Deep sigh.) (EMs.)

JK: *Just notice what you are feeling—it doesn't have to have words. Stay with what you are feeling now.* (EMs.)

Whitney: I just feel that! At that moment, it went into all of my pores. Every part became that. I can't tell you how awful that feels to me, that moment!

Whitney is experiencing an abreaction, but also appears to continue to have good orientation to the safety of my office. Just to be sure, I ask specifically if she is able to maintain dual attention.

JK: *Can you feel it right now?*

Whitney: I can *feel* it!

JK: *Can you stay with it, and know you are still here, too, so that with half your awareness you are here and you are safe—it was a long time ago—but go back with the other half of your awareness and feel it as fully as you can, in all your pores.*

Whitney: Yes. (EMs.) It is so much for such a young child.

JK: *Yes.*

Whitney: But I am telling you, I know now that is what happened. Now, right this minute, I know that is what happened. (EMs.)

JK: *Go back again, and look at this little baby, and let's say the feelings of upset, of shame, of "I'm a whore"—let's say that was a "10" when we started today. Look at this child right now, and what do you get now?*

Whitney: It is just a little bit farther away. I can't quite connect with it right this minute, for some reason.

JK: *Okay. So when you try to connect with it, what number do you get?*

Whitney: Probably a "6." I just have the feeling left over.

JK: *So, look at the whole incident again, on purpose. And it is a "6." It is not a "4" or a "0." It is a "6" right now. Talk about that "6." You know it is a "6," somehow. Talk about that "6."*

Whitney: Maybe it is less than a "6" right now. I just know because of my internal stress level right now, in my stomach. (EMs.)

JK: *Say what you get right now, when you think of it.*

Whitney: Not a lot! (Smiles.) (EMs.) I feel so much more relaxed now.

JK: *Good. I'm glad.*

Whitney: I don't have the angst!

JK: *Good.*

Whitney: (EMs.)

JK: *Go back and think of it again. Think of all the worst parts of it—the shock of the baby, the feeling of "I'm a whore." Go through it all in your mind so you can review it again. What do you get now, when you think of that?*

Whitney: There still is some of it. It is a "2" now. Maybe a "3." (EMs.) I am feeling so much better.

JK: *Good.*

Whitney: I think this insight today is huge for me, that moment in time when I became, truly became this whore, through all of me. It is like in *all my DNA*. It almost felt like it went through all my DNA, and it was there for good.

JK: *I almost have a visual image of that. So go back and think of it again—*

that exact moment. Think of it on purpose. What do you get, right now, when you think of that exact moment, of that happening?

Whitney: I feel detached from it. I can see it happening. I can almost visualize it, too, but I don't feel connected to it. It is like . . . I see it happening. But I don't have any feelings around it right now, for some odd reason. (EMs.)

JK: *When you look at this child right now, and see this child's DNA . . . the transformation that has happened in every cell of her body . . . what do you see right now, when you look at that?*

Whitney: (Pauses.) I don't see it! (Smiles.) (EMs.) I mean, I can kind of feel activity in this body, but it doesn't feel like the whore activity. It is just an activity. I don't know. It is bizarre.

JK: *So, look at her again, and see if you can see any trace of that "whore" kind of sensation in her feelings in her body. See if there is any trace if it, anywhere.*

Whitney: There is still a little bit . . . I think right now it is just because she doesn't have any clothes on. And that is bothering me. (EMs.) I am so mad at my dad. I just want to say, put some clothes on me! That is what I want to say. There is nobody there to help me get these clothes on. Nobody! It is just that . . . you get this happening to you, and then the person who does it doesn't even . . . like you are not even a human being, or something. You know? You really are an object. That is how it feels.

Since we are nearing the end of the session, I offer two cognitive interweaves to help her accelerate processing, so that she can reach resolution before we stop.

JK: *So go ahead. Do whatever needs to happen here.* (EMs.)

Whitney: I could put some clothes on her. I want to tell her something, but I don't know how to say it.

JK: *If she said to you, "I'm just a whore," what would you want to say back to her? She can't talk, but if she could, what would you want to tell her?*

Whitney: She's not!

JK: *Tell her what she is.*

Whitney: She is a sweet little girl. (EMs.)

JK: *Can she hear you?*

Whitney: Yes. (EMs.) That is nice.

JK: *Good. Look and see if there is any shame left in her DNA.*

Whitney: That helps me, to see that she is a sweet little girl, because she is. (EMs.)

JK: *As you say that to her, does it feel true?*

Whitney: Yes. (EMs.)

JK: *We will be out of time in a minute. What are you coming to understand today? What was useful about this for you? It looks like it was useful.*

Whitney: It was *so* useful for me. I don't know, it just feels like I am getting rid of all that.

JK: *Yes. This cellular DNA idea of shame is really an interesting idea.*

Whitney: I don't know how that even came into my mind.

JK: *Well, we can't know for sure, but I think it was putting into words what you experienced as a child. You the adult have words, but when you were a child without words, you were experiencing something awful, and those are the words that say it.*

Whitney: This was very helpful. The feeling is very different.

In the weeks that followed, this client reported a surprising and deeply felt change across virtually all of her relationships. She said that her feeling of "badness," which previously had been so intrinsically interwoven into all of her interactions with people, was now simply absent in those interactions. In both her appearance and in her report, she was free of depressed affect. Briefly, for a week or two after this session, she reported a certain disorientation, as she noticed again and again that her long-held "angst" and negative sense of herself simply weren't there anymore (except as a memory), even when she would deliberately search for them. She said, "It is like when I got new glasses, and suddenly could see everything more clearly." Within her new definition of self, she was able to relate to others more comfortably, realistically, and appropriately. These gains were maintained during the remaining 3 months of her therapy, at which time she successfully terminated.

SHAME ORIGINATING IN PERVASIVE
CHILDHOOD TRAUMA AND NEGLECT

"Elizabeth" was a 48-year-old woman referred by her lawyer for EMDR following a violent attack and attempted rape by her previous employer. This attack, which had occurred several years prior to her entering therapy with me, had triggered in this client a period of several months of self-hatred and dissociative numbness. When she first began therapy with me, she could only remember brief fragments of the actual attack and the time that followed. There were other dissociative symptoms. She generally interacted in sessions in a way that appeared very "normal," but when something came up that was a reminder of the attack (such as seeing someone on the street who resembled her assailant), or when we were discussing her family of origin, she would go into a very different state of mind, quickly switching into feeling extremely depressed, "spacy," and "numb," and expressing hatred for herself. When I would mention positive information about her, as evidence that she was a satisfactory person, she would say, "I know you are not lying when you say that, but I feel guilty, because I must not be telling you the truth of how bad I am." Similarly, when we were discussing the assault, she would say, "Why did he pick me? There must have been something about me that made him do it." There was no evidence whatsoever that she was responsible for the attack, and she could intellectually acknowledge that this was true. But her hair-trigger shame was so strong that facts and logic had no importance. In her sense of self and feelings, she was totally bad, and therefore she was totally to blame for the attack.

As we discussed the assault, it became clear that a dissociated state of self-hatred would arise at any attempt to directly target this event. This state had its origin in childhood, from the many years of physical neglect and physical beatings by her psychotic mother. These sources of her "badness" identity would need to be processed prior to working on the more recent attack by the employer. Figure 4.5 represents "Elizabeth's" ego state structure prior to the first transcripted session.

In order to find an appropriate point of intervention, I asked her the following question: *"When you think of that feeling of badness, that core sense of being a bad person, what event in your life gives you the* strongest evidence *that you are bad? What events taught you that lesson about yourself, that you are a very bad person?"* She had had many childhood traumas, including a sexualized assault by an emotionally disturbed second-grade teacher. But the situation that came up for her, immediately, in response to my question, was one that recurred over and over between 5 years old and adolescence. On weekends, at her house, it was her job to make coffee in the morning, and then take it to her mother who was still in bed. Her mother would often remain in bed for a day or more at a time, leaving her five children hungry. Sometimes, when her mother was finished with the coffee, Elizabeth would

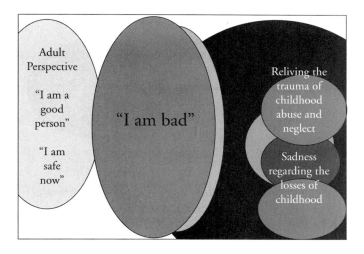

Figure 4.5 "Elizabeth"—Structure of dissociated parts of personality before the initial transcripted session

ask her to get up to prepare some food for her and the other children. Many times, her mother reacted to this type of request by going into a rage, beating Elizabeth with a stick, and sending her to her room for hours. Little Elizabeth would then stay in her room and hate herself for causing her mother's upset. The representative picture for this repeating situation was one of Elizabeth the child, at the bedside, asking her mother to get up. This was the image that gave her, the adult, the strongest evidence for the NC "I am bad." When I asked her what an alternative positive thought about herself might be, in connection with this old memory, she said, "I can't think of that." When I suggested the words, "I am a good person," she said, "But *that would be a lie*!! I hate myself when I think of that." The intensity of her vehemence, proclaiming her badness, suggested to me that this shame might be functioning as an entrenched defense against the fear, loneliness, abandonment, and perhaps even the physical hunger that she repeatedly experienced as a child.

She said that the SUDS level of shame connected with the bedside memory was a "10+," with physical sensations of numbness "all over." The high SUDS and her report of numbness indicated that she might be on the edge of dissociation, so I altered the targeting to make it more

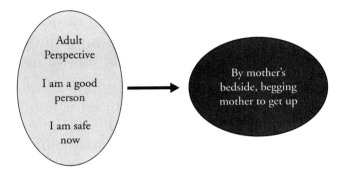

Figure 4.6 First, Elizabeth is asked to bring to mind the image that most represents her identity of shamefulness

structured, in order to make it safer for her. She appeared to be caught in a loop—a chain of sequentially activated ego states that led her, again and again, into a hopeless and dissociated state of shamefulness. We proceeded to dismantle the loop in the following way: First we fo-

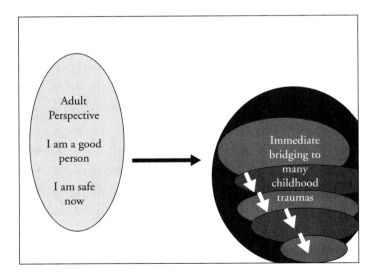

Figure 4.7 Elizabeth then experiences a highly disturbing bridging to many childhood traumas

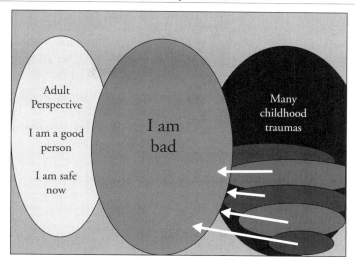

Figure 4.8 To contain the intense affect of the many traumas, the defense of shame is activated

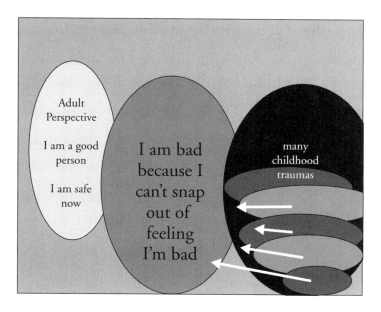

Figure 4.9 Elizabeth's feeling of shame is a trigger for increased shame, creating a loop—a downward spiral of disturbance. The targeting question for the first transcripted session (in the childhood trauma situation) is, "What is better, to be *scared and lonely,* or to be *bad*?"

cused on her shame about feeling shame, shifting from "I feel such deep shame, and that proves I am a bad person" to "I am a normal person who feels intense shame feelings when I think of childhood events." This was progress, but was not sufficient. In the second transcripted session, with Elizabeth more able to maintain an adult orientation, I used an Affect Resetting procedure (see Chapter 17, by Katie O'Shea) to neutralize the remaining aspects of her shame defense, which opened the way to direct EMDR processing of the fear, loss, and sadness of her childhood posttraumatic stress disorder (PTSD). The sequence of targeting dysfunctionally stored information, over the course of the two transcripted sessions, below, is visually represented in Figures 4.6–4.12.

In the first transcripted session, I asked a question intended to help Elizabeth see that her decision, as a child, to blame herself for the troubles with her mother, wasn't bad, but was reasonable.

JK: *So the decision to be bad . . . what exactly do you do that makes you bad?*
Elizabeth: I beg her to get out of bed and feed us.
JK: *Yes, and you knew in advance everything that would follow from that.* (Elizabeth has tears.) *She would spank you and send you to your room and you wouldn't have breakfast. So, as you are standing there, and you haven't asked her yet, what's better: to be scared and lonely, or to go ahead and ask her to get out of bed, which makes you bad? Which one is better, to be scared and lonely, or to be bad?*
Elizabeth: To be bad is easier. I just am bad because I don't control myself.
JK: *Yes. So bring up this moment: She just finished drinking her coffee and you haven't decided yet what you are going to say. Can you just hold that moment in mind? On the one hand you can do this, on the other hand you could do that. Can you just stay with that moment?* (Elizabeth nods.) *And what are you feeling physically, in that moment?*
Elizabeth: Just that I *am* bad. (Tears.)

Because the client is beginning to become disoriented as she dissociates into "reliving" the traumatic memory, I ask to do something that will help her become more oriented to the present situation.

JK: *Let's do something right now.* [With a pillow in hand] *Can you catch this?*
Elizabeth: (Nods yes. The pillow is tossed back and forth.)

With this procedure, Elizabeth's affect changes. This is the usual result of a game of "catch" with a client who is on the verge of a dissociative abreaction. Tossing a pillow (or a tissue, or a pen, or a paper clip) seems to activate the orienting response and take a person out of traumatic "reliving." This result usually happens quickly and shows the client that the memory is not so powerful and impossible to escape. The client is then more able to maintain an observer status with regard to the memory.

Elizabeth: Thank you. I feel better.

JK: *Okay, so you were in this memory and now you feel better. What would you say is different from a minute ago?*

Elizabeth: If I need to, I can picture it like a picture and it's not like I'm going through it.

JK: *Okay, does it help to realize you can do that?*

Elizabeth: (Nods yes.) (EMs.)

JK: *So can you stay aware of this office, but also be aware of the moment when your mother just finished her coffee? Can you hold both awarenesses, almost like a split screen? See if you can do that.*

Elizabeth: It's hard for me not to just go back into it. I really go back there.

JK: *So did you just go back there right now?*

Elizabeth: Yes, maybe halfway.

The "pull" of the memory material appears to be too strong, so another intervention is used to help her come "back in the room."

JK: *So, just listen right now for the next car that drives by in front of my office.* (Car goes by.)

Elizabeth: (Nods yes.) Hmm . . . I'm all the way here.

JK: *Does that feel better?*

Elizabeth: Yes. (EMs.)

With sufficient orientation to the present now clearly restored, I ask her to go back to the target.

JK: *Let me ask again the same question I did before. Think again of the moment before you asked her to get out of bed, when you are feeling scared and alone. What's better, at that moment—to be scared and alone, or to be bad? Which is better?*

Elizabeth: To be bad.

JK: *Can you stay with that, that it is better to be bad?!* (EMs.) *Notice how it is better. Good, now take a deep breath. Let it go. That's good . . . Just think out loud right now.*

Elizabeth: I just know logically it's not . . . logical, she's gone and I'm here and I can't get . . . I can't stay on the logical side of me. Why can't I just snap out of it?!

This segment of this transcript illustrates a shortcoming of strictly cognitive approaches to the problem of low self-esteem. Elizabeth knows full well that her self-referencing NCs are irrational, but she experiences that fact, together with her continuing emotional disturbance, as a self-imposed "guilt trip." I use a reframing interweave to help her begin to see that our therapeutic focus is not on her negative thoughts, but on the more visceral feelings of "badness" that continue to drive those thoughts.

JK: *Well, in the past you might have said, "The reason I can't snap out of it is because I'm so bad!"* (Elizabeth laughs, with recognition.) *So why are you bad? Because you can't snap out of being bad! But that's just more of the same. Come back to this basic puzzle . . . You're with someone right now who likes and respects you; you're here, you're working hard on some-thing that is important* and *you have a feeling of being bad!—which doesn't make a lot of sense. I've been here with you for the last 20 minutes, and yet I haven't seen you do anything bad, and yet you* feel *like you're bad. You have a feeling of "badness." Maybe "badness" is the word we should use. Because, it's more of a feeling of* being *bad. There are bad peo-ple in the world, but you aren't one of them. And you know that—I'm not just reassuring you.*

Elizabeth: I know that, logically. I know that logically, but emotion-ally, I can't convince myself.

JK: *Well, yes, you have been trying to convince yourself all these years. What we are doing here is different. We're looking without any judgment at this feeling of badness and saying, okay, this is a feeling that has been there all along, all through your adult life, even though it doesn't make sense. What can we make of it?*

She accepts this shift in focus, and we go back to target.

JK: *Let's go back to it again. Go back to the moment before you said any-*

thing to your mother to ask her to get out of bed, and again, it's a choice point. On the one hand: scared and lonely. On the other hand: badness. Which one do you choose?

Elizabeth: I always choose being bad. (Tears.) (EMs.)

During the next 15 minutes, as we went through channels of information with sets of EM, Elizabeth was able to report that the memory was gradually losing some of its emotional intensity.

Elizabeth: I can stay in the room, here, more easily now. It helps for it to be a picture instead of that I am doing it. (EMs.) But I was bad and stupid to keep asking her to get up! I knew she would spank me, but I did it over and over again. *Why,* when I *knew* I was being bad!?

JK: *Consider this. I've asked you a few times—"Is it better to be lonely and scared or is it better to be bad?" And, every time, your answer is that it feels better to be bad. And yet you're saying that when you were actually 8 years old and you chose to be bad over and over again, that that was irrational and stupid. I'm confused. Do you see why?*

The "I'm confused" cognitive interweave is useful when a client is stuck in an internal debate. The therapist verbalizes the conflicting viewpoints, and the client then resolves the contradiction, ostensibly as a way of helping the therapist. Processing is then freed up to continue, with additional interweave questions to draw the client's attention to how reasonable it was for her to assume a role of "badness."

Elizabeth: (She nods yes.) Even though it made me feel less scared, it's as if I was connected to someone. At least I was *alive*, and she *noticed* me. (EMs.)

JK: *Which way did she notice you more?*

Elizabeth: When she spanked me. (EMs.)

JK: *So when that happened, did you know who you were?*

Elizabeth: Did I know who I was? . . . Yes. (EMs.)

JK: *Now compare that with how you were in the kitchen before you decided, when you are still alone and scared. At that moment, do you know who you are?*

Elizabeth: (Long pause.) I don't think so. I think it was an automatic response I had . . . to be bad. (EMs.) The "lonely and scared" was really scary, and it was easier to be spanked and bad. At least I knew I still existed. I wasn't just numb and scared. (EMs.)

JK: *Does that help to realize that?* (Elizabeth nods yes.) (EMs.) *What are you seeing here, as we are looking at this situation that repeated over and over again when you were a kid?*

Elizabeth: I am amazed I can just look at it and not be in it. I mean I can see a picture but I don't just fall into it. I can stay here more!

JK: *When we started talking about this, your sense of badness and shame was a "10+." Go back and think of it again right now. What would you say?*

Elizabeth: It's about a "4," maybe.

JK: *What's different from when it was a "10+," compared to now? What would you say?*

Elizabeth: I have more understanding of why I did it— why I didn't have control over that.

In the weeks that followed this session, Elizabeth reported that she was not only feeling better about herself, but also that she continued to be able to see this particular repeating childhood incident, and many other similar incidents, with a more objective adult perspective. In our sessions, she often would say again how useful it had been for her to re-alize that she wasn't "crazy" for being so convinced of her "badness" during her growing-up years. In spite of this progress, she still remained vulnerable to a sudden surge of shame feeling, both in her daily life and in our sessions, whenever we would go back to discuss difficult child-hood events. The loop in her thinking, though weakened, still remained. This loop, expressed in the previous transcript, went as follows:

1.   When she would think of any incident of interpersonal conflict, or even frustration with another person, she would immediately be aware of a feeling of shame.

2.   She then would try but be unable to "snap out of" those feelings of shame.

3.   Her inability to "snap out of it" would be felt as proof of her bad-ness, which then would lead to

4.   an intensification of the shame feeling, and on into an increas-ingly disturbing downward spiral of disturbance.

This is a pattern that seems to occur in many clients with a shame-based depression: "I am so critical of myself. What's *wrong* with me,

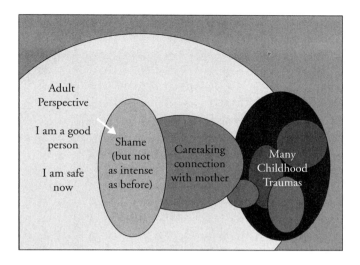

Figure 4.10 Second transcripted session. To break the loop of shame causing more shame, a different targeting question is used: "What does shame look like?"

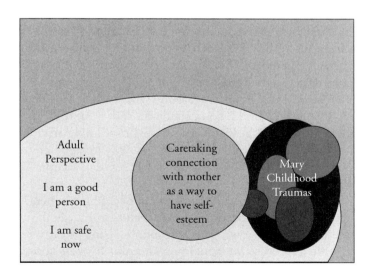

Figure 4.11 Following resolution of the shame affect, she becomes aware of and reassesses a codependent attachment to mother

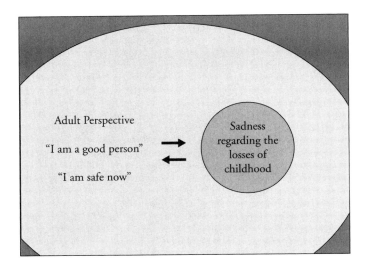

Figure 4.12 Finally, with defenses resolved, *standard EMDR trauma processing* was used to directly target the remaining feelings regarding the losses of childhood

that I am so critical of myself?" In order to help Elizabeth break this loop, I used a procedure that was developed by Katie O'Shea, a skilled and creative EMDR therapist from Spokane, Washington. O'Shea's procedure, which is described in detail in Chapter 17 of this volume, follows from the observation that people who *feel* ashamed are often not objectively shameful. (You could also make the observation that people who *do* act shamefully often appear to be shameless!) Katie asks her clients an odd question, repeatedly, with the clients' answers accompanied by sets of BLS. The question is, "For you, right now, what does shame look like?" In Elizabeth's case, I used this Affect Resetting procedure during a later part of therapy, as a way to help her break this dysfunctional loop that had perpetuated her sense of shame. The transcript that follows illustrates several things. First, I explain the whole notion of Affect Resetting and how it might be helpful to her. Then we do the actual resetting procedure, which results in Elizabeth no longer being able to access her own shame response. This, in turn, results in her being able to process the remaining stimulus triggers and dysfunctional information that had previously bound and maintained her shame identity. At the end of this session, she was experiencing some disorientation (since a feeling of shame had been an intrinsic part of her experience throughout her life!). She was also experiencing the relief of letting go of the shame, as well as compassion for herself, seeing that she was a good and normal child who had not received the love and nurturing she deserved.

At the start of this second transcripted session, we looked once again at the bedside memory, and Elizabeth told me that she still was experiencing some shame and guilt (SUDS = 4) because, in her words, "I still feel so strongly that I was causing trouble for her." The transcript of this videotaped session begins from that point, with a set of alternating right-left hand taps.

JK: *Here you are, a little kid, 5, 6, 7, 8 years old, bringing coffee to your mother. As far as I can tell, the whole sequence of events, any objective observer would look at that and say, "Hmm. Is this kid the troublemaker here? Or is this parent someone with a problem?" Can you see the objective truth of that?*

Elizabeth: Yes, especially if I think of anyone other than myself. But, the sadness—it is the guilt I feel. I knew what would happen.

These statements show Elizabeth's progress, in that she is now able to see the irrationality of her "troublemaker" feelings, but she still is emotionally unresolved.

JK: *If you knew that was happening to any other child, there is absolutely no doubt about how you would feel. It is just that the rules are different for you, when you think of the child being you. Is that right?*

Elizabeth: Yes.

JK: *So perhaps there is something that still is tangled, or the wires are crossed, or something like that, with regard to one of your very normal and natural responses, the response of shame. Let me explain what I mean. We all have shame at times. Shame is natural.*

Elizabeth: Okay.

JK: *Shame has a purpose for any person in the natural course of life, as a part of being healthy. Shame is a way to know if you are doing something wrong—and you should stop doing it, and really resolve something so that you don't do something like that again—because it is destructive to another person, or destructive to the self. That is what shame is for. If we didn't have shame, we would be shameless!*

Elizabeth: It would be a mess.

JK: *Actually, people wouldn't have brakes. Shame is like the brakes. If you are going in the wrong direction, put on the brakes. Shame is like that. And that is the natural purpose of shame. So, I would like to do some procedures here today that can help you untangle all that, so that shame only comes up for you when you have done something wrong, truly wrong. So when you get to the point of resolving this, you can actually feel in your core: "When I haven't done anything wrong, I can feel good about myself. I can just do that." Not as a big struggle, but as something that you automatically know and feel. So, that is the purpose of what we will be doing.*

Elizabeth: Okay.

JK: *So I will ask you just to look at certain things. And it is a kind of structured procedure, but you will see right away what we are doing. So here is a question, and with your permission, I am going to tap your hands.*

Elizabeth: Okay.

JK: ([Tapping] while he continues talking.) *Just notice the tapping, first of all. Just notice the back and forth, the right and left. That's right. Good. And right now, what does shame look like, for you? Right now, just see whatever comes into your mind when I ask that question.*

Elizabeth: Me! (Tears.)

JK: *Stay with that.* (Taps.) *That's right. Notice the feelings that go with that. Just talk.*

Elizabeth: I have done so many shameful things in my life!

JK: *Stay with that.* (Taps.) *If this starts to get too hard, or you start to go into that numb, dissociated place, you tell me right away. Okay? Is it already happening?*

Elizabeth: It started to. I just felt a flood of how bad I was as a kid.

JK: *Okay. So, right now, are you more in the memories or are you more with me here in the office?*

Elizabeth: I'm right here with you right now.

JK: *Good. You are all the way here?*

Elizabeth: Yes.

Elizabeth still has dual attention. I ask a question to help her become even more oriented to the resource of present orientation and safety.

JK: *Good. What is good about being here?*

Elizabeth: It is not happening. And I am with someone who doesn't think I am bad!

JK: *Yes! That's true. So that helps, doesn't it. Stay with that.* (Taps.) *Say whatever is on your mind.*

Elizabeth: Well, right now, I'm here right now, but at first when you asked me to think of that, I thought of . . . everything. I got spanked so much. (Tears.) I couldn't do anything right.

JK: *So, you had a flood of images all of a sudden. Okay. So right now, what do you get?*

Elizabeth: That I am here, and I'm okay.

JK: (Taps.) *I am going to ask the same question again, and just say whatever the answer is, at this point, for you. What does shame look like? Right at this point, for you? The answer might be the same, or it might be different.*

Elizabeth: I am blank.

JK: *Is it a numb, dissociated blank, or is it just a neutral blank?*

Elizabeth: Just blank.

JK: (Taps.)

Elizabeth: That confuses me.

JK: *Yes.* (Taps.)

This shift to an emotionally neutral state is a typical result when this Affect Resetting procedure is used (O'Shea, in Chapter 17 of this volume). With her shame response no longer so potentiated, processing of additional channels of information regarding her long-held shame identity can now more easily occur. We go back again to target.

JK: *Let's go back and check again. Right now, what does shame look like, right now? There might still be something left. What do you get?*

Elizabeth: I know the feeling I had, that it was me, and I can go back to that if I think about it too hard, but right now I'm just blank.

JK: *Is it a blank that is kind of okay?*

Elizabeth: I can't think what shame is.

Elizabeth is disturbed and disoriented that her shame feelings are not presently in her awareness. To help her become more oriented, I ask questions to demonstrate that her shame response is still part of her personality, if she needs this response to provide moral direction. It is only the irrational, pathological shame that has lost its reactivity.

JK: *If you happen to do something shameful this afternoon, like cheat somebody, or lie to somebody, or do something hurtful to somebody—make a guess right now: Do you think you would feel ashamed afterward?*

Elizabeth: Yes.

JK: *Okay. And that would be an appropriate thing, wouldn't it?*

Elizabeth: Yes.

JK: (Taps.)

Elizabeth: It confuses me because I have never been blank.

Even though she is still processing disturbing emotions and information, she is now able to do so more easily, without the disruptive effect of intense shame affect.

JK: *Just talk right now.*

Elizabeth: It didn't matter how hard I tried, I just always got in trouble. (Tears.) (Taps.)

JK: *As you think of that, does it seem like you are reliving those times, or are you just looking at those memories and able to stay here?*

Elizabeth: All the way here.

JK: *Great. Just kind of notice that. Is that a relief that you can come back here?*

Elizabeth: Yes. I don't remember being able to do it this quick.

JK: (Taps.) *It is a nice ability to have.*

Elizabeth: It is a relief! It helps me to know that I am not doing anything bad right now.

JK: *Yes. You are not doing anything bad.*

Elizabeth: That bad feeling is just shut off! Sometimes, I wanted to hurt her and make her mad. And she would always tell me that my begging her was what was causing her unhappiness. It is kind of confusing.

JK: *Say the confusion.*

Elizabeth: When I start to think that maybe I didn't do something wrong, I get very confused. That makes me think that I am not telling you something.

JK: *Yes. Okay.* (Taps.)

Elizabeth: But I don't know what it is. (Taps.) I feel blank. (Taps.)

JK: *Just pause for a moment. Look out the window. Be here.*

Elizabeth: Blank is different from not remembering things.

JK: *Yes, it is. And it is different from the dissociation.*

Elizabeth: Because I am still here! I just feel blank! It is like I always have just listened to everybody else's opinion, and never have had my own. (Taps.)

JK: *Can you look, now, and see the time by your mother's bed, and all of these times from childhood, with an adult perspective, and see it with all of your skills as an adult, all your adult understandings. What comes to mind when you take that point of view?*

Elizabeth: I am shocked I can look at it that way, because I don't remember being able to look at it my adult way. (Taps.)

JK: *As you look at it through your adult eyes, what do you see?*

Elizabeth: Everybody is pretty screwed up! (Taps.)

JK: *What else do you see?*

Elizabeth: I was the target. (Taps.)

JK: *What can your adult self say to the child about that?*

Elizabeth: I was just a little kid who wanted a mom. I didn't have a real mom. Part of me wanted to take care of her. I didn't want her to be sad. (Taps.) I couldn't separate hating her from hating me and hating the situation. As an adult, I can hate the situation.

Elizabeth is talking about her need to take care of mother, as part of an affectionate bond. She may still be holding some idealization of the bond with her mother, and that idealization may be preventing full awareness of the pain of these childhood events. In order to explore this possibility, I ask her to access images or information connected to her affection for her mother.

JK: *Talk about your love for her. Can you think of a time that really brings to mind your love . . . something she did, or some moment with her . . . maybe the best moment with her that you can think of?*

Elizabeth: That makes me feel guilty—I can't think of anything.

JK: *Can you think of your mother with fondness right now . . . and love?* (Elizabeth nods yes.) *Okay. What is the thought you have about her that is a nice thought?*

Elizabeth: That other people liked her. But some specific thing that I felt cared for . . . that was only when I was waiting on her.

JK: *So, when you waited on her.*

Elizabeth: It made her happy.

JK: *When she was happy like that, when you waited on her, what was the feeling you had?*

Elizabeth: I was glad she wasn't sad anymore. (Taps.)

JK: *And stay with the feeling you have, right now, when you think of her, that fondness for her. (Taps.)*

Elizabeth: I would always take care of her, when no one else wanted to be with her.

JK: *How did you feel about yourself, when you were the only one who could really take care of her?*

Elizabeth: I felt good about myself. (Taps.) It is so different to really be here, and think of these things, and not fall completely into it.

JK: *Yes. Isn't that something!*

Elizabeth: My emotions are still there, but I don't lose sight of being here.

JK: *Yes.*

Elizabeth: (Blowing nose.) How is it possible to have this much mucus in your head, and not know it until you start crying. (Laughs.)

JK: *What are you figuring out here that helps you?*

Elizabeth: That I can stay here. I can think of it, and not . . . I mean, I feel the emotion, but I am not stuck there where I'm just going to be devastated for weeks.

JK: *Yes. Right. Good for you. So, here is the other question. Right now, what does shame look like, for you, right now?*

Elizabeth: I can't think of anything that is appropriate. It is like being blank. (Taps.) I know what I just told you. I can repeat it, but I'm not feeling it. Oh, it is confusing!

JK: *Yes. Would you say it is even disorienting?*

Elizabeth: Yes. I'm not used to it!

JK: *I think we are reorganizing the circuitry.*

Elizabeth: Yay!

JK: *Well, check and see, tomorrow morning when you wake up. Think of some things that usually would make you feel ashamed. And just see what is going on with that. And you might still have some feelings, but notice if there is a difference. What do you think right now, when you think of doing that?*

Elizabeth: That it is *very* different. It boggles my mind right now, to feel such emotion but know that I am still okay.

JK: *Go back again right now. Just check and see . . . what does shame look like right now?*

Elizabeth: Not me! (Taps.)

JK: *Is it okay with you that this has happened?*

Elizabeth: I don't feel like a huge liar. I just feel a little tug of some kind of feeling, but it isn't shame.

JK: *There may be some more to this. We can get to it next week when you come in. This is really good work. What did you come to see? What did you come to understand today about your feeling of shame? Check and see.*

Elizabeth: That I had reason to believe I was shameful, but I wasn't.

(Taps.) And, you know, that is a whole different ache. Because if I wasn't bad, why did I have to go through all that?!

JK: *Yes. So, what you just said was, "If I wasn't bad . . ." Finish that.*

Elizabeth: I must have been okay!

JK: *Does that feel true to you, right now?*

Elizabeth: Yes . . . I think so. It does.

JK: *Ask yourself, what does shame look like right now? And see what you get.*

Elizabeth: I'm okay . . . This will be interesting.

JK: *Yes. Good for you. Good work here. Is this a good stopping point?*

Elizabeth: Yes. I'm not bad!

JK: *Yes. Isn't that weird! Isn't that amazing!*

In the weeks that followed this session, Elizabeth was able to rapidly become oriented to living without the constant triggering of her shame response. She reported feeling more whole, more worthy, more courageous in speaking up for herself, and more optimistic as she considered her future. The other traumas of her life were now much more accessible to successful standard EMDR processing. In fact, she derived some satisfaction from going back in her mind, between sessions, to situations that had previously been overwhelming to her, and rethinking them, empowered by the new resource of knowing she was an "okay" person. When she remembered these other traumatic events, it was as though she had now exchanged shame feelings for sadness, and she reported, "That is a good trade. I can feel the sadness fading." As she was winding down the therapy process, an unfortunate event occurred that served as a test of her therapeutic progress. While she was visiting friends in another state, she was attacked by a large dog and was hospitalized for a week to treat her physical injuries. When she returned to therapy with me, she said, "You know, it is so incredible. This happened, and I didn't go into the 'badness' feeling. And it gave me a whole new perspective on when (the employer/assailant) attacked me. I survived both him and the dog! I think I'm pretty strong!"

CONCLUSION

These cases illustrate how a modified EMDR approach can be effectively used with depressed clients who present with separate, dissociated ego states. For both of these individuals, the resolution of shame—first the cognitive aspect and then the nonverbal sensory aspect—was directly associated with a dramatic and lasting improvement in self-esteem, felt energy, and a lifting of depressed affect.

The transcripts here illustrate some ways that standard EMDR procedures may be supplemented when working with people who come to therapy with conflicted, dissociated ego states. Within an ego state model, it is appropriate and often helpful to ask the client such questions as "What is the child feeling right now, in that trauma situation?" "Where does the child feel that emotion in *her* body?" and "How is that different from what you, the adult, are experiencing right now?" In the therapy of these individuals, psychological defenses—particularly avoidance and idealization/shame defenses—are likely to be much more prominent, and those defenses must be taken into account to achieve comprehensive therapy goals. Within this model, the client is often asked to "look" from one ego state to another. To ask an adult part to simply "look at" the child in the trauma implies both connection and distance from the potentially overwhelming traumatic memory material, and can help clients begin to reverse problematic dissociative fragmentation. This procedure, described in detail elsewhere (Knipe, 2007), is a way to give the child part something that was never there before: the experience of caring attention from a sympathetic adult. The numerical ratings of SUDS and VOC scores are not always used with this approach, since asking about numbers seems to pull the client back into the adult ego state, and this sometimes interferes with the goal of enhancing access to the experience of the child part. All of these variations are true to the Adaptive Information Processing model, in that, in each instance, the client is accessing dysfunctionally stored memory information, while remaining oriented to the safe present, and moving that information to resolution through sets of BLS. The cases here illustrate how individuals, caught in a distress they did not choose, can, through a series of therapy steps, become free of needless self-doubts. The therapy paths of these clients provide evidence that an identity of shamefulness does not have to be a permanent impediment to the joys and meanings that this life can offer.

REFERENCES

Bradshaw, J. (2005). *Healing the shame that binds you* (rev. ed.). Deerfield Beach, FL: Health Communications.

Damasio, A. (1999). *The feeling of what happens: Body and emotion in the making of consciousness.* New York: Harcourt.

Fraser, G. A. (2003). Fraser's dissociative table technique revisited, revised: A strategy for working with ego states in dissociative disorders and ego state therapy. *Journal of Trauma & Dissociation, 4*(4), 5–28.

Knipe, J. (2002). It was a golden time: Healing narcissistic vulnerability. In P. Manfield (Ed.), *EMDR Casebook.* New York: Norton. (Reprinted from *Extending EMDR,* P. Manfield, Ed., 1998, New York: Norton)

Knipe, J. (2005). Targeting positive affect to clear the pain of unrequited love: Codependence, avoidance and procrastination. In R. Shapiro (Ed.), *EMDR solutions: Pathways to healing* (pp. 189–211). New York: Norton.

Knipe, J. (2007). Loving eyes: Procedures to therapeutically reverse dissociative processes while preserving emotional safety. In C. Forgash & M. Copeley (Eds.), *Healing the heart of trauma and dissociation with EMDR and ego state therapy* (pp. 181–225). New York: Springer.

Liotti, G. (2004). Trauma, dissociation, and disorganized attachment: Three strands of a single braid. *Psychotherapy: Theory, practice, research, training, 41*(4), 55–74.

Liotti, G. (2006). A model of dissociation based on attachment theory. *Journal of Trauma and Dissociation, 7*(4), 55–74.

Nathanson, D. L. (1992). *Shame and pride: Affect, sex, and the birth of the self.* New York: Norton.

Popky, A. J. (1994). *EMDR protocol for smoking and other addictions.* Presentation at the Annual Meeting of the EMDR Network, Sunnyvale, CA.

Popky, A. J. (2005). DeTUR, an urge reduction protocol for addictions and dysfunctional behaviors. In R. Shapiro (Ed.), *EMDR solutions: Pathways to healing* (pp. 167–188). New York: Norton.

Shapiro, F. (2001). *Eye movement desensitization and reprocessing: Basic principles, protocols, and procedures* (2nd ed.). New York: Guilford Press.

van der Hart, O., Nijenhuis, E., & Steele, K. (2006). *The haunted self: Structural dissociation and the treatment of chronic traumatization.* New York: Norton.

Chapter 5

Attachment-Based Depression

Healing the "Hunkered-Down"

Robin Shapiro

PEOPLE WHO LEARN EARLY THAT THEY CAN'T ELICIT ATTENTION, APPROVAL, and joyful play from their caregivers, give up on the endeavor. They may "buck up" and become extremely self-reliant (dismissive attachment). They may lose their inborn capacity for positive affect: smiles, joy, and play. If their neglect is coupled with abuse, chronic disapproval, or the distress of an anxious or overbearing caregiver, they can get caught between overlapping states of anxiety (insecure attachment and an unmyelinated ventral vagal state) and depression (dorsal vagal shutdown) and become "hunkered down" (HD).

You see this condition in a wide range of clients, from the chronically dysthymic but high-functioning professional, to the disorganized, highly dissociated, extremely depressed, and barely functioning client. On the low end of the continuum, they won't make eye contact. On the high end, they will look you in the eye, but the contact is tentative, perfunctory, or anxious. You may not feel completely "met" by their gazes. Some come across as inert, some as anxious. All manifest depression. They often look younger than their natural ages. Their chests are caved in. Their heads are forward. They breathe shallowly. Their feet are often on tiptoe or crossed, making it impossible for them to completely connect to the ground and their own internal states. They can be appeasing, hypervigilant, or checked out. Their complaints may include procrastination, passivity, trouble in making decisions, and codependence. They tend to be extremely nice people, easy to be around. They are rarely as-sertive. Many, but not all, of them fit Elaine Aron's description of "highly sensitive people (Aron, 1996) and Alice Miller's sensitive "gifted children" (Miller, 1997); being constitutionally sensitive to their environment, especially their social environment.

Caregivers' interactions with children shape the growth of neural networks that contain and regulate emotion (Schore, 2003; Siegel, 1999). When babies' actions and reactions bring forth mirroring (for giggling and play) or soothing (for distress), the babies grow up know-ing that they have efficacy ("I made my Mom laugh." "I made my mom pick me up." "I'm powerful!) and worth ("My mom/the envi-ronment responds to me. I must be a big deal."). When caregivers are unable to respond effectively, children lose their external regulation and the development of efficacious neural networks.

Ogden, Minton, and Pain (2006) wrote:

> Hyper- and hypoarousal are both involved in the infant's psychobiologi-cal response to frightened or frightening caregivers, with whom the so-cial engagement system is functionally off line for much of the time. Disorganized/disoriented attachment patterns in children have been as-sociated with behavior that may indicate increased dorsal vagal tone, such as stilling, going into a brief trance, unresponsiveness, and shutting down (Schore, 2001). . . . When sympathetic arousal cannot be regulated, a quick shift to hypoarousal may occur. The body undergoes "the sud-den and rapid transition from an unsuccessful strategy of struggling re-quiring massive sympathetic activation to the metabolically conservative immobilized state mimicking death associated with the dorsal vagal complex" (Porges, 2001, p. 136). . . . These negative states leave the child with a compromised social engagement system. . . . Whereas over stimu-lation and inadequate repair are inevitable outcomes of trauma, inade-quate stimulation, insufficient mirroring, and a lack of responsiveness by the caretaker accompany neglect. Such inadequate stimulation can be life-threatening to an infant, forcing the child to autoregulate by becom-ing disengaged and hypoaroused (Carlson et al., 1998; Perry et al., 1995; Schore, 2001). Individuals who have experienced chronic childhood trauma characteristically . . . remain between hyper or hypoarousal zones for extended periods of time. (pp. 57–58)

Many HDs did not experience abuse. The small *t* traumas of misat-tunement or an anxious mother stimulated hyperarousal, then hypoarousal in these children. Some HD clients come from families who faced external pressures from poverty, danger, or even extreme pressure for conformity. Some, but certainly not all, families in some upper-class enclaves or fundamentalist religious organizations shame or punish nonconforming children, causing some of them to "hunker" in attempts to fit rigid social expectations.

Imagine an active 2-year-old who learns that his exploration and high spirits continually distress his anxious mom. He's never abused and is well cared for. The tension in his mother's body and her slight withdrawal in response to his exuberance are his only messages. If he's rowdy and playful, she withdraws. If he yells, she tightens up. He can't live without her. He must stop the "bad" behavior. The only way he can curb himself is to inhibit his whole system. He becomes "good": quiet, compliant, and nearly unmoving. He waits for permission before every action. He hangs out in a zone between anxious attention to his mother's state, depressed affect, and squelched aliveness.

INTAKE

Pay careful attention to attachment issues in your intake. The HDs all had caregivers who were distressed, anxious, overburdened, critical (if not abusive), grieving, or just not a good "fit" for your clients. Ask questions about what was going on in their families when your clients were born, and the few years before and after. Was Dad gone to war? Did Mom lose one of her parents? As small children, did the clients spend a lot of time unattended? Were there many other little children around? Aggressive or abusive older brothers? Financial difficulties? Marital difficulties? Drug or alcohol use/abuse? In what communities did they live: religious, social, class, region, ethnicity? What were the parents like when the clients were children? Critical? Distant? Anxious? Needing all the children's attention? Preoccupied? Angry? Abusive? What were the interactions like at the dinner table? Did someone make fun of the children? What happened when the children made a mess? Were "bad"? Were inattentive? Needed comforting? Were rowdy and rambunctious? Wanted to be alone? Wanted attention? Watch your clients' reactions to all these questions. You may learn more from their reflexive cringing than from their words. Ask about the quality of their relationships with other authority figures: teachers, bosses, coaches, and so on. Find out about their current and historical social lives and love relationships. Are there friends? Are they able to say "no" and "I want" to their friends and partners? Do they have the capacity to know what they want, especially around other people? Can they express anger, love, disappointment, or conflict around others? Do they feel lovable? Understood? Responded to? Do they deserve response? (Great Negative Cognitions arise from these questions. Take notes.)

This may not suit your style, but I have had great luck with these clients, with declaring, after a thorough intake, that the diagnosis is "hunkered-down" and that our therapy is about "dehunkering." I say to clients: *You learned to pay close attention to your parents' every move in order to do the right thing. You forgot how to notice what you wanted. It wasn't as important as pleasing/avoiding that criticism/not getting hit/your mother's needs/keeping your mom from getting anxious. You do the same thing with people in your current life. Keeping yourself hunkered-down stops you from noticing and following your internal compass. Our job, as I see it, is to clear out that old hunkering response, so that you can notice what you want and learn how to reach for it, even when you're dealing with another person. I think that your depression may start floating away, halfway through the therapy. After that, we'll work on some skills you never got to learn, about negotiating, having conflict, and standing your ground. That's often when the rest of the depression goes away.* Clients tend to like this nonpathologizing diagnosis and the clear treatment path. One client said, "I feel seen for the first time!"

First Steps

Assess the depression. It's possible to have attachment-based depression concurrent with endogenous or big "T" trauma-based depression. You may have to use EMDR to clear the big traumas before you can go after the more subtle relational targets. Your very depressed clients may need to take omega-3's, add in exercise, knock down alcohol consumption, and/or take antidepressants to bring them up to a treatable level. Many of the HD clients I've worked with didn't need these interventions. Some did.

Build a strong relationship. These clients are generally easy to like. They tend to be compliant and pleasant and grateful for nearly anything you do. You need to have a strong enough sense of them to notice when they are complying when they should be complaining. Track them carefully and respond, respond, respond. They need to know that you can tolerate any feeling or thought that they are having. Their parents couldn't do that and HD clients tend to project that you, the therapist, are either too fragile or too overpowering for them to be themselves in your presence. Let the therapeutic relationship be a laboratory for the clients to learn that you're different from their parents, and that they can be exactly who they are.

If HD clients have body awareness, it is usually a heightened reaction to their own social anxiety. Send them "inside" to connect with any feeling. Ask, *Where are you feeling that?* Combine body awareness with good Diana Fosha (2000) relational words: *What do you feel inside when I tell you how happy I am when you show me who you really are? Where do you feel that?* Teach grounding techniques. *Put both feet flat on the ground and sit up a little straighter. Feel gravity holding your feet to the ground and the rest of you to your chair. Notice your breathing and notice that if you straighten a little more, you can breathe into your belly. Good job! You can use this grounding and breathing whenever you get too nervous or are having too much of any feeling. You can let the emotion flow through you, right into the ground. Breathe those feelings right through you.*

When you do the standard EMDR preparation steps (Safe Place, visualizations, etc.), watch for overcompliance. For instance, make sure there really is a Safe Place. These folks want to please you too much. You can't do trauma processing until you know that your clients will tell you the truth about their experience. Become trustworthy as fast as you can. And make sure that they become trustworthy, too.

EMDR TRAUMA PROCESSING

Here are three ways to bring EMDR trauma processing into your work with HD clients. I give the clients a choice about where to start. (I try to give these clients many choices, in order to help them discover how they know what they want.) *Do you want to start with the early relationship with your parents and move, step by step, up to the present? Would you prefer to start with some current interaction and "float back" to its roots in the past? Or we can start in your body and move from there.*

Chronological

If they choose the chronological processing of Maureen Kitchur's Strategic Developmental Model (2005), I often start with: *Imagine that you're an infant in your mother's/father's arms, looking up at her/his face. You don't have to remember this for it to work. Imagine that face. What do you notice in your body right now?* If there's any tension or anxiety, we clear it. If the exercise brings up feelings of being loved and comforted, we install them. Then we move on to the next developmental phase. For people who were neglected, I try, *Imagine that you are a little baby in your crib. You cry for attention, but no one comes. Notice what you feel in your body.* You may see the depressive symptoms arise before your eyes, as your client moves from agitation to extreme agitation to abrupt spaced-out depression. Keep processing through that dorsal vagal state until the client is back in the room, oriented, and well connected with you.

I've found many juicy targets between 1 and 4 years old. If they don't remember a specific incident, and there's no discernable body feeling at a certain age, you can try universal targets: *What would happen when your mother walked in on you after you had emptied out the lower cupboards of the entire kitchen?* If your client shrinks into an inhibitory crouch, set up the Standard Protocol on that target. Another good target is the child crossing her arms and saying, "NO!" to either parent. Again, you may see the trajectory of defiance, then fear, then HD depression. Process through the depression/repression. It's not the end point.

Floating Back

Clients tend to pick one of two current situations from which to float back. The first is an interaction with an authority figure or a significant other: "I couldn't say 'no' when my husband asked me when I wanted to go camping. I don't really like to camp and I have too much to do this weekend." The other is an inability to make a decision: "He asked me what I wanted to do, and I don't know. It's like I can't know." From either of these, float back: *When you think about that situation, what are you saying to yourself about yourself? . . . What feeling is there? . . . Where in your body? . . . Float back to the first time you remember feeling that way. What's happening? Who is there?* When you get the target, set up trauma processing. Often the processing will jump from node to node, covering many bases. If it doesn't, you can continue to float back from current targets. After clearing the old targets, don't forget to float forward, clearing the current issues, and when you've processed them, to float further forward to future manifestations of the issue.

Starting from the Body

If we're starting with the body, I ask HD clients to feel the tension/collapse in their chests and upper torsos and to exaggerate it (Negri, 1981, personal communication). *What age does this feel like? What's happening there? Who is there? What are you saying to yourself about yourself when you hold this stance?* (Usually "I'm not safe." Or some variation on "I'm not acceptable.") Find the Positive Cognition (PC). Get the Validity of Cognition (VoC) (usually extremely low). *What emotion are you feeling?* (Usually fear and/or shame.) *How big is that, 0 to 10? And where are you feeling that in your body?* You often end up with an incident that happened between 2 and 4 years old. It's Mom saying, "I'm ashamed of you!" or "Stop it," or similar words. Processing often moves through many nodes of similar situations. It may take several sessions to clear all the related inhibitory incidents. Start each session with the body, and floating back, until there are no more targets. As the clients clear, their bodies begin to change. They sit up. Their shoulders migrate back. Their necks lengthen. They get taller, and as they do, they begin to breathe more deeply. Eye contact becomes less tentative. Then it's time for the present. *Your mom/dad is sitting on that chair looking mad/tense/disapproving.* If the client goes back to full slump, insert the Standard Protocol: *What are you saying to yourself about yourself,* and so on. If/when the client can hold on to an erect posture and open stance, ask: *Feel that power in your body. What do you want to say to your parent, right now?* (BLS [Bilateral Stimulation].). Keep processing until nothing new comes through. At this point in therapy, I've heard clients tell their imaginary parents, "I used to be afraid of you, and now I realize that I'm grown up and you can't hurt me." "I thought I was bad, when you got nervous, and now I know that you're always nervous." "I'm not bad. You're just a perfectionist!" Ask, *Where do you feel that truth in your body?"* Install until the client is completely full of that new belief.

Jean: Clearing Relational Trauma

Jean is a retired helping professional in her 60s. She's beautiful, intelligent, sensitive, engaging, funny, anxious, and moderately depressed. She wants to feel better, heal the wounds of a failed relationship, and "know who I am." She'd like less anxiety and more energy and pleasure. At the intake, we find a middle-class Southern family. Mom was narcissistic. Dad was mostly gone. The culture of the small town bred conformity and inhibition, especially in its female members. One of the first memories: Jean is 2, sitting on the kitchen floor, playing with baking pans. Her mother rushes into the room, yelling, "We don't play on the floor. That's for trash!" Mom doesn't connect with Jean and is either oblivious to her or overinvolved with Jean's appearance. Jean was molested by a neighbor boy. She was continually shamed by her older sister. She grows up charming and feeling empty inside. She's been married and divorced, but no relationship ever sustained her. She has good friends, but isn't often "real" with them.

After the usual preparation, Safe Place, explanations, and so on, we clear the molestation in three sessions. Then we go after Mom: *You're an infant in your mother's arms. Look up at her face. What do you see?*

Jean: It's like a mask.

RS: *When you look into that mask, what do you say to yourself about yourself?*

Jean: I'm not okay. . . . In fact, I'm not . . .here.

RS: *What's the opposite?*

Jean: I *am* here. I exist!

RS: *When you're a baby, looking into you mom's face, how true, 1 to 7, does it feel in your gut, that you exist?*

Jean: Not very true, a 2, maybe. She feels empty, in her core, a 6 SUDS (Subjective Units of Disturbance Scale) for emptiness, tinged with anxiety. As we process, she goes from empty to tense to mad to sad. "I was there. She (Mom) wasn't there! She didn't know what to do. I was okay. I always existed. . . . But I really didn't have a mother. (Sad affect, tears. Several more rounds of processing. Finally, spontaneously and strongly) I deserved to have a mother who was there and I didn't have one.

RS: *Go with that!*

We finish the session with installing, "I exist and I deserve attention." When we're done, this petite woman seems a head taller.

In the next session, we target the kitchen floor incident, then we do five sessions of other interactions with her mother. Jean realizes that the molestation and an incident of being stuck on the roof were due, in part, to her mother's inattention. She begins to see her mother's internalized pressure to conform, as a Southern woman, as an inheritance from her mother's family. Jean sees her mother's competition with her for her father's scant attention. The more she clears, the more she knows, "It wasn't about me. It was about who my mother was. I was okay and I'm still okay." Jean begins to move through grief near the end of each session as she realizes how her family's dynamic squelched her aliveness. As we process through the grief, she always comes to "But I can be different now." And we always install it.

The depression lifts as Jean begins to experience weekly epiphanies. "I've reorganized my house so that it's comfortable for me, not for how it looks. I've bought a big comfortable chair for me. I may never let anyone else sit on it. It's my throne. I'm the queen of my house." Other weeks she talks about how her social life is shifting. She's become more of a leader, and more spontaneous. Sessions become more oriented to the present, bringing new skills into her current life.

Mark, Clearing Trauma

Mark is in his late 30s. He's bright, funny, and boyish. He uses gentle, self-deprecating humor as a defense against the judgment that he projects on me. His chest is slightly caved in, his head is forward. He makes good eye contact, but there's something held back. He's well married and has two small children for whom he is often the primary parent. He is a skilled artisan with a successful small business. He wants to be able to take more risks in his life, to know what he wants to do and go for it. Mark comes from a religious family. His mother was anxious and critical. His father was more distant, and is still critical. His father was the enforcer. There was no abuse, no big trauma, no neglect. Mark spent many childhood hours roaming the countryside around his small town, where "nobody could tell me that I was doing anything wrong." He was considered the "bad kid" in his adolescent years for refusing to comply with some of the family strictures.

He breezes through the Safe Place (out in the countryside of his childhood) and other preparations. He's smart and quick and makes good use of the BLS. He chooses to process chronologically.

RS: *You're an infant in your mother's arms, looking up into her face.*
Mark: God, she's so nervous!
RS: *What does that say about you?*
Mark: Something's wrong . . . with me.
RS: *What feeling goes with that?*
Mark: I'm kind of nervous and kind of frozen. (SUDS 8)
RS: *Where do you feel that in your body?*

Mark: Everywhere! Mostly my stomach.
RS: *Go with that.* (BLS.)

We clear it out. We install, "I'm okay, I was just a kid" and "I'm safe."

In the same session we are able to clear a solid memory of feeling frozen and terrified when his mother yelled at him for making a mess as a 3-year-old. At one point I ask him what he'd say to that kid. He drew on his own experience as a father and had a lighthearted discussion of big messes with this younger self, while the BLS continued. He finished with a stronger posture and a stronger gaze, and again, "I'm safe" and "I'm an adult now." Over the next 10 sessions, we cleared many instances of his mother's criticism and both parents' disappointment. We spent three sessions on his teenage years, after which he realized that he was and had been intelligent and a reasonably good kid. (My response, *"Well, of course! Go with that!"*) His posture continued to straighten, his voice deepened. The boyishness fell away and I felt that I was in the room with a grown man. His progress seemed to prove Maureen Kitchur's (2005) contention that chronologically clearing trauma creates a developmentally older client at each session.

SKILL BUILDING

Your client has moved through the fear and shame of her childhood trauma, through the anger about that it happened, and through the grief about how her life force was occluded for so many years. She's sitting up straight, looking you in the eye, and feeling like an adult. She still has trouble figuring out and saying exactly what she wants. It's time for skill building and practicing new ways of being. Before she can assert herself, the client needs to learn how to know what she wants. Here's an exercise for finding her inner compass:

I'm going to give you a series of choices. None of them are binding and some of them are silly. When you choose one, I want you to notice from where in your body you made that choice. Go inside to notice the choice and then tell me where it came from. Some will be instant, some will take longer. There's no pressure. Ready? Romantic comedies or thriller movies? . . . Cats or dogs? . . . Chocolate or vanilla or strawberry? . . . Democrats or Republicans? . . . Meat or tofu? . . . Coffee or tea? . . . and so on. If clients have trouble finding "inside" answers, I use the Two-Hand Interweave (R. Shapiro, 2005):

Put "coffee" in one hand and "tea" in the other. Weigh them each, and just notice what you notice. (BLS.) That's right. Keep going with that. What do you notice? Usually there is some differentiation. If we've successfully found inner correlates to her choices, we send her off with an assignment: *We all make hundreds of choices each day. I want you to stop about five times a day and notice exactly where inside you you're making some choices. Do it at the grocery store, at the restaurant, when you're choosing your clothes for the day, and when you're deciding what to do with your leisure time. Just notice how/where you know the answer to what you want. That's your inner compass. Your compass may live in different parts of your body for different decisions. That's normal. So is having just one place.*

The decidedly undecided may use the Two-Hand technique for out-in-the world decision-making. *In one hand hold chocolate; in the other hold vanilla. Got it? Watch my fingers and notice what happens. (BLS.) What do you notice now? Your right hand is lighter? Go with that. (BLS.) What do you get now? Definitely right hand/chocolate? Where do you feel that choice in the rest of your body? When you do your five choices each day? You can put a choice in each hand and slowly open one hand while closing the other. Then keep alternating.*

Recovering HD clients are often lacking simple information about boundaries and appropriate behavior in relationships. I sometimes assign *Breaking Free: A Recovery Workbook for Codependence* (Mellody & Wells, 1989) or other codependence books. And we discuss and practice new behaviors. EMDR's Future Template helps in this process:

RS: *Imagine telling your husband that you can't go camping with him.* (She tenses up, but not as much as she would have before the trauma processing.) *What would happen?*
Client: He'd be disappointed.
RS: *What would that say about you?*
Client: I'm bad, because I'm making him unhappy.
RS: *What would you be saying after we fix your attitude?*
Client: It's okay to say what I want.
RS: *Could you make an I statement out of that?*
Client: I'm acceptable, even if I'm assertive.
RS: *When you think about telling your husband about not camping, how true is it that you're acceptable, 1 to 7?* and so on.

After we've run through the protocol and installed "I'm acceptable, even if I'm assertive," the tension is gone. Her chin is up, her shoulders square.

RS: *So imagine telling him now and him being disappointed and maybe a little angry.* (BLS.)
Client: I can deal with that.
RS: *Go with that.* (BLS.) . . . *Is there a way you can support him in his disappointment and still stand your ground?*
Client: Yeah.
RS: *Go with that.* (BLS.)
Client: I didn't know that I could do that. Wow! (BLS.)
RS: *What's it like to know that?*
Client: I feel like an adult who is dealing with another adult, not a scared kid dealing with a fragile, angry mom.
RS: *Go with that!* (BLS.)

The last part of therapy contains many such epiphanies. As clients get more centered in their own lives, their relationships change. They renegotiate some of their interpersonal contracts. They start living Robin's Rule of Healing Hunkering: *Notice inside what you most want to do, and choose that.* Doormat behavior lessens. Some friends accept the new contracts. Some leave. Families often resist: "You used to be so nice. What happened?" (I try to minimize the possibility of this interaction by differentiating between aggressive and assertive behaviors. In some families, even assertion is not condoned.) I sometimes lend clients the line, *I've gone from being "nice" to being happy. I hope you can support me in that.* The family system usually adjusts to their newly assertive, happy member.

Jean: Skill Building

Jean's mother needed help to close down the family home and move into assisted living. Before Jean flew out of state to help her mother, we had two future-pacing sessions:

Jean: I'm afraid that I'll be totally absorbed into my mother's needs.
RS: *You're there. Imagine the space. Your mother is distressed and relentless. What are you saying to yourself about yourself?*
Jean: I can't say no. I have to do everything. I'm not enough.

RS: *What do you want to say?*

Jean: I have limits and can enforce them. . . . I have choices. (VoC 3.5, anxiety, SUDS 7, in stomach.)

We cleared it and installed "I have choices." Then:

RS: *So let's run through how you can exercise those choices. How can you set it up from the beginning? You're a highly sensitive introvert. How do you take care of that kind of person?*

Jean: I'll need breaks from my mother. I'll need to walk every day. I'll need to have regular meals. And I shouldn't stay in the chaotic house because it would drive me crazy.

RS: *Great, how would you set that up?* (She talks about the details, and tells me that the worst part will be telling her mother about her plans to stay elsewhere.) *When you think about telling your mom, how big is the anxiety?*

Jean: 6, in my throat.

RS: *Go with that.* (BLS.)

Jean: It's going down fast. A 2. (BLS.) . . . I do have a choice, even if it makes me nervous. It's hard to say no to my mom. (BLS.) I can do it. I have to take care of myself.

RS: *Great. I want you to run through the phone call and your mom's likely reactions. Then we'll run through a bunch of scenarios that are likely to occur when you're there. Start with the phone call. Imagine dialing the phone to tell your mom that you're not staying at the house during the move.*

Jean: I can do it. I feel resolved. (BLS.)

Jean moves through that and several scenarios involving her mother, the amount of work to do, family members, and other people. We use the BLS on any twinges of anxiety, which become less and less as she progresses through the various tasks and scenarios of the trip. When she returns from the trip, she is triumphant. She had opportunities to stand her ground, and she did. Mostly, she noticed what she needed, took care of herself, and stayed reasonably calm and grounded throughout the trip.

Later, when we used the mix of problem-solving and clearing anxiety during Jean's dating experiences, she was able to use her newfound sense of entitlement to avoid further dates with inappropriate men. "I used to wait for them to pick me or drop me. Now, I can pick them or drop them if they're not right for me." She holds her ground, connects fully, and seems to be on her way, in her mid-sixties, to her first differentiated, adult relationship.

COMPLEX CASES

Complex cases with more big "T" traumas take much longer to heal. First, you must move through some of the "I'm not going to survive" traumas in order to build a sense of safety in the now. Severely traumatized clients may not be able to feel into their own bodies without triggering abreactions or full-blown dissociation. These people will often project their frightening or unresponsive parents on you and you will use your therapeutic relationship as the arena for them to practice new behaviors. *You looked pretty scared when you asked me if we could change the appointment time. It looked like it took real guts. What was that like for you?* It's possible to set up a tightly controlled EMDR session (Kiessling, 2006; York & Leeds, 2001) around issues like this. If the client is abreactive, keep them out of their bodies and in this moment.

RS: *What do say to yourself about yourself when you think of asking me for something you need?*
Client: I don't deserve it.
RS: *How true does it feel that you do deserve it, 1 to 7?*
Client: Not much. A 2, sort of.
RS: *Think of asking for me to change the appointment, and that you don't deserve it. What feeling do you get? Anxiety? How big? 9? Go with that. (BLS.) When you think about asking me, what do you get?*

This is EMD, used by Kiessling (2006) to keep complex clients from flooding when working on a specific problem.

Client: I feel a little less scared.
RS: *Go with that. (BLS.) So, when you think of asking me, what do you notice?*
Client: Even better. You know, you didn't seem mad when I asked earlier.
RS: *You mean I might not be the same as your mom?*
Client: Yeah!

RS: *Go with that!* (BLS.) . . . *Now, when you think about asking me, what do you notice?*

Client: It's okay.

RS: *Do you deserve to ask me for what you want?*

Client: 100%.

RS: *So think about asking me for something bigger, something I'll be sure to say no to you about. And notice if you deserve it, even if I say no.*

Client: Can I move in with you and have you take care of me for the rest of my life?

RS: *Nope. . . . What do you notice?*

Client: A little shame.

RS: *Kids that don't get their needs met think it's because they're bad. Are you bad?*

Client: No!

RS: *Go with that!* (BLS.)

Client: I deserve to move in with you, even if I can't.

RS: *Right!*

Notice how we kept the processing in the here and now. We used humor and play. We used the relationship itself as part of the target, and kept it safe. As treatment progresses, and the client stabilizes, we will be able to use the full EMDR protocol on attachment-based and other trauma, proceed to skill building, and then full therapeutic integration.

CONCLUSION

EMDR processing, in the context of a strong therapeutic alliance, assists in healing attachment-based trauma, removing blocks to new ways of interacting, and integrating new skills. Targets may be processed chronologically, from body sensations, or by floating back from current distress. Depressive symptoms often spontaneously lift as clients clear the HD stance from their bodies.

REFERENCES

Aron, E. (1996). *The highly sensitive person.* New York: Broadway Books.

Carlson, V., Cicchetti, D., Barnett, D., & Braunwald, K. (1998). Finding order in disorganization: Lesons from research on maltreated infants' attachments to their caregivers. In C. Cicchetti & G. Carson (Eds.), *Child maltreatment: Theory and research on the causes and consequences of child abuse and neglect* (pp. 494–528). New York: Guilford Press.

Fosha, D. (2000). *The transforming power of affect.* New York: Basic Books.

Kiessling, R. (2006, September). *From BLS to EMDR: Treating survivors of trauma, natural disaster, and combat along a time and stability continuum.* Presentation at EMDRIA Conference, Philadelphia.

Kitchur, M. (2005). The strategic developmental model for EMDR. In R. Shapiro (Ed.), *EMDR solutions: Pathways to healing* (pp. 8–56). New York: Norton.

Mellody, P., & Wells, A. (1989). *Breaking free: A recovery workbook for codependence.* New York: HarperCollins.

Miller, A. (1997). *The drama of the gifted child* (rev. ed.). New York: Basic Books.

Ogden, P., Minton, K., & Pain, C. (2006). *Trauma and the body: A sensorimotor approach to psychotherapy.* New York and London: Norton.

Perry, B., Pollard, R., Blakely, T., Baker, W., & Vigilante, D. (1995). Childhood trauma, the neurobiology of adaptation, and "use dependent" development of the brain: How "states" become "traits." *Infant Mental Health Journal, 15,* 271–291.

Porges, S. W. (2001) The polyvagal theory: Phylogenetic substrates of a social nervous system. *International Journal of Psychophysiology, 42*(2), 123–146.

Schore, A. N. (2001). The effects of early relational trauma on right brain development, affect regulation, and infant mental health. *Infant Mental Health Journal, 22,* 201–269.

Schore, A. N. (2003). *Affect regulation and the repair of the self.* New York: Norton.

Siegel, D. J. (1999). *The developing mind.* New York: Guilford Press.

Shapiro, R. (2005) The two-hand interweave. In R. Shapiro (Ed.), *EMDR solutions: Pathways to healing.* New York: Norton.

York, C., & Leeds, A. (2001, June). *The gate theory.* Presentation at EMDRIA Conference, Austin, TX.

UNIT II

TREATING EATING DISORDERS

Chapter 6

The Why of Eating Disorders

Andrew Seubert

"BUT WHY!?" TWO DESPERATE PARENTS, PLEADING AND QUESTIONING AT the same time, were asking of their 16-year-old daughter. "Why do you want to *starve* yourself? It makes no sense!"

They sat across from me on a couch, their daughter, Shana, in a separate chair, pouting, arms crossed. Shana wouldn't even try to make sense. They just wouldn't get it. All she knew was that it helped her feel better.

At first look, eating disorders (EDs) don't make sense. Nor does cutting or severe risk-taking. But as any clinician will tell you, every behavior has a purpose, and the purpose is typically ego-syntonic. "I just feel better when I don't eat."

Most clinicians regard EDs as among the most difficult, complex, and challenging conditions to treat. The very fact that there are so many etiological explanations of EDs reflects the multidimensional character of these disorders. The origins can go back as far as the moment of conception.

Genetics can play a significant role in EDs. "The majority of family studies have shown that EDs are familial (Strober, Freeman, Lampert, Diamond, & Kaye, 2000; Treasure, Schmidt, & van Furth, 2003). This includes inherited predispositions toward depression, anxiety, and other forms of mental illness and certain temperaments. Activity level, readiness to approach new experiences, self-esteem, and social comfort level are temperamental factors that can influence early attachment and possibly predispose a person to an ED. Perfectionism and obsessive-compulsive traits are quite common, typically accompanied by anxiety.

Slade (1982) suggested that perfectionism is one of the "setting conditions" for the development of anorexia nervosa (AN) and that it leads to a need for total control over some area of the individual's life. "Dissatisfied" (or "neurotic") perfectionism (in which there is an inability to derive pleasure from one's successes because the performance is never good enough) is considered to be particularly important (e.g., Kiemle, Slade, & Dewey, 1987; Slade. Newton, Butler, & Murphy, 1991).

Dysfunctional family interaction and attachment history are significant factors that can increase a person's susceptibility to an ED. Enmeshment or a detached pattern of relationship leaves a person relationally handicapped and less able to deal with stress, life challenges, and abuse. This happens when the sense of self is truncated and diminished without the proper attachment experience. And the likelihood of an ED increases even further if one or both of the parents are concerned about body image and food.

Attachment and relational injuries, those of omission and commission, create dysfunctional templates of relationship, as well as debilitating patterns of emotional regulation and expression. If a person experiences loss and abuse in addition to such injuries, she can develop a great need for something to distract, to help her feel in control, and to deaden unwanted feelings.

In *Why She Feels Fat*, Johanna McShane and Tony Paulson (2008) write to the caregivers of those suffering with an ED: "Eating disorders are powerful coping mechanisms that help an individual manage the parts of life that feel too much to bear. [Your loved one] . . . experiences her eating disorder as a source of support even though its symptoms are, in reality, harmful to her. Your loved one doesn't feel threatened by it. To the contrary, she feels threatened without it."

The cultural environment that idealizes thinness plays an enormous role, particularly for women. Way (1993) wrote:

> As a preschooler, I remember staring wide-eyed at the beautiful, glamorous, reed-thin models on the covers of magazines while I waited with my mother in the supermarket checkout line. I studied the cover girl mannequins; I looked up at my mother. Those women weren't like Mother. They wore beautiful clothes, exotic makeup, and windswept hairstyles. They were chic and glamorous. They were very, very thin. (p. 25)

In *Reviving Ophelia*, Mary Pipher (1994) brought much-needed attention to the plight of girls and young women in a society that glorifies a particular look, one that is unnatural for a majority of women. Bloom, Gitter, Gutwill, Kogel, and Zaphiropoulos (1994) found that as many as 85% of American women diet chronically and 75% are ashamed of their body size and shape.

In light of such cultural influence, puberty has become a time during which girls succumb quite readily to EDs. It is a time when the increase of body fat in the female body, a normal and necessary stage of physical maturation, seems like a betrayal to girls who are, quite literally, dying to be thin. Weight gain becomes painful and embarrassing, so that an age-appropriate physiological event becomes shameful within a culture of thinness. They go to war with their own bodies; food becomes the enemy.

The impact of trauma and loss further compromises a system that is already weakened from genetics, culture, and experience. When this occurs in a society that exalts thinness and avoids emotional pain, you have the perfect soil for the growth of EDs and dissociation. EDs seem to mask underlying dissociative ego states, adding psychological complications to the clinical picture.

Even with no prior signs of the biochemical or psychological disturbances associated with EDs, culturally induced dieting can easily lead to those conditions. Restricted eating, regardless of the motivation, can cause an ED. Most clients struggling with an ED never intend it. It typically begins with a diet and a desire to lose "a few pounds."

The effects of semi-starvation were seen in the Minnesota Starvation Experiment, a clinical study performed at the University of Minnesota between November 19, 1944, and December 20, 1945. The investigation was designed to determine the physiological and psychological effects of severe and prolonged dietary restriction. The subjects were 36 conscientious objectors who wanted to serve their country in some other capacity. They volunteered for the experiment in order to provide information that would aid in the dietary rehabilitation of a devastated Europe following World War II.

The study revealed that the men who had enjoyed mental and physical health before the experiment revealed significant increases in depression, irritability, hysteria, hypochondriasis, and self-mutilating behaviors. Other noticeable effects were a preoccupation with food, loss of concentration, and impaired cognitive judgment.

In discussing the observations from this experiment, Ancel Keys

(Keys, Brozek, Henschel, Mickelsen, & Taylor, 1950), the project coordinator, noticed that the social and psychological effects of starvation approximated those experienced by patients with EDs. These effects took place without the cultural, genetic, and familial influences of clients with EDs.

In other words, the physiological disturbances created by disordered eating can readily beget an ED and its symptomatology. Dieting, for example, can create a vicious and unrelenting loop because a pattern of restricted eating will slow down the body's metabolic rate. The body's main purpose is to survive, and so it holds on to whatever little food it is offered. The dieting person experiences this as "getting fat," restricts even more, resulting in, among other things, mood imbalances and a body that can no longer tell if it is hungry or sated.

The more we learn about the biology of appetite and weight regulation, the more it appears that disordered eating can readily prepare the way for an ED, and that EDs are self-perpetuating. Furthermore, alterations in brain chemistry are part of the collateral damage from EDs, strengthening the very existence of the disorder. "Morphological brain alterations are most likely a consequence of endocrine and metabolic reactions to starvation, regardless of whether starvation leads to an underweight state" (Treasure et al., 2003, p. 89). More research is needed. "Functional neuroimaging, neuroendocrine and candidate gene studies will help to further elucidate the central mechanisms maintaining low appetite and weight in AN [anorexia nervosa], and the drive to overeat in BN [bulimia nervosa] and BED [binge eating disorder]" (Treasure et al., 2003, p. 77).

What are the reasons for the existence of an ED? Neurobiological? Cultural? Developmental? Familial? Psychological? Trauma history? They all contribute, but their relative degree of influence is debatable. We live in a time when multiple factors support a somatic disconnect, one in which our bodies, more so than ever, are being nailed to the cross of thinness and false identity.

Just as it takes a village to raise a child, it will require enormous collaboration among therapists, psychiatrists, medical professionals, creative art therapists, and nutritionists to begin the work of healing from this cultural epidemic. The chapters in this section are contributions from therapists who have struggled to find ways out of the clinical labyrinth created by these disorders. It is our hope that they will provide light and a few guideposts to those of you who are willing to take this journey with your clients.

REFERENCES

Bloom, C., Gitter, A., Gutwill, S., Kogel, L., & Zaphiropoulos, L. (1994). *Eating problems: A feminist psychoanalytic treatment model*. New York: Basic Books.

Keys, A., Brozek, J., Henschel, A., Mickelsen, O., & Taylor, H. L. (1950). *The Biology of human starvation* (2 vols.). Minneapolis: University of Minnesota Press.

Kiemle, G., Slade, P. D. & Dewey, M. E. (1987). Factors associated with abnormal eating attitudes and behaviors: Screening individuals at risk of developing an eating disorder. *International Journal of Eating Disorders, 6*, 713–724.

McShane, J., & Paulson, T. (2008). *Why she feels fat*. Carlsbad, CA: Gurze Books.

Pipher, M. (1994). *Reviving Ophelia: Saving the selves of adolescent girls*. New York: Putnam.

Slade, P. D. (1982). Towards a functional analysis of anorexia nervosa and bulimia nervosa. *British Journal of Clinical Psychology, 21*, 167–179.

Slade, P. D., Newton, T., Butler, N. M., & Murphy, P. (1991). An experimental analysis of perfectionism and dissatisfaction. *British Journal of Clinical Psychology, 30*, 169–176.

Strober, M., Freeman, R., Lampert, C., Diamond, J. & Kaye, W. (2000). Controlled family study of anorexia nervosa and bulimia nervosa: Evidence of shared liability and transmission of partial syndromes. *American Journal of Psychiatry, 157*, 393–401.

Treasure, J., Schmidt, U., & van Furth, E. (Eds.). (2003). *Handbook of eating disorders* (2nd ed.). West Sussex, England: Wiley.

Way, K. (1993). *Anorexia nervosa and recovery: A hunger for meaning*. New York: Huntington Park Press.

Chapter 7

Integrating Eating Disorders Treatment into the Early Phases of the EMDR Protocol

Janie Scholom

EATING DISORDERS (EDs) ARE COMPLEX CHRONIC ILLNESSES WITH PHYS-ical, social, and psychological ramifications. The threads of obsessive concern about food, weight, and appearance, inappropriate eating behavior, and body image distortions run through anorexia nervosa (AN), bulimia nervosa (BN), and binge eating disorder (BED). The same threads run through disordered eating, that is, problematic eating behavior where one eats, not out of physiological hunger, but to soothe, numb, comfort, or avoid.

EMDR can be a framework for treatment with EDs. Apart from genetic factors, experiences within families, social milieu, and culture dramatically impact the development of EDs. These experiences may not be adaptively processed, becoming the contaminated lens by which subsequent experience is incorporated into our personal schema (R. Shapiro, 2005). EMDR processing targets specific aspects of the ED, as well as the underlying traumas and the traumas developing out of the disorder itself. For example, Sally had several plastic surgeries to "improve" her looks. She was never pleased with the surgeries, filled with greater self-hate for having them. We'll track Sally's case throughout the chapter. By processing her early trauma from attachment deficits and abuse, we were able to bring her to a place of acceptance for her body and her self.

I conceptualize EDs, in part, as an affect management problem, with roots in early attachment relationships. The style of our early attachments to primary caregivers is crucial in determining personality development. Affect regulation develops out of these early attachment experiences.

EATING DISORDERS AS AN AFFECT REGULATION PROBLEM

ED symptoms are major defenses erected to keep people from experiencing and examining certain feelings, thoughts, conflicts, and fantasies (Bloom, Gitter, Gutwill, Kogel, & Zaphiropoulos, 1994). Anorexics restrict food to feel in control, strong, acceptable, and powerful; bulimics and binge eaters turn to food as their primary source of comfort, coping, and emotional fulfillment. Thus, affect regulation is expressed via the eating disorder: ". . . defense mechanisms are, in essence, forms of emotional regulation strategies for avoiding, minimizing, or converting affects that are too difficult to tolerate" (Cole, Michel, & O'Donnell, as cited in Shore, 2003, pp. 27–28). How do we develop affect regulation? Simply stated, unconscious to unconscious, mother to infant, strategies for affect regulation are encoded through psychoneurobiological mechanisms for coping with stress. These internal representations continue to be accessed as blueprints for future interactions (Shore, 2003). Infants do not have the capacity to regulate negative affect. If they are hyperaroused, for instance, crying to get needs met for too long, without the attuned intervention of the caregivers, their parasympathetic nervous system will activate to quiet the hyperarousal and the infants will dissociate/go numb.

IMPORTANCE OF ATTACHMENT

Sroufe defines attachment as the dyadic regulation of emotion (as cited in Shore, 2003). The baby attaches to the modulating caregiver who expands opportunities for positive and minimizes negative affect. According to Shore (2000) the early social-emotional environment mediated by the primary caregivers directly influence the final hard wiring of the brain circuits that are responsible for future social-emotional development. The child uses the output of the mother's right cortex (the emotional brain) as template for the hard wiring of circuits in her own right cortex that will come to mediate her developing affect regulating capacities, that is, unconscious to unconscious, each re-creating a psychophysiological state similar to the other. This nonverbal emotional attunement between infant and caregiver shapes the development of the baby's right brain stress coping system. A secure, healthy attachment facilitated by emotional attunement is critical to the development of affect regulation. The baby becomes attached to the modulating caregiver who generates greater opportunities for positive experiences while lessening negative ones. When attachment problems occur, the growing person's capacity for affect tolerance and regulation is compromised. People with insecure attachments are also more vulnerable to low self-esteem and body image issues.

Affective instability, vulnerability, powerlessness, and shame are common to EDs across the spectrum. For the ED person, food becomes the avenue to express significant aspects of the self. Food symbolizes the time when merger of mother with baby was or should have been a soothing experience. "Feeding interaction between mother and child is one of the first and primary areas in which communication occurs. The nonverbal, presymbolic transaction that occurs lays the groundwork for neurophysiological and intrapsychic schemas that will organize the infant's experience" (Johnson & Connors, 1987, p. 95).

The binge eater lacks an internal soothing presence to manage anxiety and turns to food, symbolic of the good mother. The cycle of discomfort, eating, self-reproach, and anger at not being able to eat continues endlessly. Similarly, the bulimic displaces her split-off needs, conflicts, and feelings onto food. Spoken or unspoken, parental and cultural expectations are internalized. The bulimic, like the anorexic, pushes herself to be the best, though false, self she can be. Perfectionistic and striving toward control, she is compromised in her abilities to manage stress. The bulimic hides her shame, conflict, and despair. She compulsively, as if in a trance, consumes food to fill the emptiness, and then, feeling invaded, must purge the beast. She shares a core emptiness and denial of feelings with the anorexic for whom food represents the rejecting, traumatizing object to be denied.

Lack of psychological differentiation between self and other leads the eating-disordered person to feel out of control, distrustful, and inadequate. She cannot tell how or what she feels. Though the body is the concrete representation of the boundary between me/not me and the means to play out control issues and intrapsychic conflicts, the ED person is detached from her body. She cannot sense somatically what she is feeling.

EMDR gets at the early nonverbal internal object relations visually imprinted and stored in the right hemisphere. EMDR treatment of early negative experiences fostering Adaptive Information Processing paired with emotional, empathic attunement within the therapeutic relationship gives the ED person opportunities to reparent and rectify attachment problems. The experience of being better cared for by self and therapist enables the client to reconnect with the pain, mourn the losses, and free herself to disconnect these losses from food and body obsession as she learns her needs can be met and she is not bad for having them.

PHASE ONE: HISTORY AND TREATMENT PLANNING

Sally

Sally is the second of five girls. She experienced maternal neglect within an enmeshed family, tolerating no individuation. She was singled out as the "bad" child, denigrated by her mother, ostracized by her sisters, and abandoned by her father after a modeling career with him ended at 10 years old. She came into treatment with panic (especially when alone or perceiving rejection) depression, laxative abuse, bingeing and purging, compulsive stealing and spending, sexual addiction, and body loathing. She was in recovery from alcohol abuse.

As a child, Sally was sexually abused by an uncle. Sexual boundaries in the family were blurred across generations. She had few friends, was often "picked on." Sally presented with a preoccupied attachment style. She tended toward anxiety, was overwhelmed by her feelings, and felt tremendous anger, rage, and shame. Negative Beliefs were "I'm not good enough. I'm fat and ugly. I'm all alone. I'm worthless." It took many months of treatment before Sally could identify a nurturing figure as well as a Safe Place. She had little tolerance for positive or negative affect. Treatment centered around the independence-dependence conflict Sally experienced in all of her relationships, including with me. Over the many years we worked together, Sally took several sabbaticals whenever she felt too close, dependent, and needy. She had a difficult time identifying and managing feelings, usually "disconnecting" or depersonalizing when overwhelmed. Through treatment, Sally was able to trust me as a consistent, safe, and nonabusive person. We had to front-load affect management skills before she could stay present to do the reprocessing work. Her presence was fostered by her developing connection to me as her partial container, as well as her growing ability to allow positive experience.

History/Intake

When working with EDs, we are interested in learning how the person experiences and behaves in her world, what led her here, and what is necessary to enhance her life now and in the future. Pay particular attention to attachment history, psychosocial development, trauma, and history of the ED. Several questionnaires are useful in facilitating information gathering, in addition to the Dissociative Experiences Scale (DES). These include, but are not limited to, Garner, Olmsted, and Polivy's (1983) Eating Disorder Inventory, and George, Kaplan, and Main's (1985) Adult Attachment Interview.

I find genograms to be useful illustrations of family patterns over generations, enabling the clinician and the client to see experiences in context: the coincidence and impact of life events, relationships, transitions, and traumas. Maureen Kitchur's use of genograms is a particularly helpful guide (Kitchur, 2005).

Attachment History

In the absence of the actual Adult Attachment Interview, eliciting a narrative history is more than adequate toward understanding how the client experienced their primary caregivers.

1. *Starting as far back as you can remember, describe your relationship with your parents.*

   Sally: My mother was critical, saying I was the cause of all the family problems. I had a special relationship with my father until 10.

2. *What are five adjectives describing your relationship with your mother? Your father?* For each adjective it is important to probe for memories and incidents, as specifically as possible. How the person reveals these details indicates something about their attachment

style. For example, a person with a "preoccupied" style is likely to ramble or become extremely absorbed and preoccupied by these memories, whereas an idealized depiction cannot be substantiated by specific memories.

3. *What were separations like? How did your parents respond?*

   Sally: I would pretend I was sick so I could stay home from school. My mother let me.

4. *How did your parents discipline?*

   Sally: Once my father punched me, my mother did nothing.

5. *How did they respond when you got upset, hurt, sick?*

   Sally: They told me to get over it, that I exaggerated.

6. *Why do you believe your parents behaved as they did?*

   Sally: They came from pretty crazy families themselves. I see that now.

7. *How do you think your childhood experiences impact on you now?* It is important to describe and evaluate the effect their relationship with attachment figures had on their development (Fonagy & Target, as cited in Shore, 2003), thus revealing their ability to step back and reflect on their experience. According to Siegel (Solomon & Siegel, 2003), how a person makes sense of past experiences in his family reveals a certain integration of functioning within the mind. Linear telling of a story is a left-hemisphere operation. Autobiographical narratives require the left hemisphere to connect with the subjective emotional self-experience stored in the right hemisphere, forming a coherent story. Blockages lead to incoherent narratives. Self-reflection is necessary to experience and regulate emotion or distance from it.

8. *Losses: of parents and significant others. How did these impact you?*

9. *What is your current relationship with your parents like?*

   Sally: My mother still singles me out as the problem. She is very close with my sisters.

10. *Other disruptions: surgeries, significant illnesses.*

11. *Peer relationships: quality of friendships. Teasing?*

    Sally: I drank at 12. I always felt outside the group.

Attachment Styles

Attachment styles tell us about the person's quality of relationships and will provide us with core beliefs to focus on in treatment as well as to inform us of the person's strengths, needs, and deficits. This explanation came from Wesselman (2000).

Secure: Has a balanced, realistic view of oneself and others. Is generally trusting and enjoys healthy relationships. Is able to self-regulate and is resilient under stress. Secure attachments are fostered by a caregiver who skillfully attunes to the child's needs.

    Core Beliefs: I am lovable. My feelings and needs are okay.

Preoccupied: Early relationships were characterized by overinvolvement, dependency, and enmeshment. Tends to be anxious and overwhelmed by feelings, requiring more focus on emotional regulation and containment. Views self as not good enough. May be angry, distressed, ashamed, or ambivalent toward attachment figures. Is common in eating disorders, especially in bulimia nervosa.

    Core Beliefs: I am unlovable. My feelings and needs are not okay.

Dismissive: Relationships characterized by emotional distance and lack of mutuality. Often represses memories of vulnerability and rejection by significant childhood figures. Denies importance of relationships. Avoids uncomfortable feelings, is usually not reflective. Looks for ways to feel in control. Self-esteem is tenuous, may be grandiose. Wants quick fix. Tends to be defensive. This style is common in anorexia nervosa.

    Core Beliefs: I can't trust anyone. I don't need closeness.

Fearful/Disorganized: Others are untrustworthy. Puts up walls, desires yet fears closeness. Childhood memories may be confused, frightening, and trigger extreme emotions. Hypervigilant with others.

    Core Beliefs: I will be hurt. I am unlovable.

Lilly

Understanding attachment styles can inform our interventions, from the extent of preparation necessary to the way in which we interact with the client. Lilly comes from an alcoholic home. Her mother was obese, always dieting and including Lilly in these diets. Mother was unpredictable, volatile, and would periodically threaten to leave the kids. Lilly seemed to have a fearful/disorganized style, wanting closeness yet fearing it. Bulimia represented this dilemma, as well as offering Lilly a means to self-soothe. When troubling memories arose, Lilly spaced out in confusion. The spectrum of dissociation is common in this population, from "spacing out" to detaching from one's body to the development of more distinct ego states and/or parts. Lilly required a lengthy preparation phase to ground in the present, gain mastery in managing emotions, and time to trust me as a consistent, reliable and empathic "caregiver."

RESOURCES

It is important to identify positive attachment experiences for use as resources, including mentors, pets, other family members, teachers, and friends. These can be utilized as an "inner coach" or form part of the "inner support team" (Foster, 2001a, 2001b) the client can incorporate imaginally and reinforce with BLS (Bilateral Stimulation) as part of resource building. Positive networks are necessary in order for EMDR processing to forge new connections between the targeted dysfunctional memory network and those holding more adaptive information. If no positive experiences are reported, these need to be built in during the preparation phase.

EATING DISORDER HISTORY

Understanding the client's relationship with food from family messages to identifying the triggers (*what, where, when, how often, antecedent events?*) that propel the ED behavior is essential. This includes:

Past weight: Most, least, desired. Weight fluctuations? Diet history: First diet? Types of diets? Typical food intake. Meals/day? Vomiting, laxatives, diuretics—how often? Exercise?

Eating in family: Parental control over eating? Meals together? *What were these like? Pleasant, forced, punishing? Imagine family dinner at your parents, any time, real or fantasy. What feelings come up about each person? What is the atmosphere like? How do you feel? Now go back to your childhood. Any similarities then and now?* (Orbach, 1998).

Family Messages:
My mother's message to me about/My father's message to me about

    food was_____

    eating was_____

    weight was_____

    my body was_____

    having needs was_____

    my feelings was_____

    handling feelings was_____

    satisfaction was_____

TREATMENT PLANNING AND
CASE CONCEPTUALIZATION

As we explore the history, notably of the adaptive function of all aspects of the ED symptoms, we begin to identify themes, patterns, core beliefs, deficits, and potential treatment targets from positive and negative events. It is important to begin making connections with the client, between the symptoms and the deeper issues of dependency, need, shame, vulnerability, and the self and body–hate they camouflage. We are fostering the client's ability to identify the feelings they so tenaciously defended against.

Affect Bridge and Floatback (Zangwill, in F. Shapiro, 2001) will be helpful in identifying the touchstone experiences for EMDR processing, specifically targeting episodes of bingeing, starving, or other symptoms that function to keep the client from effectively managing her needs, issues, wants, and feelings, as well as traumas identified in the history.

Through the floatback, Sally was able to connect her present body loathing to the time she was told she could no longer model because she was too big.

In my experience, once safety and stabilization are in place, that is, the client may still be symptomatic but weight is stable, caloric intake is sufficient, binge/purge episodes are no more than several times a week, and the client has developed the necessary affect management skills to enable state change, I do trauma processing first. While trauma reprocessing can be destabilizing because of the overwhelming emotions triggered, if the client is sufficiently prepared, she can manage this more effectively. These experiences are fueling the ED symptoms and, once processed, seem to facilitate the sense of control and mastery necessary to tackle the lingering ED symptoms directly. Most ED clients are ambivalent about giving up these symptoms because of the protection from feelings they experience, but they can be more comfortable with this prospect as their affect tolerance and sense of control build. Body image disturbances, the most intractable of the issues to resolve, are the last cluster of targets to reprocess. Despite the processing of many of the traumas, Sally continued to doubt her appearance, seeking repeated reassurance from me.

PHASE TWO: CLIENT PREPARATION

Because EDs are profound protections against disturbing emotions, these clients need extensive affect regulation front loading to enhance their sense of control, power, and competency.

Client Readiness for EMDR Processing

Questions to consider as we conceptualize the treatment plan include: Is the client able to access experience and allow processing to occur without fear of fear? Can the person change states? (Can they calm themselves when in fear?) Can they soothe/calm themselves sufficiently to stay in the present? Are they able to maintain dual awareness, that is, "go inside" during BLS while maintaining external contact with the clinician in the present? Are there significant health risks? For EDs, are they malnourished? Severely restricted eating impairs cognitive functioning. Some additional red flags include active suicidal and or homicidal ideation, extreme denial (common), poor impulse control (self-mutilation, stealing, spending, and substance abuse), significant dissociation, difficulty acknowledging/tolerating positive experience, unstable therapeutic alliance, or current crisis.

Psychoeducation: Knowledge Is Power!

Psychoeducation includes information about EMDR and basic facts about EDs, especially medical ramifications; nutrition; importance of exercise; neurobiology of affect and the role of the autonomic nervous system in response to stress. Understanding how our minds and bodies operate can be liberating. Our clients often do not understand how we get into habitual patterns psychologically or physiologically. This information can move them away from shame and self-blame.

I present the model of attuned eating, that is, eating when hungry. Since most ED clients can't identify body sensations, I find Somatic Experiencing (Levine, 1997) techniques especially helpful. Sally could not distinguish hunger, nor could she identify calm in her body. I worked with her to identify and track body sensation and to manage the negative sensations by shifting focus to where in her body she felt calm or neutral. It was frightening for her to bring her attention into the body from which she was detached. As we worked at sensing positive sensations using pleasing images, she became more comfortable with her body as a source of pleasure. It's important to move slowly to ease into the experience to minimize evoking the ED defenses. As Sally gained body sensation awareness and the ability to manage the distressing sensations, she began to entertain the possibility of living comfortably in her body.

We spent time exploring and understanding her pervasive and debilitating shame. Shame has its roots in our early disrupted attachment experiences, leaving us feeling alone and disrupting our sense of self to the core (Fosha, 2003). Sally blamed herself for the dysfunctional family behavior, patterns that repeated over generations. She felt defective, damaged, and worthless.

Ego State (Watkins & Watkins, 1998) work is useful with this population, offering us a way to conceptualize healthy vs. dysfunctional aspects of ourselves. Ego states can be delineated by traits, functions, or roles (the anxious state, the part that starves, the critic). They may have a normative imaginal function and they can change and adapt. Therapists use imagery to access various ego states as well as facilitating the development of inner resources. They invite ego states to a conference table meeting as another way of accessing various parts. When clients dialogue with an ED part, it can illuminate the conflict, strengthening the observing ego. Sally thought of her binge eating as the "bad child." She had a "nurturing grandmother" ego state that she anchored to her right hand, ever ready to remind her that she could soothe the "bad child" when negative feelings arose. We strengthened this imaginal scene with several short sets of BLS.

Affect Management Techniques

BLS may be used to enhance the positive experience, with several short sets of four–eight movements. Longer sets run the risk of activating negative material.

1. *Safe or peaceful place.*
2. *Container:* A repository of disturbing experiences, thoughts, feelings, memories. A specific feeling can be placed in the container at any point, until an appropriate opportunity to deal with it occurs. Examples: file cabinet, bank vault with safety deposit boxes to hold clustered experiences, army tank, bomb shelter. (See Chapter 17 for a complete discussion of containers.)
3. *Movie screen/video with remote:* To titrate the intensity of feelings by adjusting the volume, pausing, or fast forwarding. This can be practiced in preparation for use, if needed, during reprocessing.

   Sally managed her overwhelm by visualizing an experience on a TV screen. She could slo-mo the picture as well as decrease the volume.
4. *Inner coach, guide, helper, protector:* To provide support, strength, and reassurance.

   Sally used an image of her grandmother, perched on her shoulder, to whisper reassuring reminders that she is a good person and could delay her binge, even if it was only a few seconds. We reinforced this image with several short sets of BLS.
5. *Resource Development and Installation*: "a set of EMDR protocols focused on strengthening connections to resources in functional (positive) memory networks while deliberately not stimulating dysfunctional (trauma) memory networks" (Korn & Leeds, 2002, p. 1469). Remember, we need positive networks to do EMDR processing.

   Sally identified assertiveness as a resource to manage the powerlessness she frequently slipped into. She tapped into a memory where she appropriately set boundaries with a boss.

6. *Mindfulness:* Being in the moment. The ED client moves at the speed of light from affect to behavior without thinking. Often they are in a trancelike state as they approach a binge/purge episode. I especially like the exercise below to help slow them down.

Exercise*: Just sit for a few seconds with the feeling or urge. What's it like? How does it feel? What do you notice in your body? What else comes up? Just notice without judgment.*

This is both diagnostic of their ability to hold a feeling and useful toward developing awareness. It can be practiced at home. Stretching/prolonging their ability to sit with the urge/uncomfortable feeling will not only yield a sense of control and competence, it will expand the range of resiliency to tolerate greater negative affect.

7. *Protective cover:* Bubble, shield, or layer that is porous, allowing in positive, manageable feelings and experiences while keeping out negative. *Imagine a protective layer—it can be a bubble, a membrane, whatever you want—that will keep out the negative and allow only the positive in.* Reinforce with BLS. This exercise reinforces body boundaries as well. This is a popular tool with all my clients.

8. *Future Template:* As an imaginal rehearsal for coping skills and mastery experiences. Positive memory networks may be created as the person imaginally practices various scenarios. *What needs to happen to feel better? Imagine doing that.* Reinforce with BLS.

Sally visualized managing the panic she experiences with rejection without bingeing. She appreciated she could use relaxation to lessen the anxiety before it moved into panic.

9. *Marsha Linehan's Emotional Regulation and Distress Tolerance Skills:* These are extremely helpful (Linehan, 1993; Lovell, 2005).

Sally's relationships were volatile. She experienced euphoria with the reconciliation following a blowup. Identifying options to handle the emptiness and aloneness she felt enabled Sally to step back and begin to separate from these dramas.

SUMMARY

EDs are challenging to treat because of the complexities of their underlying issues and because of the potential life-threatening nature of their symptoms. The early negative attachment experiences and traumas encoded in memory are part of the genesis of this pathology. EMDR, as you will see in subsequent chapters, is effective as part of an overall, comprehensive treatment approach. In light of the enormous dysregulation this population experiences, devote as much time as your client needs obtaining a thorough history and front-loading affect management skills.

REFERENCES

Bloom, C., Gitter, A., Gutwill, S., Kogel, L., & Zaphiropoulos, L. (1994). *Eating problems: A feminist psychoanalytic treatment model.* New York: Basic Books.

Fosha, D. (2003). Dyadic regulation and experiential work with emotion and relatedness in trauma and disorganized attachment. In M. F. Solomon & D. J. Siegel (Eds.), *Healing trauma: Attachment, mind, body, and brain* (pp. 221–281). New York: Norton.

Foster, S. (2001a). *From trauma to triumph: EMDR and advanced performance enhancement strategies.* Workshop presentation, Bethesda, MD.

Foster, S. (2001b). *Using EMDR for performance enhancement in career and in the creative and performing arts.* Workshop presentation, Bethesda, MD.

Johnson, C., & Connors, M. E. (1987). *The etiology and treatment of bulimia nervosa: A biopsychosocial perspective.* New York: Basic Books.

Kitchur, M. (2005). The strategic developmental model for EMDR. In R. Shapiro (Ed.), *EMDR solutions: Pathways to healing* (pp. 8–56). New York: Norton.

Korn, D. L., & Leeds, A. M. (2002). Preliminary evidence of efficacy for EMDR resource development in the stabilization phase of treatment of complex posttraumatic stress disorder. *Journal of Clinical Psychology, 58*(12), 1465–1487.

Levine, P. A. (1997). *Waking the tiger: Healing trauma.* Berkeley, CA: North Atlantic Books.

Linehan, M. (1993). *Skills training manual for treating borderline personality disorder.* New York: Guilford Press.

Lovell, C. (2005). Utilizing EMDR and DBT techniques in trauma and abuse recovery groups. In R. Shapiro (Ed.), *EMDR solutions: Pathways to healing* (pp. 263–282). New York: Norton.

Orbach, S. (1998). *Fat is a feminist issue.* London: Arrow Books.

Shapiro, F. (2001). *Eye movement desensitization and reprocessing: Basic principles, protocols, and procedures* (2nd ed.). New York: Guilford Press.

Shapiro, R. (2005). EMDR with cultural and generational introjects. In R. Shapiro (Ed.), *EMDR solutions: Pathways to healing* (pp. 228–240). New York: Norton.

Shore, A. N. (2000). *The neurobiology of attachment and the origin of the self: Implications for theory and clinical practice*. Workshop presentation at the EMDRIA Conference, Toronto, Canada.

Shore, A. N. (2003). *Affect regulation and the repair of the self*. New York: Norton.

Solomon, M. F., & Siegel, D. J. (2003). *Healing trauma: Attachment, mind, body, and brain*. New York: Norton.

Watkins, J. G., & Watkins, H. H. (1998). *Ego states: Theory and therapy*. New York: Norton.

Wesselmann, D. (2000). *Treating core attachment issues in adults and children*. Workshop presentation at the EMDRIA Conference, Toronto, Canada.

FURTHER READING

Zerbe, K. J. (1993). *The body betrayed: Deeper understanding of women, eating disorders and treatment*. Washington, DC: American Psychiatric Press.

Chapter 8

The Neurobiology of Eating Disorders, Affect Regulation Skills, and EMDR in the Treatment of Eating Disorders

Linda J. Cooke and Celia Grand

WHY DO SOME PEOPLE DEVELOP EATING DISORDERS (EDs) WHEN OTHERS don't? Many studies point to the comorbidity and familial co-occurrence of ED and obsessive-compulsive disorder (Uher & Treasure, 2005). EDs are usually preceded by a stressful life event or challenge that strains the individual's coping resources. This results in a sense of helplessness that alters physiological and psychological systems. Advances in neurobiology have given us a dynamic understanding of how stress impacts ED symptoms. As the genetic and neurobiologic picture unfolds, the perception of EDs as a psychiatric disorder changes to a primarily biologically based disorder with secondary psychiatric manifestations.

A basic understanding of the appetite mechanism is important to our understanding of EDs. The hypothalamus or "metabolic furnace" controls many important functions, including appetite and the stress response. The ventromedial region of the hypothalamus appears to be the main center for satiety and thermogenesis (the increase in energy expended due to an increase in caloric intake). This center "reads" the genetically predetermined set point for normal body composition and ensures that the body keeps in balance by effecting appropriate feedback mechanisms such as appetite and thermogenesis. EDs may stem from not only a "mis-setting" or "mis-reading" of the set-point reference, but from problems in the malfunctioning of the feedback corrective mechanisms. This results in an overshooting in obesity or an undershooting in anorexia (Hoek, Treasure, & Katzman, 1998).

THE ROLE OF STRESS

The limbic system, our emotional control center, controls the hypothalamus. Under stress, the limbic system sounds an alarm, which stimulates the hypothalamus to release cortico-releasing hormone (CRH). CRH stimulates the pituitary gland to release adrenocortico-tropic hormone (ACTH). In response the sympathetic nervous system releases norepinephrine and epinephrine, which increase heart rate and respiration and blood flow to prepare for danger, igniting our fight-or-flight response. The adrenal glands respond to ACTH by releasing cortisol, which tells the limbic system when the danger is over. The alarm shuts off and the body returns to balance.

However, under chronic stress, the ongoing secretion of cortisol exhausts the adrenal glands. Chronic activation of the HPA axis (hippocampus-pituitary-adrenals) inhibits its ability to respond appropriately to further stress. Overactivity of the HPA axis occurs in conjunction with an alteration in the serotonergic system, with loss of appetite as a secondary feature. Studies with rodents and monkeys have shown exaggerated HPA and Sympathetic Nervous System (SNS) responses to separation, resulting in dendritic shrinkage and causing a decrease in hippocampal volume (Hoek et al., 1998). Similar results have been shown in humans. Children with disorganized attachment who are under chronic stress are subjected to prolonged exposure to cortisol. High levels of cortisol released during stress are associated with loss of neurons and dendritic branching (Liotti, 1992).

NEUROBIOLOGICAL VARIANCES IN EDS

The research on the neurobiological variances of various EDs is complex. Functional neuroimaging research points to lesions in frontotemporal circuits as significant to the genesis of EDs (Uher & Treasure, 2005).

The Neurobiology of Anorexia

Anorexia is a multifaceted disorder that should be viewed from a biopsychosocial perspective (Garfinkel & Garner, 1982; Garner, 1993;

Strober, 1991). Recent studies explore a neurobiological perspective that adds insight into the complexity of the disorder. Puberty generates a window of vulnerability in the system controlling body-mass composition. In females, the percentage of fat tissue increases by 17%–25% of body weight resulting in an adjustment in set point, which does not occur in males. This is one reason that girls are at greater risk of developing an ED. During the active myelination process of adolescence, abstract cognitive processing is already challenged. Starvation compounds the problem and negatively impacts brain and cognitive development. Studies indicate that the IQs of anorexics are, for the most part, average, yet their ability to outperform suggests the presence of personality traits of persistence, perfectionism, obsessionality, and low-reward sensitivity. These personality traits often predate the disorder. EMDR treatment that is focused on enhancing effective problem solving and coping strategies can help prevent the oversensitive HPA system from perpetuating the spiral of severe weight loss.

The Neurobiology of Bulimia

Single Photon Emission Computed Tomography (SPECT) scan studies show that bulimics have temporal hypermetabolism, changes in the frontal areas of the brain that cause them to overeat, and higher levels of blood flow in frontal regions of the brain before feeding, than in controls. When bulimics are shown images of high-caloric foods, blood flow increases in the amygdala, insula, and anterior cingulate areas. After feeding, there is a reduction in blood flow in the bilateral inferior frontal, left temporal, and right parietal regions. The research suggests that overeating in bulimia may result in reduced activity in these limbic regions (Hoek et al., 1998).

The limbic region is responsible for processing emotions and is the area most activated in posttraumatic stress disorder (PTSD). Developmental adversity and trauma are likely to result in difficulties handling stress by causing abnormalities in the HPA axis and lower levels of serotonergic system. Low levels of serotonin decrease satiety, resulting in a person needing to eat large amounts of food before satiation is achieved. Studies clearly indicate that abusive experiences increase an individual's vulnerability to develop an ED, especially bingeing and purging. These abnormalities predispose bingers to the negative effects triggered by an episode of dieting. People with a family history of obesity and a fear of being fat have a higher set point and are more at risk of dieting. In these individuals, homeostatic mechanisms controlling appetite and weight function normally. Their bodies resist weight loss, resulting in a self-perpetuating trap of weight gain (Hoek et al., 1998).

Though the significance of these findings remains uncertain, neurobiology is the lens through which we see our patients with bulimia. Binge eating and purging help them avoid distressing emotions, decreasing activation of schemata related to threats of safety, well-being, and self-esteem. EMDR can counteract the effect of prolonged emotional stress and strain by decreasing activation of these perceived threats, thereby improving neurobiological function.

The Neurobiology of Binge-Eating Disorder

The hypothalamus integrates several neural and hormonal messages, controlling hunger and satiety, and influencing the deposition and utilization of energy stores. As in bulimia, obesity is caused by frontal damage resulting in hyperphagia, or voracious overeating, and not from any associated metabolic disturbances (Anand & Brobeck, 1961, cited in Hoek, 1998). The homeostatic mechanisms controlling weight and appetite are very complex and beyond the scope of our knowledge, but the concept of set point controlling weight is useful (see Figure 8.1). The hormone leptin is expressed in fat tissue. Normally, satiety occurs as the fat cell releases leptin, which stimulates the hypothalamus to send a signal of satiation in order to stabilize weight. Recent studies of the ob mouse, known to be fat, infertile, and inactive, indicate that their leptin gene seems to be dysfunctional. If the mice are given leptin, their appetite decreases, metabolism increases along with increased activity, their weight falls, and fertility improves. In humans, dieting through cognitive control of intake results in lower levels of nutrients so fat levels become depleted. There is less availability of leptin, so the signal of satiation is inhibited. In addition, lower levels of nutrients cause an increase in Neuropeptide Y (NPY), a peptide that decreases satiety and inhibits metabolic control. Hence, dieting attempts fail (Hoek et al., 1998).

BEHAVIORAL ISSUES IN EDS

Studies of rodents with histories of early maternal separation show an increased activity in the amygdala and hypothalamus. Their stress response remains elevated and the CRH receptor in the pituitary re-

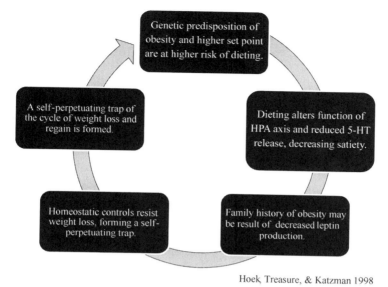

Hoek, Treasure, & Katzman 1998

Figure 8.1 Dieting and Obesity Cycle

mains down-regulated throughout the course of their lives. Infant monkeys with early maternal separation demonstrate insecure attachment styles, are reluctant to explore novel situations, and are more anxious.

Similar effects are known to occur in children with histories of insecure attachment and early distress. In adolescence, the brain goes through the process of "neural pruning" in order to make the brain more efficient. In individuals with trauma or early attachment disruptions, the pruning does not rid them of the survival pathways, but rather results in these pathways becoming more rigid and automatic. Survival needs create a form of "addiction" to a pattern of hypervigilance that interferes with the ability to self-regulate. These patterns of automatic dysregulated defensive responses are the underpinnings of the rigidity and affect dysregulation of individuals with EDs. The crisis of weight control for girls occurs at a critical time of psychosocial development. Girls at age 19 eat 12% less than at age 10 yet gain more fat stores. This is compared to boys at 19 who eat 20% more than at age 10 but don't gain fat. As identity development occurs, there is an increased self-awareness and concern for body image. It is a time of establishing roles among peers and sexual attraction, as well as a time of seeking approval from society. The female body remains the vehicle through which tensions are expressed.

Temperament and Personality in Anorexia

Classic traits of anorexics are emotional restraint, avoidance of novelty, perfectionism, obsessiveness, self-doubt and worry, compliance, and perseverance in the face of nonreward. Strong evidence links serotonergic mechanisms to restraint of reward motivation for exploring novel environments, modulating feelings and sexual behavior, and regulating the sensitivity of neurobehavioral systems to stimulus events. Although there is an increased serotonergic activity after weight restoration, the temperament and personality traits of anorexics remain unchanged (Lock, le Grange, Agras, Dare, & Agras, 2001). Girls reluctantly relinquish their culturally reinforced thinness. Girls' quests for achievement and autonomy make it difficult to believe that anorexia is not vanity, but a true disorder. It's important to be sensitive to the fact that female identity and role expectations are more fundamental than "cosmetic" concerns about body image.

Temperament and Personality in Bulimia

Bulimics are emotionally dysregulated and often engage in thrill-seeking behaviors. They have a tendency toward dysphoria in response to rejection or nonreward. These features may predispose them to periodic lapses in control and dietary chaos. There are two models for bulimic behavior: (a) the starvation model, which states that restriction leads to binge eating and loss of control, and (b) the blocking model, which we support. In the blocking model, eating is an escape from awareness (or dissociation) and is stress related. Negative emotions and exaggerated cognitive representations of threat trigger a pattern of cognitive and behavioral avoidance. Binge eating is triggered by negative moods, threats to self-esteem, and subliminal abandonment cues rather than calorie deprivation. Treatment needs to focus on identifying what triggers the individual and how to develop self-regulatory abilities in the activities of daily life.

Temperament and Personality in
Binge-Eating Disorder

Individuals with binge-eating disorders (BEDs) experience as much body dissatisfaction as other subtypes of EDs. They experience a significant amount of functional impairment and psychosocial stress in their concern with eating, weight, and shape, all connected to physical appearance and self-evaluation. They share commonalities with anorexia and bulimia and should be considered to have "subtypes" or "subthreshold" disorders.

Treatment goals for individuals with EDs require an approach that enhances self-control within a well-structured daily life. This requires the therapist to be more understanding of the individual rather than trying to get them to eat more or less. Collaborative engagement between the therapist and client helps to calm limbic activation, which brings the frontal lobes online. Engagement also helps overcome clients' ambivalence to treatment. Reframing the ED behavior as a survival mechanism gives clients an opportunity to expand their repertoire of responses versus relying on habitual patterns of survival reactions that have become ineffectual and self-harming.

EMDR TREATMENT

Phase One Treatment (History Taking): In EDs, include medical issues and assessment of external support systems in your assessment of client readiness for EMDR. Assess the client's internal coping strategies, which are often underdeveloped or nonexistent. A client's impairment in the ability to cope with connection with herself (self-regulation) or with another (interactive regulation) makes treatment interventions difficult. Clients often present with symptoms of dissociation, little body awareness, and little affect tolerance, and they are chronically emotionally dysregulated. Their limbic systems are activated and constantly alarming, making connection intolerable and hindering their capacity to learn new information. Dual attention is necessary to promote stabilization of limbic activation. In the initial phase of treatment, we focus on teaching clients to regulate their affect. We establish trust and safety as clients learn to calm their nervous systems from their constant states of emotional dysregulation. You and your client can plan affect management skills that will be needed in the Preparation Phase, so that, eventually, underlying traumas and triggers can be processed with EMDR. (See Chapter 17.)

Phase Two Treatment (Preparation): In this phase of treatment, preparation skills stabilize presenting symptoms while diagnosing what the client can tolerate in treatment. After installing a Safe Place, some clients may have the tolerance and dual attention capacity to be able to start trauma processing. However, since most ED individuals have difficulties managing their affect, it is necessary for the client to learn new skills to cope with overwhelming affect. We have identified four areas to consider: (a) building internal resources, (b) overcoming ambivalence, (c) inoculating the client's system with trauma fragments to increase emotional tolerance, and (d) managing affect. Clients need mindfulness, often lacking in traumatized individuals, to successfully negotiate these four areas. Mindfulness will help to develop their capacity for dual attention, a prerequisite for successful EMDR treatment (see Figure 8.2). During Phase Two, both affect tolerance and dual attention help build the client's capacity to process trauma.

The indicators of stabilization include that: (a) the client tolerates state change, (b) the client does not fluctuate between hyperarousal and hypoarousal, (c) the client is able to easily allow connection and interactive regulation by the clinician, (d) the frontal lobes are online so the client has intact cognitive capacities and can manage symptoms, and (e) the client can be mindful or hold dual attention. When internal resources are developed, there is a balance of the client's ability to tolerate both intense affect and the experience of symptoms. It is at this juncture that the Standard Protocol can be initiated.

STABILIZATION CONSIDERATIONS FOR EACH TYPE OF EATING DISORDER

Clients with anorexia often have an ambivalent attachment style and defend against affect. Build a strong therapeutic relationship to enable the client to foster a sense of self and a new narrative. Overwhelming feelings can be titrated by weaving cognitive strategies and body-oriented techniques through mindfulness, which engages the frontal lobes and helps to regulate arousal.

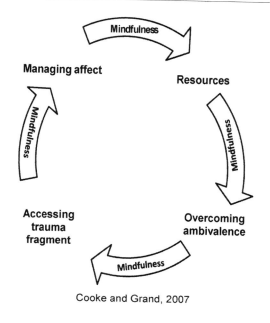

Cooke and Grand, 2007

Figure 8.2 Stabilization through Mindfulness in EMDR

Janie

Janie came to treatment following a long residential program. She had severe trauma symptoms of hyperarousal, feelings of terror, difficulty feeling safe and trusting of others. She had difficulty staying on her food plan, was unable to work, avoided intense feelings, and was unable to report the trauma event that led to her recent bout of anorexia. She never felt connected to her inpatient therapist and was told she was a difficult client because she had a hard time opening up. While inpatient, she had had two sessions of EMDR and thought it might help her now. She had a history of being anorexic since high school, with periods of remission. In the first phase of treatment, Janie was taught the pendulation protocol (Grant & Grand, unpublished) to help stabilize dysregulated limbic activation so she could self-regulate intense somatic feelings. The pendulation protocol uses Bilateral Stimulation (BLS) to stabilize intense affect by alternating from a neutral place in the body to an identifiable distressed place in the body. Janie held on to the tappers and I asked her to identify a place in her body that felt neutral, interesting, or pleasant. Janie replied it was in the palms of her hands. I asked, *"What's the sensation you notice in your hands?"* She answered, "It's like a soothing, calming sensation." I directed Janie to spend a few moments there. Afterward, I asked to rate her level of distress on a scale of 1 to 10. Janie denied any distress. Then I asked her to find a part of her body where she felt distress and to describe the sensations to me. She noticed tightness in her stomach. Janie stayed with the distress for a few moments. Then I asked Janie how distressed she was on a scale of 0 to 10. She indicated a 7. Then I directed her to go back and forth (pendulate) between the neutral place and the distress place, reassessing her level of distress after spending a few moments each in the neutral and distress places. Alternating between these states with mindfulness allows for a discharge of the negatively aroused state, resulting in "state to state" change. As Janie learned how to titrate her symptoms, she felt safe enough to trust in the therapeutic relationship and could begin to tell me her story. We initiated the EMDR Standard Protocol on the recent adult trauma event. Through EMDR, the activating trauma material remitted enough for therapy to focus on recovery issues related to the anorexia: following her food plan and eventually returning to work. If Janie had been unable to tolerate stabilization of the habitual negative arousal states, then I would have stopped pendulation until Janie could stabilize her arousal through grounding, centering, or another somatic resource.

In bulimia, stabilization often includes working with a disorganized (dissociated) attachment style. (See Chapter 13.) It's essential to establish dual attention to rebuild affect management structures that may have been truncated by trauma, loss, or childhood adversity.

Annie

Annie came to treatment with a long history of bulimia. She reported that she was in a chaotic love relationship that exacerbated her feelings of emptiness and aloneness and triggered her binge/purge cycles. Although insightful and aware of how her love relationship triggered her symptoms, Annie could not tolerate feelings that she would cease to exist if not loved by another. We used the Back of the Head Scale (Knipe, 2008), which helps a client track and report verbally on her ability to be present in moment. By using a hand signal, I asked Annie to show me how present she was in the moment. *"Annie, place your hand out in front if you feel very present, at eye level if you feel somewhat present, or toward the back of your head if you do not feel present at all."* Annie placed her hand close to eye level. Since she was somewhat present, I suggested doing a centering exercise. *"Place one hand on your heart and the other on your belly and just breathe into your hands. How do you feel now?"* Annie said she felt more present. *"Great, you are feeling very present."* Annie was able to slowly begin to regulate intense feelings of emptiness and loneliness. Recognizing that her present feelings were the same emotions she had experienced from childhood enabled Annie to separate the past from the present. Practicing this skill gave Annie a tool to help her decrease overwhelming feelings and to know she will not cease to exist in the face of intense feelings.

Stabilization considerations for binge eaters may include: (a) working with an anxious (hypervigilant) attachment style, (b) developing orientation to self versus caretaking or orienting to the environment, (c) teaching auto regulatory skills of all feeling states, and (d) developing coping strategies that inhibit compulsive eating.

Jules

Jules came to treatment because she was unhappy about a recent weight gain following a long period of dieting. She felt frustrated that she could not sustain her previous eating habits and keep her weight down. Jules wanted to do EMDR for her compulsive eating. Initially, she appeared to have good internal coping strategies and to be highly functional as a professional. In her relationships, she was a caregiver who was very supportive, loving, and accommodating. During the Preparation Phase, Jules agreed to follow a food plan that suited her. The goal was to bring up the associated affect when the food was controlled. At this phase, Jules became conscious that she binges when she is angry at her husband, especially when he minimizes her feelings and needs. Jules would find herself seeking comfort in a glass of wine, overeating, or reaching for something sweet. We used York and Leeds (2001) affect management protocol to address Jules's ego dystonic anger. I asked her to bring up the feelings of anger she felt toward her husband. I asked Jules the following questions to help her deepen into mindfulness. *"Where do you feel the anger in your body? Does it have a color? A shape? Does it move? Now what negative belief do you have about yourself or that feeling state? And what would you rather believe about your-self or that feeling state?" On a scale of 1 to 7, how true do those positive words feel to you now, where 7 feels completely true and 1 feels completely false? And when you bring up the anger and the negative words, are there other feelings that go with it? On a scale of 0 to10, how disturbing does it feel, where 10 is the highest and 0 is neutral. Where do you feel that in your body?* (Start BLS. After 2 sets, if it turns into an EMDR processing session, continue on. If the affect gets more overwhelming, do an "adaptive cognitive interweave.") *Jules, I want you to think of your place of comfort. Notice what happens in your body as you think of this special place. What happens now? Great it feels good . . . notice how you did that.* (BLS. BLS continued until Jules felt less overwhelmed by her anger.) *Now Jules, even with the distress left, what is the most positive thing you can say about yourself? Great, notice how that feels as you hear the words, "I can cope."* (BLS.) (Do another Subjective Units of Disturbance Scale [SUDS], end with a few positive visualizations or other positive coping strategies.) Her binge behavior remitted and she was able to tolerate her angry feelings. Then we did EMDR to address the earlier developmental trauma Jules experienced growing up in a family in which women were submissive to men.

IN THE STABILIZATION PHASE

Before ED clients can begin the Standard Protocol, they must have the necessary internal resources to balance symptoms and manage the associated affect. ED clients typically lack internal resources. They have (a) inability to self-care, (b) inability to identify stress and/or stress-related symptoms, resulting in not feeling grounded or centered in the face of stress, (c) difficulty in orienting to inner and/or outer experiences, (d) unremitting trauma symptoms, (e) inability to manage intense affect, or (6) difficulty allowing movement in the body. For example, Tina is a 40-year-old married woman with an early history of trauma and severe neglect. When activated, she goes into a freeze response. As a child, she kept very still by focusing on one point on the wall so as not to cause her abuser to go into a rage. When triggered by intrusive memories, Tina becomes still for hours at a time, regresses to a child state, and loses time. During sessions, I taught Tina to ground herself and to orient to the present by naming pleasant objects in the room. This helped decrease Tina's limbic activation while enhancing her internal capacity to regulate strong affect. When oriented to the present moment, titrating small voluntary movements such as moving her big toe or her fingers enabled Tina to experience movement safely without being overwhelmed and feeling unsafe.

OVERCOMING AMBIVALENCE IN THE
STABILIZATION PHASE

Clients feel that the compulsions that drive their disordered eating are too big to overcome. They project fears onto their bodies to be or feel successful in treatment. Align with their attachment style to help overcome ambivalence. Normalize the attachment style as having been an adaptive survival response rather than a deficit to help relax defensiveness in treatment. Provide psychoeducation about how ego states, or parts of self, help to compartmentalize what feels like a whole body experience. Name and validate the internal experience of the inner conflict to engage the client in exploring the parts of self that create overwhelm. These techniques (a) foster mindfulness, (b) decrease self-criticism and judgment, and (c) increase motivation to complete actions for change. In the *Haunted Self*, van der Hart, Nijenhuis, & Steele, 2006, state that the mental level of action tendencies are composed of two factors; mental focus and mental efficiency. These have a dynamic relationship and each plays a role in regulating arousal, enabling the individual to identify triggers, patterns, and survival resources. In the presence of intense affect or trauma activation, low levels of mental focus and efficiency impair integrative capacity and actions that include the ability to plan, begin something, be engaged in or complete actions for healing. Teaching clients how to regulate their arousal somatically through mindfulness techniques, such as grounding and centering, or by describing thoughts, feelings, inner body sensation, movement, and the five senses (Ogden, Minton, & Pain, 2006) helps clients to improve both their mental focus and mental efficiency. When clients have the capacity to be engaged, therapy is less triggering and they can participate in safely addressing trauma-related content. As they engage and participate in therapy, they gain more motivation for change. With increased motivation and regulation of the overactivated limbic physiology, they have greater capacity to hold dual attention and can begin to deal with the underlying traumas, losses, or wounding that is fueling the ED. As a result, the addictive compulsions and behaviors have an opportunity to relax. When they don't, treatment needs to shift to challenging the addictive cycle.

CHALLENGING THE ADDICTIVE CYCLE

When clients achieve abstinence or have established a normal weight, they may experience an increase in PTSD symptoms. When their disordered eating is no longer managing the traumatic symptoms, it increases their physiological urges to relapse. The PTSD symptoms cause a vicious cycle of going in and out of the relapse. The only way out of the cycle is for clients to learn to manage the impulses to relapse (Fisher, unpublished data). To modulate these urges with the motivated client, start by teaching grounding, orienting, and centering techniques, or the two-hand interweave (see R. Shapiro, 2005). For example, Lucy is a food addict who had become isolated from people and only left her house for appointments. Lucy had many psychiatric hospitalizations due to abuse memories and a life of immobility because she was afraid of what else she would remember. To quell her terror of nighttime, she would begin to overeat in the early evening, continuing into the night so she could avoid sleeping. Lucy was very motivated to end this cycle. The therapist used the two-hand interweave to help her overcome her ambivalence to *mental content,* which were the fears of what she'd remember and her uncomfortable symptoms. Lucy held the part of her that used food to quell her feelings in one hand, and in the other hand she held the part of her that wanted to end the cycle. After experiencing a few rounds of BLS, dual attention enabled her to get a new perspective on the internal conflict. She was then capable of being more engaged in treatment, managing her feelings and learning new coping strategies. Lucy was able to use the two-hand technique at home, holding the two conflicting parts of her while she alternately open and closed each hand.

WORKING WITH TRAUMA FRAGMENTS
IN STABILIZATION

When we refer to *trauma fragments* we are referring to titrating trauma activation rather than attempting to process a past event or developmental triggers. There is often a particular event that triggers the ED, as in

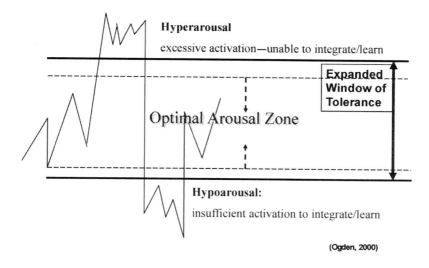

Figure 8.3 The Modulation Model

the case of Janie, or there is underlying developmental missing experience, as in the case of Jules, in that she learned girls were "less than." Either events or developmental triggers might exacerbate overwhelming feelings or hypoarousal, creating impulses to engage in ED behavior.

The modulation model (Ogden et al., 2000) shown in Figure 8.3 teaches the client to track their arousal patterns when triggered by an old memory, development deficits, a current intrusive thought about body image, or fears of giving up behaviors. Lucy had both past event trauma (childhood sexual abuse) and missing developmental experiences (not being attuned to or understood), and she lacked the ability to reach out for help. She would mitigate overwhelming feelings, the night after her sessions, by bingeing. In therapy, Lucy learned that her body was physiologically trying to help her deal with overwhelming affect. She experienced immediate relief as she realized that she was not a failure or defective. She was better able to tolerate distress, which increased her motivation for change. She became able to use pendulation and the two-hand interweave techniques to cope whenever she reexperienced trauma fragments. With this ability to tolerate her feeling states, her bedtime bingeing decreased so that she could sleep 6–7 hours a night, reach out to friends, and maintain her food plan.

The key to affect management is to go slowly so that gradual changes can create change in the neural networks. By dropping the story and focusing on the physiological arousal, clients are more apt to decrease the physiological effects and increase frontal lobe activity. The more fluent clients become with managing their arousal, the more capacity they have to integrate new information. This indicates that the clients have the ability to manage their affect. Treatment can then shift to resource building or to processing underlying trauma events with the EMDR Standard Protocol.

Another useful technique is from *Brain Lock* (Schwartz, 1996). This psychoeducational tool helps with the "undoing" of obsessive thinking associated with compulsive behavior. Schwartz's five steps are: (a) *relabel* the thought: "This is my thought"; (b) *reattribute* the thought and identity: "I am not my thought"; (c) pause and *"drop the content"* by just breathing and letting go of thought; (d) *externalize* the thought by locating the somatic and emotional response in the body: "Wow, my heart is beating really fast"; and (e) remain *mindful* of what is happening internally. Using these steps brings the frontal cortex online, which unblocks cognitive negative energy, which in turn increases client stabilization. Separating out the obsessive thought from feeling and body states helps shift the traumatic overwhelm. Consider the case of Annie who came to treatment overwhelmed after a relationship ruptured. She had been purging several times a day. As she learned to separate her thoughts about the ruptured relationship ("I will cease to exist if I am not loved"), she could access the deep feelings of aloneness and how her body sensation fueled her uncomfortable feeling state ("this is just a thought," pausing to breathe, and becoming aware of emptiness in her belly). This increased her ability to stay mindful while a memory emerged of being a toddler and being left alone with little contact. This deep unconscious wounding was brought to the foreground where she could then "make sense" of the depth of her triggered reactive state to her boyfriend's unavailability. Once stabilized with her frontal lobes online (as evidenced by the feeling "making sense"), the hyperarousal that had been the culprit of her reactive state could then be managed so she was no longer hijacked into the purging behavior.

MANAGING AROUSAL
DURING STABILIZATION

Shame is often the underlying affect that disables the client's ability to manage affect because shame magnifies helplessness. The compass of

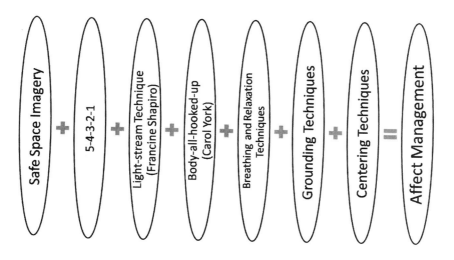

Figure 8.4 Affect Management Skills

shame gives us a template for understanding the effects of shame within the arousal system (Nathanson, 1992). In treatment, shame is primarily reflected in the self-hate and rage clients experience toward themselves because of their EDs. Coupled and reinforced by their feelings of being out of control, a downward spiral takes them into feelings of desperation, guilt, helplessness and hopelessness, and depression. (See Chapter 4.) It is challenging to shift these states because clients' observing egos are offline as they shift into this hypoaroused state. If shifts to child states occur, then shifting out of the shame affect is even more difficult, especially if clients exhibit perpetual fluctuations between hyper-arousal and hypoarousal states. At this moment in treatment, affect management techniques such as grounding and centering are imperative for enabling small, gradual changes in affect. It's also useful to increase the ability to tolerate positive affect when targeting shame affect. The affect management protocol targets the smallest positive ability to interrupt the negative affect overwhelm by adding BLS to the positive capacity.

Lizzie

For example, Lizzie experienced the traumatic death of a family member, which triggered her symptoms of anorexia. Within 6 months of the death she had become almost skeletal. It was evident on intake that she would be unable to process the trauma with the EMDR Standard Protocol for two reasons: (a) She was experiencing overwhelming associated feeling states of grief, aloneness and shame, and (b) her main support system, other family members, were experiencing their own intense grief and into their own coping strategies. I decided to initiate the affect management protocol to target her grief and aloneness, and then to target her shame of becoming anorexic. She immediately became overwhelmed. Inoculating the system with small positive shifts in her ability to cope in the moment increased her ability to tolerate distress to what was previously such overwhelming trauma material. Lizzie had emotional distress when she recalled the moment the police came to tell her family of the family member's death. Prior to the police visit, she and her family were sitting around the kitchen table eating cake. After told of the death, Lizzie had intense negative feelings toward the family member and at that point displaced her anger at the death by saying to herself that she would not eat again. Interrupting the ego-dystonic rage by having her use a coping strategy when dealing with food started to improve her ability to cope with the anger. At first, I had Lizzie work with her breath. I had her imagine sitting down to a meal with her remaining family members and everyone's unspoken grief. I would have her feel her breath through her body and use her breath to ground her. She would press her spine against the back of the chair, breathe a heart-centered breath, and when her overwhelm dissipated, BLS could be initiated. From this small shift we built on to greater coping strategies to deal with the range of her feeling states and moving toward positive action steps.

Adding BLS to positive coping strategies (being able to ground herself, using her breath to stay with her body, and visualizing herself taking positive actions) helped Lizzie to increase her capacity to deal with her overwhelming feeling states and better tolerate her grief.

PUTTING IT ALL TOGETHER: SPECIAL CONSIDERATION FOR USING EMDR IN TREATING EDS

Within each phase of ED treatment (stabilization, processing trauma, and reintegration), homework is essential to enhance integration of these skills into daily life. For there to be fluidity between each of these

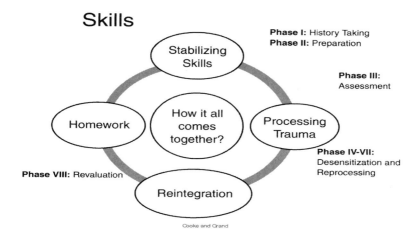

Figure 8.5 Affect Management Skills

phases, it may be necessary to reestablish stabilization, whether it is during or after processing trauma, or in the reintegration phase. We can't overemphasize collaboration with the client when assessing and developing targets for processing. To ensure safety, do ongoing assessment of the client's resources and ego strength before beginning trauma processing. (See Chapter 11.)

EMDR PROTOCOL: PROCESSING THE TRAUMA

During trauma processing, looping or abreactive states can occur that require "titrating" the trauma material. Continually identify emotional triggers and use graded exposure or mastery experiences to process the emotional material, if the client can tolerate it, or by using a previously learned stabilizing technique as a cognitive interweave. If the client cannot resume with trauma processing, then it is essential to return to the stabilization phase. It is important to make sure that the client is within the "window of tolerance" (Figure 8.3) before going to the underlying trauma; otherwise limbic activation shuts off the observing capacity of the frontal cortex and the trauma material becomes hard to integrate. When the client is able to process the feeling states and trauma material, she will be more able to identify areas of mastery. In Janie's case, once she was able to tolerate her overwhelming feelings and engage in treatment, we set up the EMDR target of being stalked and assaulted that caused her relapse into anorexia. During the Desensitization Phase, Janie would sometimes become too overwhelmed with the memory of what happened to her. If cognitive interweaves failed to keep the processing moving, we would temporarily suspend EMDR trauma processing and Janie would use the pendulation technique, alternating awareness between a place in her body that contained good feelings and a place that contained distressing sensations and feelings. Once Janie could regulate her emotion, I instructed her to return to the target and we resumed processing. This titration of trauma material with Janie's increased ability to manage the intense affect kept her stabilized and her ED unactivated.

REINTEGRATION: USING THE FUTURE TEMPLATE TO PREVENT RELAPSE

Reintegration is beneficial for many reasons. Recovery from the ED itself can trigger the person as their body changes and they let go of the behavior that has often been their identity. They also deal with the impact this change has on their relationships, having new experiences, and facing the future without the ED. Utilizing a variation of future template at the end of each EMDR processing session will help to prevent relapse by the integration of new information. You may weave in a modified Positive Cognition (PC), or a daily envisioning of the new skill or belief acquired in the session, or add a movement that embodies the newly acquired skill.

Annie

Annie began EMDR with a target of not being able to stand up for herself, which permeated love relationships, friends, family, work, and her favorite recreation, dance. The first target that Annie could tolerate working on was losing her step when dancing to the point she would get injured. Soon into processing she made associations to her feeling states connected to not having a voice or standing up for herself. She brought up memories of childhood in which she was put into dangerous situations, which led to dangerous situations in most of her adult life. Her inability to say no and to be disapproved of by others caused her such great distress that she would go along, even at her own expense. The first session ended with a SUDS of 5. After doing a modified PC (*"What is the most positive thing you learned about yourself or experienced today?"*), she was able to say, "I am worthy." BLS was added to the modified future template directive, *"Feel your worthiness now, feel what it feels like in your body."* (BLS.) *"Now see yourself leaving the office and feeling worthy all evening."* (BLS.) *"Now see yourself going through the week, holding this sense of worthiness."* (BLS.) Keep adding BLS to the positive shifts as the clients embody the new positive state and can see themselves in the near future holding on to the positive state. Any of these strategies will enable clients to incorporate a new way to deal with impulses that may trigger relapse.

After processing trauma targets, it's vital to use Future Templates. In cases where there is anticipatory anxiety, it is often helpful to use the "float forward" (Zangwill, 2005) to quell the fears associated with not utilizing the old, unhealthy coping strategies. For example, Molly anticipated attending a buffet with a group of her coworkers. I asked her to imagine walking into the restaurant and noticing what she experiences. She imagined all of her favorite foods and strong urges to binge. She immediately imagined using one of her resources and felt calmer. Using BLS on this state change, she saw herself having more ability to connect with her coworkers and noticed she was less obsessed with the food around her. Again, we deepened this state change with BLS. The following week, Molly came to therapy and related that she had a wonderful time at the buffet and did not overeat.

CONCLUSION

We have delineated physical and behavioral aspects and the use of EMDR in the treatment of EDs. Since many clients with disordered eating have impaired ability to regulate affect, we emphasized the importance of developing affect regulation skills before beginning the EMDR Standard Protocol. In our experience, clients with a trauma history rely on disordered eating behaviors to manage their trauma symptoms, and over time these behaviors take on an addictive quality. As treatment progresses and behaviors diminish, there is a greater potential for trauma fragments to surface, which can trigger an increase in ED symptoms. We cannot overemphasize the importance of returning to the stabilization phase to stabilize affect and maintain clients' motivation before proceeding with trauma processing. Once they're stabilized, we collaborate with our clients before moving on to trauma processing in Phase Two treatment. The clients' ability to regulate affect is essential to eradicating the addictive cycle of ED behavior.

REFERENCES

Garfinkel, P. E., & Garner, D. M. (1982). *Anorexia nervosa: A multidimensional approach.* New York: Brunner/Mazel.

Garner, D. M. (1993). Binge eating in anorexia nervosa. In C. G. Fairburn & G. T. Wilson (Eds.), *Binge eating: Nature, assessment and treatment* (pp. 50–76). New York: Guilford.

Hoek, H. W., Treasure, J. L., & Katzman, M. A. (1998). *Neurobiology in the treatment of eating disorders.* New York: Wiley.

Knipe, J. (2008, June). The CIPOS method—procedures to therapeutically reduce dissociative processes while preserving emotional safety. EMDREA Conference: London, England.

Lock, J., le Grange, D., Agras, W. S., Dare, D., & Agras, W. (2001). *Treatment manual for anorexia nervosa: A family-based approach.* New York: Guilford Press.

Nathanson, D. (1992). *Shame and pride: Affect, sex, and the birth of the self.* New York and London: Norton.

Ogden, P., Minton, K., & Pain, C. (2006). *Trauma and the body: A sensorimotor approach to psychotherapy.* New York and London: Norton.

Schwartz, J. (1996). *Brain lock.* New York: Regan Books.

Shapiro, R. (2006). The two-hand interweave. In R. Shapiro (Ed.), *EMDR solutions: Pathways to healing* (pp. 160–166). New York and London: Norton.

Strober, M. (1991). Disorders of the self in anorexia nervosa: An organismic-developmental paradigm. In C. Johnson (Ed.), *Psychodynamic treatment of eating disorders.* New York: Guilford.

Uher, R., & Treasure, J. (2005). Brain lesions and eating disorders. *Journal of Neurology, Neurosurgery & Psychiatry, 76*(6), 852–857.

van der Hart, O., Nijenhuis, E. R. S., & Steele, K. (2006). *The haunted self: Structural dissociation and the treatment of chronic traumatization.* New York and London: Norton.

York, C., & Leeds, A. (2001). Gate theory: An accelerated information processing model for developing functional state change. EMDRIA Conference, Austin, TX.

Zangwill, W. (2005). Float back technique. *EMDR and Training.* Available at www.emdrandtraining.com.

Chapter 9

Treating Bulimia Nervosa with EMDR

DaLene Forester

BULIMIA HAS BEEN THE FOCUS OF NUMEROUS SELF-HELP BOOKS, WORK-books, 12-step programs, and therapeutic treatments. Typically, if you treat bulimia you have been well versed in cognitive behavioral therapy (CBT). Research in the field of eating disorders (EDs) has relied heavily on CBT, largely because it is an easily replicated therapy with well-defined interventions. I have been treating individuals with bulimia in both individual and group therapy for 13 years. Because I was also trained in EMDR, it seemed natural that I would incorporate EMDR in the treatment of individuals with bulimia.

Many clinicians have noticed the tendency for bulimia to start as a coping mechanism when the rest of a client's life feels out of control. An out-of-control life coupled with a decision to diet or lose weight (to gain some control) often results in a long-term battle with bulimia. When we view bulimia as a coping mechanism and the act of bingeing and purging as a state change or way to regulate affect, it makes sense to use EMDR. A central element of bulimia treatment is teaching affect regulation using healthy state changes and working to process original traumas and the negative beliefs about the self that both drive and support the bulimia. Once the original traumas have been processed, the EMDR therapist engages the Three-Pronged Protocol at the heart of EMDR to process current bulimia triggers and establish Future Templates.

In a recent research project (Forester, unpublished), I administered the Trauma Symptom Inventory (TSI) and the Eating Disorder Inventory-3 (EDI-3) to a group of 6 bulimic women. For one half of the group I

administered the TSI and EDI-3 followed by a 8-week treatment phase
that included a 1-hour history-gathering session, a 1-hour Safe Place
development session, six 90-minute EMDR sessions, then a second administration of the TSI and EDI-3. Following an 8-week break, I
brought them back for a third administration of the TSI and EDI-3. The
second half of the group received the TSI and EDI-3 and was then
placed on a waitlist for 8 weeks. At the end of the 8 weeks they received a second administration of the TSI and EDI-3 followed by a 1-
hour history-gathering session, a 1-hour Safe Place development
session, six 90-minute EMDR sessions, and a final administration of
the TSI and EDI-3 measures. Between the 1-hour history-gathering session and the 1-hour Safe Place development session for both groups,
the participants were asked to make a list of the 10 worst experiences
of their lives. The list was then used as targets for the EMDR sessions.

Six women with bulimia is a very small sample size; however, at
the end of the study 3 of the 6 women reported that they were no
longer bingeing and purging after only six 90-minute sessions using
the basic EMDR protocol. One woman from the study who reported
stopping all bingeing and purging behavior had initially reported the
daily use of vomiting, laxatives, and diuretics for the past 23 years.
Though this is the first formal study I have conducted, I have been
treating bulimia this way for the past 14 years and have observed significant success in a considerable majority of the clients I have treated.

Bulimia reduces affect tolerance. Over time, as an individual turns
to bingeing and purging to cope with upsetting emotions, the individuals train themselves to reduce their affect tolerance. Eventually, any
emotion becomes a trigger for a binge-purge episode and bulimia becomes the dominant coping mechanism.

Most of us have a wide range of affect tolerance. We don't like all
the emotions we may feel but we tolerate them and return to normal
within a reasonable period of time. With coping mechanisms such as
bulimia, binge-eating disorder (BED), and other addictions, the individuals shorten their ability to tolerate emotions to the point that almost anything triggers an episode. For this reason individuals with
bulimia need to learn to tolerate emotions, need to learn healthy state
change techniques, and need to learn to deal with the habit of the
binge-purge more than how and why it developed. Viewing bulimia as
a coping mechanism, I see a strong need to identify triggers and build
on the idea of learning healthier coping mechanisms and breaking the
habit of bulimia.

PHASE ONE—CLIENT HISTORY

When treating a bulimic client, I use the first four to eight sessions gathering history, developing a therapeutic relationship, and developing the foundation for treatment. As part of a comprehensive history, I have the clients help me construct a timeline of the major events in their lives. This timeline is an invaluable tool in selecting targets for EMDR, especially in seeking the first, worst, and most recent examples of a cluster. I look for cluster targets, a type of trauma, either big "T" or little "t," that has occurred multiple times. An example of a cluster trauma would be when a client has several instances of molestation, domestic violence, or verbal abuse.

I also obtain a history of their bulimia. I ask:

How long have you had an issue with food?

How did you first come to use bingeing/purging?

How old were you when you first binged?

How old were you when you first purged?

How did you learn about bingeing and purging?

What else was going on in your life when bulimia first became a problem?

Has there ever been a time when you stopped bingeing and purging since you started?

Have you ever binged and not purged? If so, what was that like?

What thoughts did you have about yourself when you binged but did not purge?

What thoughts do you have about yourself now?

Does anyone else know about your bulimia? If so, how did the person(s) find out?

What do you believe people and/or family members think of you?

How is the bulimia helping you? How do you see the bulimia as harmful to you?

Non-EMDR sessions typically last 50–60 minutes, with 90–100 minutes for EMDR sessions. It is essential to have more time when doing

EMDR to allow for more comprehensive treatment. In private practice, I am able to set this pace. Individuals working in agencies and inpatient facilities typically do not have this luxury. The first EMDR session is set for 90–100 minutes, followed by a 50–60-minute session to process the outcome. This second session is followed by another 90–100-minute EMDR session followed by another processing session. This dual protocol may happen three to five times while the bulk of the initial EMDR targets are processed. Over time, the individual begins to process faster. When I see that happening, the EMDR sessions naturally reduce to 50–60-minute weekly sessions. This allows for the individual to progress at a comfortable pace and the bulk of the core work is handled in the earlier stages. During every session I pay attention to emerging Negative Cognitions (NCs) and newly uncovered EMDR targets.

Target Order

In determining target order I tend to be client centered. I ask the client, *"When you think of all of the events that have impacted your life, which ones stand out the most?"* or *"Which one do you think had the biggest impact on your developing bulimia?"* However, on occasion, I see the connection between the clients' sense of shame and an earlier life event that I believe is key to helping them deal with their bulimia. In that case I will offer that particular event as something I see as valuable to target. I then ask their permission to use that event and target it in the EMDR Standard Protocol.

Treatment Planning

In developing a treatment plan, I keep the Three-Pronged Protocol in mind. In doing EMDR to treat bulimia or any other trauma-related disorder, a comprehensive treatment plan that covers: (a) past contributing events; (b) present triggers; and (c) the development of Future Templates usually results in the highest degree of bulimia resolution.

Life Events vs. Traumatic Events in Bulimia

Risk factors associated with the development of bulimia include being female, dieting, low self-esteem, a history of sexual abuse, and other adversities such as parental divorce and nonsexual trauma (Jacobi,

Hayward, de Zwann, Kraemer, & Agras, 2004). Bulimia has been linked with traumatic experiences such as rape (Faravelli, Giugni, Salvatori, & Ricca, 2004) and physical abuse (Steiger, Gauvin, Israel, Kin, Young, & Roussin, 2004). But the most compelling argument for utilizing EMDR in the treatment of bulimia came from a study by Smyth, Heron, Wonderlich, Crosby, and Thompson (2008) who reported that the development of bulimia could be predicted from a trauma history. This study was able to predict bulimia based on an individual's history of trauma, defined in this study as the number of traumatic incidents and a severity rating of the respective traumatic events, including higher levels of severity for the death of a loved one, divorce or separation by parents of the individual, and higher ratings on violent trauma. This further proves the importance of all trauma consideration, big "T" and small "t," to the development of bulimia. EMDR is my treatment of choice for releasing the grip of trauma.

In my bulimia study, the most common events listed on the "10 worst" lists were parental divorce, the breakup of a long-term relationship, being the victim of domestic violence, experiencing a major move as a child, and experiencing a hospital or surgical trauma.

Resource Development

Resource Development and Installation (RDI) can be used to stabilize clients prior to using EMDR. Bulimic clients utilize bingeing and purging as a coping mechanism for a wide range of emotions, both positive and negative. Due to an inability to tolerate emotional experiences, these clients may require developing other coping mechanisms and developing new internal resources. RDI (Leeds, 1998) is the installation of strengths or coping skills from the client's repertoire. Roy Kiessling presented a chapter in the first *EMDR Solutions* that is very helpful in developing RDI skills (Kiessling, 2005).

PHASE TWO—PREPARATION

In the preparation stage of treatment after I have given the client an explanation of EMDR, I work with the client to develop a state change experience such as the Safe Place (Shapiro, 2001). The Safe Place helps the bulimic client develop an alternative way to tolerate difficult emotions. The act of bingeing and purging is intended to produce a state change. The individual feels an intense emotion, stress, or expectation from the world and will immediately turn to bulimic behaviors to change the intolerant state of experiencing the feelings. Therefore, to address the trait of using bulimic behaviors in response to all emotions, negative and positive, individuals need to learn alternative healthy ways to change their state. I have had many clients tell me that prior to learning the Safe Place or the "light stream" exercise (F. Shapiro, 2001), they felt they had no choice but to binge and purge. Then, with learning a healthy way to change their state, they had options. Of course they may still choose to binge and purge, but they begin to realize they have a choice. (See Chapter 17, by Katie O'Shea, for several state change examples.)

Containment

At times it is necessary to teach the individual with bulimia the ability to contain difficult memories and feelings. In fact, in discussions with other therapists who treat bulimia with EMDR, some do not even begin EMDR without first doing sufficient containment work. Because of the preparation work and the structured initial 90–100-minute EMDR session, specific containment may not be necessary for EMDR processing with all clients. However, when clients present needing a way to "contain" difficult emotions between sessions, I have them imagine a container of their own design. I help clients imagine all the possible details, such as how big the container should be, the shape, what material it should be made of, how the emotion will be safely contained, and so forth. When they have as much of the details as they need to feel protected and not vulnerable, I ask them to imagine putting the overwhelming feelings and/or memories into the container. I say to the clients, "*I am going to start the Eye Movements [EMs] and I want you to imagine putting the feelings and/or memories in the container and give me a hand signal when everything is in.*" Then I proceed with Bilateral Stimulation (BLS). (Again, see Chapter 17.)

Containment work may be more necessary if the clinician is limited to 50–60-minute EMDR sessions. It is also possible that, because I treat clients in private practice, I see a less fragile population of ED clients. Therefore, I would recommend you be familiar with containment work. (See Chapter 7 by Janie Scholom.)

Sufficient Trust for Honesty Regarding Bulimia

As stated previously I typically spend four to eight sessions developing a solid therapeutic relationship. Often in those early sessions, I address the need for honesty in EMDR work. The roots of bulimia are often fertilized with shame. Telling lies, while common in EDs, perpetuates the shame and further belief that the individual is deserving of that shame. Practicing being honest about the ED, even if only with the therapist, is immensely healing. But be warned: Individuals with EDs have a difficult time being truthful, and you, as the EMDR therapist, will need to take your time developing the relationship prior to trauma processing. Always keep in mind, when your client tells you she has reached a 0 on the SUD Scale, she may be trying to be a good client or make you feel good about your work.

Intense Emotions and Increased Bulimia in Initial Stages

It is important to caution individuals with bulimia that bulimic symptoms frequently increase in the initial stages of therapy. Bulimia has developed as their best friend and the number one coping mechanism. In the early stages of treatment, when you as the therapist are asking intense history-gathering questions, they will often turn to what they know and trust. It is best to address this up front by letting the client know you are not going to take their ED away from them. You may need to educate them about the coping qualities of bulimia. You may need to share with them that in the early stages you need to gather a lot of information and they are not going to have any other coping mechanism to deal with their feelings. However, you can assure them that over time you are going to be teaching them much more effective and satisfying coping mechanisms that will help work the bulimia out of a job.

Unrealistic Expectations

It is important to address the individual's expectation for a rapid cure. Bulimia is a notoriously treatment-resistive condition. While EMDR therapists are working hard to educate the public that EMDR is not an instant cure, individuals still hold the belief that EMDR can change anything and everything in a few sessions. You may need to explain that the negative belief systems are the result of memory networks of associated events that took years to hardwire into the brain. *EMDR is like doing a root canal on each one of these memory networks. Treating bulimia with EMDR is very hard work; it takes commitment and time to do multiple root canals.* That being said, in the simple study I did in my private practice with 6 bulimic individuals, 3 of those individuals no longer met the diagnostic criteria for bulimia at the end of six 90-minute EMDR sessions.

PHASE THREE—ASSESSMENT

Top 10 Most Disturbing/Distressing Events

During the Assessment Phase, I ask the client with bulimia to either choose a target from the list of the top 10 worst things that have happened in their lives or I recommend a target based on the history-gathering and treatment-planning phase. Sometimes clients have a particular memory they want to work on. Once we have an agreed-upon target, I ask the individuals to hold the most upsetting part of that event in their mind and tell me what that makes them believe about themselves now. Most often individuals can easily state the NC. I have little difficulty getting a self-referencing negative belief because individuals with bulimia seem to have a lot of self-referencing negative beliefs such as "I am unlovable," "I am not good enough," or "I don't deserve." Once we have established the NC, I move along developing the Positive Cognition (PC), the Validity of Cognition (VoC), the Emotion, the Subjective Units of Disturbance Scale (SUDS), and location in the body as in any other EMDR session, following the Standard Protocol.

The Bridging or Floatback Technique

At times, the client has a strong NC that I hear continuously throughout the sessions that has not been identified while processing any of the agreed-upon targets. In these instances, I utilize the Bridging Technique (Parnell, 1999, 2007). The Bridging Technique, also referred to as the Floatback (Zangwill, in F. Shapiro, 2001), is best used with clients who have sufficient ego strength and enough processing of past material to be able to deal with spontaneous distressing material. First, I work to activate the associated memory network with the NCs by asking the clients to identify the NCs, a recent time the NCs came up for them, and the emotions and any sensations associated with them. When the clients have as much of the associated memory network lit up as possible, I ask them to close their eyes and follow the experience back to the earliest time they can remember feeling that way. I then use this image as the target for EMDR processing.

Eating Disorder Myths and Blocking Beliefs

Eileen Freedland presented her work that involves working with ED myths and blocking beliefs (2001, 2002, 2003). She created a worksheet (in full, at the end of the chapter with her permission) that helps clients identify myths and blocking beliefs that interfere with EMDR processing. This sheet can be helpful in developing a treatment plan or assisting the therapist when processing becomes stuck. The ED Myths and Blocking Beliefs sheet can be used in the history-gathering phase of EMDR, again in the Preparation Phase, and throughout EMDR processing. Freedland has also developed an EMDR Worksheet for ED Targets, specifically for identifying ED targets (also at the end of the chapter and used with her permission).

Body Sensations

At times individuals with bulimia have difficulty identifying body sensations. When this happens I spend time helping them recognize body sensations. Francine Shapiro called this "sensitivity training" (Shapiro, 2001). This training involves asking the client to close her eyes and tune into her body. I ask the client to close her eyes and tune into her body and notice how her body feels and I say, *"Now, I want you to think of the memory we were just talking about."* I pause and ask, *"Tell me what you first noticed."* Having the client close her eyes and then bring up the memory allows her to recognize body sensations and the connection more clearly. If necessary, I will spend a whole session helping a client learn to identify body sensations.

PHASE FOUR—DESENSITIZATION

I usually start all EMDR sessions with EMs unless a client either cannot tolerate EMs or has had EMDR in the past and requests taps or audio BLS. I personally prefer the EMs because it is easier to tell

when and if a client begins to dissociate, common in this population.

In general I use the train metaphor for EMDR processing but have
also used the VCR/DVD metaphor. If clients have difficulty maintaining dual attention (in other words, they get pulled into the memory
and are no longer able to be present in the room with me), I will suggest that they allow the image to go to black and white. This seems to
be enough to reestablish dual attention processing. Many distancing
techniques work well, including having clients imagine the memory as
if on TV or placing the memory behind glass or out a window. Almost
any distancing technique will work.

During the Desensitization Phase I have the clients teach me
what they would like to use as a stop signal. I suggest that EMDR is
like driving through a tunnel. If they take their foot off the accelerator they will slow down. If they keep their pedal to the metal, they
will get through the tunnel faster and out the other side. That said, I
do not push clients beyond their capability. Most clients report back
at some point that they could see how easy it would have been to
stop too soon. They often report that they thought about what I said
and, even though the emotions were intense, they were grateful
they kept going. But again, my clients may be unique to my setting
and I recommend you rely on your knowledge of your clients to
guide you.

Length of Sets

I always start with a set of approximately 24 horizontal EMs and either
increase or decrease, depending on the clients' needs. I have found that
most of my clients process better with longer sets of around 36, but I always start with 24 and experiment with what works best. I tend to stay
with the horizontal EMs the majority of the time and only change direction when processing gets stuck or clients begin to loop.

PHASE FIVE—INSTALLATION

When the SUD rating is a 0, or when it's an ecologically sound 1, and
when the VoC is rated as a 7, or as high as it can possibly be, I begin the
installation phase. I have the client hold the memory of the original tar-

get and the PCs and, using BLS, install the PCs with the target memory with a short set of approximately 12 EMs.

PHASE SIX—BODY SCAN

If the Body Scan is clear and there is time, I will move to identifying and targeting current triggers. Occasionally, I will have time in the session to do a Future Template but there's usually not enough time.

If the Body Scan is not clear, I have a client hold the original memory along with the PCs and target the area in the body that seems to be blocked. I target the blockage by asking the client to notice where it is in the body and ask if it has a shape, size, color, texture, or smell. This is done to activate as many of the senses as possible prior to engaging in BLS.

PHASE SEVEN—CLOSURE

If the session has come to completion, I remind the clients that they will likely continue processing and recommend that they keep a log of issues that may come up. I tell clients they can send me a short e-mail or leave me a quick voice mail. I remind them that I am probably not going to call them back but the e-mail or voice mail is simply so they have a way to share with me what has come up in a way that best works for them and in a way that they will not forget or lose the information. I have never had clients abuse these options.

If the session is incomplete, I will shut the session down as an incomplete session and either contain what is left to process later or have the client practice a state change like the Safe Place or something tailored to the client's need.

PHASE EIGHT—REEVALUATION

At sessions following an EMDR session, I reevaluate the SUD level of the target we have processed. As I mentioned earlier, I tend to have a 90–100-minute EMDR session followed by a 50–60-minute non-EMDR session. During the non-EMDR session I reevaluate the SUD level and ask about times that they may have been triggered since the last time I saw them. I find out what is going well and how they are feeling about their progress. Then at the next 90–100-minute EMDR session I begin by reevaluating the previous EMDR target memory. If the target has stayed a SUD level of 0, I move on to current triggers and Future Template work.

ED Myths and Blocking Beliefs
By Eileen Freedland

1. ____ If I eat, I'll get fat.

Challenge: _____

2. ____ I need to (binge, purge, cut) to not think about my problems.

Challenge: _____

3. ____ I need to (binge, purge, cut) to not feel (sad, anger, anxiety).

Challenge: _____

4. ____ I need to (binge, purge, cut) to (calm, comfort) myself.

Challenge: _____

5. ____ I have to be thin to be happy.

Challenge: _____

6. ____ I have to be thin to be (successful, special, admired).

Challenge: _____

7. ____ I have to be thin to be loved.

Challenge: _____

8. ____ Eating fills up my emptiness.

Challenge: _____

9. ____ If I have my eating disorder people will take care of me.

Challenge: _____

10. ____ I can get at my parents by having my eating disorder.

Challenge: _____

11. ____ I won't have/be anything if I give up my eating disorder.

Challenge: _____

12. ____ My feelings aren't important.

Challenge: _____

EMDR WORKSHEET FOR ED TARGETS
Developed by Eileen Freedland

Name _____ Date _____

Speed/Modality _____

Safe Place _____

Resource(s) _____

ED Myth → NC:

Challenge → PC:

Picture that represents ED Myth → Target:

VoC: 1   2   3   4   5   6   7

Emotions:

SUDS: 0   1   2   3   4   5   6   7   8   9   10

Body:

REFERENCES

Faravelli, C., Giugni, A., Salvatori, S., & Ricca, V. (2004). Psychopathology after rape. *American Journal of Psychiatry, 161,* 1483–1485.

Forester, D. (unpublished). *EMDR as a treatment for bulimia nervosa in a clinical private practice setting.*

Freedland, E. (2001, June). *Using EMDR with eating disorders.* Conference session presented at the annual EMDRIA Conference, Austin, TX.

Freedland, E. (2002, October). *Using EMDR with eating disorders.* Conference session presented at the annual EMDR Association Canada Conference, Vancouver, BC.

Freedland, E. (2003, May). *Using EMDR with eating disorders.* Conference session presented at the annual EMDR Association of Europe Conference, Rome, Italy.

Jacobi, C., Hayward, C., de Zwaan, M., Kraemer, H. C., & Agras, W. S. (2004). Coming to terms with risk factors for eating disorders: Application of risk terminology and suggestions for a general taxonomy. *Psychological Bulletin, 130,* 19–65.

Kiessling, R. (2005). Integrating resource development strategies into your EMDR practice. In R. Shapiro (Ed.), *EMDR solutions: Pathways to healing* (pp. 57–87). New York: Norton.

Leeds, A. (1998). Lifting the burden of shame: Using EMDR resource installation to resolve a therapeutic impasse. In P. Manfield (Ed.), *Extending EMDR: A casebook of innovative applications* (pp. 256–281). New York: Norton.

Parnell, L. (1999). *EMDR in the treatment of adults abused as children.* New York: Norton.

Parnell, L. (2007). A therapist's guide to EMDR: Tools and techniques for successful treatment. New York: Norton.

Shapiro, F. (2001). *Eye movement desensitization and reprocessing: Basic principles, protocols, and procedures* (2nd ed.). New York: Guilford Press.

Smyth, J., Heron, K., Wonderlich, S., Crosby, R., & Thompson, K. (2008). The influence of reported trauma and adverse events on eating disturbance in young adults. *International Journal of Eating Disorders, 41*(3), 195–202.

Steiger, H., Gauvin, L., Israel, M., Kin, N., Young, S., & Roussin, J. (2004). Serotonin function, personality-trait variations, and childhood abuse in women with bulimia-spectrum eating disorders. *Journal of Clinical Psychiatry, 65,* 830–837.

Chapter 10

Image Is Everything: The EMDR Protocol in the Treatment of Body Dysmorphia and Poor Body Image

DaLene Forester

YOU ARE SITTING ACROSS THE ROOM FROM YOUR CLIENT WHILE SHE DE-scribes how acne has ruined her life. She describes being chronically late and having daily anxiety, depression, and suicidal thoughts resulting from her skin problems. She has spent hundreds of dollars from her minimum-wage jobs on visits to dermatologists and skin treatments. No matter what she does the acne is always there. You furtively search her face and body for the debilitating acne she describes, but you can't see any of it.

WHAT IS BODY DYSMORPHIA?

Body dysmorphic disorder (BDD) is a total preoccupation with a slight bodily flaw or perceived flaw that causes significant distress and is not otherwise accounted for by another disorder (generalized anxiety disorder, obsessive-compulsive disorder, panic disorder, a major depressive episode, separation anxiety, or another somatoform disorder). The preoccupation leads to compulsive mirror checking, picking of the skin, excessive time attempting to camouflage the flaw, social anxiety, unnecessary treatments and surgeries and, sometimes, self-inflicted injury or suicide. Most individuals report the preoccupation begins in adolescence or early adulthood and occasionally following a particularly traumatic time in the individual's life (Phillips, Menard, Fay, & Weisberg, 2005).

Individuals with BDD often seek therapy to deal with the loss of a job, difficulty remaining in or completing college, anxiety issues, or relationship issues that arise from living with BDD rather than for the treatment of BDD. Most individuals with BDD have a difficult time believing that their perception is flawed. This is why most individuals with BDD seek a dermatologist or plastic surgeon rather than a therapist. One client came to me only after being put on academic probation because she could not make it to her classes. Her ritual of face picking would sometimes take up to 4 hours, making it difficult for her to get to class on time. Another client came for couple counseling. His belief that his hair was thinning was consuming his thoughts and created intense arguments with his wife because he would not be seen without a hat, even by his wife. He only agreed to counseling after she threatened divorce.

EMDR TREATMENT OF BDD AND
POOR BODY IMAGE

I have used EMDR with BDD and individuals who do not meet the full BDD criteria but do have significant issues of poor body image. I have found that using the EMDR Standard Protocol (F. Shapiro, 2001) can bring relief and resolution to clients suffering from an intense, irrational focus on a perceived body flaw. In 1997, Brown, McGoldrick and Buchanan reported the sussessful treatment of five out of seven individuals with BDD following only one to three EMDR sessions. I have not personally experienced this level of rapid resolution of BDD but I have seen several successes. I have found that a more complete treatment plan with substantially more EMDR sessions is necessary for the resolution of BDD or body image issues.

Nieziroglu and Khemlani-Patel (2003) and others have reported significant trauma as common in the history of individuals with BDD. Therefore, it would make sense to utilize EMDR in the treatment of BDD and body image issues in a similar way that one would treat a trauma based disorder.

History-Taking Considerations—Phase One

When treating clients with perceived body flaws, I take my time in gathering history and developing a therapeutic relationship. It takes time to develop a treatment plan with awareness that the clients are highly anxious and have a core belief that there is something seriously flawed. These clients tend to be resistant to acknowledging that their perceived flaw is not a flaw to others. In addition to a comprehensive history, I have the clients help me construct a timeline of the major events in their lives as well as a history of when this focus began. This helps in target selection for EMDR sessions.

During the history-gathering phase individuals with BDD or poor body image often describe frequent and persistent teasing about their appearance or the area of perceived flaw. Regardless of the validity of how many times an individual was actually teased about having a large nose or acne, the initial feelings of humiliation and shame permeate the clients I have treated. Other times the individuals report a family emphasis on appearance and perfectionism whereby they interpret that their worth is based on their appearance. In my experience, individuals with BDD and severe body image issues have a traumatic event that could be linked to the origins of the BDD or body image issue. Therefore, when treating BDD and poor body image issues I let the Adaptive Information Processing (AIP) model (F. Shapiro, 2001) guide my treatment plan.

I obtain a history of their developing awareness of the body image issue or perceived flaw by asking:

How old were you when you first noticed the problem?

Has the same area always been of concern or do you sometimes focus on other areas of your body?

How do you deal with this issue?

How much time do you spend hiding or covering up this area of concern?

What else was happening in your life when you first became aware of this area?

Has there ever been a time when you were not focused on this area?

Does anyone else in your family have the same or similar concerns?

When you think about this area, what does it make you believe about yourself?

What do friends and/or family say when you make negative comments about this area?

Sessions typically last 50–60 minutes while I gather history, build the therapeutic relationship, and prepare the client for EMDR, with 90–100 minutes for the early EMDR sessions. It helps to have more time when doing the initial EMDR sessions to allow for processing of initial targets. After the majority of initial targets are processed, EMDR sessions go back to the 50–60-minute format.

Treatment Planning

In developing a treatment plan, I focus on the AIP model and the Three-Pronged Protocol. I review the history and help the client develop a trauma timeline. In doing EMDR to treat body image issues or BDD, a comprehensive treatment plan that covers: (a) past traumatic events; (b) past incidents of teasing, shame and humiliation; (c) present triggers; and (d) the development of Future Templates usually results in the highest degree of symptom resolution.

Using EMDR with BDD and body image issues, as with the treatment of eating disorders (EDs), complex posttraumatic stress disorder (PTSD), and other complex issues, requires a strong commitment from the client and is not an easy fix. Full resolution can require multiple EMDR sessions on multiple targets.

Phase Two—Preparation

In the preparation stage of treatment after I have given the client an explanation of EMDR, I work with the client to develop a state change experience such as the Safe Place (F. Shapiro, 2001). I use the Safe Place exercise with Eye Movements (EMs) initially to detect dissociation even after administering the Dissociative Experiences Scale (Bernstein & Putnam, 1986). The Safe Place helps the BDD client develop an alternative way to tolerate difficult emotions. The act of engaging in picking, mirror checking, or camouflaging is calming and reduces tension.

The Safe Place exercise or the "light stream" exercise (F. Shapiro, 2001) can be used to replace or interrupt picking, mirror checking, or camouflage behaviors.

Once I have established that the client is not prone to dissociation, I will work with the client to discover what mode of Bilateral Stimulation (BLS) they prefer. The BDD population can sometimes focus better with eyes closed, necessitating either tapping or audio BLS.

Resource Development

Clients with BDD or body image issues may need stabilization with Resource Development and Installation (RDI) prior to using EMDR. RDI (Leeds, 1998; Leeds & Shapiro, 2000; Shapiro, 2001) utilizes EMs to install strengths or coping skills from the client's own experiences. Roy Kiessling presented a chapter in *EMDR Solutions* that is very helpful in developing RDI skills (Kiessling, 2005). I recommend spending one to two complete sessions on the development of resources that the client believes they may need to work on the issues of past traumas or in learning to recognize when the BDD behaviors are being triggered.

Containment

Often, it's necessary to teach individuals with BDD or body image issues how to contain difficult or overwhelming memories and feelings. When I think a client could benefit from a way to "contain" memories and emotions between sessions, I have them imagine a container of their own creation. I help the client imagine all the possible details of their container such as the size, shape, what material it should be made of, and so forth. I have helped clients develop huge cargo containers made of sturdy metal, small treasure boxes with soft pillowy insides, and a whole array of garbage cans. When they have as much of the details as they need to feel confident the memories and feelings can be safely contained, I ask them to imagine putting the feelings and/or memories into the container. I say, "*I am going to start the Eye Movements and I want you to imagine putting all the feelings and/or memories in the container. When you feel everything is in, I want you to give me a hand signal.*" Then I proceed with BLS. I recommend you be familiar with containment work in Chapters 7 (Scholom) and 17 (O'Shea).

Phase Three–Assessment

Target Selection

When developing the target order I review the trauma timeline that the client and I created in the treatment planning phase. I ask the client what incident or incidents from their trauma timeline they believe may have contributed to the development of the BDD or body image issue. If the client is unable to decide, I determine which target I think is most closely related to the development of the BDD or body image issue.

Once the traumas that may be the origin of the development of the BDD or body image issue have been targeted with EMDR, I focus on the clients' perception of the first or worst incident involving the perceived flaw. I ask the clients, *"When you think of the events that have impacted your focus on (this area of your body), which one(s) stand out the most?"* or *"Which one do you think had the biggest impact on your life and how you perceive yourself now?"* I then ask their permission to use that event as the target using the standard EMDR protocol. If the clients have a difficult time finding a connected incident, I have them focus on the perceived flaw and do the Bridging Technique (Parnell, 1999), also referred to as the Floatback (Zangwill, in Shapiro, 2001). I may have the clients look in a mirror or put their hand on the perceived flaw to more fully access and light up the associated memory network. Once we have a target memory, incident, or image, I proceed to the development of the NC and PC.

Negative Cognitions

When asking the client with BDD or body image issues for an NC, it is important to remember the basics of a NC. An NC is a negative, currently held self-referencing belief that is not true. Do not accept statements such as *"I hate my nose"* as the NC. When I ask the BDD client, *"When you think about your (perceived flaw), what do you believe about yourself?"* I commonly hear, *"I hate myself"* or *"I hate it."* I then ask the client, *"When you think about how much you hate (the perceived flaw), what does it make you believe about you as a person?"* This allows for the client to access the deeper, underlying erroneous belief, which may be *"I am not good enough,"* *"I am not lovable,"* *"There is something wrong with me,"* *"I am flawed,"* or *"I am a disappointment."* I find that taking my time to develop the NC and PC that are the core of the memory, incident, or image, pays off strongly in the most complete processing and symptom reduction.

Positive Cognitions

When asking the client with BDD or body image issues for a Positive Cognition (PC), it is important to remember that while the PC should correspond to the NC, it is not simply the opposite of the NC. The idea of a PC like *"I am good enough"* may be rated a *"1"* on the Validity of Cognition (VoC) Scale and completely beyond the realm of possibility for the BDD client. It may be more appropriate to develop a PC such as *"I can begin to accept myself"* or *"I can learn to accept my (perceived flaw)."* Get to know your client and guide the process of developing the PC based on your knowledge and clinical skills.

Phase Four—Desensitization

By the time we have reached the desensitization phase I have a full understanding of the client's history to draw on. We have developed a strong rapport and I am as confident as I can be that the client is going to be honest with me in their processing. We have practiced state change exercises and developed whatever resourses the client and I think we might need. We may have developed a container for difficult emotions and/or memories and we have agreed on a stop signal that the client can use if they feel overwhelmed. We have agreed on the target memory or image and we have a well defined NC and PC. The VoC has been determined, the emotion labeled, the SUDS level and the location they feel the disturbance in their body has been determined and we begin the desensitization phase.

I generally use the train metaphor for EMDR processing but have also used the VCR/DVD metaphor. If the client has difficulty maintaining dual attention (in other words they get pulled into the memory and are no longer able to be present in the room with me), I suggest they allow the image to go to black and white or image a window or plate of glass between the memory and themselves. This seems to reestablish dual attention processing. Any distancing technique you currently use will work well here. Sometimes I just stop and say to the client *"remember, I just want you to notice the memory while staying present here with me."*

As I mentioned earlier, I have the client establish a stop signal. However, I find it helpful to tell my clients that, while I do not want them to go beyond their capability, EMDR is like driving trough a tunnel. If they take their foot off the accelerator they will slow down and remain in the tunnel. If they keep their pedal to the metal, they will get through the tunnel faster and out the other side.

Length of Sets

I always start a set of approximately 24 horizontal EMs and increase or decrease depending on the client's needs. I have found that most of my clients process better with longer sets of around 36, but I always start with 24 and experiment with what works best for that client, knowing that some clients process wonderfully with just 24. If I am using taps or audio BLS, I start with longer sets of approximately 30–40 BLS and experiment from there. I have noticed that with taps and audio BLS clients seem to prefer and process better with longer sets.

Phase Five—Installation

When the SUD rating is a 0, or when ecologically sound, a 1, and when the VoC is rated as a 7, or as high as it can possibly be, I begin the Installation Phase. I have the client hold the memory of the original target and the PC and, using BLS, install the PC with the target memory with a short set of approximately 12 EMs or 25 taps or audio BLS.

If I used a mirror initially I will have the client look in the mirror again when the SUD rating is a 0. This often brings the SUD up slightly and we continue processing until the SUD is 0. If you are using a mirror, I recommend keeping track of time and allow yourself enough time to close down an incomplete session should the SUD rating remain high.

Phase Six—Body Scan

If the Body Scan is clear and there is time, I will move to identifying and targeting current triggers. Occasionally, I will have time in the session to do a Future Template, but this is rare given how much time has usually passed.

If the Body Scan is not clear, I have the client hold the original memory along with the PC and target the area in the body that seems to be blocked. I target the blockage by asking the client to notice where it is in the body and ask if it has a shape, size, color, texture, or smell. This is done to activate as many of the senses as possible prior to engaging in BLS.

Phase Seven—Closure

If the session has come to completion, I remind the clients that they will likely continue processing and recommend that they keep a log of mirror-checking, picking, or camouflage behavior. I have them record how often and for how long they engage in the behavior and describe the circumstances. I then use these targets to process current triggers after the past triggers have been processed.

If the session is incomplete, I close the session down as an incomplete session and either contain what is left to process later or have the client practice a state change such as the Safe Place. As homework I sometimes have the BDD client practice a cognitive-behavioral technique called the Alarm Clock Technique. The client and I determine what they believe is an appropriate amount of time to spend mirror checking, picking, or camouflaging. I then ask the client to set a timer or alarm clock for that amount of time and when the timer goes off they are to stop the behavior. Most clients report resetting the timer or clock several times initially, but eventually the number of times the clock is reset is reduced and can be a tangible indicator of progress for the client. The Alarm Clock Technique can also be used imaginarily as a target for Future Template work.

Phase Eight—Reevaluation

At sessions following an EMDR session, I reevaluate the SUD level of the target we have processed and ask about times that they may have engaged in picking, checking, or camouflage behavior since the last time I saw them. I then go right into EMDR if the SUD is above an ecologically sound 1. If the target has stayed a SUD level of 0, I move on to current triggers and Future Template work.

REFERENCES

Bernstein, C., & Putnam, F. W. (1986). Development, reliability, and validity of a dissociation scale. *Journal of Nervous and Mental Disease, 174,* 727–735.

Brown, K., McGoldrick, T., & Buchanan, R. (1997). Body dysmorphic disorder: Seven cases treated with eye movement desensitization and reprocessing. *Behavioral and Cognitive Psychotherapy, 25*(2), 203–207.

Kiessling, R. (2005). Integrating resource development strategies into your EMDR practice. In R. Shapiro (Ed.), *EMDR solutions: Pathways to healing* (pp. 57–87). New York: Norton.

Leeds, A. (1998). Lifting the burden of shame: Using EMDR resource installation to resolve a therapeutic impasse. In P. Manfield (Ed.), *Extending EMDR: A casebook of innovative applications* (pp. 256–281). New York: Norton.

Leeds, A. M., & Shapiro, F. (2000). EMDR and resource installation: Principles and procedures for enhancing current functioning and resolving traumatic experiences. In J. Carlson & L. Spery (Eds.), *Brief therapy strategies with individuals and couples* (pp. 469–534). Phoenix, AZ: Zeig/Tucker.

Neziroglu, F., & Khemlani-Patel, S. (2003). Therapeutic approches to body dysmorphic disorder. *Brief Treatment and Crisis Intervention, 3*(3), 307–322. Retrieved October 2, 2008 from http://brief-treatment.oxfordjournals.org

Parnell, L. (1999). *EMDR in the treatment of adults abused as children*. New York: Norton.

Phillips, K. A., Menard, W., Fay, C., & Weisberg, R. (2005, July–August). Demographic characteristics, phenomenology, comorbidity, and family history in 200 individuals with body dysmorphic disorder. *Psychosomatics, 46*(4), 317–325. Retrieved August 13, 2008, from http://psy.psychiatryonline.org

Shapiro, F. (2001). *Eye movement desensitization and reprocessing: Basic principles, protocols, and procedures* (2nd ed.). New York: Guilford Press.

Chapter 11

Addressing Retraumatization and Relapse When Using EMDR with Eating Disorder Patients

Janet McGee

THE EMDR COMMUNITY HAS PROVIDED US WITH EXCELLENT ASSESSMENT tools, history-taking procedures, specific setup protocols, resourcing techniques, affect regulation tools, treatment plans, and blueprints for Future Templates for a variety of populations. The previous chapters in this section provide a comprehensive treatment approach for eating disorder (ED) patients. This chapter will address reevaluation of targeted material, relational issues, and treatment effects. "Rapid treatment effects can have immediate repercussions intrapsychically and interactionally" (F. Shapiro, 2001, p. 200). Therefore, responsible EMDR treatment includes vigorous reevaluation of factors contributing to treatment effects. ED patients present with a variety of comorbid issues, both characterological and organic. Their ED behaviors are both physiologically and psychologically traumatizing. Because of this complexity, treatment effects can cause destabilization and retraumatization and impede recovery and healing. Those who have difficult experiences with EMDR subsequently become afraid to continue using it as a treatment. In treating both patients and therapists who have been traumatized by treatment reactions, it is essential to consider reevaluation vigorously throughout treatment. With ED patients specifically, a difficult EMDR session that is *not* understood and *not* handled carefully can be retraumatizing on many different emotional levels, resulting in patients turning to the only coping mechanism they know, their ED.

The EMDR protocol simultaneously brings up the patients' cognitions and emotions. We must hear and evaluate the emotion-laden thoughts of our patients for a positive treatment experience. ED patients' thoughts and feelings often reveal the dissociated emotional triggers related to their food and ED behaviors. Therefore, ongoing reevaluation of processed material, assessment of spontaneous processing between session, notation of any newly activated material, and careful evaluation of the patients' ability to manage treatment effects are necessary in organizing a safe treatment approach. Reevaluation at the beginning of each session provides a compass and measuring scale, informing your direction and how to get there. It is an opportunity to help reframe material, to consider how to pace sessions, and to determine essential targets to address. This will enable patients to move forward and will provide them a different way to understand how triggers contribute to their relapses.

WHAT IS RETRAUMATIZATION?

Retraumatization can occur when a patient has an experience, emotionally, physically, mentally, or spiritually, that parallels a previous traumatic event and invokes a similar response, consciously or unconsciously. Often, unconscious reaction occurs that can sabotage recovery and healing by activating overwhelming traumatic material. Retraumatization happens for a variety of reasons on a number of different emotional levels. ED patients are especially vulnerable to this phenomenon because their presenting problem is often the tip of the treatment iceberg. As therapists we have been trained to deal with what occurs in our office. It is essential, however, that we recognize, assess, and reevaluate the EMDR treatment process in a holistic way. EMDR is a powerful tool and its Three-Pronged Protocol (Past, Present, and Future) with ED patients can be too linear and cause retraumatization. Acute clinical attunement with ED patients during EMDR processing allows the therapist to adjust pacing of processing or make a necessary shift in the intervention. Dissociation, depersonalization, freezing, numbing, quick ego-state shifts, and excessive somatization indicate that a particular patient is susceptible to retraumatization during EMDR processing.

WHAT FACTORS CONTRIBUTE
TO RETRAUMATIZATION?

When we have done our best to ensure a safe therapy experience, our patients may still be retraumatized. Here are some fundamental considerations that need to be addressed in all complex ED (and other) cases.

Complexity of Case

An incomplete patient history can be a setup for retraumatization. What a patient consciously answers may be remarkably different than what later unfolds. ED patients can be so focused on food, their bodies, and their eating behaviors that they discount many of the early neglect and attachment issues, core traumatic conflicts underlying their addictive behaviors. They often don't understand that past traumas contribute to their ED. Frequently they are in denial about the harm their ED behaviors have had, not only in their lives, but to their bodies. Carefully assess affective and dissociative disorders because of the possible ripple effects of treatment. Again, we have creative protocols and resource strategies to help process and integrate material. Excessive time spent on ruminating about food and resourcing material up front can often inhibit central processing of necessary targets. An "easy does it, but do it" philosophy can go a long way.

Level of Activation

Assess the level of activation that occurs with Bilateral Stimulation (BLS) for each patient. ED patients are often activated by getting in touch with their bodies and need very slow, gentle BLS. A patient who gets overactivated can become somatically and emotionally overwhelmed and feel out of control. This can be distressing for any patient; for the ED patient it can trigger a relapse. In the first phase of EMDR it's important to evaluate how a patient experiences internal activation somatically and emotionally. Ask patients to consider how they feel about beginning therapy or EMDR treatment. Next, have them focus on any activated feelings they have in their body, along with their thoughts about treatment. Encourage them to keep focusing on the sensation and notice what happens. Check in on the intensity of the sensations or feelings. Evaluate the visual field; if they feel more activated on right or left side; their audio experience in how they experience volume and sounds; and how they experience speed or intensity. When you do this, it provides insight into how a patient responds to different BLS, which can be used to titrate and pace processing. Evaluation of BLS not only provides information for the therapist, it engages the patient in a "we" process and lends reinforcement to the fact that *they* are processing material and that EMDR isn't something "being done to them."

The Therapeutic Relationship

Issues in the therapeutic relationship can cause retraumatization. EMDR is a powerful clinical tool inextricably tied to the transferential relationship. Regardless of your theoretical orientation, the patient/therapist relationship is *the* essential component in healing. If you are reading this, we can assume you are committed to doing no harm. However, transferential issues get complicated with ED patients and EMDR. These patients have a relationship with food that can be incomprehensible We are not just clearing out trauma (the easy part), we are touching all of the relational issues involved with a primary need. We will be seen as their mothers and fathers, their hated doctor or nutritionist, their resented thin friends, their lost loves that couldn't bear them, and "all those people who don't understand." They will invoke many feelings in us. It is important to understand the countertransference experienced as an induction of feelings coming from the patient. It will help us understand how they are feeling and can guide our interventions.

Previous chapters discussed ego state work. Reevaluation at the beginning of each session provides a clue about what ego states are showing up for treatment. I have found it invaluable to ensure that an adult part leaves the office. ED patients often get lost in a loop of panic and frustration. It's imperative to listen for the phases that indicate that a younger part is being overwhelmed. Disassociated emotional memories can get confused with emotional material that parallels the experience of their EDs. Here is a common presentation: A patient is processing how overwhelmed she is with the stress of work, money, and children. She feels depleted, not taken care of, and out of control. Her focus shifts to how can she possibly deal with her ED. She begins a loop: "I can't, I don't know what to do, it's too much, it's too hard, it's the only thing I have," and so on. A state shift is felt, expressed explicitly by the patient or felt implicitly in a shift in the countertransference to the patient-processing experience. Most often answers to all of the panic questions regarding their food and ED behaviors have been gone over many times. Of course, this type of material can be connected to numerous important issues in the patient's life. However, timing is everything, and it is critical that you leave enough time to ground the patient as material is being processed. Patients not taken care of in this regard can be retraumatized, and feel abandoned and confused. Using the "here and now" therapeutic relationship can help gain equilibrium for both the patient and you. The transference and countertransference can clearly inform the therapist in how to organize what "needs" must be met to maintain stability and pace treatment.

Abstinence and Relapse

In addition to the trauma of ED behaviors, food has many deep emotional connections that may not be congruent with the ED behavior. Moreover, recovery isn't always a linear route. You must see stabilization and symptom reduction in the context of overall healing. Consider recovery as a forward-moving process, as relapse will reinforce patients' negative beliefs about their disease. Most ED patients have had numerous defeats regarding their abstinence. It can be retraumatizing when patients are doing deep work to heal, and feel that they aren't getting better.

Whether a patient binges, starves, obsessively overeats, restricts, spits, or purges, they come into treatment focused on wanting to gain "control" of their ED. Then they find out that the ED behavior is the only time they feel in control. Unlike most other addicts, the ED patient has to engage in eating every day, making abstinence elusive for many. Abstinence has different meanings in different theoretical orientations. It's important to define the boundaries and regularly reevaluate abstinence with each specific patient. The EMDR protocol provides an opportunity for patients to connect with their own internal truths about their personal abstinence.

JANIE

Complexity of Case

Janie, a 40-year-old single mother, actor, and singer, battled her ED since she was a child. Her family of origin was dysfunctional and she suffered an enormous amount of neglect. Food was her only source of comfort and childhood obesity created many traumatic experiences.

Over the years Janie vacillated between anorexia, restricting, and compulsive overeating. She has body dysmorphia and her weight has ranged over a 70-pound range. She battles with anxiety and depression congruent with her eating behaviors. She has been in out-patient programs and inpatient programs and has tried every nutrition program around. Every emotional experience of Janie's life is penetrated by the trauma of her ED. She has developed an inability to tolerate emotional distress, making abstinence elusive. Like many ED patients, she continually externalizes her power and is victim to feelings of no control. Her self-loathing and loneliness are a constant reexperience of her neglect and abandonment as a child.

Janie experienced EMDR in her last 30-day intensive ED inpatient program. During her inpatient EMDR sessions Janie had a controlled environment that provided much support, but was flooded with traumatic memories. At that time, she got her compulsive overeating under control despite being at her highest weight.

Retraumatization

After treatment, Janie found an EMDR therapist who was well trained. This therapist used a light bar and sat far away from Janie (possibly trying to stay "out of the process"). Once again, Janie was flooded and overstimulated, but this time there was no containment of affect, leaving her destabilized. This reexperience of neglect and abandonment was retraumatizing but wasn't addressed with the therapist. Experiencing such destabilization over a few sessions, Janie began to restrict food and slowly moved into anorexia. She stopped treatment and once again raged at herself for her failure to be abstinent.

Emaciated, Janie came into treatment with me 1 year later. She was very reluctant to do EMDR although she believed in its powerful effects. Her complex case needed to be organized in a way that would keep her stable. Providing answers about her past experience with EMDR was our first order of business. I assured Janie that our process would move slowly and that recovery would be addressed from a number of different perspectives. Along with getting support from a sponsor, Janie committed to a food plan that she knew worked for her.

Level of Activation

Janie was very sensitive to BLS. We used low, slow oceanic sound, which calmed her autonomic nervous system as she processed. We used sets of Eye Movements (EMs) to reinforce positive shifts and connections. When we processed her negative EMDR experience, Janie connected with her beliefs about her past therapist not meeting her needs. She believed she was "too needy" and no one could ever take care of her.

Abstinence and Relapse

Next we spent time on defining what her goals were, considering a new conception of abstinence. Recovery from her ED would "include" abstinence and not be defined by it. She had to have stabilization between sessions in order to reduce her level of anxiety. Because of her history with EMDR, I insisted that there be close examination of her between-session processing. I made myself available via e-mail and phone, providing Janie with grounding and reassurance when needed. This helped to identify patterns of sabotaging thinking and behaviors as they unfolded. When overstimulation would happen during EMDR processing, I'd have her take off the headset and ground by having her focus on a part of her body that felt most calm. We used very slow EMs to install the sense of forward recovery. This was true even during times when her ED behaviors "flared up." I kept track of the micro-movements toward recovery that she would have easily dismissed. I framed EMDR sessions around her triggers/Negative Cognitions (NCs) and emotions, not her ED behaviors. Janie began to understand the complexity of her disease and triggers in a new way. She learned to accept her ED as a chronic illness that resulted in longer periods of abstinence. Janie's flare-ups decreased in duration and intensity and were no longer considered relapses.

Therapeutic Relationship

Janie was a difficult patient. She would present in many different ways, inducing countertransference reactions that provided me with information about what she was feeling and what she might need. I integrated many different techniques within EMDR to support her treatment. Ego state work and integration were essential in enabling her to function in the adult world. Her younger parts, full of anger and fear, would consistently use her ED as a punishment and distraction from self-responsibility and recovery. Her despair, self-loathing, and helplessness would induce similar feelings in me about her treatment. She at times would lash out about therapy and EMDR. It was essential that

I continually addressed the "process" and not the content of her expressions. This linked to Adaptive Information Processing, enhanced the alliance of the therapeutic relationship, and shifted a distorted perspective.

Reevaluation

We evaluated treatment effects session to session to consider the progress of the resolution of material. Initially regular positive "state changes" emerged but were not sustained. Janie would often have clarity about her ED, life, and recovery that appeared to be positive shifts in her treatment. Inevitability, a slow regression would happen and her abstinence would slip toward restriction or bingeing. Over time together we detangled the matrix of negative emotional and cognitive information that had made it impossible for her to sustain recovery. Slowly, a "trait change" evolved that contextually felt very different for both Janie and me. This internal shift of integration and healing brought abstinence into reach. She finally began to notice and integrate the small, subtle differences in how she felt about herself and how she experienced the world.

This treatment approach works with attention to the whole person. A complex case can easily erupt without notice. Therefore it is important to always consider careful evaluation of processing. ED cases are always challenging but we have a unique opportunity to provide deep healing and real recovery. To provide stable treatment the therapist must organize these cases using a comprehensive approach that addresses the vulnerability and fragility of abstinence. An organic shift in patients' relationship to food and themselves happens over time and is measured by the reevaluation of treatment effects. Reevaluation provides the essential information needed to navigate the unpredictable emotional storms that can interrupt recovery.

REFERENCE

Shapiro, F. (2001). *Eye movement desensitization and reprocessing: Basic principles, protocols, and procedures* (2nd ed.). New York: Guilford Press.

Chapter 12

Desensitizing Desire: Nonverbal Memory and Body Sensations in the EMDR Treatment of Eating Disorders

Catherine Lidov

CONSIDER TWO YOUNG WOMEN: THE FIRST IS A TEENAGER IN TREATMENT FOR A *mood disorder who is struggling with tantrums and the beginning of disordered eating. She is gaining weight and is overweight for the first time in her life. She tells me that she has great difficulty when she is in a store and sees something she wants. "The feeling of wanting it and not being able to have it overwhelms me. I cannot get it out of my mind." Similarly, at home she frequently experiences intense desire for sweets. "I just have to have it or I can't do anything else." The second is a college student in treatment for anorexia who has reached a healthy weight for the second time in her treatment process. However, she remains unmotivated to eat or to do anything in life. She tells me that she cannot want anything, because if she wants one thing she will be completely overwhelmed by everything she wants. "I can't care because I care too much."*

Disordered eating can be both an expression of and a response to problems with the experience of desire. Binge eating can offer a way of obtaining something wanted, either as a substitute or as displacement, and can effectively suppress other desires. Restricting and purging can be displaced means for trying to control desire. And eating to self-soothe or for a sense of company can quiet the longing for human connectedness when secure attachment is absent. While disordered eating behaviors are multidetermined symptoms that cannot be reduced to one cause, function, or meaning, for some clients disordered eating can be a way of expressing or managing problems associated with desire. In this chapter I discuss using EMDR to target experiences of desire that contribute to disordered eating.

Desire is an urge to have something that is currently absent. For the purposes of this chapter, desire will be considered as a spectrum of internal states that include wanting, longing, missing, and disappointment, and the word *desire* will be used interchangeably with other states on this continuum. Desire motivates behavior to attain what is wanted or needed. When desire occurs together with the expectation of getting what is wanted, it is experienced with excitement and anticipatory pleasure. When desire occurs with the expectation of not getting what is wanted, it is experienced with emotional pain (sadness, anger, shame, or guilt). In keeping with Shapiro's (2001) Adaptive Information Processing (AIP) theory, I assume that a person's experience of desire is shaped by her memories of associated experiences. Dysfunctionally stored memories of experiences associated with desire can thus become sources of current dysfunctional behavior.

BACKGROUND

Desire starts very early in life, including hunger and the desire to be held. While basic needs and securely attached relationships are primary objects of desire for most people throughout life, other objects of desire transform with the developing child, adolescent, and adult. Desire helps us to identify what we need, what our preferences are, and what we value. This awareness is important in the development of a sense of self. The ability to tolerate both wanting and disappointment is a prerequisite for adaptive self-care and for working toward long-term goals. When a person can tolerate paying attention to what she wants without immediately acting on the urges associated with it, she can figure out what is important to her, her values, her likes and dislikes. She can organize her behavior to work toward something she wants that is currently (uncomfortably) absent. And she can adapt to disappointment without giving up or defending against the experience of wanting in the future.

The body sensations associated with desire can be intense. Much of parenting is focused on soothing babies and teaching children to self-soothe. This helps them tolerate delays in getting their needs met and, later, learn to delay gratification and accept disappointment. Disruptions in this learning process lead to problems with tolerating the experiences of wanting, longing, missing, and disappointment. A child may develop negative internal states in response to problems tolerating desire. These may include shame ("I'm selfish"), guilt ("It's my fault I didn't get it"), sadness ("I'll just be disappointed again"), and anger ("I never get what I want").

In the absence of secure attachment and appropriate attunement, a baby or child may develop significant difficulty modulating all forms of desire. When there are problems modulating desire, a person may feel overwhelmed by the body sensations and fear that she is out of control. This can lead to maladaptive efforts to control her experience. When this pattern is repeated over time, body sensations themselves can become a source of fear, independent of the event that triggers them. In these situations, when a person is fearful of feeling desire, preoccupation with shame, guilt, anger, and sadness can enable her to avoid experiencing desire directly.

Given that experiences of desire are present very early in life, precognitive memories may be present in these body sensations (Shapiro, Kaslow, & Maxfield, 2007). It may be that some of the individuals for whom the body sensations of desire are overwhelmingly distressing are reexperiencing very early disruptions in attunement and attachment. When a baby's physical and attachment needs are not met, the baby's safety is threatened. Therefore, disturbances associated with very early desire, as felt in the body, may be experienced with intense distress.

The Standard Protocol of EMDR (Shapiro, 2001) can be used to address problems in the ways clients manage and respond to experiences of desire. According to the AIP model, if early experiences of desire were accompanied by significant stress or distress, there is a strong possibility that these memories were dysfunctionally stored. Desensitization and reprocessing should, therefore, result in the client making connections between these memories and the currently available information that she can survive, tolerate, and even learn to accept wanting, longing, missing, and disappointment. This, in turn, should lead to an increased ability to effectively reprocess current triggers for disordered eating and to develop a template for responding adaptively to experiences of desire and disappointment without disordered eating in the future. Theoretically, the approach outlined here should be applicable for clients who express or manage dysfunctions of desire in ways other than disordered eating.

What follows is an illustration of the application of EMDR in the treatment of binge eating, with a discussion of modifications and important aspects of each phase of the Standard Protocol.

EVALUATION AND TREATMENT PLANNING

Clients with eating disorders (EDs) can be fragile. It is critical to consider when in treatment it is appropriate to directly process experiences of desire. Because of the bodily intensity with which people experience desire, I have chosen to target desire only after a client is stable and able to tolerate and regulate anger, shame, sadness, and pleasure. (See Chapter 7 for information on treatment planning.)

Sarah

Sarah is 52 years old and has struggled with disordered eating since she was 13. She has a history of binge eating with periods of physician-prescribed fasting to lose weight and periods of restrictive dieting. She had a 15-year history of treatment prior to being referred to me, including extended psychodynamic and cognitive-behavioral psychotherapy. Over the course of her treatment we used EMDR to resolve the series of traumas associated with her parents' separation and her mother's alcoholism (which prompted the start of her ED) and her first memories of believing she was overweight. Attempts to address her current fears of intimacy and her shame and anger related to her body were less successful. We worked with her current relationship with her aging mother and with several life transitions (with notable improvement) and helped her develop an extended support system of friends and family. She engaged in extensive yoga training to increase mindfulness and attunement with her body. While we made progress in decreasing her general distress, improving the quality of her life, and moderating some of her eating behaviors, she continued to binge and to believe that she was too heavy to ever be in an intimate relationship. Over time she identified that if she believed that she were lovable and could have intimacy, she would be overwhelmed by the intensity of her longing and be unable to maintain healthy boundaries in relationships.

PREPARATION

There are two aspects of preparation specific to targeting desire. First, the client needs to be educated regarding all of the emotions on the spectrum of desire and assisted to identify how she experiences them in her body. Second, it is important to discuss the goals of tolerating disappointment and living with wanting something that she does not have. She must be able to perceive these as adaptive outcomes, at least in theory, or reprocessing will get stuck in efforts to avoid disappointment.

Sarah was frustrated that our extensive work in self-care, affect regulation, and trauma treatment had not resolved her ED. She started another fasting regime, then decided that she could no longer tolerate fasting, and returned to a restrictive diet of protein and vegetables, alternating with periods of binge-ing. As we continued to track the triggers for her binges, I started exploring with her what it was like for her to feel longing and to want something without obtaining it. She alternated between feeling impatient to get what she wanted and feeling hopeless about ever fulfilling her desires.

IDENTIFYING TREATMENT TARGETS

To establish specific targets for EMDR and to open the door to early memory, I focus on the body sensations of desire. Body sensations provide the starting point for the Floatback technique. In keeping with Francine Shapiro's (2001) theory of the Touchstone Event, it is important to identify and reprocess the earliest available memories of disturbance associated with desire.

To identify our treatment targets, Sarah focused on what she felt in her body during a recent experience of wanting to binge. I asked her to focus on the physical sensations, to close her eyes, and to allow her mind to float back to the earliest time she could remember having those feelings in her body. With each memory, I asked her to maintain her focus on the body sensations and see if there was anything earlier. Sarah floated back to a memory she had never brought up before: "I've always remembered this time when I was in my crib, in a room off the kitchen, and my parents were in the kitchen. I remember this intense feeling of wanting my parents' attention and I remember holding the rails and rocking my body back and forth with such force that I actually made the crib move, which brought them running to me. I have another memory around the same time of my father carrying me, pacing back and forth in the apartment, and I was crying. My mother has told me that she wasn't feeding me enough. She was breast-feeding me and didn't realize that a lot of my cry-ing was due to hunger."

We listed the other memories that came up during the floatback. At age 8 she had wanted to tell her parents why she was struggling during her piano lessons, but felt that she could not. At age 9 she saw her father drive by from a window at school and felt an intense urge to run out to him.

ASSESSMENT

During the Assessment Phase, Negative Cognitions (NCs) and Positive Cognitions (PCs) should reveal beliefs associated with desire. Examples include:

Negative Cognitions	Positive Cognitions
I can't tolerate disappointment.	Sometimes I get what I want and sometimes I don't, and I'm okay either way.
I'm selfish.	My needs matter.
I don't care.	What I want is important to me.
I care too much.	I can care and be okay.
My needs don't matter.	I deserve.
If I let myself want it, I'd go crazy.	I can tolerate disappointment.
If I don't get what I want, it will kill me.	I can feel this and be okay.
If I don't get what I want, it means I did something wrong.	I deserve to be loved.
I have to be perfect in order to get my needs met.	I'm good enough to be loved and cared for.
There is no point in trying.	My efforts matter even when I don't succeed.
My needs are too big; I'm too big.	My wants and needs are normal.
I can't trust myself.	I can tolerate wanting something and still make good choices for myself.

Sarah chose to start with the memory of her father holding her and pacing as she cried. Her NC was "My desire is too big and I won't be able to control it." Her PC was "I can be with these feelings without cake."

DESENSITIZATION AND INSTALLATION

Desensitization should lead to the reprocessing of the sense of disturbance associated with desire. The goal is that the client becomes comfortable with wanting something and to believe that she is okay, whether or not she obtains what she wants. Often desire continues after reprocessing, and clients may report a Subjective Units of Disturbance Scale (SUDS) higher than 0. It is important to check whether this is the ecologically valid experience of wanting something that is not present or whether it is a sense of disturbance about that experience that requires further reprocessing.

After five 60-minute sessions working on the target of her father holding her and pacing while she cried, Sarah's SUDS level was 0 and her Validity of Cognition (VOC) Scale was 7. During these weeks, Sarah described the following changes: She was more aware of hunger and satiety cues and more often able to choose to stop eating, she joined a spiritual community and started to feel connected there, and she had more frequent periods of feeling grounded. However, she continued to binge on weekends, overeat during the week, and have difficulty recognizing times when she needed rest.

BODY SCAN

Body sensations associated with wanting, longing, and desire may continue after reprocessing. This is especially true when working on a Future Template, which involves being able to tolerate wanting something that the client does, in fact, currently want. Again, the goal is for these sensations to be experienced without disturbance or distress.

During the Body Scan Sarah experienced a number of pleasant feelings in her body, including some sexual arousal, which was initially comfortable but then led to thoughts of intimacy with a man that generated disturbance. As this seemed to be a part of her Future Template, I asked her to refocus on the current target and PC without projecting into the future. With the memory and her current belief that she can be present with her desire in mind (without acting on it), her Body Scan was clear of disturbance.

REEVALUATION

It is important to recheck the SUDS level of the previously processed memory, and to see if it has generalized to any other memories, before choosing the next target.

At the beginning of the next session, the initial target remained at a 0 SUDS. Sarah's two other earliest memories were also now at a 0 SUDS.

We started working on her memory of a piano lesson. NC: "I'm not lovable

*when I want help." PC: "I am lovable when I want help." This memory chan-
neled into the memory of seeing her father drive by and led to intense processing of her body hatred. At the beginning of the second session on this target,
she noted increased body awareness, increased ease with her current diet, and
a stronger sense of a spiritual presence in her life. It took three sessions to fully
clear this memory, during which she went through a period of intense reprocessing of her relationships with both of her parents. Toward the end she saw
them sitting at either end of a table and she practiced coming and going from
the table, listening to her body's hunger and eating what she wanted, while
her parents stayed as a protective presence at either end of the table, neither
leaving nor intruding. Eventually the image faded. When we returned to the
target, her SUDS was 0.5 (sadness, but no disturbance) as she saw herself
waving good-bye to her father. She revised her PC to "I'm lovable and I can
feel connected without overeating." Installation went quickly and her Body
Scan was notable for no discomfort and many pleasant sensations in her body.*

*At our next meeting she announced: "It's almost miraculous. I've been able
to eat what I want to eat and then stop. I've been able to not eat and be okay
with that. I've missed some snacks and not even thought about it. I have a piece
of chocolate cake in the freezer and another one got moldy in the refrigerator—
that's never happened before." She had put on a pair of tight jeans, "and it was
no big deal. It was just tight jeans. That was it. None of the usual self-hatred.
No diet promises." Even more notably, she had had a serious family situation
over the weekend that recapitulated a number of traumas from her adolescence.
She weathered it with compassion for her mother and herself, and she made
them both brownies and ice cream and had one serving. For the first time in her
adult life, food and eating were not an issue for her. This was different from her
previous "good" periods, which were times of effective adherence to her diet
plan. As the session ended, she expressed strong feelings of connection in the
treatment relationship, including awareness of my care and concern for her.*

PAST MEMORIES, PRESENT TRIGGERS, FUTURE TEMPLATES

In keeping with the Three-Pronged approach of EMDR, symptom resolution is unlikely to be sustained until present triggers and future concerns are addressed.

*Sarah returned the next week stating that she had felt overwhelmed by her
sense of connection to me and had had problems with overeating all week. The
SUDS levels of all of her past memories remained at 0, so this experience of*

feeling connected became the first present trigger target for EMDR. Her NC was "I don't deserve to be cared about." Her PC was "I deserve to be cared about." She reprocessed her fear that the desperateness of her need to feel loved will cause her to ignore her own boundaries, as it had in the past. She resolved her anxiety about feeling that I cared about her, and expressed the belief that she could trust herself to choose healthy relationships.

A log of current experiences of desire that trigger disordered eating can be developed both prior to starting and during the reprocessing of past memories. One of the most important current triggers to address is the body sensation of desire. This is similar to targeting the physical sensations of fear in the treatment of a phobia (Shapiro, 2001). Hunger is a state of physical wanting that can be triggered *by* desire and also be a trigger *for* desire. Like emotional desire, the body sensation of hunger can become a source of fear in itself and may need to be targeted.

To target the experience of desire itself, Sarah identified a recent incident of longing for intimacy that was followed first by hopelessness and then by the urge to binge. It was difficult for her to identify the state of longing separate from the hopelessness, but she was able to clearly identify the desire to binge. With the image of driving to the grocery store, feeling the wanting in her body, her NC was "I am weak and unattractive and vulnerable." Her PC was "I am attractive, desirable, and strong." The sensations were located "everywhere in my body." Reprocessing this experience was very intense for her and involved revisiting a number of past experiences, but it cleared within one session and Sarah finished with a VOC of 7, feeling strong, grounded, and clear.

In following sessions we reprocessed other triggers she had identified and ones that came up along the way. As we worked, she continued to experience more frequent and longer periods of freedom from disturbances related to food, eating, and body image.

Because current desire is often about future goals, attending to current desire is likely to identify targets for Future Templates. Future Templates can also be identified by exploring what fears arise when the client imagines having what she desires or living with disappointment. At some point, the Future Template needs to include a sense of self as able to tolerate both wanting and disappointment while working toward future goals.

Sarah experienced both intense desire for intimacy with a man and intense fear of being unable to form or maintain a healthy relationship. She longed to feel less alone in the world, wanting both human support and a spirituality that would help her feel held and safe. Future Templates included images of herself wanting and being open to an intimate relationship with a man, trust-

ing her ability to assess people, practicing relationship skills while wanting intimacy, experiencing setbacks without giving up, and wanting and staying open to a sense of connection with a loving divine power.

CONCLUSIONS

We all have things we need in order to survive, things we need in order to thrive, and preferences. Discerning among these is an area of great confusion in our culture, where preferences are spoken of as needs and thriving is considered a luxury. It is even more confusing for individuals who experienced problems with attachment and other threats to their well-being at young ages, whose preferences were consistently invalidated in childhood, or who were taught that their wants and needs were not important. While our desires are not road maps, they are important guides that help us identify who we are and what is important for our well-being, from survival to self-development.

Some individuals with EDs have lost these guides, as the adaptive functions of desire are blocked by the distress and dysfunctional behaviors that are triggered by desire. Using EMDR to target disturbances associated with desire—the urge to get what is wanted or needed—appears to offer a direct and powerful route to access and reprocess key experiences that perpetuate dysfunctional feelings and behaviors. When this is effective, the ED behaviors that expressed and managed these problems can become irrelevant and more easily extinguished. The client is then free to explore the qualities that develop from feeling desire without disturbance: the ability to distinguish between brief, fleeting desires and lasting, meaningful needs; the ability to work toward long-term goals; the ability to sustain motivation through difficulty and disappointment; the ability to inhibit acting impulsively in ways that go against her best interest; and the ability to define her values and have a sense of deeper purpose in her actions.

REFERENCES

Shapiro, F. (2001). *Eye movement desensitization and reprocessing: Basic principles, protocols, and procedures* (2nd ed.). New York: Guilford Press.

Shapiro, F., Kaslow, F. W., & Maxfield, L. (2007). *Handbook of EMDR and family therapy processes*. Hoboken, NJ: Wiley.

Chapter 13

The Case of Mistaken Identity: Ego States and Eating Disorders

Andrew Seubert and Judy Lightstone

> The time will come
> when, with elation,
> you will greet yourself arriving
> at your own door, in your own mirror,
> and each will smile at the other's welcome
> —Derek Walcott, from "Love after Love"

ANDREW SEUBERT AND JUDY LIGHTSTONE HAVE WORKED FOR MANY YEARS with clients with eating disorders (EDs). Both have discovered the need to work with ego states and dissociation in bringing about change with this population, yet, each has had different experiences in using EMDR. Andrew primarily works with clients suffering from anorexia nervosa (AN), and Judy with clients engaged in binge-eating disorders (BED) and bulimia (BN). This chapter describes their individual approaches and their use of Bilateral Stimulation (BLS).

ANDREW'S EXPERIENCE

The more painful, consistent, and repeated an experience, and the more absent the presence of healthy attachment, the greater the need to disconnect from the feelings, body sensations, and self-experience generated by trauma. If I am not able to tolerate who I think I've become due to trauma, then I must create a new identity, or at least displace the shameful and painful aspects of experience elsewhere, in an identity that is perceived as a "not-I." Protective avoidance is the need, and dissociative strategies are the mechanisms of achieving that protection.

Discovering the presence of dissociation in clients with EDs was essential in shaping my therapeutic approach to this very difficult population. These clients slip into forms of restricted consciousness, at times called polarities (Polster & Polster, 1973), ego states (Watkins & Watkins, 1997), or parts (Schwartz, 1995). I will use "parts" and "ego states" interchangeably to refer to these aspects of the self. In extreme cases, a client will enter the realm of dissociative identity disorder (DID) or dissociative disorder not otherwise specified (DDNOS). Here, however, I will be referring to clients whose dissociation falls midrange on the dissociative continuum.

The personality is not a fixed, monolithic entity. Rather it appears to be made up of parts or states, some of which mature with the organism, others that become fixed or frozen in time at an earlier developmental stage. These arrested states typically form at the time of a traumatic experience.

When clients are not able to tolerate that experience, they create ways of disconnecting or dissociating from it, forming a new ego state or part around the unfinished experience, as well as the strategies for disconnecting from the trauma. In such moments a restricted and false sense of self comes into existence. Therapy then becomes a process of unraveling a case of mistaken identity and of reclaiming or remembering the real or whole self.

EMDR conceptualizes these parts as dysfunctionally stored experiences unavailable to the corrective and healing powers of the prefrontal cortex (F. Shapiro, 2001). Essential to these negative experiences are the false stories the clients begin to believe about themselves and the subsequent identities formed to survive the way the clients experience the world.

Eating Disorder Strategies

EDs, and here I will specifically refer to AN, employ various kinds of dissociation in order to tolerate the intolerable. The ED, often referred to by clients as "Ed," becomes a new identity or at least a best friend that imbues the client with a false sense of strength and control, often quieting internal self-critical thoughts. It helps distract the client from painful emotions and events by developing a sense of control over food and body weight and displacing psychic pain onto the body. It also allows the client to experience some relational empowerment, if not with an actual person, at least with a substitute in the form of food.

Gloria was the younger of two daughters, both parents, but especially the father, possessing critical and perfectionistic traits. Her older sister suffered from multiple sclerosis and demanded much of her parents' energy and attention. Gloria learned quickly not to stress her parents, since their personal reserves were minimal. She became the good girl who never dared to argue, act out, or show anger.

Gloria later married a man who, in her words, "bulldozed" over her. She had nowhere to go with her anger and anxiety, particularly after her husband insisted on her having an abortion, much against her will.

"So where did all that anger go?" I would ask her.

"Oh, that was easy," she answered. "I cleaned a lot, over and over, until the house was perfect. And I sort of stopped eating. The angrier I got, the less I ate. Kind of made me feel better."

"So you never get angry?" I continued.

"I don't dare! If I do, the Zone will get after me."

"The Zone?"

"Right. The Zone tells me what to do and what not to do or say. He just takes over if I start to get angry and punishes me if I don't do what he tells me to do."

Gloria dealt with life from a very young consciousness or "part." In conflictual moments, she was a frightened child (young ego state), intimidated by a critical part (the Zone) that resolved the internal civil war (to speak up or not) via restrictive eating and compulsive cleaning.

Scapegoating the body is another ED-identified dissociative strategy. The body becomes the place where shame, grief, and sadness are displaced and stored, so that the client doesn't have to experience them. As long as the body can be controlled and, to some extent, punished, by the ego state identified with the disorder, then the painful feelings remain buried, yet buried alive.

Katie had an abuse history, which included sexual abuse by her father and other adults, gang rape and subsequent abortion at 17, extensive drug and alcohol addiction, and ongoing promiscuity, eventually leading to severe anorexia. Most of her painful history took place during her teen years. Consequently, the parts of her internal world that held most of the pain and resorted to the ED to disconnect from her feelings were developmentally arrested in adolescence.

In one session, Katie recalled that during several years of ongoing alcohol use and sexual abuse by a man for whom she had been babysitting, she began to lose weight. As the memory processed, she remembered the compliments she was receiving about how good she looked and noticed that her shame and her guilt were diminishing. Looking good seemed to mitigate feeling bad.

"And as the shame is diminishing," I asked, *"is the abuse continuing?"*

"Yeah, it's still going on, but I don't feel as bad about it."

"Where did it all go?" I briefly interjected, while continuing the processing (Eye Movements [EMs]).

Katie was quiet during the BLS. Her eyes widened, and when the processing came to a pause, she related the following:

"It's like the thinner I got, the less shame I felt. The shame is in my body, my flesh! That's where I put it, and that's why I freak out if I gain half a pound!"

Katie's shame-based adolescent part protected itself from painful feelings by investing in being thin. She displaced her intolerable feelings onto her body, then tried to make that body disappear through starvation.

Yet another dissociative strategy is to make food the relational enemy. John Omaha (1998) references object relations theory in his conceptualization of addictions, EDs being among them. Rather than viewing the relationship to food, be it overeating or avoiding, as a way to soothe difficult emotions and reactions, this model understands the disorder as an opportunity to compulsively reenact primary relationships that have been absent, painful, and often abusive. In rejecting or purging the food, the client replays the original relationship in which there had been no control for the client, now, with some perceived control.

I have found this conceptualization quite helpful, and would refer the reader to Omaha's work to learn how he guides the client in discovering which relationship(s) the client-food process is repeating. With Sonja, it was obvious.

Sonja could never be good enough for her father. As fine a dancer as she was from grade school years on, he rarely attended her performances and never had a good thing to say. Years later, as Sonja was studying dance in New York City, she began to realize that her need to "be the best" at whatever she tried was not happening with her dance career. She was good enough for a second-level dance troupe but didn't have the talent to make it to the top level.

"So I decided that if I couldn't be the best at dance, then I would at least have a body that my dance instructor (the embodiment of her critical father) could never criticize," she related to me during a session.

Food became that which kept her from being good enough. So she simply made it the enemy and conquered it, but then became so physically compromised that she was admitted to an inpatient treatment facility. As with Gloria and Katie, Sonja developed a part or internal state at the time she realized she would never be good enough for her father or her dance instructor. Indirectly and without resolution, that part enlisted the ED to create a sense of control in the face of relationships that left her feeling never good enough, invisible, voiceless, and without power.

One of the first indications that I wasn't going to be able to "speak rationally" with these clients, much less process traumatic material, was when I would hear statements such as the following:

"I know it sounds crazy (*adult consciousness*), but I know that if I let myself feel happy, that will make me fat! (*younger consciousness*)."

"I'm not allowed to be angry, because I'm bad if I do, and I'll be punished." When asked who would punish her, the reply was, "The Zone! (*self-critical and self-punishing ego state*). The Zone tells me that I have to clean the house and just not eat instead of feeling angry!"

"I don't believe I thought this way for years (*adult consciousness*), but if I couldn't be the best at something, dancing, for instance, then I wouldn't eat and would at least have a body that my dance teacher couldn't criticize (*younger consciousness*)."

How do we contact and communicate with these states or information nodes that were at the source of such irrational and, often, self-destructive thinking processes? It requires a great deal of Preparation Phase work to get to know the arrested states that drive the disordered behaviors.

The Phase Approach (Phases 1–6)

Some preparation begins during the first few sessions (front-loading) to take the edge off of presenting symptoms (panic and anxiety, for example), but in any good trauma treatment, we need to start with *evaluation and treatment planning*. Since this phase, as well as Phases 7–8, has been addressed in other chapters, I will make reference to specific aspects of evaluation and treatment planning including dissociation (Dissociative Experiences Scale [DES], Dissociative Disorders Interview Schedule [DDIS]) and attachment status (Steele, 2007) since they are typically part of the story. I evaluate both of these and take a general history, trauma history, and an ED assessment (Garner, 2004).

The case formulation follows, which makes the connection between the trauma history and the presenting problems. I see the case formulation, which needs to be shared with the client in nonclinical terminology (Greenwald, 2007), as the fulcrum of the evaluation phase. The history taking and assessments inform the case formulation, which in turn leads to goal setting and treatment planning.

Goal setting is particularly important since many clients are not willing to give up the ED. Yet, it's critical to align with your clients' goals. The least common denominator in goal setting is keeping the client alive or out of an inpatient facility. Once this goal is agreed upon, then the need to change eating patterns can be supported. I don't deal directly with the eating behaviors (this is the task of medical colleagues and ED clinics), but I can establish a goal to reduce the clients' anxiety, as long as they have to eat in order to achieve this goal. The treatment plan follows based on the established goals, which (much like the trauma list) is often an ongoing work in progress.

The *Preparation Phase* is often quite prolonged and tedious, with frequent setbacks. I typically conceptualize the Preparation Phase in three parts. The *first part of preparation* involves stabilization and case management. The physical eating patterns are addressed by someone other than myself. Clients critically need support at home and in therapeutic groups.

Physical health must be attended to immediately. I will not work with a client with an ED unless they are under the care of a physician or clinic that is competent in the assessment and treatment of EDs. Working with the irrational belief structures of various ego states is impossible if the brain is being starved by an anorexic client.

This change in the symptomatic patterns of eating serves the purpose of bringing up the feelings and unfinished business from the past (which the ED was covering), reinforcing the case conceptualization, and encouraging eventual cooperation in trauma processing.

The *second part of the preparation* involves clients learning about and relating to the various ego states, while developing skills and resources that can be part of internal stabilization, attachment repair, and trauma processing. Clients learn strategies for working with emotions, self-soothing, and, particularly, tolerating and dealing with anxiety. (See Chapters 8, 17, and 19 for greater detail.)

This chapter can't give an in-depth treatment of ego state work and attachment repair. For this, I encourage you to review these references at the end of this chapter (Forgash & Copely, 2007; Holmes & Holmes, 2007; Paulson, 1995; Schwartz, 1995; Watkins & Watkins, 1997), and read Chapters 4, 5, 17, 18, and 19 in this book. Both ego state work and attachment repair are important in dealing with EDs, which often mask an underlying dissociative process. The trauma is contained in the dissociated parts, which avoid or bury the traumatic experience through the distraction and diversion of EDs.

Ego state work is not only a requirement for trauma work with EDs, but also enhances the development of skills, resources, and attachment repair taught within an ego state framework. Typically it's a younger part, not the adult consciousness, that needs to realize that one has to eat to survive. I impart information and skills to this arrested ego state, since it is committed to starvation as a way of managing otherwise intolerable experience.

The adult consciousness must compassionately understand the various ego states, particularly those identified with the ED. Each part was created with a purpose. The meaning of the disordered behavior must be understood, so that we might suggest more helpful and appropriate ways of functioning, rather than through the disorder.

Katie could identify an internal state that blocked our work and seemed to sabotage success in her daily living. She carried a great deal of rage and disgust toward that part, which held the shame, rage, and grief over ongoing sexual abuse, gang rape, and abortion as a teenager. Understandably, the adolescent part was quite angry at the adult consciousness for being blamed, shunned, and neglected, repeating the experience she had with her biological parents.

After creating a meeting place where Katie could dialogue with her adolescent part, I suggested she ask the adolescent several questions in order to create more mutual understanding. At the beginning of this process, the adolescent simply refused to communicate. Over the course of time she began to respond. I used BLS to enhance this dialogue.

"Why do you do what you do?" asked Katie. *"I mean the starving, the drinking and getting stoned, the cutting?"*

"Because I deserve it, and then I don't have to feel anything else," the adolescent replied.

"And what else don't you want to feel?" Katie asked with a little coaching.

"How disgusting I am, and how pissed off I am about everything I did! And everything that happened to me. I'm a total fuckup, but I'm making sure no one else sees that."

Katie and I had been exploring why she was so angry at the adolescent. I encouraged her to make herself known to the teenager about why she had disconnected herself from the younger part.

"Well, what I want you to know about me," ventured Katie, *"is that I'm totally afraid of you. I'm afraid that if I get close to you I'll feel the disgust and the anger and a lot of anxiety."*

Thus began the mutual understanding that led to a collaboration between adult and adolescent parts. Katie had disconnected herself from her painful experiences, which were stored in a fixed adolescent identity attached to the ED in order to survive. Given the fact that the adolescent had displaced her shame onto her body, restricted eating made sense. Once there was dialogue, the purpose or meaning of the behavior could be supported, while suggesting healthier ways of achieving the same goals.

It is critical for the client to realize that a part is not the whole. The "whole" is one's true Self or Essence, characterized by qualities such as love, compassion, kindness, strength, and courage. Once there exists an alliance between the client's larger or real Self (based on awareness, mindfulness, and positive resources) and internal parts, then the work can move forward. Without this cooperation, a civil war takes place and the identity of the ego state with the ED rigidifies.

With the reinforcement effect of BLS, I often teach awareness (Seubert, 2006) of being in the place of the real or essential Self (thoughts, feelings, breathing, body sensations that go with that). Positive memories of being connected to the Self are also of great assistance in this task: "When were the times you were grounded in your Self and were operating from the best in you?"

Clients often slip into a confluence with a part, saying: "I'm so disgusting! I hate myself! I just want to be thin!"

When this happens, I combine BLS with a Gestalt practice of preceding any reaction with the words: "I am aware that/of . . ." In such cases, I teach clients to change their statements to: "I'm aware that a part of me feels disgusting," and so on. This linguistic shift, combined with BLS, supports the needed separation between Self and parts.

During this phase of treatment, I employ BLS whenever there is the possibility that the stimulation will enhance the development of a new resource (a model or a memory), a new skill (awareness), or a new way of handling a situation (reduced anxiety when eating). I will at times employ BLS as the client is entering into a dialogue with a part. I do, however, omit the BLS when my clinical instincts tell me that what we are learning or exploring needs to move slowly.

While I refer the reader to the reference list at the end of this chapter for more detail regarding ego state work, I suggest a number of basic questions to ask of parts attached to the ED in order to create understanding and compassion:

1. *How old are you? When did you come into existence?*
2. *What's your purpose? What are you trying to accomplish?*
3. *What do you want me to know about you?*
4. *What are you most afraid of?*
5. *Are you tired of constantly having to think about food? Tired of hating your body?*
6. *Are you happy? Would you be interested in feeling better? Stronger?*
7. *Would you be interested in working together to feel better/stronger, perhaps in a way that doesn't hurt you or your body?*
8. *What do you need from me (adult consciousness)?*

These questions are just the beginning of creating a relationship with internal parts. This relationship must be developed if the state that contains the trauma, the dissociation, and the ED identity is to heal, move forward in time, and catch up with the rest of the psychic economy. Again, BLS is often helpful, particularly tapping the client's hands (creating simultaneously an experience of nurturing touch), throughout this exchange.

Attachment injury is also more efficiently repaired when the larger, adult consciousness is present to and compassionate toward younger ego states. The lack of healthy attachment experience is almost as predictable as the presence of trauma in clients with EDs. Two useful approaches to attachment work are the Imaginal Nurturing strategies of April Steele (Steele, 2007) and the Developmental Needs Meeting Strategies of Shirley Jean Schmidt (Schmidt, 2006).

One client, Jackie, had made contact with the ego states that were most deeply tied to the ED. There was "Claw" and "Blob," names the client offered. (I do not encourage naming parts as a matter of practice.) There was also a very angry and recalcitrant teenage part ("the teenager"). An agreement was made to begin to process the earliest memory that gave rise to the ED state: being teased by her two siblings about being fat when she was 7 years old.

In order to prepare the younger ego states for this work, we agreed
to process an even earlier memory. From her history, I wasn't aware of
any outstanding attachment injury. This was a major oversight on my
part, corrected almost immediately in the course of the processing.

Jackie was 5 years old when she and her family were visiting her
mother's relatives in Puerto Rico. Her mother was an extremely efficient and busy person, more dedicated to getting things done than
being present to her children. In the memory, Jackie recalls hanging on
to her mother's leg, fearing that her mother would return to the States
without her.

In processing the memory, the absence of secure attachment became evident, and the need for some attachment repair obvious,
before moving on to later trauma. Without reparenting very young aspects of her own psyche, Jackie would not have the resources to deal
with the trauma that gave rise to dissociation and then the ED at the
age of 7.

Future and corrective movies comprise the *third part of preparation*.
Future movies or Future Templates, as well as corrective reruns of mis-
handled events, combined with BLS, give the client the opportunity to
rehearse problematic situations (not major events or incidents connected to parents or family) with the inclusion of skills and resources
that lead to desired outcomes. Scripting these "movies" gives the therapist and client more control than the free association process of
EMDR. These tightly scripted scenarios lead to greater strength and
confidence.

"Movies" are useful in learning to tolerate the anxiety that arises
when clients with AN experience food in their stomach. The clients
typically agree to at least "take the edge" off of the anxiety experienced
when eating. We create a mental movie of the last time the clients had
to eat or the next time the clients expect to eat, incorporating relaxation
response skills and resources to tolerate the feelings that arise when
eating.

Trauma processing (Phases 3–6) can be quite complicated. To begin
with, it is often difficult to convince various ego states to do the work,
as they have become rigidly attached to a disordered existence, their
means of survival. Convincing ego states that there are better ways of
dealing with unprocessed experience is often a daunting challenge.

The greater the resistance to change, the more I find the presence of
adolescent ego states that stubbornly insist on doing it their way.
Jackie's world was similar to a family situation in which an acting-out

teenager was running the show. Claw and Blob were beginning to soften, but the adolescent dug her heels in.

The adolescent appeared in Jackie's mind dressed in jeans and a T-shirt. Jackie began the conversation.

"So what's going on with you?" Jackie asked.

"They can't make me eat!" came the reply. "I'm so pissed off at both my parents, especially my father."

"What about him?"

"He keeps me from going to dances, from branching out. I feel so friggin' trapped. He like hovers over me and feels he's got to protect me from *every*thing."

"Okay, what do you want then?" asked Jackie.

"I want things more *my* way. I'm tired of doing things my parents' way, tired of being the ugly one and not feeling good about myself. And I hate the thought of getting bigger, putting on weight."

And so begins the process of finding common goals with the adolescent and brainstorming healthier ways of achieving them.

When doing trauma processing with this population, there is an almost inevitable regression into the ED. Despite months, even years, of preparation work, this still occurs. Yet, at a certain point, both my clients and I sense a need to get to the bottom of the dysfunctional behaviors, rather than dealing symptomatically.

It's crucial to forewarn the client that some relapse may occur, so that there are as few surprises as possible, reframing any "relapse" as a signal to pause or break, rather than a failure. If regression occurs after a session of processing, then we step back into the Preparation Phase in order to ground and soothe the part that is finding the trauma work intolerable without the ED.

I do this by acknowledging the client's progress, pausing, and shifting to a positive emotional state or resource. We might then continue with the processing. At other times we titrate the material via various forms of closure, returning to the memory within the next one or two sessions.

In order to close a session, I will often ask the adult self to go back in time and take the younger, traumatized part out of the memory and forward in time to a safe or peaceful place. I call this "reparenting." It is a way of inviting the child state to begin to share in and connect with an adult adaptive resource. At the beginning of the subsequent session, I often ask for a Subjective Units of Disturbance Scale (SUDS) level on the incomplete memory. Almost inevitably the SUDS is lower. This may be due to ongoing processing between sessions, and it may well have to do with introducing a stuck part to adaptive resources and adult consciousness.

In Katie's case, this stop-and-go has continued over the course of years of therapy, yet she is able to recognize progress, albeit very gradual. Jackie, however, is still in the process of convincing her adolescent ego state to collaborate with trauma processing. The younger parts (Claw and Blob) are willing, particularly after seeing the progress that Jackie's 5-year-old part is making after several weeks of attachment healing. What often convinces one part to cooperate is seeing improvement in other parts, which leaves us hopeful with regard to Jackie's stubborn adolescent part.

After trauma processing, we must continuously address the need for relapse prevention, framing any return to the disorder as understandable and fear-based, rather than as a failure. We deal with such events as they arise, apprising the client ahead of time that such occurrences are quite common. In Chapter 11, Janet McGee covers this phase of treatment in detail.

JUDY'S EXPERIENCE

When I first started offering psychotherapy with a specialization in EDs in 1984, my treatment approach was most strongly influenced by the anti-diet feminist relational model taught at the Women's Therapy Centre Institute (see Bloom, Gitter, Gutwill, Kogel, & Zaphiropoulos, 1994). According to feminist relational theory, BN and BED, like self-mutilation (Farber, 2000), enable clients to tolerate otherwise unbearable attachment-deprived internal states so they can function, and sometimes at rather high levels. In his book *Traumatic Stress,* Bessel van der Kolk (van der Kolk, McFarlane, & Weisaeth, 1996) explains how self-mutilation, which triggers a release of endorphins, can become a physiological addiction because the endorphins also medicate unbearable emotional pain. Without the bingeing and purging or restricting, the clients cannot access the endorphins that regulate their "vehement emotions" (van der Hart, Brown, & van der Kolk, 1989), nor can they prevent them from intruding into day-to-day life, or from causing potential decompensation.

This understanding is key to working with people with EDs—the symptoms contain the affect that cannot be integrated (or digested) because it is too toxic. Just like the person who suffers from food poisoning, the bulimic person must purge to stay alive psychically. Respecting the symptom as the client's only available means of survival at the time is a core concept of feminist relational theory. It is not too far a leap, then, to learn to respect the ego states that act out those symptoms.

I have named the approach I use with EDs PSI, which stands for PsychoSomatic Integration. This model integrates the anti-diet feminist relational approach to eating and body image problems with somatic, ego state, and EMDR-derived resourcing and trauma-processing models of healing.

The Anti-diet Approach

The anti-diet approach involves the following four steps in developmental order, and incorporates working on body image issues throughout:

1. Finding your hunger—learning to distinguish physiological hunger from emotional triggers and to also distinguish different degrees of hunger.
2. Feeding your hunger—getting off externally imposed diet regimens and eating when physically hungry that which you are hungry for.
3. Breaking into the binge/purge/diet cycle (see cycles below).
4. Stopping at satiation—learning to distinguish different degrees of physiological satiety and to stop eating when satisfied and before becoming overly full.

These steps integrate readily with the eight phases of the EMDR protocol, much of this work taking place within the Preparation Phase. Their effectiveness also increases with the incorporation of ego state, somatic, and EMDR-derived protocols.

According to EMDR's Adaptive Information Processing (AIP) theory, trauma becomes "frozen in time, isolated in its own neuro network and stored in its original state specific form" (Shapiro, 2001, p. 42), making it particularly resistant to change. The anti-diet relational approach addresses compulsive eating symptoms directly and, in so doing, uncovers the ego states previously hidden behind the symptoms. That is why those of us using this approach in the early '80s

often found ourselves with clients with previously unreported dissociated trauma. The hardest and most important lesson I learned from the
early days was that if I didn't work with the ego states that acted out
the symptoms, the symptoms would keep recurring. Fortunately, by
the time I discovered this, feminist relational theory had already
primed me to work with ego states.

Ego State Therapy and the Anti-diet Approach

Ego state therapy (Watkins & Watkins, 1997) was originally developed
with the dissociative disorders in mind and offers especially effective
techniques to use with BN and for some people with BED, both of
which can have strong dissociative components (Lightstone, 2004). A
relatively recent development in ego state theory is the structural theory of dissociation (van der Hart, Nijenhuis, & Steele, 2006), which
incorporates an understanding of psychosomatic (mind/body) split-
ting (referred to as somatoform dissociation by the authors), which is
especially relevant to the type of dissociation often seen in EDs.
Trauma-based parts of the personality, relating to the AIP's dysfunctionally stored material (Shapiro, 2001), are created by repeated
trauma-initiated and truncated survival action states where neither
fight nor flight is a safe option (as, for example, in relational developmental trauma). *Emotional Parts* (EPs) of the personality, then, are
frozen in uncompleted fight, flight, submission, and/or freeze-action
states. This leaves the *Apparently Normal Part or Parts* (ANPs) of the
personality to function at higher levels than the entire personality
could otherwise. Ego states that binge, starve, and/or purge typically
fall into one of the EP categories (fight, flight, freeze, or submit).

For example, Jane had two distinct EPs that were bingeing and
purging. Her binges were acted out by a flight EP frozen in a state of
perpetual panic. When triggered, this EP would flee frantically from
store to store, cramming food into her mouth as she drove. The purges
that followed this were quite violent, acted out by a perpetrator-identified fight EP, who would jab a spoon or chopstick into her throat several times to trigger purge after purge. Although the fight ego state
was so dissociated as to not experience Jane's body as her own, this
was not DID because there was no amnesia for the behavior. Neverthe-
less the body/mind dissociation was quite pronounced, as is often the
case in bulimia.

Engaging a perpetrator-identified fight ego state requires a certain amount of finesse, especially when the state is so dissociated that it does not experience the bodily consequences of its behavior. EMDR cannot be effective at this point, as there is no somatic awareness, a prerequisite to reporting SUDS and Validity of Cognition (VoC) levels, and an inability to benefit from dual attention. First the EPs must be gently encouraged to develop awareness of cause and effect at the felt-sense level. Naturally they have avoided such awareness, even to a phobic degree (van der Hart et al., 2006) and so need to be introduced to embodiment at a carefully titrated pace.

Using the anti-diet hunger/satiation model developed at the Women's Therapy Centre fits in nicely here, as it addresses the ego states' main concerns (eating and gaining weight) while simultaneously introducing awareness of internal bodily states (hunger and fullness). Here is an example of working with step 2, finding your hunger, during the Preparation Phase:

Jane: I had a huge binge last night.

JL: *Were you hungry?*

Jane: Yes, I was starving, but I couldn't stop eating and I couldn't stop running from store to store. I was putting away food like I would never eat again—I just shoveled it in. It was disgusting.

Judy: *That is an understandable way to eat when you are starving. How did you end up getting so hungry?*

Jane: No. You didn't see it—there was nothing normal. I mean, I ate straight from the containers—things that were meant to be cooked.

Judy: *You must have been terribly hungry. How did that happen?*

Jane: Well, I had had such an awful binge last Sunday that I decided I could go the rest of the week without any food. I've done it many times before. But this time I was such a weakling.

Judy: *I don't agree. There's nothing "weak" or "bad" about feeding yourself when you are hungry. We would do better to explore this idea that you have to starve yourself any time you have a binge. Now it's looking to me like some of these "binges" may really be perfectly normal reactions to abnormal deprivation. In order to work through the "real" binges, we must first be able to distinguish them from binges that are in response to starvation. The only way to be sure is to ask yourself if you are physically hungry first. If the answer is yes, then please, see if you can enjoy your food.*

One ego state was in flight mode because she believed that she was going to starve in reaction to a maladaptive introject/fight EP that was telling her she could never ever eat again and threatening violent purges should she try. As I empathized with the frightened flight EP, the angry fight EP got angrier (and curious) about what I was doing.

I then joined empathically with the fight EP by understanding its terror of fatness and all that "fatness" represented to it/Jane (lack of control, weakness, victimhood, and associations to being teased as a fat child), addressing the fight state's need to get rid of the food and avoid fatness, and finally introducing the possibility of a new "job description." I suggested that the state become responsible for observing hunger levels and helping the flight EP learn to wait until hungry before eating. In this way, it is in both ego states' "self-interest" to become more aware of somatic sensations.

Here we can see how the anti-diet hunger/satiation model acts as a form of somatic resourcing. "Somatic resources comprise the category of abilities that emerge from physical experience yet influence psychological health. . . . Cognitive reflections are stimulated by the experience of the action itself: Through the act of pushing, clients realize that they have the right to defend themselves; through the act of reaching out, they understand that they can ask for help" (Ogden, Minton, & Pain, 2006, pp. 207–208).

Through the act of becoming aware of hunger, Jane developed a resource that let her know that eating when hungry was a good thing. As she learned to distinguish physical hunger from a binge urge, she was developing a body-based ability (resource) that was a first and critical step in interrupting the binge-purge cycle. At this point, I often use BLS to enhance positive felt states.

Additional somatic resourcing can be taught to ego states at this point, using techniques such as "Put Your Best Foot Forward," an EMDR-derived somatic protocol developed by Krystyna Kinowski (2003). Kinowski directed clients to assume a physical posture that would represent how they would feel if their presenting problem were resolved. In that position and felt sense, the client is asked to intuitively derive three images that act as resources in the face of the problem. The client's attention is then moved from resource images to a titrated part of the problem/memory, then back to the images, while the therapist adds BLS. The result is a relatively gentle processing, which enhances confidence, courage, and resilience, and, often, a reduction in the SUDS.

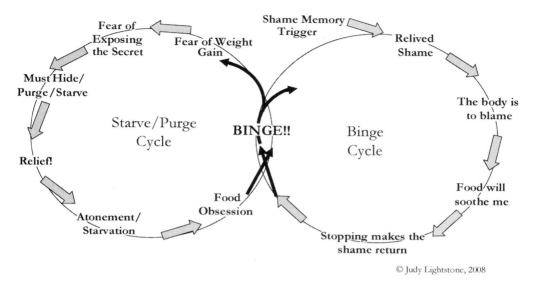

Figure 13.1 The Binge/Purge/Starve Cycles

Breaking the Binge-Purge Cycle

Figure 13.1 is a graphic representation of the work involved in directly engaging the bingeing and purging as seen in Jane's case. The trigger for the behavior is often not available to conscious awareness, and even less so is the original "trauma" (capital "T" and/or small "t") that the trigger links back to. The binge cycle above occurs at lightning fast speed, and must be slowed down and "joined" in with the client, so the client does not reexperience it alone or at its original intensity.

I begin with the binge behavior and work slowly backward to help the client identify the binge trigger. The cycles above describe what I have seen again and again when I have engaged with clients in this process. The trigger is quickly redirected at the body, so that the shame associated with the original trauma gets projected onto what becomes a "shameful" body image. Food is then sought out to both explain and medicate the shame (the bingeing becomes "shameful") and must continue lest the actual source memory leak through. In helping the client slow down by reporting the behavior mindfully, increment by increment, some of the dissociated affect or memory can become symbolized. By having a "compassionate witness" (Miller, 1984) to the traumatic reenactment, the client may be able to verbalize what was unspeakable before. Once a nonsymbolic (e.g., somatic) symptom becomes verbal, it becomes unnecessary to reenact it, as it can now be "talked" about.

Case Example

JL: *What do you think made you go for the Oreos at 2 p.m. yesterday?*

Jane: Well, as you know, that's when I get home from my job, and then I have an hour to get to class. I always binge then. I have trouble with transitions.

JL: *Yes, that seems to be a hard time of the day. Can you remember what made it so hard yesterday?*

Jane: I'm just stupid . . . it's stupid, that's all. I used to see Joey during my break when we lived together . . . but that was so long ago and so that can't still be it.

JL: *So you feel ashamed about still missing Joey? You should be over it by now?*

Jane: I never get over anything. I'm so clingy and needy—no wonder he left me.

JL: *So remembering that you used to see Joey then reminds you of the shame you feel for still needing him?*

Jane: It makes me sick to think about it.

JL: *Is that why you reached for the Oreos, do you think? Because of that sick feeling?*

Jane: Yes, but they just make me feel sicker! It doesn't make sense!

JL: *Well, it kind of makes sense if you wanted to forget the sick feeling about Joey, that you might cover it with a sick feeling about eating, which maybe doesn't feel as shameful.*

In this scenario, the "trigger" has been found. The trigger is not the trauma, but it points to the trauma, which no longer has to remain hidden since somatic awareness has already increased due to prior somatic resourcing. Once the trigger is identified, a somatic floatback (floating back on the "sick feeling" in her stomach) (Zangwill, in Shapiro, 2001) can be used to identify the "source memory" (original trauma). Trauma treatment options then become available, and it becomes possible to introduce the SUDS and VoC Scale as reference points once body awareness has been developed.

Ego state therapy combined with somatic resourcing and the mind-fulness required in breaking the binge-purge-starve cycle can offer a safely paced process for uncovering trauma and attachment-based triggers and for integrating "vehement emotions" and split-off parts of self.

PsychoSomatic Integration Protocol

The PSI ED protocol I have subsequently developed involves three phases of trauma treatment: preparation, trauma processing, and integration.

Phase I: Preparation and Stabilization:

1. *Taking an "eating symptom history" and evaluating* for lethality and dissociation are essential components of developing a treatment plan (EMDR Phase One: History Taking and Treatment Planning). As Andrew mentioned above, it is important to get medical backup when working with EDs. If a client is engaged in risky behavior, I ask that they see an M.D. (and sometimes a dentist, for bulimia) who is familiar with EDs and will stay in communication with me.
2. *Teaching client how to find and identify hunger.*
3. *Teaching client how to feed physical hunger.*
4. *Somatic Resourcing*—Developing intrapersonal and interpersonal somatic resources as described in *Trauma and the Body* (Ogden et al., 2006) and developing positive somatic associations to feared behaviors (such as eating) with the *Best Foot Forward* protocol (BFF) (Kinowski, 2003).
5. *Psychological Resource Development and Installation* as described by Andrew Leeds (2001) and/or building a *Healing Circle* consisting primarily of adult resources (nurturing, protective, and the core-self) (Schmidt, 2006).
6. *Breaking into the binge/purge/diet cycles* (see above).
7. *Body image work*: Asking the client to keep track of the "negative body voices" is a relatively simple way of identifying symptomatic ego states. Clients are instructed to keep a journal in which they write down the negative beliefs and messages they aim at their bodies, and this is then grist for the therapeutic mill. For example, one "voice" may say, "You're a disgusting pig—no one will ever

want you," and this can be distinguished from a voice that says, "I'm going to be good and control myself, and then maybe I will fit in."

8. *Ego state mapping*: In the previous examples, the first "voice" is most likely a perpetrator identified fight EP, whereas the second might more likely be a victim/child ego state or an ANP. Once the primary symptomatic ego states are identified, they can be "mapped" according to their internal relationships with one another, their "reasons" for being, their roles, their ages, and which traumatic experiences need to be processed. After the ego state system is mapped, trauma processing can proceed.

Phase II: Trauma Processing

In working primarily with bulimia and compulsive overeating, I have often found EMDR processing to be too intense for my clients, even with the extensive preparation I describe above. Consequently, I typically choose strategies other than those described earlier by Andrew. There are, however, three methods that I use that can complement EMDR and ease some of the intensity of the processing phase.

Sensorimotor sequencing (Ogden et al., 2006): This involves moving ego states that are frozen in fight, flight, submit, or freeze to somatically complete their truncated action using mindfulness and somatic tracking.

> Sensorimotor sequencing is a therapeutic technique that facilitates the completion of these involuntary bodily actions that are associated with traumatic memory. Instead of executing actions wilfully and voluntarily, sensorimotor sequencing entails slowly and mindfully tracking, detail by detail, the involuntary physical movements and sensations that pertain primarily to unresolved autonomic arousal, orienting, and defensive reactions. (Ogden et al., 2006, p. 253)

If a client is observed tightening a fist, the content of the memory is placed aside and the client's entire awareness is brought to observe the fist and to be open to what needs to happen (somatically) next. There is no "doing," but rather an allowing of the body to unfold and release what has been frozen by trauma. Empowering action is completed on a body level, thus making the return to the memory content more effective.

Rescue scripts, such as those found in Lifespan Integration (Pace,

2005) and other ego state or inner child work support trauma processing by inviting clients to imagine bringing their adult-selves into the scenes of the original trauma to rescue the child-selves, and to then bring them up to the present. This intervention serves the AIP function of bringing current information to an old, stuck, dysfunctional neural network and is often used as an interweave during EMDR trauma processing. This is similar to the strategy that Andrew calls "reparenting" and can also be effective in closing down an incomplete session.

Fractionated abreaction: A memory can be processed piecemeal, one part of the memory at a time. This is referred to as fractionated abreaction by Richard Kluft (Fine, 1993; Kluft, 1988, 1990) and its application to EMDR is described more fully by Sandra Paulsen (1995) and by Forgash and Copeley (2007). Kluft wrote, "Fractionated abreaction technique . . . allows for the recovery of experiences in discrete bits with a minimal experience of the associated affect, which is allowed to emerge later on" (1990, p. 528).

After a small part of the memory is processed, the work is interrupted and is discussed verbally, keeping affect at a minimal level, or the client is asked to shift attention to a positive resource.

Phase III: Integration

In addition to what others have mentioned about the final phase of treatment, I would add the following necessary considerations in supporting the client's return to an integrated life:

1. *Stopping at satiation:* Learning to stop eating when satisfied but not overly full often brings up issues of grief and letting go. This can be felt in the transference, as the letting up of the ED also may signal the termination phase of therapy, but for those with a presenting eating problem, it will first be felt in the "relationship" to the food. Using the food as a metaphor for other loss, and learning to say "good-bye" but also "I'll see you later when I'm hungry again" addresses the lack of object constancy or the irrational beliefs that often undergird an eating problem. I use the Future Template to help clients imaginally practice and reinforce stopping at satiation.

   Therapist: *Imagine the next time you are eating that you're paying attention to your body and feeling the sensations of being full. Part of you may want to continue eating. Your body is done. What thoughts about yourself arise?* (Negative Cognition [NC].) *What would you like to think about yourself and the situation?* (Positive Cognition [PC].) *What emotion? How big? Where is it? Go with that!* (BLS.)

You can practice this exercise targeting a future time when the client might be distressed and leaning toward bingeing.

2 *Integrating ego states:* Once the traumas held by the symptomatic ego states have been identified, they can be processed one trauma and/or ego state at a time. When the processing phase is completed, there is at times a natural internal movement toward an integration of the various ego states, particularly with moderately dissociated self-systems. At other times, it's not necessary at all, and all that is left to do is to make sure that cooperation continues, with every part being faithful to the new job descriptions. The therapist can also facilitate such a process by inviting all of the parts into one place, directing them all to look out of the eyes while BLS is applied, and while thinking of such supportive statements such as "We are one" or "We are I" (Paulson, 1995).

3. *Somatic integration into healthy functioning*: This involves guiding the client to somatically remove blocks to healthy attachments and functioning. Learning to literally "reach out," "hold on," and "let go" are examples of somatic skills taught during this phase. You may use these movements as interweaves during the second (current/present) and third (future) prongs of the EMDR Three-Pronged Protocol. Notice when your client is physically holding back or dysfunctionally holding on and coach her during processing through the movement she needs to be able to do.

Therapist: *As you feel that need to connect, what happens if you lift those arms out to that person? Do that right now, as we process, slowly, feeling each muscle. Just notice.*

Case Example

After several months of working on her compulsive overeating, Rita had gotten off her restrictive diets and was doing well with feeding herself when hungry. She had become more assertive and was liking herself a good deal more. She was still having trouble stopping when full and was continuing to binge, resulting in visible weight gain. I hung on to my anxiety as I watched her get larger, exploring as best I could what Rita might be trying to "show" me.

A turning point occurred when she felt safe enough to tell me her secret. "I have been bingeing in the strangest ways. Yesterday, after one of my patients left my office, I turned off the lights and reached into my desk drawer and pulled out a handful of Mars Bars. I was frantically ripping off the wrappers while stuffing them into my mouth. Some parts of the wrappers got into my mouth, and some of the chocolate got onto my face. I practically swallowed them whole while I cleaned off my face with a paper towel. When my next patient arrived, I turned on the lights and tried to act like every thing was fine."

This binge sounded like a violent reenactment of something to me. The turning off of the lights, the "cramming" into the face, the mess on the face, the secretive nature of the binge, and the shame and cover-up after her patient arrived all pointed to a disguised flashback; but to Rita it was a mystery. I stayed with her in that mystery until it could reveal itself to her. What we did know was that Rita felt enormous shame and had been keeping this behavior a secret up until now, even from herself.

As we slowed down binge after binge, Rita began retrieving dissociated memories of being sexually abused by her grandfather, who lived with her during ages 8–13. She remembered how she used to sit in her bedroom afterward and rock. She remembered imagining that her mother would see her rocking and come over and ask her what was wrong. She also remembered that her mother never did.

Rita continued the painstaking process of working through her compulsive eating and body image problems. We had uncovered dissociated abuse and had begun to make connections to dissociated ego states. We were then able to map Rita's ego state system and process the trauma, as it was now available to conscious awareness. Rita identified the child that had rocked on the couch, her fat self, and her thin self as being currently active in her adult life. The dissociated memories had belonged to the child, the thin self was a people-pleasing ANP of the personality developed at an early age, and the fat self had come to represent her newfound sense of empowerment, and who she was to become as she became more integrated.

The integrated Rita knew that she was safe, that she was strong, and that she could tolerate her feelings. She no longer needed to binge to contain either her disconnected states or the overwhelming affect that they contained.

The dialogue between Andrew and Judy continues. It is their hope that these pages will stimulate further exploration and exchange among clinicians who work with EDs, work that can be quite daunting. Those held hostage by the power of an ED deserve every bit of collaborative effort clinicians and caregivers can muster.

It takes a village to raise and to free a child, so that our clients can come home to who they truly are, their true identity.

REFERENCES

Bloom, C., Gitter, A., Gutwill, S., Kogel, L., & Zaphiropoulos, L. (1994). *Eating problems: A feminist psychoanalytic treatment model.* New York: Basic Books.

Farber, S. K. (2000). *When the body is the target: Self-harm, pain, and traumatic attachments.* Northvale, NJ: Jason Aronson.

Fine, C. G. (1993). A tactical integrationist perspective on the treatment of multiple personality disorder. In R. P. Kluft & C. G. Fine (Eds.), *Clinical perspectives on multiple personality disorder* (pp. 135–153). Washington, DC: American Psychiatric Press.

Forgash, C., & Copeley, M. (Eds.). (2007). *Healing the heart of trauma and dissociation with EMDR and ego state therapy.* New York: Springer.

Garner, D. (2004). *EDI-3.* Lutz, FL: Psychological Assessment Resources.

Greenwald, R. (2007). *EMDR: A trauma-informed treatment approach.* New York: Haworth Press.

Holmes, T., & Holmes, L. (2007). *Parts work: An illustrated guide to your inner life.* Kalamazoo, MI: Winged Heart Press.

Kinowski, K. (2003). *Put your best foot forward: An EMDR-related protocol for empowerment using visual and somatosensory priming of resource experiences.* Victoria, BC, Canada: Author.

Kluft, R. (1988). On treating the older patient with multiple personality: Race against time or make haste slowly? *American Journal of Clinical Hypnosis, 30,* 257–266.

Kluft, R. (1990). The fractionated abreaction technique. In D. C. Hammond (Ed.), *Handbook of hypnotic suggestions and metaphors* (pp. 527–528). New York: Norton.

Leeds, A. M. (2001, December). Principles and procedures for enhancing current functioning in complex posttraumatic stress disorder with EMDR resource development and installation. *EMDRIA Newsletter, Special Edition,* 4–11.

Lightstone, J. (2004). Compulsive eating and dissociation. *Journal of Trauma and Dissociation, 5*(4), 17–32.

Miller, A. (1984). *Thou shalt not be aware:* Society's *betrayal of the child* (American ed.) New York: Farrar, Straus, and Giroux.

Ogden, P., Minton, K., & Pain, C. (2006). *Trauma and the body: A sensorimotor approach to psychotherapy*. New York: Norton.

Omaha, J. (1998). *Chemotion and EMDR: An EMDR treatment protocol based upon a psychodynamic model for chemical dependency*. Paper presented at the EMDRIA Annual Conference, Baltimore, MD.

Pace, P. (2005). *Lifespan integration: Connecting ego states through time* (3rd ed.). Bellevue, NY: Author.

Paulsen, S. (1995). Eye movement desensitization and reprocessing: Its cautious use in the dissociative disorders. *Dissociation, 8*(1), 32–44.

Polster, E., & Polster, M. (1973). *Gestalt therapy integrated: Contours of theory and practice*. New York: Random House.

Schmidt, S. J. (2006). *The developmental needs meeting strategy: A model for healing adults with childhood attachment wounds*. San Antonio, TX: Author.

Schwartz, R. (1995). *Internal family systems therapy*. New York: Guilford Press.

Seubert, A. (2006). The power and peace of awareness. Retrieved April 26, 2008, from http://www.clearpathhealingarts.com/publications

Shapiro, F. (2001). *Eye movement desensitization and reprocessing: Basic principles, protocols, and procedures* (2nd ed.). New York: Guilford Press.

Steele, A. (2007). *Developing a secure self: An attachment-based approach to adult psychotherapy*. Gabriola, BC, Canada: Author.

van der Hart, O., Nijenhuis, E. R. S., & Steele, K. (2006). *The haunted self: Structural dissociation and the treatment of chronic traumatization*. New York: Norton.

van der Hart, O., Brown, P., & van der Kolk, B. A. (1989). Pierre Janet's treatment of post-traumatic stress. *Journal of Traumatic Stress, 2*(4), 379–395.

van der Kolk, B. A., McFarlane, A., & Weisaeth, L. (Eds.). (1996). *Traumatic stress: The effects of overwhelming experience on mind, body, and society*. New York: Guilford Press.

Watkins, J. G., & Watkins, H. H. (1997). *Ego states: Theory and therapy*. New York: Norton.

PERFORMANCE, COACHING, AND POSITIVE PSYCHOLOGY

Chapter 14

EMDR and Performance

David Grand

EMDR IS HIGHLY EFFECTIVE WITH ALL TYPES OF PERFORMANCE ISSUES, BIG or small, public or private. EMDR practitioners have done performance work with athletes, performing artists, graphic artists, writers, public speakers, business people, and test takers (Foster & Lendl, 1995). By widening the definition of EMDR performance work, we can include all clinical issues that impact behavior. Emotional suffering and confusing thoughts affect our behavior. Any "doing" is a form of performing: performing on a job, in a relationship, or behind the wheel of a car. We usually reserve "performance" for something that is done and evaluated in front of others, sometimes large groups. However, we are performing all day, every day, even when we serve as our own audience. And oftentimes we are our own harshest critics.

Clients who come for EMDR are often suffering from symptoms of trauma, depression, or anxiety (F. Shapiro, 2001). Pain drives people to pursue help when they cannot resolve or manage symptoms on their own. But people also seek help for impairment or loss of function. If they can't arrive at work on time or complete tasks when they're there, if they've broken down in their ability to parent their children, or if they're are too afraid of elevators to board one, their condition is a performance problem (Grand, 2002).

We tend to separate these daily performance problems from those of the golfer who freezes in front of a 3-foot putt, the actor who is terrified of auditions, or the stock trader who has become impulsive and veers off on a destructive losing streak. When we separate the daily, personal performance issues from what we generally view as performance situations, we are creating and perpetuating an artificial divide. Fear of public speaking is an anxiety condition and writer's block is an inability to do one's task that may have roots in earlier life trauma. When we see all performance situations under a wider umbrella, it illuminates the overall condition and expands our ability to understand and resolve them (Grand, 2001).

The central elements in EMDR performance work are *identifying the block, exploring and understanding it, targeting and processing it through* (Prongs 1 and 2) and then *bringing the new adaptive behavior to the future* (the third of the Three-Pronged Protocol).

Blocks come in many shapes and sizes and are often below the surface, dissociated far from consciousness. They reveal themselves in anxiety, avoidance, procrastination, inhibition, and confusion when we anticipate or confront a task. Comprehensive history-taking for performance clients needs to include a personal history and a performance history. The goal of the work has one particular challenge—measurable behavioral change. This change can be reflected by a client addressing a group feeling little or no anxiety, striking a tennis ball crisply and accurately, driving on the highway, or completing reports on time. While the treatment goals of feeling less symptomatic have wide latitude, performance goals are usually precise and measurable. This success/failure ratio can put pressure on therapists and can lead the client to unrealistic expectations of change in a specified time frame. These expectations often lead to client critical self-judgment, intensifying the vicious cycle of avoidance, performance anxiety, and failure (Grand, 2001).

THE 15 GUIDELINES FOR
EMDR PERFORMANCE AND
CREATIVITY ENHANCEMENT

During my 14 years of using EMDR with performance issues I have developed guidelines to understand and treat issues of performance with general clients and "performers" who perform given tasks in front of observers and spectators (Grand, 2002). Performance tasks are specific and assessed as success or failure by referees, reviewers, authorities, and audiences. Some performers are judged with immediacy on the field or stage. Some, like writers and painters, are evaluated long after their performance is over. Because of the observing audience, athletes, stage actors, singers, dancers, and stand-up comedians tend to have more performance anxiety. And writers, painters, sketch artists, and architects can have blocks to the point that their work can be interrupted or completely stopped. Anxiety feeds every block, which leads to more anxiety, which leads to more blocks.

The guidelines are a mixture of EMDR, performance work, and other good clinical practice. They give both background and foreground information and conceptualizations that translate into direct application.

1. Body Relaxation Is Essential for Performance Enhancement

All athletes and performers will tell you that they perform best when they are relaxed: feeling calm, safe, grounded, and focused (Greene, 2001). The technology and procedures of EMDR can be molded specifically to promote body relaxation quickly, especially before a performance (Grand, 2002). Bilateral Stimulation (BLS), especially when slow, gentle, and fluid, is parasympathetically deactivating, slowing down the heart and relaxing the muscles. The negative thoughts and anxiety held in the body can be counteracted by having clients shift their awareness from the part of the body that holds distress to the body resource (the place in the body where they feel calm, relaxed, safe, and grounded) (Levine, 1999). Combining gentle BLS with attention to the body resource, especially directly before a performance, can quickly foster deep body relaxation, promoting the zone experience and natural flow. I have taught clients to do this on their own by practicing it in session and have received impressive feedback of released anxiety and breakthrough performances. I say: *Notice where you feel the distress in your body. Now notice where you feel the most calm, relaxed, or grounded in your body. Holding that awareness, now loosely squeeze your left fist/right fist/left fist/right fist. Let your mind drift wherever it goes.* (After 30 to 60 seconds:) *Now notice where you feel most relaxed in your body. Resume the hand squeezing.* At the end I guide the client to return to the body distress and notice how it has changed.

2. A Balanced and Quiet Mind Is Necessary for Performance Enhancement

The ongoing presence of trauma and the resultant spikes of fight, flight, or freeze underlie performance anxiety (Scaer, 2001). Freeze is the most lasting and responsible for the most pernicious, enduring, and inexplicable performance problems. The brain is in the optimal state for performance when it is quiet and balanced. This is often experienced as being centered in the body and calm blankness, a Zen state, the quiet, attuned preparedness that is optimal when entering a performance (Kogan, 2002).

A few years ago I was involved in an fMRI (functional magnetic resonance imaging) study in which we did EMDR with trauma survivors right in the scanner, shooting brain images every minute. When examining the pictures, we observed that in the beginning, in the activated state, there was considerable brain activity (blood flow) distributed unevenly between both hemispheres. Sometimes the left hemisphere was more lit up; sometimes it was the right. By the end, when a 0 on the Subjective Units of Disturbance Score (SUDS) had been attained, the subject's brain appeared quiet and the activity was more evenly distributed between the hemispheres.

3. Positive Reinforcement Enhances and
Negative Reinforcement Impedes Performance

We were taught in Psych 101 that positive reinforcement is more effective for lasting change than negative reinforcement. Positive reinforcement, or support, promotes a sense of safety and activates the parasympathetic nervous system (PNS) and enhances performance. I have observed that negative reinforcement, or criticism and ridicule, activates the sympathetic nervous system (SNS) and inhibits performance (Sands, 2002). That explains why criticism, ridicule, and screaming by coaches, teachers, and directors usually fail, and why they get short-lived results. Negative reinforcement has a cumulative effect and has been an underlying factor in the distress of many who seek help. Conversely, patient encouragement paired with respectful corrections and critiques help in the short run and accumulate, paying off in the long run.

4. Performance Work Needs to Be
In-depth and Comprehensive

Provide attention to the person who gives the performance. Don't view the performance as separate from the person. EMDR works deeply and widely explores experiences from early life through the present (F. Shapiro, 2001). Comprehensive work that starts with the earliest performance trauma can sequentially process many buried, forgotten events that have shaped our performance selves. Narrowly focusing on the performance block will either not yield results or will prematurely open up the underlying issues, which can be disruptive to the person and the performance. Performance is best seen in the context of a person's entire life history, present experience, philosophy of being, and sense of self. Performance is limited when viewed solely in terms of conscious phenomena: sensory input and response, thought (beliefs) and reaction patterns (Grand, 2002).

5. Performance Is an Every-day, All-day Issue of Life

Shakespeare said, "All the world's a stage," and I would add, "And every day is a performance." We are performing all day, every day, and accordingly we serve as our own audience. Oftentimes we are our own harshest critics, especially if we have grown up with unfair criticism and humiliation at home and in school. Opening our eyes in the morning raises the curtain and closing them at night brings the curtain down. Choosing our clothes, putting on makeup, and shaving are all preparing to face the day and face the audience, whether real or imagined. Driving to work, interacting with others, and performing tasks all have strong performance components. Social anxiety and insecurity undermine our daily performance as therapists or athletes or singers. And performers also have to confront their own every daily life performance experiences as well as those they perform in front of others (Grand, 2002).

6. Performance Starts at the Beginning of Life

How we experience performance in the present is determined by the accumulation of all performance experiences dating back to birth (and intrauterine experience). How our parents and caretakers responded to our early performances of nursing, rolling over, smiling, cooing, walking, talking, and toilet training formed the foundation of our later performance experiences. Many parents respond with positive mirroring reflecting: "Look what Ellen did! She rolled over," or "Billy, what a wonderful picture!" However, some parents respond adversely with criticism or perhaps, more damagingly, by ignoring these early "performances." This can result in the accumulation of negative experiences, which develop into a performance sense of "I am bad" (shame) or "I don't matter" (invisibility). Early social experiences with young peers in nursery school and kindergarten are crucial aspects of our performance histories as they are the first structured group performance and evaluation experiences of our lives. EMDR processing of present-day performance anxiety often yields humiliation memories from kindergarten and elementary school that can be targeted and released (Grand, 2002).

7. Performance Anxiety Is a Dynamic Phenomenon

The disappointing early performance experiences of life (cited in Guideline 6) are the foundation of (mostly unconscious) negative self-beliefs and self-perceptions. For the performer, these inner perceptions are silently projected out into the minds of the audience and then erroneously experienced as on the outside. The performer believes the audience sees him as a failure and a fraud and reintrojects these projected negative self-beliefs. The performer's original anxiety and shame are then reinforced, further affecting both internal experience and actual performance, which completes this negative loop (Dunkel, 1989). The result is a downward spiral that can result in the avoidance and cessation of performing. I have worked with many actors, singers, and dancers with stage fright who have been caught in this vicious cycle. Clients found it extremely helpful for me to identify and educate them about this phenomenon. I identified these dynamics during the history-taking phase, which set the stage for identifying and processing the EMDR targets underlying this projection/reintrojection matrix. I frequently found it helpful to target the imagined picture of a critical and unforgiving audience. One actor caught in the grips of stage fright literally saw the audience as a firing squad. EMDR processing unearthed more memories of being judged, criticized, and rejected in childhood (Grand, 2001).

8. Dealing With the Critic on Our Shoulder

Delving deeper into the dynamics outlined in Guideline 7, I observed that the projected negative self-perceptions, beliefs, and self-statements (which we identify as Negative Cognitions [NCs]) can be traced back to distinct ego states, even in nondissociative clients. These are self-critical and/or attacking parts that can be called out, identified, and worked with directly. An interesting way of understanding the NC is to recognize it as the voice of critical self or the critic or "devil" on your shoulder ("You always mess things up," "You're not good enough," "You deserve to suffer"). These self-critical ego states are in need of healing as they usually feel powerless and disenfranchised, and are suffering. They also, when healed, have energy, assertiveness, and determination that can serve the overall self. Other selves (parental or spiritual) can be brought to the aggressive self for healing and direct protocol work. For those of you not familiar with parts or ego state work, or if you are and want to see how they can be used with EMDR, I recommend *Healing the Heart of Trauma and Dissociation with EMDR and Ego State Therapy* (Forgash & Copeley, 2007).

9. Secondary Gains and Identity Issues
Affect Performance

When you plumb "resistance" deeply enough you often find that it is emanating from an early and/or primal survival mechanism. However, you need to consider and evaluate performance blocks as expressions of secondary gains. Hidden secondary gains can play a role in avoidance and escape. The child or adolescent prodigy wonders, "Who am I performing for, my parent/coach/teacher or myself?" This issue continues into the adult life of the blocked prodigy who may be unknowingly rebelling or calling out for recognition or help. Prodigies are often abused in childhood, especially in relation to the development of their giftedness. In my practice I have worked with many gifted athletes and musicians who, as children, were physically and verbally humiliated by parents, teachers, and coaches when they made mistakes.

Celebrities are often treated as commodities by corporations and fans and accordingly experience being divorced from their true selves. "They don't like me for who I am, they like me for what I do." This deepens the traumatic experience of abandonment and exploitation and tends to intensify the performers' need to defensively rely on narcissistic and dissociative defenses. "Star-gazing" is a pitfall to assiduously avoid in conducting performance work with those in the public eye. The client needs to know that you both are attuned to the loss of their true self and are committed to addressing and not repeating it in the work together. Although the presenting problem is behavioral and the ultimate outcome of the treatment will be assessed in these terms, the behavior has to be reintegrated into the self-experience. The question, "What does my performance mean to me?" naturally flows to the larger ones, "Who am I?" and, "What do I want out of my life?" These serve as valuable EMDR targets and can reveal repeated wounding experiences in childhood and adulthood (Grand, 2002).

10. Educating Our Performance Clients Is Necessary

As with all EMDR work, it is essential to educate the client about the process. With more education, the client can feel choice, control, and safety. Performance clients need to know that it will usually be necessary to explore and work with both their personal history and performance history. They need to know that if their performance block or anxiety is deeply entrenched and started in childhood trauma or attachment, the therapy will mean personal and affective exposure (to themselves and you) (Grand, 2002).

11. Don't Forget the Follow-up

In performance work, the three most important things are follow-up, follow-up, and more follow-up. A shift or reprocessing in a therapy session is no guarantee of improved performance. The follow-up session(s) gives the chance to see what has shifted and what hasn't. My first performance work painfully illustrates this rule. A high school tennis coach brought his male doubles team to me. Individually they were successful but they couldn't transition effectively to playing together: They lost match after match. I did EMDR performance work with each player individually and then I worked with them together. We targeted badly lost matches, negative thoughts, anxiety, and lost confidence. I was startled at how quickly and efficiently they processed through trauma after trauma, loss after loss. We finished by installing the Future Template of anticipated successful matches. Even I emerged feeling like a real winner. But I forgot one crucial detail. I didn't educate the coach or the players up front that follow-up is crucial and necessary. And I didn't educate them, especially the coach, that performance work is unpredictable and sometimes the immediate result can be turmoil before the results and resolution set in. So here's what happened. The doubles team went out and played as poorly as ever—but they felt relaxed and handled the loss well. Needless to say, the coach never brought them back.

Follow-up sessions provide the opportunity to install and deepen the positive changes that occurred in and after the previous session (a reality template similar to the Positive Cognition [PC]). Then, unshifted targets or remaining negative experiences can be targeted and processed with EMDR. Often as sessions proceed, the positive experiences accumulate and expand and the negative ones diminish. Sometimes, in-office sessions are not enough to accomplish the performance goals. In these cases in vivo work, on-site during practices or before performances, can make all the difference in the performance world. It is best when you are present, but if that is not possible, cell phone contact can be a reasonable substitute.

There can be value in working simultaneously with two parallel targets and protocols, one present day and behavioral, the other historical and underpinning the performance inhibition. Back and forth shifting between these protocols will oftentimes accomplish synergistic movement in both. I treated a golfer who froze at the top of his swing on tee shots, unable to move the club off his shoulders. During processing he remembered being beaned at the plate while playing high school baseball. His frozen stance was the same as the position he couldn't release at the tee. This incident occurred the day before the pro scouts came to watch his team. He was one of the players they were coming to observe. The next day he tried to hide the fact that he suffered a concussion and collapsed during pregame warmups, knocking him out of the lineup. The scouts never came back. For the golfer his trauma extended beyond the beaning and fixated on the lost opportunity. We processed each of the two separate targets (the frozen swing and the beaning and the lost opportunity), spending at first 10 minutes on one before switching to 10 minutes on the other. As we continued, progressively less time was spent on each target until we shifted back and forth every 30 seconds. This approach resulted in a synergistic increase of the power and speed of the EMDR processing and a more effective resolution his performance block (Grand, 2002).

12. Always Keep to the Contract

Always remember that the goal, unless changed by mutual consent, is the client's definition of behavioral improvement. It is a mistake to let performance work evolve into primarily personal work without an ex-plicitly new contract with the client. Performance clients need to be guided and supported to determine when they have satisfactorily met their original goals and more toward termination, even if more per-sonal work remains to be accomplished (Grand, 2002).

13. Sports Injuries Are Neglected Traumas

Sports injuries, especially in childhood and adolescence, often underlie later performance anxiety or inhibition. The most pernicious end re-sults of injury-derived performance problems are called the "Yips." This dreaded condition (actually feared to be contagious by some ath-letes) is derived from the golfing greens where the players attempting a short putt (usually 4 feet or less) jerk or freeze their wrists reflexively and miss badly. Most people are able to shake off this random occur-rence as an aberration. However, by the second or third time this oc-curs, it spooks the vulnerable golfer. And when it becomes habitual it can end the career of even top pros, including Ben Hogan. In every "Yips" case I've treated with EMDR, a series of earlier sports injuries has emerged. Take Jim, who found he was freezing at the most un-likely position—the apex of the backswing on his tee shot. We targeted this image, the NC of "Watch Out!" and the feeling of lock in his wrists and pain in the side of his head. While wearing headphones listening to one of the BioLateral CDs, I had Jim stand in the afflicted position. He immediately flashed back to getting beaned at the plate while play-ing high school baseball. His frozen stance at the plate mirrored this frozen swing while attempting to hit a drive. Once this was processed through, another memory emerged of being blindsided while playing football. Some earlier family issues surfaced and released and Jim was able to swing his club fluidly. The "Yips" not only affects athletes in all sports, it can cripple surgeons, painters, electricians, and others doing technically precise jobs. Dancers, singers, and actors are injured in practice and onstage more than you know, leading to "Yip-like" freez-ing onstage.

An athlete or performer recovering from injury or surgery often will suffer from fear of reinjury and loss of confidence in the efficacy of their body integrity. This "fear of reoccurrence" trauma symptom is very responsive to EMDR, which can release the negative imagery and thinking that accompanies the fear, allowing the client to confidently return to the field and stage (Grand, 2002).

14. Both Adaptive and Dysfunctional
Dissociation Affect Performance

Performance in front of an audience, whether on the sports field or acting stage, requires you to be able to "adaptively dissociate" or "creatively dissociate." Dissociation is the only way that a hitter can connect with a darting, spinning ball traveling at 95 mph or a stage actor can morph into another personality under the scrutiny of screaming fans and demanding audiences and critics. The problem arises when adaptive and creative dissociation is infiltrated by trauma-driven dissociation. There is a thin line between these two states of mind. The triggering of traumatic dissociation leads to the perception of imminent threat, mental and physical hyperactivation or hypoactivation, muscle tensing, reflexive freezing, the impulse to escape, and depersonalization and derealization (Scaer, 2005). This is usually the cause of most intractable performance anxiety and inhibition as well as inexplicable inabilities to perform tasks that would ordinarily be simple. And of course these phenomena come from earlier, profound trauma, often in the same endeavor. Dissociation, especially in its severest forms, has to be correctly diagnosed and treated before its performance components can effectively addressed. You'll see this in the example of Maria the singer (below) (Grand, 2002).

15. Performance Anxiety Is
Also Clinical Anxiety

Many performance experts separate out performance anxiety from the clinical anxiety we treat in our offices every day. Some actually split the treatment between the performance expert and a separate psychotherapist (Foster & Lendl, 1995). Performance anxiety flows from the same stream of any other condition on the anxiety spectrum. That is why it is essential to take a full clinical history as well as performance history with our performance clients. You nearly always find a family history of anxiety and significant trauma in and out of the realm of performance with these individuals. Ask enough questions and you will likely find that anxiety expresses itself in nonperformance areas of the person's life. When we explore performance anxiety, we may find a wide and complex variety of other anxieties. Posttraumatic stress disorder (PTSD) symptoms, including traumatic dissociation, often present as performance anxiety and blocks. I have often found performance clients exhibiting social phobia, panic disorders, and obsessive-compulsive disorder (OCD). Failures in performance work result when these conditions are not properly diagnosed and treated. Psychopharmacological evaluation is often required for performance clients. Medication is often the fulcrum between their success and failure (Grand, 2002).

Case Example: Maria: Audition Anxiety

The story of my former client Maria, a gifted, trained singer, reflects how debilitating performance anxiety around auditioning can be intertwined with personal and performance history. In this case illustration I will highlight where the 15 guidelines directly apply. My work with Maria illustrates how EMDR can be a powerful tool for untangling both the underlying issues and the performance struggles. Maria was referred to me by a friend of hers, another singer. Maria had never seen a therapist before and didn't know what to expect from the first session. She came to see me 3 years after an audition meltdown; she hadn't auditioned or performed since the meltdown. Maria was a gifted singer both of opera and popular music. She grew up in a musical family, her mother an opera singer, her father a composer, and her older brother a concert violinist. She started taking voice training at age 6. By 7 she was performing at opera recitals. She never liked auditions, but she loved to perform, so she tolerated her mild audition anxiety. In her early 20s she tried out for the lead in a local musical, which she had been dying to play all her life. Maria overprepared, went in with minimal anxiety, and gave the best audition of her life. She knew she had scored the role until she discovered it went to her high school rival who hadn't given half the audition she had. Maria was inconsolable. When the play was performed she couldn't bring herself to attend. She was ashamed of her avoidance but found it too painful to watch someone else doing "her" role, especially knowing she could have done it better.

The following season Maria auditioned again for the same theater company. The stakes were not so high because she was going for a secondary role in a musical that didn't excite her. She prepared, but without her usual zest. Waiting to go in, she saw her rival who again was trying out for the lead. Maria smiled faintly at her and wished her good luck. When it was Maria's turn to audition she started to feel a burning in her chest. She thought it might be heartburn from a late lunch or too much coffee. Then her breathing started to become labored and her neck tightened up. An experienced performer, Maria covered her discomfort with a smile and proceeded to sing a tune from the show. She strained to reach the upper octaves and started to panic. "What is happening to me?" flashed through her mind. Maria white-knuckled her way through the audition and was still better than most of the other singers. She even got the part. But she was so thrown by the experience that she started to doubt herself even though she acquitted herself nicely in the show.

A few months later Maria was asked to audition for a church choir. She enjoyed these performances and agreed. The night before the audition she had a nightmare that she was auditioning and lost her voice. She then froze when the people she was auditioning for asked her what had occurred. Maria woke in a panic, drenched in sweat. She started to dread the audition, even though it wasn't much of a challenge for her. As the day neared she felt like she was facing her execution. When she finally went up her knees and hands were shaking visibly. Maria started singing the aria; her voice trembled and she struggled with the key (see Guideline 14—dissociation). Halfway through she stopped and walked off humiliated, crying hysterically. The audition was actually pro forma as the choirmaster knew her work and had already decided to invite her to join. Maria refused. She did not attempt another audition for 3 years, passing up opportunities she desired. She continued to practice at home hours a day, where she sang beautifully. But she was terrified of a repeat performance. It wasn't until I took Maria's personal history in her first two sessions that the source of her audition anxiety was revealed. She was born in South America and her family moved to the United States when she was 11. This was primarily to give Maria's brother, who had become a violin virtuoso, a chance to study and perform at the highest levels. While her brother flourished, the transition was difficult for Maria. She left behind her friends and beloved music teacher (see Guideline 9—secondary gains). Everything in her new country was different; the people, the music, the smells, the food, and most of all the language. In school she became shy and self-conscious. She felt more comfortable hiding in the back of the classroom. When called on, she often couldn't find the proper words and her teacher humiliated her repeatedly by marching her to the front of the class to give the answer. She stood there speechless while her classmates laughed at her. To make things worse, Maria's first voice coach in her new country was extremely strict. Every time Maria made a mistake the coach would suddenly slam her hand down on the table, sending a shock wave through Maria's body. She quickly learned to avoid any mistakes (see Guideline 3—positive/negative reinforcement). But for the next year she had nightmares almost every night. Maria loved singing opera, but she also was drawn to both the traditional music of her homeland and the popular music of her new country. These were frowned upon by her parents, who wanted her to maintain her focus on classical music and follow her brother's success. In her room at night she secretly sang her favorite popular songs into her pillow.

Although close with her brother, her parents often compared the two of them. Maria knew she was gifted, but felt inadequate compared to her brother's genius and amazing ability to practice 5-plus hours a day. Secretly she fantasized besting him and wresting away the unconditional approval of her parents she felt he had. But these thoughts also made her feel guilty and she viewed herself as bad (Guideline 9— secondary gain).

At age 15 Maria developed pneumonia. She walked around with it for weeks, coughing and wheezing. It quickly advanced to a crisis when she couldn't breathe and was rushed to the hospital. The needed medical care saved her but the recovery period was lengthy. All this time she worried about the damage she had done to her vocal cords, and she was told not to sing until fully recovered. She was afraid her voice was impaired or, worse yet, lost. When Maria was ready to try it out she felt anxiety burn in her chest before she attempted to sing. When a beautiful song emerged unaffected she was relieved and the anxiety dissipated (see Guideline 13—injuries).

At age 20 Maria was involved in a serious car accident. She was being driven home from a date with a young man when the car skidded off a country road. She was uninjured but he suffered cracked ribs and a punctured lung. It took 2 hours for help to arrive. Maria was afraid to leave to find assistance, fearing he would pass out or worse. She felt trapped and alarmed as his breathing was labored. She stood by the side of the road with her hands and knees shaking. Finally help arrived and he was taken to the hospital, where he recovered. Maria noticed it was the same facility that she had been brought to when she had pneumonia.

Maria was resilient and determined. But when, years later, she lost out on the coveted leading role she felt she had earned in audition, she was unprepared to understand her emotional and bodily reactions.

She was clueless regarding where these triggered reactions came from, which made the problem worse. But Maria was only reexperiencing her life history of larger and smaller traumas that accumulated silently and emerged in the audition experience. The emotional and physical responses in her disastrous auditions then became conditioned and associated to the entire audition process itself, leading to a series of failures and losses. But in truth, it had been her life history that led up to the outbreak of the audition anxiety (see Guideline 6—performance history).

In the third session, after completing the history taking, treatment planning, and preparation, we were ready to start EMDR targeting and processing. The choice of first target is significant in all EMDR treatment, especially performance work. The traditional EMDR approach is to start with the first, worst, or most recent incident, but with performance work the choice can be either a performance or personal incident. I leave the selection up to the client, which can be a revealing projective approach. I asked Maria what she wanted to target first regarding her struggles with auditioning and she responded, "The nightmare." This was a reference to the dream the night before the fateful audition she had recounted during the history taking.

I asked, *"What image comes to you from the nightmare?"* She answered, "I am in the church standing in front of the choirmaster and her assistant. I can't creak out a word. They are looking at me like I am crazy." *"Can you hear or smell anything?"* She responded, "I can smell the wood and I hear some murmuring in the background." Oftentimes in EMDR so much attention is given to the images that the other senses are neglected. Sound, smell, and taste hold encoded memory traces not found in images. These four senses are also visceral pathways into the deeper brain and body and as such promote meaningful nonverbal processing. And performers rely heavily on their senses to both act and react.

"What negative, distorted thoughts or words come to you? Maria replied, "It's over." Succinct words and phrases can also be overlooked potent contributors to an effectively developed EMDR protocol. I then asked, *"What would you like to believe about yourself?"* and she answered right away, "I can!" NCs and PCs that do not overtly match, like "It's over" and "I can," oftentimes can be more directly associated than they appear at first glance. *"How true does 'I can' feel to you if 1 is totally false and 7 feels totally true?"* Maria quietly said, "2."

I proceeded, *"If you hold the image and the smells and sounds in the*

church together with the words 'It's over,' what emotions come to you now?"
"Terror, it's still painful to think about," she replied. I continued, *"How intense is the terror if 10 is the worst and 0 is none?"* Her answer was "9." When I asked where she felt the distress in her body she answered, "My chest is burning, it's hard to breathe, and my neck is tense." In my opinion it is no accident that the body sensation is the last part of the EMDR protocol setup before the processing begins. Everything that leads up to locating the body experience serves the purpose of cumulatively activating and being held in the body. Although others disagree, I see EMDR as a somatically oriented therapy and that a great deal of its success rests therein. Even the bilateral eye, sound, and tactile activations that are foundational to EMDR are all direct body activators (see Guideline 1 on body relaxation).

I guided Maria to track my fingers moving slowly left and right and to observe inside wherever things went for her. I find slower Eye Movements (EMs) are helpful with high-distress clients, especially when targeting performance anxiety. I have found it promotes processing with a simultaneous calming, parasympathetic quality. It also can avoid the retraumatization that I've seen occur when the anxiety spikes and/or continues for too long (Guideline 1 again).

In the first set Maria saw the nightmare replaying over and over. After a few more sets the dream faded away and the processing took off. Maria said in wonderment, "It's like watching a film with all the sequences spliced together randomly. But then again, it's really not that random." She described how first she was back in South America, then on the stage performing, then back in the hospital with pneumonia, then on to the painful audition, then to the classroom humiliation, then to watching her competitor get the role she coveted, followed by envious memories of watching her brother perform, then the car accident, and finally back to the audition and actually feeling her knees shake as she recalled it. After this rapid-fire processing, things slowed and scenes of the audition meltdown began to replay over and over. "I'm stuck," Maria groaned. I asked, *"Where do you feel stuck in your body?"* and she croaked, "It's all in my throat. I can't get it out." Regrounding clients in their body sensation of the moment can deepen and open up the processing and is very effective with performers who rely so much on their bodies. I restarted the gentle, flowing EMs and encouraged Maria to hang in there. I reassured, *"Give yourself all the time and space you need and see what happens."* This kind of guidance is a remarkable antidote for stuckness and looping in all clients as it takes the performance pressure off not only the client but the therapist. The guidance worked and after a short while Maria started deeply sobbing, reflecting on everything she had lost in her life, especially the last 3 years of not being able to perform. When Maria said, "I feel so sad!" I again went for body regrounding by asking for the location of the sadness. She replied, "My heart." For clients healing from trauma and performers recovering from performance anxiety, the emergence of sadness is often a turning point in the process. The onset of grieving is a stage that emerges when the traumatic anxiety ebbs and the realization of the loss flows. This sadness can then be processed, especially where it is held deep in the body, subsequently leading to the next phase of healing.

We proceeded for a long set of EMs and suddenly Maria offered with surprise, "My throat is clear." I asked her to be aware of the clear feeling in her throat and see what happens. In EMDR we are used to targeting distress in the body and miss the opportunity to capitalize on processing in a spontaneously emerging positive body sensation or body resource. This is particularly powerful when the site of the body resource was the original container of the body distress (Guideline 1).

After a series of sets that resulted in deepening relaxation and positive imagery, I asked Maria to bring up the nightmare. She replied, "I can't. It's gone." I decided to check out the memory of the worst part of her final audition, which had followed the day after the nightmare. The dream and the audition meltdown were tied so closely together that I decided to proceed without setting up a new EMDR protocol. I also wanted to keep the process moving, as flow is so important to performers. When I asked about the audition image Maria reported, "It's faint now. It's about a 2. My knees are shaking a bit." Holding the image, the NC "It's over," and body sensation together, we resumed the EMs. The residual distress released in another 5 minutes of processing. Maria finished with, "I can go on." Referencing back to the original PC, I asked, *"How true does that feel to you now, from 1 to 7?"* She replied, "7," before I could finish the question. I again went for grounding the PC in the body, which deepens its hold further. *"Where do you feel that 7 in your body?"* and Maria replied, "All over," with a smile. I guided, *"Just go with that, as well as the feeling of the smile on your face."* It can be valuable to install and deepen the positive that reflects in facial expressions of joy and relief (Guidelines 1 and 2).

The initial process of healing significant performance anxiety is not always this rapid, especially with performers with serious panic disorders or significant histories of childhood abuse (Guideline 6—history). However, I have found that people who are gifted artists or elite athletes have amazing neurophysiological pathways, both by birth and by development, that can lead to lightning-fast processing. But don't be fooled into believing that the healing and resolution in the office leads to the same on the stage or in the athletic arena. There can be miles of difference in between the two scenarios. In Maria's case, her remarkable initial experience was not enough to fully resolve her performance anxiety (Guideline 11—follow-up). But it had begun the process of releasing her from the frozen traumas of her past in addition to her re-traumatizing audition experiences. Maria needed an additional five 90-minute sessions of EMDR during which we specifically targeted her issues with her parents, her sibling rivalry, the wrenching move to the United States and its dislocation of culture and language, her pneumonia, and the vicarious traumatization during her car accident. I introduced the use of the BioLateral sound CDs that I have produced, which allowed Maria to close her eyes and have longer sets, eventually leading to continuous stimulation. Some in the EMDR field warn against clients processing with their eyes closed, believing that it can promote dissociation and loss of present-moment orientation. I have never found that to be true; in Maria's case, and those of others, I have observed it deepen and accelerate the processing. The CDs use healing music and nature sounds that phase-shift gently. This, as with slower EMs, supports parasympathetic (calm, grounded, and resourced) processing, which is helpful with performance anxiety and blocks (Guidelines 1 and 2). The same is true with continuous stimulation when the sets are determined by the client going from inside to outside, with sound moving from foreground to background.

During these sessions, Maria experienced other traumatic events emerging from the shadows and then processing through. But her work wasn't completed at this point. As with most performance work, Maria needed to take the work out of the office and back to the stage for in vivo exposure, in order for her to fully process and release her trauma and anxiety. The primary obstacle for Maria was her remaining avoidance, which was still hard to shake, and the accompanying "what ifs" that had taken on a life of their own. It is remarkable how people overcoming performance struggles, even when healed from the underlying issues and the accompanying anxiety, will often be stuck in reflexive avoidance, preventing them from completing their last step of recovery (Guideline 15—performance anxiety is clinical anxiety). So we did a session that targeted this avoidance using the Future Template of anticipation of an audition. However, this would not have led to a resolution without following up with an actual tryout experience. This essential ingredient was accomplished when Maria arranged for another audition with the same church choir with which her anxiety and freeze had emerged.

We had a session 1 hour before her audition using BLS (slow EMS and sound) combined with body resourcing to help engender a sense of calm and confidence. Maria called me after the audition and said she performed wonderfully. She was so thrilled by her anxiety-free tryout that she forgot to tell me the outcome. When I pointed this out, she realized that her true victory was not the success as much as the knowledge that she had done best she could. Maria had regained the ability to evaluate herself without distortion and to rely on her own self-perception. This transcended the conquering of her performance anxiety as she had developed an honest, mature sense of self. Maria is back to singing and is able to audition without anxiety. She shared with me that the healing of painful experiences from earlier in her life was an unexpected bonus that had changed her in ways far beyond her recovery from audition anxiety.

CONCLUSION

Performance is an ever-present issue for us as EMDR therapists. As an EMDR Trainer and Facilitator I have marveled at the ubiquity and tenacity of performance anxiety found in students at the trainings and novice practitioners in consultation. Learning the varied and complex EMDR procedures and protocols can be daunting, reawakening in the experienced therapist school days that they prefer to keep behind them. EMDR generates performance anxiety in not only new but experienced EMDR therapists because EMDR magnetizes and reveals trauma unexpectedly and frequently. We all have been taken off-guard by the processing experiences or individuals who have been egregiously and repeatedly traumatized and abused in childhood. Severe dissociation can hide from the Dissociative Experiences Scale and extensive history-taking and can and will emerge in EMDR clients, even those seeking our help for performance difficulties. Many clinicians receive EMDR treatment to clear the performance anxiety tied to vicarious traumatization.

EMDR performance work is not as glamorous as many of us fanta-size it to be. It actually can be more challenging than regular EMDR work because success and failure are not judged simply by whether the client feels better. They are assessed by the gained or improved ca-pacity to perform specific tasks, whether on the tennis court or on the ballet stage. Thus we can feel the same harsh glare of evaluation on us that our performance clients have to regularly face.

Don't take this as discouragement. Performance work, especially when accelerated by the power of EMDR, is both exciting and moving. It gives us the vicarious thrill of hearing about and reliving with them the performer's highs and lows. And it can be deeply moving to ex-plore giftedness and the performer's drive to inspire others by sharing it with them. EMDR and performance—I recommend it.

The following are a few of my sayings that resonate with the perfor-mance experience:

"Perfectionists fail 100% of the time."

"We fear change yet we carry it in our pocket."

"Don't be afraid to risk healing, be afraid to not risk healing."

"The brain is always observing itself and re-creating itself in invention and art."

"The unconscious writer is expressed by the unconscious actor to the unconscious audience."

"Our fear of the future exists in the present and comes from the past."

"Shift your attention from the goal to the obstacles to the goal."

"Perseverance is a race where the winners are those who are still run-ning when all others have dropped out."

"The road to success is littered with failure."

REFERENCES

Dunkel, S. E. (1989). *The audition process: Anxiety management and coping strategies.* New York: Pendragon Press.

Forgash, C., & Copeley, M. (Eds.). (2007). *Healing the heart of trauma and dis-sociation with EMDR and ego state therapy.* New York: Springer.

Foster, S., & Lendl, J. (1995). Eye movement desensitization and reprocessing: Initial applications for enhancing performance in athletes. *Journal of Applied Sport Psychology, 7*(Suppl.), 63.

Grand, D. (2001). *Emotional healing at warp speed: The power of EMDR.* New York: Harmony Books.

Grand, D. (2002). *Natural flow EMDR,* Seminar given through EMDRIA, San Diego, CA.

Greene, D. (2001). *Audition success: An Olympic sports psychologist teaches performing artists how to win.* New York: Routledge.

Kogan, N. (2002). Careers in the performing arts: A psychological perspective. *Creativity Research Journal, 14*(1), 1–16.

Levine, P. (1999). *Healing trauma restoring the wisdom of the body.* Juilliard Performance Guides No. 3. New York: Pendragon Press.

Sands, R. (2002, October). The power of the parasympathetic nervous system. *Stress News, 14*(4), 2–12.

Scaer, R. (2001). *The body bears the burden: Trauma, dissociation, and disease.* Binghamton, NY: Haworth Press.

Scaer, R. (2005). *The trauma spectrum, hidden wounds and human resiliency.* New York: Norton.

Shapiro, F. (2001). *Eye movement desensitization and reprocessing: Basic principles, protocols, and procedures* (2nd ed.). New York: Guilford Press.

Chapter 15

EMDR and Positive Psychology

Ann Marie McKelvey

POSITIVE PSYCHOLOGY IS AN EMPIRICALLY BASED FIELD OF STUDY THAT involves the research of meaning, happiness, and "the good life" as stand-alone measures without equating them to the absence of stress or disorder. It has roots in Humanistic Psychology, which derives, in part, from the thinking of Plato and Aristotle.

As a Positive Psychology Coach Clinician and EMDR Consultant, my passion is contributing to the lives of my clients and students by discovering what they need in order to move forward. Together my clients and I let go of their story, create a view that is much larger, and step into that view. We move the action forward with EMDR and related techniques. The energy shifts. The mind and body adapt. Transformation occurs. Then we cycle through again, establishing EMDR as a strong presence in the session.

HAVE YOU EVER WONDERED WHY . . .

. . . the *DSM-IV* is for mental health, yet the emphasis is mental disorders? How is it that as clinicians we are focused on healing pathology rather than focused on virtues, positive emotions, and positive institutions?

Once elected the president of the American Psychological Association in 1998, Dr. Marty Seligman asked his colleagues for help to incorporate true mental health into the field of psychology. It was at this point that Positive Psychology emerged as a science studying and researching Signature Strengths and virtues, positive emotions and characteristics, as well as robust organizational systems. The intention was and continues to be to increase happiness in individuals and in organizations. Positive Psychology helps individuals define and live a life worth living.

Because of the vast amount of documented research, books, and college courses now available to mental health practitioners on Positive Psychology, I will be sharing the best of the interventions and applications that I utilize with EMDR. I encourage you to peruse the bibliography at the end of this chapter for books and Web sites that will further your intellectual knowledge in this ever-deepening field.

As you investigate, remember the words of Positive Psychologist Dr. Christopher Petersen in describing the premise of Positive Psychology: "that human goodness and excellence are as authentic as human flaws and inadequacies" (2006, page 11).

THE DYNAMIC DUO: EMDR AND POSITIVE PSYCHOLOGY

Singing Image of Fire by Kukai
A hand moves, and the fire's whirling takes different shapes;
All things change when we do.
The first word, "Ah," blossoms into all others.
Each of them is true.
—(Mitchell, 1993)

Why are EMDR and Positive Psychology emerging as the Dynamic Duo? Because Positive Psychology is built into the EMDR Standard Protocol. Remember Phase Three? Remember the term "Positive Cognition"? The PC is developed, then measured through the Validity of Cognition (VOC) to create a baseline. Remember Phase Five? The PC is installed. The VOC is used again during Phase Five to determine if the measurement has increased. If not, added cycles of Bilateral Stimulation (BLS) are applied to further move the client's experience into "the good life." Remember Adaptive Processing? Every EMDR training stipulates that humans have within them the power to heal. What could be more "positive" than that?

Highly functioning individuals want the most efficient and sustainable means to confidently reinvent and update themselves in this ran-

domly changing world. They have specific agendas to grow into and
live. They want the expertise of the EMDR clinician with Positive Psychology interventions and applications. How do I know this? Because I
recently polled over 100 current and former meditation students and
coaching clients, asking this question: "What is your next step in transformational growth?" Although the wording of the responses varied,
the content of the agenda remained intact: "I want to alleviate my suffering and move forward into a meaningful life while alleviating the
suffering of others."

This response is from a demographic profile of highly functioning
and resilient individuals. A client requiring deep-rooted therapeutic
growth to heal significant emotional wounding would not deliver this
response. However, as this client heals, strengths are unburied and can
be installed through EMDR. (Please see "Using the VIA [Values in Ac-
tion] Signature Strengths" below.)

EMDR and Positive Psychology build a solid foundation to increase
happiness and experience "the Good Life." A Positive Psychology therapist untangles the blocking "shoulds" that stand in the way of a client
living robustly in this present moment. The empowered client then creates and moves forward with future plans and goals.

EMDR AND POSITIVE
PSYCHOLOGY APPLICATIONS

I utilize Positive Psychology applications in almost every session. Applications give me a great deal of insight into my clients, especially in their
areas of strength. In Phase One of the Standard Protocol, I do an intake
with each client. In the beginning of our coaching relationship I am also
interested in who they are now. How do they live their lives? What gives
them passion? Where do they want to go? What is alive in them?

Here are eight Positive Psychology applications. Some utilize EMDR's
protocol. Some use pieces of the EMDR protocol, including BLS and Resource Installation. The focus is on applications for the VIA Signature
Strengths, the Signature Strength Gratitude, and the Pillars Exercise.

USING THE VIA SIGNATURE STRENGTHS

The three steps in applying the VIA Signature Strengths are: (a) Take
the VIA Signature Strengths assessment; (b) identify top five Signature

Strengths; and (c) use the EMDR Standard Protocol to incorporate the Signature Strengths more consciously in daily life (Peterson & Seligman, 2004).

Step 1: Take the VIA Signature
Strengths Questionnaire

As a student of Dr. Marty Seligman's Vanguard Authentic Happiness class in 2003, one of my first homework assignments was to complete the online VIA Signature Strengths questionnaire at www.authentichappiness.org. Early one Saturday morning I carved out 40 minutes to complete the 240 questions. To this day the questionnaire results are helpful to me personally and professionally. Because of the usefulness of the strengths in my own life, I encourage new clients to sit down and answer the questions to identify their top five Signature Strengths.

Dr. Marty Seligman and Dr. Chris Peterson developed the questionnaire with the initial inspiration coming from the Gallop Organization's StrengthsFinder. If you would like to read about the formation, utilization, and research of the VIA Signature Strengths, sit down for a few hours with their book *Character Strengths and Virtues* (Peterson & Seligman, 2004). The 800 pages are a guidebook for living the good life.

This invaluable Positive Psychology assessment tool helps both coaches and clients determine their top Signature Strengths. The information is documented and utilized through the University of Pennsylvania in their research studies. More than 750,000 people worldwide have taken the VIA Signature Strengths questionnaire.

Below are the dimensions and subdimensions of the 24 Signature Strengths or positive traits. Because Positive Psychology is such a new field and the Signature Strengths are continually being evaluated and tweaked to best accommodate current research, I suggest that all my clients retake the assessment every few years.

As you read the categories, think about what your own top five strengths might be. Better yet, go to authentichappiness.org (sponsored by the University of Pennsylvania) with 40 minutes to spare and answer the questions. After completing the questionnaire you will receive your top strengths. Below is a quick outline of the Signature Strengths with brief definitions.

Strengths of Wisdom and Knowledge

1. *Creativity (Originality, Ingenuity):* Thinking of novel and productive ways to conceptualize and do things.
2. *Curiosity (Interest, Novelty-Seeking, Openness to Experience):* Taking an interest in ongoing experiences for their own sake; exploring and discovering.
3. *Open-mindedness (Judgment, Critical Thinking):* Thinking things through and examining them from all sides; weighing all evidence fairly.
4. *Love of Learning:* Mastering new skills, topics, and bodies of knowledge, whether on one's own or formally.
5. *Perspective (Wisdom):* Being able to provide wise counsel to others; having ways of looking at the world that make sense to oneself and to other people.

Strengths of Courage

6. *Bravery (Valor):* Not shrinking from threat, challenge, difficulty, or pain; acting on convictions, even if unpopular.
7. *Persistence (Perseverance, Industriousness):* Finishing what one starts; persisting in a course of action in spite of obstacles.
8. *Integrity (Authenticity, Honesty):* Presenting oneself in a genuine way; taking responsibility for one's feeling and actions.
9. *Vitality (Zest, Enthusiasm, Vigor, Energy):* Approaching life with excitement and energy; feeling alive and activated.

Strengths of Humanity

10. *Love:* Valuing close relations with others, in particular those in which sharing and caring are reciprocated.
11. *Kindness (Generosity, Nurturance, Care, Compassion, Altruistic Love, "Niceness"):* Doing favors and good deeds for others.
12. *Social Intelligence (Emotional Intelligence, Personal Intelligence):* Being aware of the motives and feelings of other people and oneself.

Strengths of Justice

13. *Citizenship (Social Responsibility, Loyalty, Teamwork):* Working well as a member of a group or team; being loyal to the group.
14. *Fairness:* Treating all people the same according to notions of fair-

ness and justice; not letting personal feelings bias decisions about others.

15. *Leadership:* Encouraging a group of which one is a member to get things done and at the same maintain time good relations within the group.

Strengths of Temperance

16. *Forgiveness and Mercy:* Forgiving those who have done wrong; accepting the shortcomings of others; giving people a second chance; not being vengeful.

17. *Humility and Modesty:* Letting one's accomplishments speak for themselves; not regarding oneself as more special than one is.

18. *Prudence:* Being careful about one's choices; not taking undue risks; not saying or doing things that might later be regretted.

19. *Self-Regulation (Self-Control):* Regulating what one feels and does; being disciplined; controlling one's appetites and emotions.

Strengths of Transcendence

20. *Appreciation of Beauty and Excellence (Awe, Wonder, Elevation):* Appreciating beauty, excellence, and/or skilled performance in various domains of life.

21. *Gratitude:* Being aware of and thankful for the good things that happen; taking time to express thanks.

22. *Hope (Optimism, Future-Mindedness, Future Orientation):* Expecting the best in the future and working to achieve it.

23. *Humor (Playfulness):* Liking to laugh and tease; bringing smiles to other people; seeing the light side.

24. *Spirituality (Religiousness, Faith, Purpose):* Having coherent beliefs about the higher purpose, the meaning of life, and the meaning of the universe. (Peterson & Seligman, 2004)

Step 2: Identify the Top Five VIA
Signature Strengths

During your next session look at the assessment results with your client. Highlight his or her top five strengths. Discuss them.

These top five Signature Strengths can easily be utilized during your EMDR sessions. How? By interweaving throughout the session reminders to your client of what their strengths happen to be.

For instance, it is common for clients in the midst of transition to forget how they came upon this chapter in their life. In addition, they forget what dimensions of themselves they can fall back on.

EMDR grooms clients to step into their ever-changing world fully engaged with their VIA Signature Strengths. Using EMDR, acknowledge and remind them what strengths they can use to empower themselves. Encourage them to let their Signature Strengths trump the Negative Cognitions (NCs).

Many of the interventions below arose naturally as customized applications directly from the EMDR session.

Step 3: Utilizing EMDR to Consciously Incorporate Signature Strengths into Daily Life

Below are four EMDR and Positive Psychology applications dealing specifically with the VIA Signature Strengths to further your investigation and learning.

Application One: Dusting Off the Strength

1. Sit with your client in the position of ships passing in the night.
2. Create a safe environment.
3. Ask your clients to identify one top VIA Signature Strength.
4. Ask them to think of a time that they successfully used that strength. What are they saying to themselves about themselves? What feeling arises? Where do they feel it in their body?
5. Begin BLS. Ask them to breathe into that particular strength.
6. Continue with BLS. Ask Powerful Questions to enhance and explore the specific strengths and their innate benefits for the clients.
7. Once the Signature Strengths have become full-bodied, take them through the Standard Protocol.

Here is an example using BLS:

Clinician: *Breathing in deeply and exhaling, imagine yourself emptying out all that is not needed. That's right . . . deep inhale, deep exhale. What Signature Strength would you like to explore?*
Client: The Signature Strength Gratitude.
Coach: *Great. Remember a time you felt gratitude. Got it? What are you*

saying to yourself when you remember that time? You feel you deserve it? Great. What emotion goes with that? And where do you feel that in your body? For just a few moments let's breathe into Gratitude. Good. Imagine that you are breathing right into the middle of the Gratitude Energy Field. Are you there?

Client: Yes.

Clinician: *Great. Let your breath guide you. Would you be willing to explore the dimension of Gratitude?*

Client: Yes.

Clinician: *What does your body feel like when it is in the Gratitude Energy Field?*

Client: Open. Calm. My inner view feels soft.

Clinician.   *Okay . . . and now what are you experiencing about gratitude?* (She is contemplating. Very quiet. Her face looks calmer.)

Client: It's gold. The color of gratitude is gold. Soft, welcoming, regal looking.

Clinician: *Okay. Go with that . . . what else do you notice about your Gratitude Energy Field?*

Client: It's a country. It's a country I can live in whenever I want.

Clinician: *What is it like to live there?*

Client: My breath feels deeper. I feel whole. I'm not lacking. Everything feels like it is in its place and yet I'm curious about what will happen next.

Clinician: *What else do you know about your Gratitude?*

Continue asking Powerful Questions to help the client identify and flesh out the strength. When it feels like the strength has been revealed, ask your client to envision what characteristics the strength incorporates. Then, for homework, ask your client to create a vision board indicating the visual aspects of the strength.

Do Dusting Off the Strength application with each of the top five Signature Strengths. Depending on the needs of the client, I may do this exercise over the course of a few sessions so as to create a good container for each strength.

Notice the parallels between Signature Strengths and Kiessling's (2005) "Conference Room of Resources." Kiessling installs his resources into all three prongs of the Three-Pronged Protocol. His clients imagine having those strengths with them in the past, while facing a current challenge, and when facing future challenges. You can interweave Signature Strengths through all three prongs with any kind of client.

Application Two: Changing the Habit

Prochaska, in his book *Changing for Good* (Prochaska, Norcross, & Diclemente, 2002), documented Seven Stages of Change: Pre-contemplation, Contemplation, Preparation, Action, Maintenance, and Terminating. When clients do not experience movement (big or little) by the second or third session, they will often leave psychotherapy or coaching. This is a time when Signature Strengths can encourage and show clients how best to move forward.

I recently worked with a 72-year-old retired executive who had been a heavy smoker for 35 years. He had originally hired me to coach him through the transition of retirement. However, the agenda switched quickly when Joe began experiencing heart problems as well as the beginning stages of emphysema. For several weeks he had been contemplating (second stage of change) quitting smoking after his doctors told him to stop immediately.

By dusting off his top five VIA Signature Strengths (Leadership, Perspective, Vitality, Citizenship, and Love of Learning), we then asked each strength how to extinguish his smoking habit. During this segment we used BLS. This exercise propelled Joe from the Contemplation stage to Preparation. With the help of the Standard Protocol he moved quickly into the Action Stage. Joe not only eliminated his smoking habit; he created and implemented healthy habits.

Below are excerpts from the session beginning with Phase Two of the Standard Protocol as the NC, PC, VOC, emotion, Subjective Units of Disturbance Scale (SUDS), and body sensations are defined by the client. Please note that we have already used Resource Installation and BLS to dust off each of Joe's top five VIA Signature Strengths.

AMM: *Joe, what specifically would you like to work on today?*
Joe: I need to . . . I want to stop smoking cigarettes.
AMM: *And what arises for you when you say that?*
Joe: That there is no way I'll be able to stop smoking cigarettes. I can't stop smoking cigarettes. I never have been able . . . I never will be able to.
AMM: *What would you like to tell yourself instead?*
Joe: That I can stop smoking. I am determined to stop smoking. I've done a lot in my life. I can do this, for God's sakes! I want to be healthy!

AMM: *What feelings are arising?*

Joe: Annoyance . . . first. But really it's fear. Fear that I won't be able to stop and I'll die. I'll die before my granddaughter's first birthday.

Coach: *What would you like to tell yourself?*

Joe: That I am living a healthy life. I am doing what is necessary to have a healthy heart and healthy lungs.

The NC is "I can't stop smoking cigarettes." The SUDS is at an 8. The PC is "I am living a healthy life." The VOC measurement is 2. Physical sensations: Tight chest, thick breathing, clenched jaw. BLS begins. After several sets, the SUDS goes to 0, and the VOC to 7.

AMM: *Now, when you think about smoking cigarettes, what is the image that comes forward?*

Joe: Pink, healthy-looking lungs . . . quiet breathing . . . walking quickly without huffing and puffing . . . (Joe's voice cracks. He takes a moment to compose himself.)

AMM: *When you think about the strength that would most help you right now, what would it be?*

Joe: The Vitality Strength.

AMM: *Okay.*

Then both the client and I ask the Vitality Strength for its help in alleviating the smoking habit and creating a healthy life. The Vitality Strength responded immediately and emphatically, "I enjoy feeling healthy. Kick that habit! When you want a cigarette, do some deep breathing and go for a quick walk around the block."

What happened? Joe took the Vitality Strength's advice and began walking on a regular basis. Walking was an activity he had almost eliminated from his life. But Joe didn't stop there. When he worked with his Leadership Strength, the message was to organize other retirees to walk at 7 a.m. in the mall. His Love of Learning Strength encouraged him to then have coffee with his colleagues and discuss the latest in the world of finance. Joe was in his glory!

It's been 3 years. Joe walks 4 to 5 miles a day, sometimes in the mall, but his favorite is walking to the library and proudly waving to old friends who pass by in their cars. He is abstinent from cigarettes. Joe was released from his cardiologist's care 1 year ago.

Application Three: Positive Cognitions and Signature Strengths

One of my favorite EMDR applications is to combine PCs with the Signature Strengths. As you can imagine, there are a variety of ways to do this. The basic application is to determine which Signature Strength best corresponds to a PC that the client wants to install.

Once the Standard Protocol has been established, explore the Signature Strength with the PC during the EMDR session. The BLS will dust off the strength to enhance the installation of the PC.

Below are the 35 basic PCs, but don't limit yourself to these. It is common during an EMDR session for PCs to emerge from the client when working deeply.

Positive Cognitions

I deserve love.	I am significant (important).
I can have love.	I am okay just the way I am.
I am a good (loving) person.	I deserve to live.
I am fine as I am.	I deserve to be happy.
I am worthy.	I can get what I want.
I am worthwhile.	I can succeed.
I am honorable.	I can be myself (make mistakes).
I am lovable.	I am (can be) healthy.
I am deserving.	I am fine (attractive/loveable).
I deserve good things.	I did the best I could.
I can be trusted.	I learned (can learn) from it.
I can (learn to) trust myself.	It's over; I am safe now.
I can trust my judgment.	I can handle it.
I am now in control.	I can choose whom to trust.
I now have choices.	I can choose to let it out.
I am strong.	I can have (deserve) _____.
I can (learn) to take care of myself.	(Shapiro, 1998)
I have intelligence.	

Once the PC has arisen and is established, ask the clients, *"What Signature Strength would best enhance you living this cognition?"* Give the clients plenty of time to respond. If they say, "I don't know," review their top Signature Strengths and then ask again. If they respond once more with "I don't know," respond by saying, *"If you did know, what strength would it be?"*

Let the clients contemplate. When they respond with the strength, ask: "And how would you like this strength to help you?"

Trust the answer they give and install!

Application Four: Finding Balance

The Pillars Exercise Meets the Butterfly Hug

"I am so overwhelmed and stressed, I can't think anymore! I don't know what to do."

These two sentences have become a familiar present-day mantra in our world. With all mantras, repetition reinforces and enhances the message. The repetition of this particular mantra acts as an NC installed on a daily and sometimes on a minute-to-minute basis. In this case the focus is stress and overwhelm, which run rampant in contemporary life.

This mantra can easily evolve into a belief system, a pervasive NC that affects the physical, mental, and emotional immune systems. What is the antidote to this mantra of stress, overwhelm, and dissatisfaction? Plain old-fashioned balance, equanimity: leading the good life.

How do we guide clients to find equanimity in the midst of a high-speed life with not enough time and often no finish line? Answer: The Positive Psychology Pillars Exercise in combination with EMDR.

This is a simple yet most revealing clinical application designed by Positive Psychologist Dr. Ben Dean of MentorCoach. It creates a measurable baseline identifying life satisfaction and domains in need of self-improvement or celebration. In this way the dynamic state of equanimity resulting in the good life can be explored and gleaned. But don't limit yourself as a clinician to seeing the Pillars Exercise as only a way to find equanimity. Its infrastructure supports a multitude of processes depending on the client's needs. In this case, we will be focusing on finding equanimity in leading the good life.

The Pillars Exercise

The Pillars Exercise reveals a here-and-now snapshot of the inner and outer landscape of the client. It can be done in person or on the phone, during an intake, or multiple times over the years to measure the client's life satisfaction. The only tools required are a sheet of 8½" × 11" paper, a pencil, and two arms to do the EMDR Butterfly Hug!

1.   Place the 8½" × 11" paper horizontally in landscape orientation.
2.   Draw 12 vertical lines to indicate eleven pillars.
3.   At the top of each pillar label the domain as suggested below:

- Career
- Finances
- Physical/Health
- Spiritual
- Social Support
- Intimacy
- Family
- Learning, Growth
- Play, Fun, Creativity
- Home/Office Environment
- Overall Life Satisfaction

The Pillars guide the client straight to essence. This excerpt of the career domain contains questions, which are recycled through each pillar. However, the client's answers will differ. Remember to allow contemplative time for the client to sit with each question. Do not be surprised if this step is similar to determining the EMDR VOC measurements. This exercise steeps clients in clarity and connection regarding how they are living their life.

AMM: *Stephanie, when you think about your career, on a scale of 1 to 7 with 7 being the most satisfied and 1 not being satisfied at all, where would you place yourself on the pillar?*
Stephanie: I would say I'm at a 2.
AMM: *A 2. Okay. I'm curious. What would need to change in your life to have your career be a 7?*
Stephanie: My boss . . . my boss would have to leave the company. He's groomed me for 3 years but he just doesn't want to retire.
AMM: *And if your boss left the company, how satisfied would you be on a scale of 1 to 7?*
Stephanie: I would go up quickly to a 6.
AMM: *Great. And what would need to happen to be so satisfied with your job that you would be at a 7?*
Stephanie: I would take over . . . I would be promoted as the director of the department.

AMM: *Great. And what would be the positive cognition or affirmation that you would tell yourself to move into the 7 with confidence?*

Stephanie: Uhmm . . . I need a moment. (After deliberation the client combines three PCs.) I am succeeding. I have the experience it takes. My staff sees me as their leader.

AMM: *Great! I'm going to write that down so we can come back to it. Now let's go to the next pillar.*

The process continues for each individual domain pillar as follows: (a) The clinician in each case asks the clients where on the satisfaction scale they find themselves. The answer is noted on the piece of paper. (b) The clinician asks what would need to be done to reach a 7. (c) The clinician asks what the PC or affirmation would be to move into a 7 with confidence. For review later, the clinician tracks the clients' numbers and responses for each pillar.

After examining each pillar ask: *Which pillars have a low satisfaction score?* Then: *Which pillars are high?*

Ask your clients to color in each pillar to denote their numbered answer. The pillars now magically turn into a visual graph. Continue asking questions such as *"What do you notice? Which pillar would you like to focus on during this session to become a 7?"*

In the case of the client struggling with stress and overwhelm, ask which pillar or pillars will help induce equanimity by exploring the meta-view of the client's life. From here the clinician and client together determine a strategic plan to meet needs.

WHERE DOES EMDR COME IN?

Once the numbers are established and your client has identified the domain, it is time to discover what NCs are keeping the number down and determine what PCs would help raise the number while promoting equanimity.

Go back to our example above with the client choosing the career domain to work with during the session. This is how the session would go utilizing EMDR:

AMM: *I support you in your decision to choose the career domain to work on first to create the equanimity in your life. Do you remember that to go up to a 7 you would be taking over your boss's position as director of the department?*

Stephanie: Yes. And I would be saying, "I am succeeding. I have the experience it takes. My staff sees me as their leader."

Here are the steps that I would take to integrate the PCs into the EMDR session.

1.   Using the image of being held back from the directorship of the department, check the client's SUDS.
2.   What is the dominant NC? What emotion goes with that? How big is it? Where does she feel it. Using BLS, desensitize.
3.   Proceed directly to the incident that would give the client a 7 (promotion to director). Install the three PCs together with BLS.
3.   Continue until the numbers are at or close to a 7. Help the client install not only the PCs but also the somatic aspects of what a 7 feels like as the director of the department.
4.   Once established co-actively develop a strategic plan for the client to proceed to her goal.
5.   Check the SUDS and VOC.
6.   Use BLS to install the strategic plan.
7.   Again check the SUDS and VOC.
8.   Finish the remaining Standard Protocol phases.

Incorporating this step-by-step procedure with EMDR and the Pillars Exercise will focus the client in the best direction to reach her goals.

CULTIVATING GRATITUDE: SURPRISE +
ACKNOWLEDGEMENT + RECOGNITION

What is the most important ingredient in the cultivation of gratitude? "Surprise!" Brother David Steindl-Rast answered with a big smile. We were walking together up a path after dinner. Brother David, a lively 82-year-old Benedictine monk and Zen practitioner, has dedicated his life to the study and teaching of gratitude as a spiritual practice. His organization, The Network for Grateful Living (www.gratefulness .org), is frequented daily by over 21,000 people from around the world. Many begin their day by viewing *A Good Day* with Brother David as a reminder to focus on the amazing aspects of life that are in existence as

opposed to what is missing. (http://www.gratefulness.org/brother
david/a-good-day.htm).

This is one of Brother David's favorite poems, depicting the element
of surprise in gratitude:

"Blessings" by Ron Wallace
Blessings
occur.
Some days I find myself
putting my foot in
the same stream twice;
leading a horse to water
and making him drink.
I have a clue.
I can see the forest
for the trees.

All around me people
are making silk purses
out of sows' ears,
getting blood from turnips,
building Rome in a day.
There's a business
like show business.
There's something new
under the sun.

Some days misery
no longer loves company;
it puts itself out of its.
There's rest for the weary.
There's turning back.
There are guarantees.
I can be serious.
I can mean that.
You can quite
put your finger on it.

Some days I know
I am long for this world.

I can go home again.
And when I go
I can
take it with me.

"Blessings" is from *Long for This World: New and Selected Poems*, by Ronald Wallace, © 2003. Reprinted by permission of the University of Pittsburgh Press.

In addition to surprise, Positive Psychology adds acknowledgement and recognition of positive events to the Cultivating Gratitude Formula. Research consistently shows that living in the framework of gratitude helps individuals practice skills of emotional self-regulation, which leads to "the good life."

The practice of gratitude can increase life satisfaction levels upward to 25% while enhancing the immune system. Scientific research and self-reporting studies show benefits indicating longer and better quality of sleep, more time spent exercising, less pain, and optimistic expectations with more connection with others (Emmons, 2007).

Below are four gratitude applications. While each can be applied with the Standard Protocol or BLS, I recommend, in cases where a NC needs to be knocked out, to use the powerful Standard Protocol as the container.

Application Five: The Gratitude-Savoring List

The Gratitude-Savoring List is well known in Positive Psychology and those immersed in 12-step recovery programs. It is a common antidotal exercise to shift negative paradigms. By adding the EMDR Butterfly Hug during Phase Five of the Standard Protocol, it becomes an even more potent antidote.

To be given to the client: *Spend 3 to 5 minutes at least four times per week writing 10 things you are grateful for in your life. Here is an example.*

Today I am grateful for:
The turquoise blue skies.
My new friendship with Elizabeth.
That Mary's surgery was successful.
The referral from Peter.
The hike yesterday up in the mountains
The seedlings John gave me.
My son.
Live music at house concerts!
Being a coach.

Once you have completed your list move, into savoring by applying the But-terfly Hug and your breath to each gratitude.

For instance, begin the Butterfly Hug. Savor the first gratitude on your list by consciously inhaling and exhaling through four or five tapping cycles. Then go to the next gratitude on your list and repeat. This should take at the most 4 to 5 minutes to complete.

Application Six: The Gratitude Letter

This application produces gratitude for both the writer and the recipient. Once again, utilize EMDR Standard Protocol for the container. Install the gratitude that arises from the letter. This will often give clients a sense of well-being and the experience of deepening their experience of gratitude.

To be given to the client:

1. *Think of someone who has truly made a difference to you. It could have been a teacher, a babysitter, perhaps your first employer.*
2. *What were the benefits of that relationship? How did it contribute to your life?*
3. *Write down what you remember with as much detail as possible.*
4. *Send the letter to your benefactor. Or schedule a visit and read the letter in person.*

Application Seven: The Nightly Three Blessings

Like the Gratitude Journal, this activity helps alleviate depression and helps the client focus on the positive.

To be given to the client:

1. *Right before you turn out your reading light think about your day.*
2. *What blessings occurred that you had no control over?*
3. *Write them down in a journal.*
4. *Periodically reread them, perhaps at the end of the week.*

Application Eight: The I Am Thankful Practice

Simple and Profound

One client requested ending each session with the I Am Thankful Prac-tice. She found that interweaving her gratitudes with thankfulness softened her view of the world and deepened her appreciation of the natural environment. Although simplistic, this application had far-reaching results. Through gratitude and BLS, she became aware of the sacredness and importance of water, resulting in the investment of a water harvesting system for her home.

With each gratitude said out loud, the client adds the PC "I am thankful" while the therapist continues tapping.

"If You Want Your Dream to Be . . ."

EMDR and Positive Psychology truly are the dynamic duo. Together they help reawaken the innate impulse of strength and empowerment in the inner and outer landscapes of our clients. Both help us as clinicians to live outside the range of managing the client's inner world. Instead, as guides we facilitate the wonderment and creativity of life as it emerges.

Saint Francis exemplified the good life in how he lived. I invite you to rent the DVD *Brother Sun, Sister Moon,* a film that features him. Or go to http://www.youtube.com/watch?v=8xUx4JerVZo&feature= related and sing along with Donovan. Make it a homework assignment for you and your clients. Glean the teachings. Sing loudly and use EMDR to install! Sing so the entire world can hear you! Be an inspiration of the good life!

REFERENCES

Emmons, R. A. (2007*). Thanks!: How the new science of gratitude can make you happier.* New York: Houghton Mifflin.

Kiessling, R. (2005). Integrating resource development strategies into your EMDR practice. In R. Shapiro (Ed.), *EMDR solutions: Pathways to healing* (pp. 57–87). New York: Norton.

Mitchell, S. (1993). *The enlightened heart.* New York: Harper Perennial.

Peterson, C. (2006). *A primer in positive psychology.* New York: Oxford University Press.

Peterson, C., & Seligman, M. E. P. (2004). *Character strengths and virtues: A handbook and classification.* New York: Oxford University Press.

Prochaska, J., Norcross, J., & Diclemente, C. (2002). *Changing for good.* New York: Harper Collins Quill.

Shapiro, F. (1998). *Level II training manual* (Rev. ed.). Pacific Grove, CA: EMDR Institute.

FURTHER READING

Austin, J. H. (2006). *Zen-brain reflections.* Cambridge, MA: MIT Press.

Ben-Shahar, T. (2007). *Happier: Can you learn to be happy?* New York: Mc-Graw-Hill.

Johnson, R. A., & Ruhl, J. M. (2000). *Contentment: A way to true happiness.* New York: HarperSanFrancisco.

Kurtz, E., & Ketcham, K. (2002). *The spirituality of imperfection: Storytelling and the search for meaning.* New York: Bantam Books.

Lyubomirsky, S. (2007). *The how of happiness: A scientific approach to getting the life you want.* New York: Penguin Press.

Meyer, D. (1988). *The positive thinkers: Popular religious psychology from Mary Baker Eddy to Norman Vincent Peale and Ronald Reagan.* Middletown, CT: Wesleyan University Press.

Ricard, M. (2007). *Happiness: A guide to developing life's most important skill.* New York: Little, Brown.

Seligman, M. E. P. (2002). *Authentic happiness: Using the new positive psychology to realize your potential for lasting fulfillment.* New York: Free Press.

Siegel, D. J. (2007). *The mindful brain: Reflection and attonement in the cultivation of well-being.* New York: Norton.

Vaillant, G. E. (2002). *Aging well: Surprising guideposts to a happier life from the landmark Harvard study of adult development.* New York: Little, Brown.

Chapter 16

EMDR and Coaching

Ann Marie McKelvey

It's never too late to be what you might have been!
—Mary Ann Evans (a.k.a. George Eliot)

WHEN I WAS 30 YEARS OLD MY FRIEND DEBORAH SUGGESTED I WEAR CONtact lenses. My quick Negative Cognition (NC) response was "I'm too old." She hung up on me. I phoned her back and asked, "What happened?" "I vowed to myself never to associate with anyone who uses the excuse of age," she responded emphatically.

When I was 30 I began wearing contact lenses by affirming the George Eliot Positive Cognition (PC), "It's never too late to be what you might have been!" Fast-forward 20 years. Deborah has faded into my past. Yet the Inner Deborah continues to live inside and regularly challenges the "I'm Too Old" cognition.

This chapter is about combining EMDR and coaching to continue our own transformational growth as clinicians while helping our clients live their dreams, no matter what their age. It's about continually updating ourselves to the person we truly are. It's about living *our* life. Because, after all, it is *our life*!

WHAT IS COACHING?

The International Coach Federation in a press release dated October 25, 2007, defined coaching as partnering with clients in a thought-provoking and creative process that inspires them to maximize their personal and professional potential. Coaching is a distinct service and differs greatly from therapy, consulting, mentoring, or training. Individuals who engage in a coaching relationship can expect to experience fresh perspectives on personal challenges and opportunities, enhanced thinking and decision-making skills, enhanced interpersonal effectiveness, and increased confidence in carrying out their chosen work and life roles.

Coaching is not clinical psychology. The goal in coaching is not to diagnose and treat, but to rather help patients use their inner resources to change their lives.

THE SHIFTING ENERGY FROM
PSYCHOTHERAPIST TO COACH-CLINICIAN

I had a successful psychotherapy practice in Santa Fe, New Mexico. My specialty was trauma, utilizing EMDR as the major healing modality, and I got burned out.

What had led up to this? It wasn't depression—I was watching out for that. No, instead it was secondary traumatic stress disorder or compassion fatigue. As with many clinicians, it had seeped into my psychological marrow without any kind of fanfare. It was disguised as exhaustion, lack of sleep, feelings of overwhelm, disturbing images in my mind's eye, and an unruly dissatisfaction of the moment—any moment. It was time to dramatically change my profession.

During this time I read an article about psychologist and educator Marty Seligman and a coaching school that trained mental health professionals called MentorCoach. MentorCoach was sponsoring Dr. Seligman in his upcoming 7-month vanguard teleconference class called "Authentic Happiness." Dr. Seligman was past president of the American Psychological Association and his pet project at the time was generating a DSM for highly functioning individuals to keep them living what he calls "the good life," a true handbook for mental wellness.

While I was reading the article, a glimmer of hope began to emerge. I imagined what it would be like to work with highly functioning individuals who were focused on transformational growth, both personally and professionally. I experienced the gamut of emotions from excitement to fear to not being good enough to, of course, being too old to transition into a new profession, even with the transferable skills of psychotherapy.

So what did I do? I hired a coach. The best one I could find. I also registered and joined the weekly Authentic Happiness class of 300 clinicians from around the world. Although we were all clinicians, within the class there was a dramatic difference in how we presented ourselves. I would come on the call at noon already tired, frazzled, and looking for chocolate from having visited a suicidal client in the psych ward. There were others like me. But the ones I was particularly curious about were the clinicians turned coaches who had the full vibrant voice, the deep compassion, the rapidly synapsing brain cells with the translucent clarity and joie de vivre of a balanced life. It was those people I wanted to emulate. They were alive in every sense of the word. They were having fun! They were Coach-clinicians.

After a month the Coach-clinicians' psychological spaciousness began to rub off on me. I felt relaxed. I laughed easily and became more lighthearted. I was becoming more aware of my body and how the inhale and exhale of my breath nourished me in a way it hadn't for many months.

I began to imagine working with highly functioning and resilient individuals who were ready to move forward into the future. I worked with my coach, diligently creating a coaching business that would sustain me financially, emotionally, mentally, spiritually, and physically. I began to transform EMDR, my major source of healing, from a trauma-based modality to a modality of proactively living and breathing into the mystery of the moment. I fell in love with EMDR all over again as my clients worked with the Standard Protocol through the lens of attaining their goals and dreams. EMDR was the modality each client used to encourage the unfolding of an enhanced life while developing action steps.

EMDR TOOL KIT: MINDFUL ACTS OF
MOVING THE DREAM INTO OPERATION

How do we keep our clients motivated toward attaining their goals? How do we move our clients forward when they become afraid of failing? When they feel anxious in stepping into uncharted territories? Or ambivalent and stuck in NCs of the Inner Critic? How do we help our clients become psychologically spacious once again? Answer: Combine the three prongs of the EMDR Standard Protocol with the skillful tools of coaching. Over the years I have collected many processes, exercises, and applications to utilize in almost every situation with clients. When one doesn't land with the client, we cocreate a customized application that does land. Oftentimes the customized application arises from a metaphor that the client generates during Phase Four: The Desensitization and Reprocessing Phase of the EMDR Standard Protocol.

Why are utilizing applications essential to the coaching relationship? It's important for the client to achieve positive subjective experiences. By cognitively interweaving these experiences through EMDR, the client is able to embrace insights crucial in the coaching process, so the therapist talks more during coaching than during orthodox EMDR.

The first purpose of the application is to move clients through their fear of the unknown that resides in unfamiliar territories. The second purpose is to guide clients into robust and psychologically spacious territories where dreams and goals live with strength, resiliency, enthusiasm, and hope. I encourage you to try the applications out on yourself first, either self-directed or with an EMDR colleague to assist you. This will help you understand your clients' experience.

As I made the 100% commitment to create a coaching business, I experienced a spectrum of emotions from ecstatic gratitude to excitement to fear of the unknown. To work with the fear, I created and used my first EMDR coaching application on myself to meet the needs for safety, stability, meaning, and connection during this transition time. You will find this exercise, "My Commitment Credo," in the EMDR Tool Kit below, along with five other EMDR coaching applications.

"My Commitment Credo" is dedicated to you, the EMDR practitioner. It reminds us of whom we are, how we truly want to live, and how to create the steps toward living that life. As healers it is imperative we take care of ourselves.

Application One: "My Commitment Credo": Self-Directed Coaching with the Butterfly Hug

The application "My Commitment Credo" is a simple yet elegant process. A credo is a sacred and formal verbal or nonverbal statement of the values and beliefs that facilitate our actions. It comes from Latin meaning "I believe." This application is for those clients who are ready to reinvent or update their lives and themselves. As with all EMDR sessions, I use the Standard Protocol as the container for the coaching application, along with a few added coaching activities or questions.

Phase One: Intake. Explore client history. What is the agenda for the session? Determine stage of change (Prochaska, James, Norcross, & Di-clemente, 1994).

Phase Two: Preparation. Develop and create safety and trust within the coaching relationship. Ask Powerful Questions to determine the client's needs and expectations. Coordinate the best EMDR coaching approach to meet the needs and expectations. Coactively establish the "Safe Place." Experiment with the eye movements or Bilateral Stimulation (BLS) to determine which approach fits best.

Phase Three: Assessment. Get specific on what the client wants. Identify the agenda specifically by noting what needs are unmet. Write it down. Identify the NC(s). Develop the PC(s). Determine the Validity of Cognition (VOC). Identify the emotions and body sensations. Determine the Subjective Units of Disturbance Scale (SUDS). Initiate questions to determine where the client wants to be at the end of the session.

Phase Four: Reprocess using Dual Attention Stimulus (DAS) in combination with the coaching skills: Powerful Questions, Clearing, and Brainstorming. Notice metaphors to use with Phase Five.

Phase Five: Install PC and images while using DAS. Install positive metaphors and strategies if needed.

Phase Six: Body Scan for feedback on Installation. If body is not in equanimity, repeat Phases Four and Five. Incorporate the Body Scan during Phases Four and Five to gain immediate feedback and to determine a course correction (if needed).

Phase Seven: Closure. Cocreate homework to keep continuum going. What will you do? When will you do it? How will I know? Ask for client feedback: *Did you get what you needed from the session?*

You will use three coaching skills:

Powerful Questions:

A powerful question evokes clarity, action, discovery, insight, or commitment. It creates greater possibility, new learning, or clearer vision. Powerful questions are open-ended questions that do not elicit a yes or no response. They are derived from holding the client's agenda and either forwarding the client's action or deepening his or her learning. (Whitworth, Kimsey-House, Kimsey-House, & Sandahl, 2007, p. 300)

Clearing:

Clearing is a skill that can benefit either the client or the coach. When clients are preoccupied with a situation or a mental state that interferes with their ability to be present or take action, the coach assists by being an active listener while they vent or complain. Both client and coach hold the intention of clearing the emotionality from the situation. (Whitworth et al., 2007, p. 297)

Brainstorming:

Using this skill, coach and client together generate ideas, alternatives, and possible solutions. Some may be outrageous and impractical. This is merely a creative exercise to expand the possibilities available to clients. Neither coach nor client is attached to any of the ideas suggested. (Whitworth et al., 2007, p. 296)

Your Commitment Credo

This application can be used in two ways: with the Coach-clinician and client working together or modified as a self-directed application. Because this application is dedicated to you, the experienced EMDR practitioner, it is presented as a self-directed application to determine "Your Commitment Credo."

Create 2 hours in your life where you are alone with a tape recorder, a piece of paper and pen, or your laptop. Turn the phones off. Disconnect from the Internet. Pull down the shades. Perhaps make a cup of bancha green tea. Do whatever it takes to get settled. This is a time specifically for you with no interruptions from the outside world.

Complete Phases One, Two, and Three of the Standard Protocol.

At Phase Four do the Butterfly Hug by crossing your arms over your chest, placing your hands on opposite shoulders. In a determined way, slowly tap each shoulder one at a time. Tap so that it is loud enough to hear yet not hard enough to hurt. As you perform the Butterfly Hug ask yourself this Powerful Question: If I had a magic wand that extracted all societal "shoulds," how do I want to be living in 5 years?

Answer the question by using the coaching skill called Clearing. Clearing is stream of consciousness talking or writing on what arises as a result of the question. Working alone, I recommend recording your answers via a recorder so you can utilize the Butterfly Hug unencumbered. Talk fast. Talk without editing. Talk as though your life depends on it, because it does! Every minute or so repeat the Powerful Question out loud to keep the question and answer fresh.

Below is an example of a transcribed recording:

If I had a magic wand that extracted all societal "shoulds," how do I want my life to be in 5 years?

I will be sharing my life in a long-term relationship with a man who is kind, highly intelligent, has a great relationship with his kids and mine, is fun with a keen sense of humor, likes to read, travel, and explore, enjoys contributing to people and the planet, is financially independent and enjoys being in a committed relationship. Is understanding, appreciative, and loving with courage and chutzpa!

I will be healthy, strong, and fit in body and mind. I will not be afraid of becoming older. Instead I will be fascinated! I will seek out help when my body needs alignment and balance.

I will enjoy myself. I will continue to be an eccentric, contemplative, fun, healthy, and progressive woman filled with love and caring for others. I will be proactive and generous from the manifestation of that love.

My spiritual life will be deep and connected. I will give back to younger people the wisdom that I have been given by my mentors.

Financially I will be comfortable and able to contribute generously to projects that will benefit all peoples.

I will be a successful coach and writer, generously contributing to the planet living in a passive solar home harvesting water and generating electricity through the power of the sun and wind.

I will have long forgotten how to spell *overwhelm.*

Once you feel emptied out, go over your list looking for themes. Write down the themes and hone them into one dominant belief. Then reframe the answers from the first question into PCs and guidelines for your life.

Once you have distilled on paper the themes into one dominant belief and reframed the answers into PCs and guidelines for life, it's time to tackle the next two Powerful Questions—

What is the dominant belief system?

My outer life is a reflection of my inner life. Based on the belief system "My outer life is a reflection of my inner life," what steps do I need to implement today to live my 5-year vision fully in this moment?

This is an opportune time to brainstorm with yourself. Typically brainstorming is done with another; however, it is can also be illuminating alone as you continue to use the Butterfly Hug. Continually ask yourself the question and record any- and everything that surfaces. This is not a time to edit your thinking. It is a time to let loose and move into those juicy fertile grounds where unlimited possibilities live.

Here is an example of the transcribed recording:

Based on the belief system "My outer life is a reflection of my inner life" what steps do I need to implement today to live my 5-year vision fully in this moment?

    Belief system: My outer life is a reflection of my inner life.

Steps:

Acknowledge that I am in a long-term relationship with myself. I am my closest friend.

View dating as a numbers game.

Develop relationships with younger individuals.

Create ways to contribute to the planet.

Foster and develop old, new, and diverse relationships.

Create ways to enhance a lighthearted view of the world.

Learn how to embrace and be fascinated with the aging process.

Continue with exercising the mind and body.

Become greener: Reduce, reuse, and recycle.

Financially contribute to projects I am connected to.

Stay on top of new research on coaching and psychotherapy.

Write and submit!

Now write and record "My Commitment Credo" in present tense based on your answers to the former question: Based on the belief system "My outer life is a reflection of my inner life," what steps do I need to implement today to live my 5-year vision fully in this moment?

My Commitment Credo

- Today I embrace my longest and dearest friend . . . me!
- I am compassionate to myself as I am compassionate to all who come into my energy field.

- With love and understanding I encourage and support my son's evolution.
- Moving into not-knowing, I bear witness and let go through acts of loving-kindness.
- I am finding ways to contribute to the planet while viewing the world in a lighthearted way.
- I am in a loving, kind, intellectually stimulating relationship with a man who adores me, as I adore him.
- I am developing a strong back and a soft belly.
- I am embracing the aging process of my life and find myself fascinated with growth and learning.
- I am learning how to sustain balance as I exercise my body, mind, and heart both personally and professionally.
- My green mantra is "Reduce, reuse, recycle. Reduce, reuse, recycle."
- As I research, study, and apply new developments in the coaching and psychotherapeutic fields, I write about them for publication.
- Today I am nourishing my life with gratitude, clarity, love, connection, and contribution.
- Today I am alive!

Installing "My Commitment Credo"

Each morning before you get out of bed and each evening before you go to sleep, listen to your personalized "My Commitment Credo" recording. Incorporate the Butterfly Hug as you listen to your credo.

An extra bonus: I ask my clients who are focusing on transition in their lives to read, in addition to "My Commitment Credo," "Until One Is Committed." I have worked with these thoughts for many years. They have never failed me. Again, record it and listen as you utilize the Butterfly Hug.

Here are a few lines from "Until One is Committed:"

"I have learned a deep respect for one of Goethe's couplets:

'Whatever you can do, or dream you can, begin it. Boldness has genius, power, and magic in it.'"

—W. H. Murray (1951)
The Scottish Himalaya Expedition

WE ARE ALL PORTABLE LABORATORIES

The following four applications will be discussed via demonstration.
The transcribed integrative sessions below will show how the steps of
Application Two: Clearing the Blocked Agenda and Application Three:
Using Metaphor and Brainstorming to Solutions play out in a typical
coaching session using the Standard Protocol.

Client profile: Suzanne, 58, has a master's degree in communications and a Ph.D. in organizational development. After over a decade
of successfully working as a consultant for Fortune 500 companies,
she decided to follow her own passion and entrepreneurial instincts.
Suzanne birthed and incorporated an Internet firm working with
businesses to become sustainably green by lessening their carbon im-
print on the world. Her firm employs over 80 employees. Her current
focus is writing an e-book directed toward businesses becoming
green.

Application Two: Clearing the Blocked Agenda

Coach and client are both sitting across from each other like ships passing in the night.

AMM: *Good morning! What would you like to be coached on today?*
Suzanne: Good morning. . . . I don't know. I don't think I should even
be doing a session today. I feel stuck. Drowning in quicksand. I can't
move. I feel worthless . . . and I am so frustrated that I can't channel
my thoughts to focus on writing. I'm being flooded with thoughts.
And none of them are cohesive.

I asked her for 45 seconds to do a clearing of thoughts as they arose.
She recounted her overwhelm of too many projects with immediate
deadlines. Her cat was sick. She needed to create new designs for a

trade show. She was afraid that people would laugh at her for not being a bona fide biologist. Her favorite employee had ovarian cancer. She was overwhelmed and not enjoying anything.

When she completed the clearing, she said her breath was deeper and she felt less bottled up. We were now ready to go. We continued.

AMM: *When you think of what you would like to be coached on this morning, what would you like to be able to say about yourself?*
Suzanne: I would give anything to be in the flow of writing.
AMM: *When you think about writing, what about you stands in the way of flow?*
Suzanne: It's my thoughts. It's me. I stand in the way.
AMM: *What about you stands in the way of being in the flow of writing?*
Suzanne: I'm not good enough.
AMM: *What would you like to say about yourself?*
Suzanne: That I am good enough. That I can do this. I've done other things in my life for the first time and I succeeded.
AMM: *When you think about writing, how true (on a scale of 1 to 7) does that feel?*
Suzanne: A 2.
AMM: *When you think about writing and that you are telling yourself "I am an idiot," what do you feel?*
Suzanne: Scared. Frustrated. Annoyed. Anxious. (SUDS 9, in stomach, throat, head.)

Three sets later, her SUD was 5 and I interwove some coaching questions to help the client to move forward into the flow of writing.

AMM: *What does it mean to be in the flow of writing?*
Suzanne: It's when I sit down and I just write. I lose track of time. It feels good.
AMM: *What exactly feels good?*
Suzanne: Me. I feel good. My body is alive. My brain cells are synapsing. As I look out everything seems twinkly.
AMM: *Good. What else?* (AMM begins tapping. After two rounds Suzanne begins smiling. AMM ceases tapping.) *What are you aware of?*

Suzanne: Feeling cleared out. My mind. My body. My heart. I feel relieved. I want to go swim in the Rio Grande!

Application Three: Using Metaphor and Brainstorming to Create Strategies

Here is a session segment with Suzanne.

AMM: *Okay . . . what about the writing would you like to be coached on?*

Suzanne: I want my fairy godmother to come with her magic wand and tell me what to do.

AMM: *And with the help of your fairy godmother, what would you like to have accomplished by the end of our session today?*

Suzanne: I want to have strategies in place to complete my writing project.

The agenda is "to have strategies in place to complete the writing project."

AMM: *Shall we invite your fairy godmother into our session?*

Suzanne: Yes, yes, yes . . .

AMM: *Would you call in your fairy godmother?*

Suzanne: Yes . . . Fairy Godmother, wherever you are, I need your help to guide me in creating and putting strategies in place to write! (The client chuckles.) I feel silly, but I think she is on her way.

AMM: (After a moment . . .) *Let me know when she arrives.*

Suzanne: She's here.

AMM: *What does she look like?*

Suzanne: Wise. Quite wise with a calm nature. Her eyes sparkle and she knows how to manifest . . . she has a magic wand. She's beautiful . . . like the Good Witch of the North in *The Wizard of Oz*.

AMM: *What else do you know about her?*

Suzanne: She knows about strategies. After all, she saved Dorothy! Remember, in the poppy field she created a rain shower. She's going to save me from my own devices! (Client chuckles.) (Coach moves into Resource Installation.) (Kiessling, 2005)

AMM: *When you think about the fairy godmother helping you, what do you say to yourself?*

Suzanne: I must be worthy of her help. I am not alone. I have support. I can do this with her help.

AMM: *What feeling arises inside knowing you have her support?*

Suzanne: Gratitude. Ease. Happiness.

AMM: *Where do you feel her in your body?*

Suzanne: My stomach relaxes. My head relaxes. I just feel relaxed all over. I am actually feeling a bit excited to see what will happen.

AMM: *Go with that . . .* (and begins tapping).

Suzanne: This is great! I am really feeling her presence.

AMM: *You are really feeling her. Where does she live inside of you?*

Suzanne: My heart and head.

AMM: *Go with that.* (AMM continues tapping.) *So let's bring the fairy godmother into our brainstorming session. Do you remember the guidelines for brainstorming?*

Suzanne: No, not really.

AMM: *Brainstorming is where we can be totally outrageous and unattached with our ideas . . . whatever surfaces in response to your question,"What strategies do I need to have in place to complete my writing project?" are looked upon as important. Because a silly strategy could trigger us to pull out a strategy of brilliance from our psyche, we want to remain in a state of nonattachment.*

Suzanne: Okay.

AMM: *Would you be willing to do the Butterfly Hug as we brainstorm? That will do two things: give you practice in using a bilateral tapping and brainstorming by yourself with me as your guide as well as allow me to easily write down the strategies as they come forward. How does that sound?*

Suzanne: Okay . . . and we take turns coming up with the brainstorming ideas?

AMM: *Yes. . . . You, me, and the fairy godmother. Ready?* (Laughter from the client as she affirmatively nods.) *Great. Let's move our chairs a little closer. Now gently close your eyes and cross your arms over your chest. When you are ready, begin tapping using the Butterfly Hug.*

Moving Forward Strategies

My client and I did a typical brainstorming session. I include the Moving Forward Strategies List below because as coaches it is not unusual to do brainstorming with clients on strict deadlines. It is quite common to be their comrade in prioritizing and moving through the disempowering obstacles that hamper their success. Although in this session the focus was on writing, as the coach you can easily replace any project deadline for writing. The main gist is to help your client get out of the being-stuck-in-a- trance syndrome. For your use, this is the list of workable strategies that arose. I have only included the ones that Suzanne felt would be helpful.

Strategy List

Play piano aimlessly to get the creative juices going.

Go for a brisk walking saying, "I am the awareness of my thoughts. I am the Flow River!"

Ask the ravens for help and listen.

Make a sign that says, "Fight for the creativity!"

Trust and follow the alive thought.

Follow the yes. Follow the passion.

Write in short regular sessions.

Use a timer. Write for 30-minute blocks.

Schedule daily time for writing.

Meditate before beginning.

Ask Fairy Godmother whenever you need help. Listen for her wisdom.

Write for the fun of it!

Explore through the writing.

Get rid of all distractions.

Turn off phone ringers. Get off the Internet.

Once you begin writing, don't get up until the allotted time is up.

Free write—write without editing.

Surrender the writing session up to the Goddess of Writing.

Make writing a priority.

Write one day at a time.

Application Four: Asking Juicy Questions

Although I do an intake with each client in the beginning of our coaching relationship, I am most curious about who they are in this very moment. It is that curiosity that leads me to ask juicy questions throughout each and every session.

I ask the question. Then I sit back quietly and listen. I listen to what is being said. I listen to what is not being said. I listen to the tone and energy of the voice. I watch the little intricacies of body movement.

Here are some of my favorite coaching questions that I have gathered over the years. I invite you to use them throughout the various phases of the Standard Protocol, particularly during Phases Four and Five. And, of course, feel free to make up your own!

What's alive in you right now?

What are you truly passionate about?

What are you grateful for?

If this truly is your life, how do you want to live it?

And if you could do exactly that, what's the first step?

What motivates you when you get stuck?

How can you lock in the learning?

What support do you need to create your goal?

What resources do you need to live your dream?

How can I contribute to your life right now?

Where do you want to go from here?

Who do you love and who loves you?

The coach installs the answers the client gives. For instance, as the client answers the question "Who do you love and who loves you?" have the clients line up in their mind's eye all the people who love them. Ask them to imagine connecting with each of them and feeling that love inside.

As the client does this exercise, the coach taps.

Client: I love my dad. His arms are ready to embrace me. He's always there for me. There's my Mom. I love her so much. She was always there for me . . . and even now that she is gone I feel her inside.

Coach: *Yes, where do you feel that love inside of you?*

Client: In my chest. In every beat of my heart.

Coach: *Go with that.* (Coach taps it in.)

Application Five: Out of the Comfort Zone

Imagine you have been hired by a physicist of an international laboratory to help him transition out of developing weapons of mass destruction. His values since becoming a father have drastically changed. He now wants to develop a grassroots business helping manufacturing facilities harvest water and generate electricity through wind turbines and solar photovoltaics in India.

Together you have established goals and created a plan to move forward. His next step is to submit his letter of resignation. Yet he is not submitting it. It's been 2 weeks. You have also noticed that he is coming late to your office and is rescheduling phone sessions.

At a salient juncture like submitting a letter of resignation, it's common for the client to rescind the goals that earlier he was eager to attain. Why does this happen? Plain old-fashioned fear. Fear of failure and fear of the unknown. Bottom line: He's out of his comfort zone.

How do you stick to your client's original agenda of moving forward when he is steeped in fear? You help him by experiencing insights. I have discovered that the best way as a coach to guide your client into the realm of insights is to utilize EMDR interweaving.

Through interweaving applications, both basic and customized, our clients receive insights that bring back the confidence that fear had originally trumped. When we install the client's insights through PCs and images, as well as newly developed strategies, the client becomes aware once again of the unlimited possibilities that surround him.

The marriage of EMDR and coaching can begin to move the client at a speed that is out of his comfort zone. As a result anxiety, fear, and ambivalence may enter into his life to slow down the process of change.

When these feelings are identified, I then hand the client a list of needs originally based on Abraham Maslow's Hierarchy of Needs but now updated and used in the Nonviolent Communication model designed by Marshall Rosenberg (Rosenberg, 2003).

Needs Inventory

CONNECTION
acceptance
affection
appreciation
belonging
cooperation
communication
closeness
community
companionship
compassion
consideration
consistency
empathy
inclusion
intimacy
love
mutuality
nurturing
respect/self-respect
safety
security
stability
support
to know and be known
to see and be seen
to understand and
  be understood
trust
warmth

HONESTY
authenticity
integrity
presence

PLAY
joy
humor

PEACE
beauty
communion
ease
equality
harmony
inspiration
order

**PHYSICAL
WELL-BEING**
air
food
movement/exercise
rest/sleep
sexual expression
safety
shelter
touch
water

MEANING
awareness
celebration of life
challenge
clarity
competence
consciousness
contribution
creativity
discovery
efficacy
effectiveness
growth
hope
learning
mourning
participation
purpose
self-expression
stimulation
to matter
understanding

AUTONOMY
choice
freedom
independence
space
spontaneity

Together the client and I look at what needs are not being met. For instance, if he finds himself anxious and afraid of a new career, it would be common in this circumstance for his basic needs of competence, safety, security, and stability to be unfulfilled. In therapy, (a) first prong: You can float back to a time the needs weren't met and clear that; (b) second prong: Come to the present and meet the needs; (c) third prong: Go to the future and process through living and acting with full resources.

When the dominant needs are established, we coactively determine which PCs we can install to come back into a centered place where the future view is vast with unlimited possibilities.

Using EMDR, the client determines the incident, agenda, and unmet needs. Together we identify the NC and PC. Using DAS, we develop strategies based on the client's values brought forward in the PC. Then we install the PC along with guided visualizations and the newly developed strategies to help the client experience a more psychologically spacious and fulfilling life. The energy of fear flips and becomes the energy of excitement.

As you view the diagram below you will notice the natural evolvement from Needs to NC to PC to Strategy.

Need	Negative Cognition	Positive Cognition	Strategy
Competence	I am not good enough.	I am competent.	List of why hired
Safety	I am not safe.	I am learning to feel safe in new situations	Collaging images of safety on vision board
Security	I cannot trust this change	I have made good decisions in the past, I can trust this change.	Journal about past decisions and trusting the mystery
Stability	I am not in control.	I now have choices. I am in control.	Create an altar of stability symbols

SEVEN STEPS TO FIND "THE APPLICATION OF THE MOMENT"

There are times when the "right" application does not surface as you are doing EMDR with your client. It can be a fun and challenging experience as both the coach and the client move into the deep listening field of intuition. This process gives you and your client another opportunity to customize an application based on the specifics that have arisen during the EMDR session. To encourage the Application of the Moment to arise:

Step One: Sit in the EMDR position of two ships passing in the night.

Step Two: Acknowledge that you are both coactively looking for an application to help her experience a shift or breakthrough.

Step Three: Ask your client to take a deep breath and follow what happens in her inner landscape when you mention certain phrases and words that have been used in the session.

Step Four: Begin gently tapping her upward palms resting on her thighs.

Step Five: Ask your client what she needs to do to move forward.

Step Six: Based on the response, ask your client to search in her mind's eye for the appropriate application to contribute to her needs. Trust that the right approach will surface. If you, the Coach-clinician, receive an intuitive response, share this with your client. Remember that if it doesn't land with the client, let it go.

Step Seven: Guide the client into action mode by asking, "What steps do you need to do?"

CUSTOMIZING APPLICATIONS:
A CASE STUDY

The customized application below was designed within an EMDR session by Kate, who had been clinically diagnosed with a flying phobia. Kate had been to three other clinicians who had not been able to help her successfully alleviate the fear so that she could move into a feeling of ease when flying.

Kate needed to fly because of emergency situations with her out-of-state mother. Kate's motivation was strong. When Kate first contacted me she was exasperated. She had spent thousands of dollars and many hours trying to achieve ease in flying through analytic psychotherapy.

She knew how to "talk her story" analytically, yet she continued to be lost in how to let go of the fear.

Two different times Kate had sat down in an airplane, buckled up, and then was so taken over by utter fear that she was escorted off the plane. As clinicians we would have diagnosed the incident as a full-blown panic attack, but, because this was a coaching session and not a psychotherapeutic session, I was focused on helping her achieve her agenda goals.

Notice, as you read, how Kate's self-organizing system creates new meaning and direction around the activity of flying. Remember the agenda is to experience ease in flying.

AMM: *Do I have permission to coach you?*

Kate: Yes.

AMM: *What would you like to be coached on?*

Kate: My fear of flying. I want to find ease in flying.

AMM: *Okay. And at the end of the session today, where would you like to be?*

Kate: I want to feel confident that I am safe.

AMM: *Okay . . . take a deep breath . . . and three deep yawns to relax your body . . . that's right. What kind of feelings come up for you when you think about the last time you flew?*

Kate: AHHHHHHH! Utter and uncontrollable fear. I'm sure there are other feelings underneath but it is the fear. The fear is like King Kong going through the streets of Manhattan!

AMM: *How big is that fear, on a scale of 0 to 10?*

Kate: 9.

AMM: *Where is it in your body?*

Kate: All over. All over. In my head, my heart, sweaty palms . . . shaking hands. (At this point AMM begins alternately tapping Kate's hands . . . her breathing becomes agitated.)

AMM: *Okay. Go with that, Kate. Tell me about King Kong.*

Kate: He's violent. He ravages my body. He sucks out every rational thought I have. I am totally . . . I am unequivocally . . . under his control.

AMM: *So just for a moment would you be willing to breathe into that energy field? The energy field where every rational thought is sucked out, where you are totally and unequivocally under his control?*

Kate: Okay.

AMM: *So breathe into it . . . dip into it just for a moment . . . just for a moment, Kate . . . I'm right here with you. . . . What are you experiencing?*

Kate: It's black. A white black. It's a white-black blanket covering me . . . smothering me. (I continue tapping. Thirty seconds go by. Kate is crying.) I feel helpless. It doesn't matter what I do. King Kong is in charge.

AMM: *I'm curious. What is King Kong in charge of?*

Kate: My life. My entire life. He's covered the white-black blanket all over my life.

AMM: *Okay. So go with that, Kate. Breathe into that image. What are you aware of?*

Kate: It's the white-black blanket. . . . It has . . . it has pockets. It's black but the pockets are white. (Tapping continues.)

AMM: *What else are you aware of?*

Kate: The pockets are empty. That is what I am in charge of . . . the pockets.

AMM: *What do you need to know about the pockets?*

Kate: They are supposed to be full. They are supposed to be full.

AMM: *What else do you need to know about the pockets?*

Kate: It's King Kong's blanket but it is supposed to protect me . . . the blanket protects me from getting hurt.

AMM: *Is there a specific part of your life that the blanket protects?*

Kate: Yes . . . my survival . . . that's it . . . oh . . . that is it . . . that's it. (Kate is crying.) I don't want to die . . . not now . . . I don't want to die. . . . King Kong is my protector . . . he won't let me die. (Kate's face relaxes. Her breathing slows down dramatically.)

AMM: *So breathe into that, Kate. . . . What does it feel like to be protected?*

Kate: I feel safe. I feel like the black-white blanket is my safety blanket . . . my security blanket. (Kate begins laughing. She opens her eyes and looks at me, grinning.) King Kong is my protector. I have a security blanket!

AMM: *Great!*

Kate: (Laughs again.)

AMM: *I'm curious. What are the white pockets for?*

Kate: I don't know.

AMM: *I'm remembering that you want to find ease in flying . . . that at the end of the session you want to feel confident in your safety.*

Kate: Yes. I really do.

AMM: *Okay. Would you be willing to do some more EMDR on discovering what the pockets are for?*

Kate: Okay.

AMM: *Take a deep breath . . . good . . . and three big yawns to encourage yourself to go into that deep place once again . . . good.* (Tapping begins again.) *In your mind's eye, imagine the black-white blanket once again. Do you have it?*

Kate: Yes.

AMM: *Breathe into it . . . let yourself move into that place of curiosity . . . of wonderment knowing that the blanket is there for your safety . . . that King Kong is here to protect you. What are you aware of?*

Kate: The pockets are for me. I am in charge of the pockets. (Tapping continues. Kate's eyes are moving consistently back and forth.) There are a lot of pockets.

AMM: *What do you know about the pockets?*

Kate: I'm supposed to fill them up. Fill them up with . . . fill them up with . . . ummmm. I am supposed to fill them up with activities. Different activities. Different activities to do so I don't get scared. A different activity goes into each pocket. Each pocket of the blanket.

AMM: *Go with that, Kate . . . that's great.* (Tapping continues.)

Kate: I don't know. I don't know what to do next.

AMM: *Okay . . . how about a bit of brainstorming? Would that work for you?*

Kate: Yes. Yes.

AMM: *Now remember in brainstorming we just go wild with what emerges. No judgments . . . just knowing that what is coming forward will somehow be useful. Okay?*

Kate: Got it!

AMM: *So, Kate, what goes into those pockets?* (I am tapping. However, my eyes as well as my client's eyes are closed.)

Kate: WOW!

AMM: *WOW upside down is MOM!*

Kate: Love permeates.

AMM: *Energy.*

Kate: Breathing into the energy

AMM: *Support of your friends and family*

Kate: My protector King Kong.

AMM: *Safety blanket wrapped around you.*

Kate: (Humming) "These are a few of my favorite things!"

AMM: *Fragrance of the Eucalyptus trees when you finished the marathon.*

Kate: Steps 1, 2, 3 . . . letting go and giving it all to my Higher Power.

(The EMDR tapping brainstorming continued for several more minutes.)

AMM: *Kate, what are you aware of now when you think about flying?*

Kate: That I am totally protected. That King Kong is with me. That he'll hold the plane up . . . that I'm wrapped in my invisible safety blanket . . . all the time . . . that whenever I start getting scared I can pick an activity out of one of the pockets and do it . . . like pretend I'm Maria in *Sound of Music* and sing "My Favorite Things"! Okay . . . I am done!

AMM: *Did you get what you wanted from our session, Kate?*

Kate: Yup. I do feel ease now when I think about flying. In fact, I am kind of excited to see what it will be like!

AMM: *Feel that excitement in your body. Is there anyplace inside that needs an extra dose? Feel it expand in your body.*

Kate: Yes, I feel it everywhere now.

AMM: *What do you think would be a homework assignment that would correspond with that part of you that is ready to have ease in flying? What steps do you need to do?*

Kate: I think I should write up all the brainstorming ideas, cut them into strips, and then sew some little white pockets onto black material and put the strips into the pockets!

AMM: *Great idea. When do you want to have it done?*

Kate: Next week when I see you again.

AMM: *Okay. Fabulous work, Kate. Anything else to support you in finding ease in flying?*

Kate: Yes! I'll go to the toy store and find a loveable King Kong and he'll be flying high with me to protect me!

We both laugh.

The next week Kate came in with the safety blanket she created for her plane trips. Although she does get a bit nervous periodically during a turbulent flight, the ease with which Kate now flies has made it possible for her to not only fly out of state for family emergencies but to also travel with friends to Africa, New Zealand, Ireland, and Bhutan.

As her coach I wanted to support her by creating a physical structure for her to place in one of her pockets. I wrote a simple letter to reinforce our session. It was folded, to be included in one of the blanket pockets.

Dear Kate,

So—you are in the air! WOW! Let your body experience that WOW! WOW upside down is MOM!! Another WOW! And it's because of your love toward your mom that you have chosen to fly. What is the saying? Love overcomes all. Just for a moment remember how much you love your mom. Let that feeling permeate your body.

Even if you are feeling anxious or fearful . . . remember it is only energy. Remember when I was tapping your hands and you realized fear is energetically the flip side of excitement? Can you breathe into the excitement?

I encourage you to experience the energy of fear as the energy of excitement. Excitement, once more feel into that body experience. Anticipation. You are going home to see your mom. Your brother will be there. Your best friend is with you now . . . sitting right next to you on the airplane. Your sister phoned to welcome you. . . . Breathe into all that love . . . all that support. Rest there for just a moment. Ahhhhhhhh . . .

Here are some rememberings:

- Humming your favorite tune(s).
- The fragrance of eucalyptus.
- Tweak your nose!
- I'm okay in this moment.
- I'm getting closer to God.
- I'm using this experience to be closer to God.
- I'm walking with God.
- I'm experiencing life energy.
- Steps 1, 2, and 3 (of the 12-Step Program).
- I'm choosing to go because I love my mom and I want to see her.
- I'm following in the footsteps of other daughters who have flown to see their moms.
- Breathe in . . .
- Do positive and encouraging self-talk.
- I embrace myself so I can be fully there for my inner child.
- I am trusting God. Whatever happens is God's will.
- I am gracefully managing my inner landscape.
- This is the right thing to do for me.
- I can do this no matter what!
- I am a strong, courageous, spirited, and robust woman. I am learning how to be in places that have scared me in the past. Saying these words, I feel excited and loving towards myself.

- Identify and let go of jackal energy. Focus in on giraffe dialogue with self.
- I focus in on the beauty, grace, and tenderness of myself.
- I focus on my friend's eyes.
- I focus on my mala beads.
- Do the Serenity Prayer.
- Sing:

> Fly high, my Love . . .
> For no other reason . . .
> Fly high, my Love
> There's nowhere else to go . . .
> Put your head in her (his) lap
> And she'll wrap you in her wonder . . .
> Put your head in her (his) lap
> And she'll kiss you with her smile.

CONCLUSION

Coaching is not EMDR. But EMDR can be embedded in coaching to help clear blocks that clients encounter in moving into the place of infinite possibilities.

REFERENCES

www.coachfederation.org; press release October 25, 2007.

Kiessling, R. (2005). Integrating resource development strategies into your EMDR practice. In R. Shapiro (Ed.), *EMDR solutions: Pathways to healing* (pp. 57–87). New York: Norton.

Murray, W. H. (1951). "Until One is Committed." *Scottish Himalayan Expedition*. London: JM Dent and Sons.

Prochaska, J. O., Norcross, J. C., & Diclemente, C. C. (1994). *Changing for good*. New York: Harper Collins Quill.

Rosenberg, M. B. (2003). *Nonviolent communication: A language of life*. Encinitas, CA: Puddle Dancer Press.

Whitworth, L., Kimsey-House, K., Kimsey-House, H., & Sandahl, P. (2007). *Co-active coaching*. Mountain View, CA: Davies-Black.

SOLUTIONS FOR COMPLEX TRAUMA

Chapter 17

EMDR Friendly Preparation Methods for Adults and Children

Katie O'Shea

I DEVELOPED THESE METHODS TO MEET THE NEEDS OF MY MOST DISTRESSED clients. They are essential when targeting very early trauma. Currently they are my standard preparation methods because they provide a gradual introduction to EMDR methodology. In addition, they indicate client readiness for trauma reprocessing. Some clients will need more stabilization and preparation, but if they don't, these basic steps can increase the clinician's confidence in proceeding. If significant dissociation is not apparent initially, these methods will be helpful in illuminating it. Dissociation techniques have greatly informed these methods. The more we understand our ability to disconnect from distressing experiences, the better we are able to treat every client. EMDR therapists, especially, need training in dissociation. These procedures should not be used with highly dissociative clients unless the clinician is trained and experienced in treating dissociative disorders.

The Preparation Process requires that trust be built in three areas: the therapist, the process, and the client. Mark Dworkin, in his book *EMDR and the Relational Imperative* (2005), emphasizes the importance of the client-therapist relationship in all therapy modalities and particularly EMDR, citing the research and work of many others, including Norcross (2002) and Gelso and Hayes (1998). Clients have typically lost trust in themselves (if they ever had it) before they come to us. Each of the steps in this preparation method requires clients to "see what comes to mind" or "just notice what happens" without the therapist giving detailed instructions or suggesting any typical responses, providing an opportunity to begin to trust their Adaptive Information Processing system.

Initially, EMDR methodology seems pretty strange to most clients; it's helpful to introduce it gradually. The methods used build trust in all three areas, effectively and efficiently, by allowing the therapist to be a nurturing teacher and supportive guide; while introducing EMDR components (imagery, a "just notice" stance, and Bilateral Stimulation [BLS]).

There are three steps. I refer to them as "1, 2, 3, GO" in the booklet I put together for children to introduce them to EMDR treatment. They provide the client with the ability to:

1. Easily set aside unresolved material in an imaginary container
2. Access the ability to feel safe in safe situations via a "Safe State" cue word(s)
3. Reset automatic Emotional Circuits to a healthy level of response.

1—CONTAINER

Purpose: Provides a way to easily set aside material until it can be reprocessed.

Origin: Richard Kluft (1988), well known to anyone who has studied dissociation, created the concept of using a container image to consciously take control over the amount of material that would be reviewed during a session and to set it aside between sessions.

Neurological Rationale: Brain scans have shown that unprocessed material is held in the right hemisphere. Following EMDR reprocessing, it transfers to the left prefrontal cortex (van der Kolk, McFarlane, & Weisaeth, 1996). Using a symbolic image of a container seems to facilitate the body's natural ability to disconnect material from awareness when one is unable to give the full attention necessary for reprocessing.

Timing/When: Typically at the end of the first (history taking) session.

Assesses: The client's ability to use imagery and to set aside disturbing material.

Methodology/Language (Adults): Clinical judgment and attunement to each individual client dictate how soon to introduce the concept of a container. Most clients are ready to provide a trauma history at the first session. Teaching them to use a container as a way to set aside all that was brought up provides a natural way to close the session. When clients come in overwhelmed with distress, create the container before conducting your trauma assessment. I show clients an attractive box with a secure latch in my office. They can either leave what they need to review in that box or create their own container. An imaginary vessel that they can take home usually works better. Simply seeing a container can open up unprocessed material, so imaginary is better than a solid "real" one in their environment. Here's the essence of what I say, tailoring it to fit the needs of each client:

Our right hemisphere stores experiences, knowledge, and information until we can give them our full attention and learn all that we need to learn. We'll be using right/left brain stimulation to connect what you've already learned with whatever you haven't had a chance to review. We need to take things a piece at a time, so your system doesn't get overwhelmed. We can help our right hemisphere set things aside when we're not working on them, by having an image of a place or container to put them in. What comes to mind as a place where whatever you still need to review can be stored until you can give it your full attention? It can be an image in your mind, or you can leave it with me in my box over there in the corner. Pause. When an image of a container has come to mind, ask them to describe it so that you can be sure it has a lid or some way to ensure that material stays in. *Now, as you focus on it, let everything, past, present, or future that needs to be reviewed, go into your container, in whatever form it takes. Tell me when it's all in, or if you're having trouble.* Pause until the client indicates it has all been contained. *I'd like you to begin practicing using your container between now and our next appointment. You'll get better and better at using it. If your container changes or develops, that's what needs to happen.*

Typical Problems and Possible Solutions: If clients can't think of anything/an image doesn't come to mind, they may be experiencing performance anxiety. Because self-trust is a major goal, I don't immediately suggest containers. Instead, I say, *You may be trying too hard. It usually takes people a few sessions to get out of the habit of trying and begin to "just notice" what comes to mind. Ask yourself, "Where could I put what I still need to review?" and see what you get.* If nothing comes to mind, I'll suggest some possibilities.

If the client says material won't go into the container:

- *Are you TRYING to make it go in, or just looking at it, to see what happens?* or
- *Ask yourself, "What's the danger of letting it go in?"* or
- *Ask yourself, "What's keeping it from going in?"*

If most of the material is in the container but some pieces are still out:

Everything you need is always available. What's being set aside is only what hasn't yet been reviewed. You've already learned a lot from your experiences and that knowledge is available whenever you need it. See if what's left will go in now.

If some pieces still won't go in, and there is an urgency about the material:

Something in your system is REALLY ready to be reviewed. It is important for us to pace the work so you stay comfortable. Together we can decide when is the best time to target it, now, next session, or later. Ask yourself, "What is it that won't go in?"

If the client tries to stuff in people who have been a problem:

- *Only memories, information, or concerns need to go into our* containers.
- *Just notice what happens when you ask all concerns about* (the person) *to go in.*

For higher levels of dissociation, which will require additional stabilization methods, see Paulsen (2007) for ways to *"tuck them in, in a nurturing fashion, until the time is right."* We never put ego states in a container, though they may need to remain in a safe, contained place.

Methodology/Language (Children): The following is excerpted from my children's booklet. It's called "1, 2, 3, GO (in the office)," "1, 2, 3, STOP (on your own)." Several of my consultees use it with adults.

1. A Place for Memories and Problems

We can't learn about something if we're thinking about a whole bunch of things at the same time. We need to put away everything else and concentrate on what we're doing, right? Well, our brains are very good at putting things away when we're not working on them, unless there's something we really need to pay attention to. To do this, we actually have two brains. Our right brain (or right hemisphere) holds all the information we've taken in about the world and ourselves until we can sort through it and decide what to keep and what we don't need. When something harmful happens, it holds on to every-

thing we saw, heard, tasted, touched, smelled, thought, and felt until we can look back at it and figure out what was dangerous and what wasn't. It works just like our body does when we eat and it decides what we need to keep us healthy and sends what we don't need out the other end. Scientists call it "pruning" (like they do to trees), but we don't really know where the information branches go when they're "pruned." What we do know is, what is important to remember gets filed away in our left brain (specifically our left prefrontal cortex), where it's ready whenever we need it.

Sometimes we need to help our brain put memories away until we can give them our full attention. Some ways to do that are:

- *Let them stay in our right brain, or*
- *Make an Imaginary Place for them, or*
- *Send them to me to keep here in my box in my office.*

Where are you going to PUT AWAY whatever still needs to be sorted through until your mind can work on it or we can do it together?

Practice: Continually throughout treatment and beyond. I think we *all* need containers!

Examples: Trunks, boxes, hatboxes (sometimes in a closet), safes (sometimes locked inside something far away), Tupperware, a vase with a very long neck, a cave, a pensieve (like Harry Potter), or, for really big distress, a water tower or other big storage tank, a submarine under the ocean.

2—SAFE STATE

Purpose: When used in place of a "Safe Place" image (F. Shapiro, 2001), this method provides the client with a simple, fast, effective way to return to an ongoing state of relaxed awareness, whenever danger is not present, and ensures a neutral starting point for trauma work.

Origins: Although this state has been approached in many ways (e.g., "Mindfulness" and our traditional EMDR Safe Place Images), this methodology seems to access it more directly and efficiently, giving clients a way to easily create an ongoing sense of safety. It evolved from Brian Lynn's (2000) identification of a "Pre-Trauma State" and my personal experience. I was listening to our EMDR Institute Part I trainer teach participants how to access their own Safe Place image when the thought, "There is no Safe Place," came to mind. I was so disturbed that I conned another facilitator into skipping dinner to help me process it. My processing led to the conclusion that, from both my personal and professional experience, it *is* true, "There is no safe place. Trauma can occur anywhere." No wonder I'd never developed one for myself and so many of my clients had trouble with the "Safe Place" concept.

Neurological Rationale: "Mindfulness" seems to me to be synonymous with a "Safe or Natural State" and appears to be our natural state when emotional or physical activation is not required. Stephen Porges's (2001) polyvagal theory identifies three separate biological systems responsible for continually monitoring our environment, internal and external, for safety. In the myelinated ventral vagal state humans are capable of relaxed awareness and social engagement. His concept of "Neuroception" (Porges, 2004) has been helpful for clients who have lost trust in their body's ability to automatically scan for danger and respond as needed. Bruce Lipton, cellular biologist, describes every cell as continually monitoring its environment and stated that our automatic, subconscious responses are one million times faster than conscious ones (Lipton, 2005).

When: Typically at the beginning of the second session, if the container was used effectively.

Assesses: The client's ability to access a feeling of relaxed awareness, which provides a neutral place from which to begin reprocessing traumatic material.

Methodology/Language (Adults): After discussing the effectiveness of their container, I explain:

There is a second step that helps us function well, even when we still have material to review. Would it be okay to feel safe when you are safe, when nothing bad is happening, like right now? We can never be sure what's going to happen in the next few minutes, even the next few seconds, but we don't need to be consciously vigilant in order to be ready for whatever might happen. Our amygdala is on duty 24/7, asleep or awake, scanning every aspect of our environment, internal and external, with the ability to respond in half a millisecond. That's a million times faster than our conscious mind can. In order to feel safe when we are *safe, though, we first need to be sure that everything still needing to be reviewed or sorted through is in our* container. *Just focus on the image of your* (container *cue word) and let anything that needs to be set aside go in.* When confirmed, continue. *Your body already knows what to do, so let's rely on it. Just notice, with curiosity, how your body feels. I'll add some right/left stimulation to accelerate the process and we'll just see what happens. Is it okay if I tap your knees?* If knee taps are not comfortable, you'll need to use another form of BLS. Short sets don't seem necessary when the dysfunctional material has been contained, so I monitor physiology, checking in when I can see some relaxation has occurred.

For reassurance: *Just notice how your body feels.*

Or simply: *With everything set aside that still needs to be reviewed, just notice what happens when you simply allow your mind, body, and spirit to come together.*

Continue BLS, checking in periodically, until they reach a state of relaxed awareness, our natural state when no danger is present. *As you focus on what you're feeling now, what word or words come to mind? I want you to have a way to quickly call back this feeling.* Pause for him/her to relate what comes to mind. *Hold that word (or words) in mind while you focus on the feeling, and I'll add BLS.* Tap for about 30 seconds, then ask, *Did the word(s) stay or change?* If it stayed, explain, *You'll need to practice using it in conjunction with your container so your body will develop the habit of feeling safe when you are safe (which usually takes about two weeks), instead of being on guard.* If it changed, add BLS until a word or phrase feels right to the client. I focus on the client practicing using their container and Safe State word rather than adding more BLS because I don't want to risk opening up material before we're ready to reprocess it.

Potential Problems and Possible Solutions

If her/his body won't settle into a relaxed state: *Ask yourself what's keeping you from being able to relax right now?*

If emotional distress comes up, say: *Let that go in your container for now. We'll come back to it.*

If distress won't go in, or comes back two times, something is ready to be reprocessed: *There is something that you are really ready to review. Let's decide together whether to target it today or next week, see when it fits into our treatment plan.*

If the client continues to be unable to experience a comfortable, safe feeling, consider that you may have overlooked a significant level of dissociation and may need to use an ego state approach. If you are not trained and experienced with treating dissociative disorders, refer the client or obtain consultation.

Methodology/Language (Children): Having a diagram or model of the brain, or using your fist as a brain model, as Dan Siegel (2003) does, is helpful when describing this to kids. The following can be given to parents to read to the child or for the child to read before the session where you will actually install the Safe State, or it can be read together as you conduct the Installation. Kids usually enjoy learning about their brains, especially the strange names. Something like the following works well with 5- to 12-year-olds:

HELP YOUR AMYGDALA KEEP YOU SAFE AND READY

We have another part of our brain that checks out everything we see, hear, taste, touch, smell, everything that's happening, even inside our bodies. Scientists named it the amygdala. Its job is to make our body do whatever we need to, as fast as we need to do it, sometimes in half a millisecond. Do you know how long that is? And it's doing its job, 24/7, day and night, every day of every year! Even when we're asleep, it's checking out everything that's happening, so it can wake us up if we need to, or let us know when we need to turn over, pull the covers up, or anything else. It's especially good at watching out for danger!

Sometimes our amygdala shuts off or works too hard, making us feel like we need to hide or get away or fight back when we don't need to. Then we can't feel safe when we are safe. If that happens, we need to PUT AWAY whatever is making us feel like something bad is happening when it isn't, and remind our amygdala, "It's okay to feel safe when we are safe." Later I'll help you find out what's been making you feel upset and together we'll figure out what you need to be safe.

I'll help you help your amygdala by tuning in the "Feel Safe When I Am Safe" channel inside you. Then I'll tap back and forth (to help your brain make connections like it does when you're dreaming) until you feel safe, knowing your amygdala will always make your body do what it needs to do as fast as it needs to be done. Next we'll see what you can say to yourself to bring back that Safe and Ready feeling.

Then I put down their booklet and say:

KO: *Just see how your body feels now, while I tap, and let me know if anything changes.* (BLS.)

Child: (Reports change.)

KO: *Okay, I'm going to tap some more. Tell me if anything else changes.* (BLS.)

Child: (Reports additional change or no more.)

Children aged 6 to 12 rarely need more than 15 to 30 seconds of tapping, usually a couple of sets to reach a feeling of relaxation and no more change.

KO: *What words come into your mind when you think about how your body feels now?*

Child: (Reports what word(s) come to mind.)

KO: *Keep the word(s) in your mind and notice how your body feels while I tap, so your brain can learn the word(s) that will help remind your amygdala that it's okay to feel safe when you are safe.* (Short set of BLS.) *Let's see if this works. Take something that bugs you out of your container. Do you feel kind of upset?*

Child: Yes.

KO: *Now let it go back in and say* (their Safe State word or words). *Did your body go back to feeling safe?*

If it did, I open their booklet again and have them write the words on the line provided. If not, I add more BLS or ask some of the questions above, to try to determine what's preventing the return to a relaxed aware state.

Practice: It usually takes at least 2 weeks of conscious practice for the body to get out of the habit of being in a hypervigilant mode. I suggest consciously setting aside material and reconnecting with their Safe State before going to sleep, upon awakening, and each time they change activities during the day until a relaxed, aware state is automatic and ongoing.

Examples: "I am complete and completely connected"; "Peace"; "Effortless"; "Calm"; "I'm Safe." For some clients a physical anchor works well (e.g., holding the thumb and index finger together).

3—REINSTALL INNATE EMOTIONAL RESOURCES (CLEAR AFFECTIVE CIRCUITS)

Babies typically have no difficulty expressing their emotions, from distress to delight. Over a person's lifetime, both personal and cultural experiences can teach one to avoid, suppress, or intensify feelings. This simple method, during which no emotion is felt, has been more successful than attempting to teach clients to "manage" their emotions.

Purpose: To clear misinformation using symbolic imagery, so that emotional circuitry can function optimally during and between EMDR sessions.

Origin: Although I can take credit for the specific methodology, it would not have occurred to me if I hadn't already been using Resource Installation concepts developed by many EMDR innovators (e.g., Dunton, 1992; Leeds, 2001; Popky, 1993, 2005; Wildwind, 1993). My attempts to help those clients who could not allow feelings to be felt, which blocked processing, led me to the works of Tomkins (1995), Nathanson (1992), Valliant (1997), van der Kolk et al. (1996), LeDoux (1996), Fredrickson (1998), Damasio (1999, 2003), and Ekman (2003). Their concepts support this methodology and provided me with a deeper understanding of emotional functioning. My own work, based on Sandra Paulsen's (1994) use of a conference room and Phyllis Klaus's (1995) use of imagery in the treatment of medical and somatic disorders directly informed this technique. As we were preparing our presentation for EMDRIA in 2007, Sandra introduced me to the work of Jaak Panksepp, who identified the same Protective emotions I'd been reinstalling/resetting since 2001.

Neurological Rationale: In his book *Affective Neuroscience,* Panksepp explained why we organize our experiences via emotion: "Various environmental challenges were so persistent during brain evolution that psychobehavioral tendencies to respond to such challenges have been encoded as emotional neural circuits within the mammalian brain" (1998, p. 50). Dan Siegel (1999) described it this way in *The Developing Mind:*

> Why should emotions and their regulation be considered so central to the organization of the self? The modulation of emotion is the way the mind regulates energy and information processing. With this perspective, emotional regulation can be seen at the center of the organization of the mind. (p. 245)

My shorthand version is, "Emotions call attention to what's important and accelerate learning."

Beginning with Darwin (1872), many have attempted to understand the role of emotion, trying to determine what is based in our biology and what is learned. Both Panksepp and Tomkins described innate emotional operating systems, which are modified by life experience. Panksepp described what he called "The Blue-Ribbon, Grade A Emotional Systems" as having been reasonably well identified. He stated: "At least four primal emotional circuits mature soon after birth as indexed by the ability of localized brain stimulation to evoke coherent emotional displays in experimental animals and these systems appear to be remarkably similarly organized in humans" (1998, p. 54). Panksepp capitalizes the names of his systems to signify that he is referring not only to an emotion, but an affective brain circuit. If the FEAR circuit is stimulated intensely, an animal will run away. Weak stimulation results in a freeze response. Humans report "being engulfed by intense anxiety" (1998, p. 52). The RAGE System evokes behavior that arouses fear in opponents and is energizing. Panksepp's PANIC System is analogous to what is typically referred to as loss or grief. Because all mammals require care to survive, both parents and offspring have systems that communicate the need for care. Panksepp uses the term PANIC to emphasize the intensity of our response when that circuit is activated. He calls the system underlying all pleasurable emotion, SEEKING. Fueled by dopamine, it is what stimulates animals and humans to do what is necessary to obtain what they need. Once thought to be a reinforcement/reward system, it is actually felt as interest, anticipation, or desire.

In addition to these subcortical systems, present at birth, Panksepp has also identified what he calls Special-Purpose Socioemotional Systems that become available later. He includes sexual LUST, maternal CARE, and roughhousing PLAY, indicating they are less well understood. Neuroscience has determined "that maternal behavior circuits remain closely intermeshed with those that control sexuality, and this suggests how evolution gradually constructed the basic neural substrates for the social contract (i.e., the possibilities for love and bonding) in the mammalian brain" (Panksepp, 1998, p. 54).

My experience suggests that a SHAME circuit, and possibly COMPASSION, may also exist, but they haven't been well documented because the majority of brain research has been done with animals. Shame is a basic underlying emotion in many clinical syndromes (e.g., Nathanson, 1992; Tomkins, 1995) and is particularly implicated in disorders related to impaired attachment (Schore, 2003). Often it is the first emotion released during EMDR reprocessing because correct responsibility must be identified before resolution can occur. COMPASSION may also be one of the Basic Circuits as it appears necessary in the correct identification of responsibility. Only by feeling self-compassion, even self-pity (Hauck, 1973), can we fully realize what was unfair and no fault of our own. We need to identify what we did do, via feelings of SHAME, and what we didn't do, by allowing ourselves to feel the full impact of harm done to us or others (i.e., some level of COMPASSION). Then we accept what we have no power over and can focus on what we do have some power to change.

When: Typically, emotional resetting can begin right after the Safe State has been installed, during the second clinical session. If no blocks to experiencing emotion appear to exist, this step can be skipped and only used if the client's processing gets stuck. For clients with complex posttraumatic stress disorder (PTSD), it may be useful to recheck their images when trauma resolution is complete.

Assesses: Whether it will also be necessary to target the specific experiences, especially repeated experiences (Doidge, 2007), where the client learned about emotions (from others' behavior or their own distress, e.g., panic attacks, depression), before other trauma can be effectively cleared.

Methodology/Language (Adults): Resetting the Protective emotions first seems to make it much easier for clients to access Pleasurable feelings. Safety and the ability to obtain protection or protect ourselves seem necessary before we can relax and enjoy life. Below is my list of Basic Emotional Circuits. I see them as being on a continuum from Protective/Life Preserving to Pleasurable/Life Enhancing and Connective, terms that better describe and validate emotion than "negative and positive." As you can see, I have used LOVE and LOVEABLE for the last two. Panksepp's categories of LUST and CARE may fit, but seem awkward language for clients.

Based on your history taking and assessment, decide if you can start with simply resetting the Basic Emotional Circuits (Figure 17.1), adding SHAME and possibly COMPASSION to Panksepp's FEAR, ANGER, SADNESS/GRIEF, then SEEKING, and one of the specific Life- Enhancing Circuits. When the client has had to constrain many emotions, long-term efficiency may be served by resetting all of those listed above, beginning with SHAME and alternating between Life-Preserving and Life-Enhancing. Ultimately, the better their emotional circuitry is functioning, the faster trauma reprocessing will go.

The basic method:
1. Let all material that still needs to be reviewed go into its container.
2. Reconnect with the clients' Safe State using their cue word(s).
3. Ask what each emotion looks like, always starting with the Protective emotions.
4. Add BLS (typically knee or ankle taps).
5. Continue until the images stop changing (and Protective ones appear neutral).
6. Go to the next emotion.

−10 Life Preserving, Protective **Life Enhancing, Connective +10**
SHAME - 0 - - - PRIDE
(I caused harm)   (I caused help)
COMPASSION - - - - - - - - - - - - - - - - 0 - - - GRATITUDE
(I was harmed)   (I was helped)
FEAR - 0 - - - CURIOSITY
(Stay away, it's dangerous)   (Go toward, it's beneficial)
DISGUST - - - - - - - - - - - - - - - - - - - 0 - - - ENJOYMENT
(Spit out/reject, you're/it's toxic)   (Take in)
ANGER - 0 - - - LOVE
(You/it caused harm)   (You are beneficial)
SADNESS/GRIEF - - - - - - - - - - - - - 0 - - - LOVEABLE
(Lose/disconnect)   (Connect)

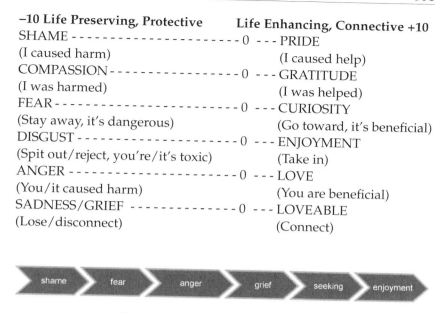

Figure 17.1 The Basic Emotional Circuits
When the picture stops changing, go to the next emotion in the Basic sequence, adding a positive emotion, like Enjoyment, to ensure positive affect is tolerated.

(Note: I use knee or ankle taps to maximize connection to the body. Sometimes the life-enhancing ones either don't go to neutral or take longer to go to a neutral image. Use your judgment about when to stop.)

The session before you begin the Resetting, explain (in age- and experience-adjusted terms): *Before we begin reviewing your experiences and relationships, we need to make sure your emotions are working the way they were intended to work. Emotions haven't been very well understood, so most of us have been taught incorrect information about them and rarely see people, other than small children, whose emotional responses are working well. Here's some information about our emotions and what each one does. You can read over it for next time, when we'll let yours reset themselves, if they need to.*

Most people benefit from basic education about the role of common emotions, so I give them a handout with descriptions of each. They may need time to review and discuss the handout before proceeding with the following. Others can proceed directly.

A computer analogy often works well with adults and kids: *Just like computer programs sometimes freeze up or don't work properly because other programs interfere, our emotional "programs" get messed up when we take in information that's not useful or doesn't fit with the way they're supposed to work. So we need to "reinstall" your emotional programs, to make sure they're working well.*

Or, from Sandra Paulsen (O'Shea & Paulsen, 2007), a car metaphor: *Many people have been taught to ignore feelings, and may even have learned that it's not okay to feel some feelings, so they disconnect from their feelings. That's like clipping the dashboard wires in our car, just because we get uncomfortable when we see a red light that says the engine is overheating!*

When you're ready to begin the Resetting, say: *First, let everything unresolved in your system go into your container and remind yourself it's okay to Feel Safe when you are safe.* Pause long enough to accomplish that. *Next I'll read a little bit about emotions just to help you get focused. Then we'll take each emotion one at a time and all you need to do is* notice *what the feeling looks like. I'll add right/left stimulation* (or *"tap your knees/ankles";* whatever you established was comfortable during Installation of the Safe State) *to help your system clear out any information that isn't useful and emphasize what you do need. When the picture stops changing, that emotion will be ready again whenever you need it, but not when you don't need it. We'll reset the protective, life-preserving emotions first, because they seem to need to be working well before we can fully experience the regenerating, life-enhancing ones. Just listen to this part.*

Our emotions protect us and enhance our lives. And they're part of us from the very beginning. If you watch a newborn baby, you'll see that nobody has to teach them to feel fear, or anger or delight or contentment. Most of us have been told to ignore our feelings at times, and may even have learned that it's not okay to feel some feelings. The truth is: Emotions call our attention to what is important and accelerate learning. As soon as our feelings are felt, or released in our imaginations, we'll automatically learn from our experiences and remember what's important. The stronger they are, the faster we learn. We won't need the feelings to call our attention to the memory or problem, so we'll return to feeling relaxed and aware, more capable of dealing with future difficulties. We want to make sure your emotions are working the way they were intended to work so you can learn from every experience.

Let's begin with (typically) Shame. What does Shame look like?

As soon as the client has a picture, say: *Just notice what Shame looks like while I add the tapping. I'll check in with you periodically to see if it's changing. Let me know if you feel anything emotionally or physically. If you do, that means memories are surfacing and need to go back into your container. When we're reviewing what we've learned about the emotions them-*

selves, there's no feeling involved.

Check in just as you would with EMDR trauma processing, but say: *What does (e.g., Shame) look like now?*

A Case Example

The client is a 66-year-old woman who was abused by her grandfather at age 2½. After explaining what we'd be doing, I simply said: *What does Shame look like?* My client responded: A big, big blob. It has living tissue in it. *Just notice if it changes.* (BLS.)

Set 1. Gotten smaller, but taller, not so fat. (BLS.)
Set 2. Smaller and not as tall, but wider. (BLS.)
Set 3. It's pink. (BLS.)
Set 4. It's kind of lying down, flattening itself out, not encompassing my whole visual field. (BLS.)
Set 5. Found myself trying to make it change and that didn't do anything. (BLS.)
Set 6. About the same except it feels a little more distant. (BLS.) *We'll just see if it changes anymore.* (BLS.)
Set 7. No change. (BLS.)

What does Fear look like? A chartreuse green mouth that's open. (BLS.)

Set 1. It grew some eyes and the whites were really prominent. I started seeing a frog. It had evil eyes, black icky eyes. (BLS.)
Set 2. It's starting to go to sleep and it's very sensitive to any movements I make. (BLS.)
Set 3. It's really small—can't see its eyes anymore. (BLS.)
Set 4. It's the same.

What does Anger look like? It fills the room, not fire but red movement. (BLS.)

Set 1. It is breathing in the room, still the same size. When it breathes in, I see there are bald-headed men like my Dad—can't see their faces. (BLS.)

Set 2. It's making a male noise and it's aimed at me and it started to get doll size. Only one figure there now. (BLS.)

Set 3. The red flame energy is leaking and as it leaks out of the space, the man can't borrow the breath anymore from the red energy. (BLS.)

Set 4. The man just fizzles out. He's not dead but he doesn't have any air left. Nothing left in the room except a very small man and I see out the window. There are some hills I can see now. (BLS.)

Set 5. I don't know if I was breathing in the pictures. Now I'm just looking at the hills and I'm aware of breathing. (BLS.)

Set 6. Still just breathing.

We reset Sadness/Grief. Then I asked, *What does Seeking look like, the circuit that allows us to feel all our Pleasurable, Life-Enhancing feelings?* Being awake. (BLS.)

Set 1. Looks like my heart and my brain walking on either side of a really bright light. (BLS.)

Set 2. The heart and the brain look at each other over the light and they have love in their eyes and they're really at peace and the light stays on. (BLS.)

Set 3. They're still walking.

After reinstalling her emotional circuits and clearing her early trauma (this client has been in and out of therapy with some of the world's best therapists for decades), plus additional past, present, and anticipated future trauma, she came to the sense that she can be "fully present" to whatever happens during the remainder of her life, something she wasn't ever able to experience before.

Typical Patterns
- Image changes seem related or unrelated, may be objects, colors, symbols, figures.
- Images often describe the emotional extremes (e.g., freeze and flight).
- Images often describe what they have not been able to experience (e.g., rage/fight).
- Images tell a story.
- Images are from actual experiences where they learned about that emotion (e.g., a shaming parent, but no distress is felt).

- Client doesn't see an image but the thoughts that come to mind are descriptive.

Potential Problems and Possible Solutions

Client isn't able to identify an image. Use wording such as:

- *What comes to mind when you think of (e.g., SHAME)?*
- *What do you think of when I say, "(e.g., Shame)"?*

If dissociation is obvious, depending on the level of fragmentation:

- *What does the part (do the parts) of you that feel(s) (e.g., Shame) look like?*

Images don't go to neutral or stop changing. (Often there has been some danger in experiencing that emotion and another one needs to be reset first.)
- Just go to the next emotion, or, if it is apparent what emotion is blocking, go to it.

   Emotions may have gotten connected/confused, seem entangled:
- Stay with the Protective Emotions.
- Go through them as many times as necessary until the essence gets teased out.

You'll know, because each one will go to neutral and stop changing, so you can confidently go to the next one.

   If *any* emotion surfaces:
- *Let whatever that's about go back into its container for processing later.*

When it's in, ask:

- *What does (e.g., Shame) look like now?*

If distress won't go in, or comes back two times, something is ready to be reprocessed.

- *There is something that you're really ready to review. Let's decide together whether to target it today or next week, or look at when it best fits into our treatment plan.*

Methodology/Language (Children): Again, this is what I give to children and their parents, or read it just before beginning the Resetting:

RESET STUCK FEELINGS

Pictures in our minds seem to make our brains work really fast. Did you know that when we're dreaming at night, our minds are sorting through what we've learned during the day and deciding what to keep, then connecting it up with other stuff we've already learned? We even have a part in our brain that's like the person in an office who puts files away and gets them when you need them. It's called the hippocampus *and it hardly ever makes mistakes. Sometimes being able to make pictures in our minds is fun, but other times there are upsetting pictures that get stuck and we see them over and over. When that happens, our mind is telling us we need to pay attention to something important. My job is to help you* learn *from the pictures you* don't *want to keep seeing in your mind or dreams, so they'll go away and you'll see pictures you* do *want to see.*

We're going to use your mind's ability to make pictures to be sure your feelings aren't stuck in ON or OFF or somewhere in between. They just need to be ready when we need them. This is how we'll do it. After we (a) put away *all the upsetting memories and problems you still need to learn from and (b)* help your amygdala *so your body is feeling calm, we'll (c) see what picture comes to mind for each of your most important feelings. You'll watch or think of the picture in your mind while I tap again. When the picture stops changing, the feeling is ready to work like it's supposed to. It won't be too strong or not strong enough anymore, just ready for you to feel it whenever it is needed.*

Then I ask, *What do Bad feelings look like—the feelings we get when we feel bad about something we did?*

A 9-year-old client said: Getting in trouble. (BLS.)
Set 1.   My mom talking to me about it. (BLS.)
Set 2.   Me fixing it. (BLS.)
Set 3.   Going outside to play. (BLS.)
Set 4.   Still playing. (BLS.)

As soon as you get no change, continue with the next Protective emotion or alternate with the Pleasurable ones, asking, *What do Proud feelings look like?* next, then: *What does it look like when you feel Sorry for Yourself? What do Thankful feelings look like? What do Mad feelings look like? What do Loving feelings look like? What do Sad feelings look like? What does feeling loveable look like?*

I haven't found a way to describe Seeking to kids, so I just pick whatever Pleasurable emotions may be blocked. Most often I reset them all, which allows the child to see we can do "feeling stuff" that's enjoyable as well as traumatic. Most of my child and adolescent clients have a hard time recalling experiences where they felt good, so I haven't had much success with Resource Development. This method is easier and builds confidence in themselves as well as the process.

Practice: None is required. The therapist (or client) may benefit from rechecking the images if processing gets stuck or when treatment is complete. Clients may want to recheck their images later in life if they realize they're overresponding or underresponding, emotionally.

Example(s): Two clients (a man and a woman), diagnosed with dissociative identity disorder (DID), who had angry, assaultive alters, have displayed no destructive behaviors in the 3 years since we reset their anger circuits (prior to beginning trauma work) in spite of numerous opportunities and a great deal of trauma (past and present) to clear.

The next example illustrates how this method can be used when trauma reprocessing gets stuck (something I try hard to avoid). It illustrates how information from our culture and training can interfere with our emotional programming. The client is a mental health professional.

Jack had made incredible progress clearing the memories of his "evil" father (who continually took his anger out on him, verbally and physically) and was feeling better about himself than he could ever remember. I was the one who felt like something was missing. We hadn't reset Compassion/Self-pity when we did the Preparation work because he was ready to get started with trauma processing and could identify his experiences as abuse. This is what happened when I did. We used tactile BLS between each response. Because he was familiar with the EMDR protocol, I didn't have to ask, *What does Self-pity look like now?* each time I checked in.

What does Self-Pity look like? The client responded: Woe is me; life sucks; looking downward; slumped over; a pity party. (BLS.)

Set 1.   Not changing. (BLS.)
Set 2.   It changed slightly to head on hands. (BLS.)
Set 3.   Not changing. (BLS.)

Did you feel sorry for the victims of Katrina? Would you feel sorry for another child who endured what you did? Was what happened to you fair? (I could also have read my description of Self-pity to him.)

If that could be self-pity, I could agree with that. Not wallowing in self-pity. (BLS.)

Set 4.   (After a long set he opened his eyes.) The picture changed. I'm just lying down with my hands behind my head, looking up. *Let's see if it will change anymore.* (BLS.)
Set 5.   Just kind of relaxed—looking up, hands behind my head. (BLS.)
Set 6.   No change.

He had always hated anger, so I wanted to be sure we hadn't missed something when we did the initial resetting. I said, *See what anger looks like now.* He responded, "Sitting in a chair. That's a stupid image!" I explained to him: *A neutral image is exactly what we want. It tells us the emotion is available but doesn't need to be activated.* Obviously we still hadn't cleared his tendency to criticize himself. His father had taught him well.

Jim Knipe includes an example of how he used a variation of this methodology in his chapter on shame-based depression. It shows how an emotion can be so locked in that it becomes impossible to successfully reprocess the experiences where it was learned.

GO—PREPARE FOR TRAUMA REPROCESSING

A description of EMDR trauma reprocessing completes the Preparation Phase. The script from my children's booklet contains essentially the same information as the handouts I give teens and adults, so will suffice as an example of my last stage of Preparation when the degree of dissociation won't interfere with reprocessing.

1, 2, 3, GO!
After we make sure all your protective and wonderful feelings are working the way they're supposed to work and you're feeling safe when you are safe, we'll start taking the memories and problems out of their container a piece at a time so you can sort through them and remember what you need to remember without any bad feelings. You won't need to worry about feelings being too weak or too strong, so it will be easier and faster. I'll add taps or sounds or help you move your eyes back and forth like you do during dreaming, so you can learn what you need to learn as fast as you can.

If we learned something was dangerous a long time ago, and we haven't had a chance to go back to it to see if we could handle it more easily now, our brain and body will keep doing things the same old way. It will have become a habit, which is a good thing, unless you don't need it anymore. Just like you get better at something the more you practice it, the longer it's been since we learned something was dangerous, the stronger the brain and body connections will be. So we'll need to let your mind and body remember where you first learned what you learned (in the past) and what you automatically do now (present) to see if there might be a better way and imagine what might happen in the future, so you know you'll be ready to protect yourself or somebody else if you need to. Our brains just want us to:

Learn from the past.
Know what to do now.
Be ready for the future.

If we haven't taken time to look back at dangerous things that happened or we know about, painful feelings will remind us we haven't learned all we need to learn. If you cut yourself and it looks like it's healed, but hurts when you press on it, it's not healed, right? We'll be doing something like that. When we tune in memories, it's like pressing on a cut. If painful feelings come back, it means we haven't learned everything we needed to learn from what happened. If a cut is really painful, you know it's important to pay attention to it and take care of it so it will heal. We have strong, painful feelings about memories, because there's something important we need to learn. Amazingly, as soon as we let the feelings be as strong as they need to be, they disappear. We've learned what we needed to learn.

FEELINGS JUST TURN INTO FACTS!

Then our hippocampus just files the facts away until we need to know whatever we need to know, like what to watch out for, so we can stay away from danger. We won't have to think about those things anymore. Kids (and grown-ups) aren't supposed to keep feeling upset. People are supposed to be playing and helping and loving and learning new things!

My job is to help you get rid of any feelings that are stuck inside. Together we'll find out where they came from and I'll help your right and left brains work together with taps or sounds or moving your eyes, so you can learn what you need to learn as fast as possible and feel better and better! We call it EMDR. A therapist named Francine Shapiro discovered it. Now therapists all over the world are helping kids and grown-ups feel better and learn faster!

CONCLUSION

These Preparation Methods seem to efficiently and effectively optimize the client's readiness for Adaptive Information Processing when additional stabilization is not required. Setting aside dysfunctionally held material via a container, accessing an internal Safe State, and resetting one or two emotional circuits that were identified during history taking as problematic (typically Shame and Fear) may be sufficient. Most often, it is safest, and ultimately saves time, to ensure the basic Protective Emotions are functioning optimally (i.e., Shame, Compassion, Fear, Anger, and Grief, plus one or two Pleasurable ones) before beginning trauma work. Your targeting sequence may need to start with those experiences where the affect intolerance began (e.g., childhood experiences with caretakers who displayed excessive emotion, punishment for showing affect, periods of depression, panic attacks or war trauma). Combining symbolic imagery and BLS has also been effective with other innate resources (e.g., parasympathetic, sympathetic, and social engagement pathways [Porges, 2004], hunger, and sexual feelings). When I'm confident my client's innate circuitry is clear, we begin taking the experiences out of their container and systematically processing them to an adaptive resolution. Because most of my clients have complex histories, yet rarely recall trauma before age 3, I typically work chronologically, beginning with my Early Trauma Protocol, which is described in the next chapter.

REFERENCES

Damasio, A. (1999*). The feeling of what happens: Body and emotion in the making of consciousness.* New York: Harcourt Brace.

Damasio, A. (2003). *Looking for Spinoza: Joy, sorrow, and the feeling brain.* New York: Harcourt Brace.

Darwin, C. (1872). *The expression of the emotions in man and animals.* London: John Murray.

Doidge, N. (2007). *The brain that changes itself.* New York: Penguin Books.

Dunton, R. (1992). EMDR Institute level II training. Portland, OR: EMDR Institute.

Dworkin, M. (2005). *EMDR and the relational imperative.* New York: Routledge.

Ekman, P. (2003). *Emotions revealed.* New York: Henry Holt.

Fredrickson, B. L. (1998). What good are positive emotions? *Review of General Psychology, 2,* 300–319.

Gelso, C., & Hayes, J. (1998). *The psychotherapy relationship.* New York: Wiley.

Hauck, P. A. (1973). *Overcoming depression.* Philadelphia: Westminster Press.

Klaus, P. (1995). *The use of EMDR in medical and somatic problems.* Paper presented at the EMDR Annual Conference, Santa Monica, CA.

Kluft, R. P. (1988). Playing for time: temporizing techniques in the treatment of multiple personality disorder. *American Journal of Clinical Hypnosis, 32,* 90–98.

LeDoux, J. (1996). *The emotional brain.* New York: Simon & Schuster.

Leeds, A. M. (2001, December). Principles and procedures for enhancing current functioning in complex posttraumatic stress disorder with EMDR resource development and installation. *EMDRIA Newsletter, Special Edition,* 4–11.

Lipton, B. (2005). *The biology of belief.* Santa Rosa, CA: Mountain of Love.

Lynn, B. (2000). Accessing pre-traumatic prenatal experience using EMDR: Uncovering a powerful resource of equanimity, integration, and self-esteem in the pre-traumatized self. *EMDRIA Newsletter, 5,* 3.

Nathanson, D. L. (1992). *Shame and pride: Affect, sex, and the birth of the self.* New York: Norton.

Norcross, J. C. (2002). Empirically supported therapy relationships. In J. C. Norcross (Ed.), *Psychotherapy relationships that work: Therapist contributions and responsiveness to patients* (pp. 3–16). New York: Oxford University Press.

O'Shea, M. K., & Paulsen, S. L. (2007). *A protocol for increasing affect regulation and clearing early trauma.* Paper presented at EMDRIA Conference, Dallas, TX.

Panksepp, J. (1998). *Affective neuroscience: The foundations of human and animal emotions.* New York: Oxford University Press.

Paulsen, S. L. (1994). *Ego state disorders.* Paper presented at the Third Annual International Conference on EMDR, Sunnyvale, CA.

Paulsen, S. L. (2007). The act-as-if and architects approaches: Treating dissociative identity disorder with EMDR and ego-state therapy. In C. Forgash & M. Copeley (Eds.), *Healing the heart of trauma and dissociation with EMDR and ego state therapy* (pp. 141–179). New York: Springer.

Popky, A. J. (1993). *Addictions specialty presentation.* EMDR Level II Training, EMDR Institute, Seattle, WA.

Popky, A. J. (2005). DeTUR, an urge reduction protocol for addictions and dysfunctional behaviors. In R. Shapiro (Ed.), *EMDR solutions: Pathways to healing* (pp. 167–188). New York: Norton.

Porges, S. W. (2001). The polyvagal theory: Phylogenetic substrates of a social nervous system. *International Journal of Psychophysiology, 42,* 123–146.

Porges, S. W. (2004). Neuroception: A subconscious system for detecting threats and safety. *Zero to Three, 32,* 19–24.

Schore, A. N. (2003). *Affect dysregulation and disorders of the self.* New York: Norton.

Shapiro, F. (2001). *Eye movement desensitization and reprocessing: Basic principles, protocols, and procedures* (2nd ed.). New York: Guilford Press.

Siegel, D. J. (1999). *The developing mind: Toward a neurobiology of interpersonal experience.* New York: Guilford Press.

Siegel, D. J. (2003). *Attachment and understanding: Parenting with the brain in mind.* Paper presented in Spokane, WA.

Tomkins, S. (1995). *Exploring affect: The selected writings of Silvan S. Tomkins (studies in emotion and social interaction).* Durham, NC: Duke University Press.

Valliant, L. M. (1997). *Changing character: Short-term anxiety-regulating psychotherapy for restructuring defenses, affects, and attachment.* New York: Basic Books.

van der Kolk, B.A., McFarlane, A., & Weisaeth, L. (Eds.). (1996). *Traumatic stress: The effects of overwhelming experience on mind body and society.* New York: Guilford Press.

Wildwind, L. (1993). *Treating chronic depression.* Paper presented at the EMDR Annual Conference, Sunnyvale, CA.

Chapter 18

The EMDR Early Trauma Protocol

Katie O'Shea

THE EARLY TRAUMA PROTOCOL EVOLVED AS A WAY TO ENSURE COMPLETE resolution of prenatal and perinatal trauma that can't be easily targeted with the Standard Protocol. Because we can't be sure when unresolved early trauma remains (few people have conscious memory of experiences before age 3), I have begun to target this time period with most of my clients. If no distress emerges, the process acts as a Resource Installation and facilitates reprocessing later material.

Most methods that attempt to repair distress remaining from very early trauma (especially adoption) and neglect have been difficult, cumbersome, or retraumatizing. The Early Trauma Protocol is a direct, simple, safe, and incredibly effective EMDR extension, based on our current scientific knowledge of early brain development (Scaer, 2001, 2005; Schore, 2001; Siegel, 1999, 2002) and the use of EMDR with infants and toddlers (Lovett, 1999; Tinker & Wilson, 1999). Its structured, sequential targeting allows for processing material, whether or not the client has conscious awareness of trauma or neglect. A list of resources that have contributed to my understanding of early trauma and provide ways to validate clients' responses can be found at the end of this chapter. Landry Wildwind (1993) first introduced me to the concept that pervasive depression often originates in early attachment disruption and can be repaired by imagining a nurturing caretaker. My experience indicates that pervasive anxiety is frequently rooted in the mother's anxiety throughout pregnancy. Stephen Porges's (2001, 2004) polyvagal theory has been especially helpful in understanding and explaining the biological impact of attachment events. Robin Shapiro's chapters in this volume, including the obsessive-compulsive personality disorder (OCPD) and Hunkered-Down chapters, many of the eating disorder (ED) chapters, and Jim Knipe's Shame-based depression illuminate additional ways to work with early childhood trauma and attachment issues. Sandra Paulsen's understanding of ego states (1994, 2007) not only informed my realization that emotional circuitry could be cleared, but provides the clinician with an efficient way to reprocess early trauma/neglect that was reinforced by later events, resulting in automatic, protective responses.

First I'll list who it's for, then an overview of the protocol, followed by a case example, and a detailed description of the components, including its use with children.

INDICATIONS OF 0–3 TRAUMA/NEGLECT

- Someone has knowledge of traumatic or neglectful experience/environment, for example:
  - adopted, multiple placements
  - traumatic pregnancy, delivery
  - Mom in distress (physically/emotionally) during pregnancy, delivery, and/or afterward
  - failure to thrive
  - early surgeries, or hospitalizations (e.g., premature birth, cleft palate)
  - abuse, neglect

- Presence of symptoms possibly resulting from or concurrent with early trauma, for example:
  - fetal alcohol syndrome
  - reactive attachment disorder or other attachment problems
  - autism, Asperger's
  - attention deficit disorder (ADD) or attention deficit/hyperactivity disorder (ADHD)
  - sleep disorders
  - eating disorders (EDs)
  - elimination disorders
  - pervasive emotional distress
    - anxiety (flight)
    - depression (freeze → helplessness → hopelessness)
    - anger (fight)

- dissociative symptoms
  - blackouts, can't remember time periods (recent or early childhood)
  - headaches (especially migraines)
  - child sits and stares, "glued" to the TV
  - daydreams, spaces out, is in a fantasy world
- somatic symptoms predominate
- (can't respond to Standard Protocol Assessment questions (memory/image, Negative Cognition [NC], Positive Cognition [PC], Subjective Units of Disturbance Scale [SUDS]/Validity of Cognition [VoC] ratings)
- Incoherent narrative (Siegel, 1999)
- Floatback/Affect scan goes to a time that feels very early or the patient senses it is

THE EARLY TRAUMA PROTOCOL

After ensuring that clients are in a resourced state:

1. Ask them to float back to the time before they were born and begin Desensitization. If you know about a prenatal event, target it. If you don't, simply direct their attention back to that time and add knee taps (or other Bilateral Stimulation [BLS] if that's uncomfortable).
2. Ask what they notice. If it's a good feeling (and doesn't transition to a distressing one), install it. If it's an uncomfortable feeling, physical or emotional, clear it.
3. Let them continue to notice what they experience. You may need to coach clients through different time periods: *Now go to the time of your birth.* (BLS.) *What do you notice?* (BLS.) *Now think about being an infant.* (BLS.) *What do you notice now?* (BLS.) Some people will spontaneously move from experience to experience and need no coaching. If you know that something distressing or dangerous occurred, target it directly: *Let your focus go to the time when you were in the oxygen tent.* Add knee taps, then ask, *What do you notice now?*
4. If "I'm going to die" or "I want to die" cognitions are present, target them as soon as clients feel safe enough to do so, directing

their focus to *the earliest time you felt this way*. Ensure that adequate safety precautions are in place and there will be sufficient time to resolve them during the session.

5. If distress (physical or emotional) occurs and doesn't release spontaneously, say, *Imagine what you needed or needed to do*. This allows them to escape from the trauma, fight back, or get protection, needs met. Go back over each time period until no distress, emotional or physical, remains and they are able to focus on that time, yet feel a sense of Safety.

6. If it doesn't occur spontaneously, say: *Imagine what would have happened if everything had been the way you needed it to be*. Go back as many times as necessary until there are no more changes and they have gotten all they needed, which will provide the physical ability to make different Choices in the future.

7. Complete the Installation and Body Scan with each time period or targeted experience, offering your own PCs when needed.

Jenny

Jenny was 52 years old and had seen many therapists for her posttraumatic stress disorder (PTSD) symptoms before she learned about EMDR. In fact, she had been asked to discontinue her participation in a university Exposure Study because she decompensated so badly after each session. Someone who had been very productive during periods of her life, she was essentially immobilized and living with her aging stepmother. Her birth mother had died of a brain tumor when she was 8 months old. After having set aside everything in her container and reconnected with her Safe State, I simply said, *Let's begin by going to the time before you were born to see if there's anything that still needs to be Reviewed, Released, or Repaired. Allow your focus to go to that time, while I tap your knees.* (BLS.)

Set 1. I seem to be relaxed and waiting for something to happen. I feel calm. (BLS.)

Set 2. I'm feeling resistance. (BLS.)

Set 3. I feel like I'm floating, lifting out of my body. (BLS.)

Set 4. I'm an embryo—a little black eye. (BLS.)

Set 5. Colors, suspended animation. My eye's most of my body. (BLS.)

Set 6.   Pink organic shapes. My body floating, almost wanting to go to sleep. My hands feel like Mom's heartbeat, distant. (BLS.)

Set 7.   I'm in an envelope. Soothing. (BLS.)

Set 8.   It's thick. (BLS.)

Set 9.   My ears and throat are closing up. I'm scared. All the colors went away. I feel like my perineum is tight. (BLS.)

This was a long set where she lifted up off the chair and expressed pain. I asked if she needed to stop or take a break and she said no.

(Spontaneously) I'm a pain in the butt! . . . I'm a pain in the butt! (BLS.)

Set 10.   He wanted a boy. He was a coach and he wanted a boy. (BLS.)

After the emotional and physical pain was released, I said, *Let your focus go back to the time before you were born and we'll see if there's anything else.* (BLS.)

Set 11.   There was no safety. (BLS.)

Set 12.   It wasn't safe. (BLS.)

Imagine what would have happened if it had been the way you needed it to be. (BLS.)

Set 13.   My mom and dad swimming in amniotic fluid and being free of worry about her health.

And what thoughts are there about yourself now?

I am safe now.

And as you think about that time of your life up to the time of your birth, how true does "I'm safe now" feel, on a scale of 1, totally false, to 7, totally true? "7."

We installed that, got a clear Body Scan, and needed to end the session, due to time. At the next session, I began by asking, *What do you get when you go back to the time before you were born?*

Client: It went immediately to after Mom was dead. I was at my god-parents' house and cut my toe. I was sledding with my cousins.

KO: *Let's start there.* (BLS.)

Set 1.   I went to the next image—the "Sunbelly" card that comes from going to summer camp. I seem really carefree and happy. It's a familiar image. (BLS.)

Set 2.   I jump to a photo of me sitting in a window of a cabin at camp. One of my goals is to have one of those rough hewn cabins. (BLS.)

Set 3.   There was a whole collage of things going on. I haven't arrived at the essence—like I've been on a road trip for thirty years— why I did leave? One of my therapists asked me, "How come you move around all the time?" Like I've been on one big camping trip. I did live with the gypsies. There's something about being really driven, but part of me is more like the grasshopper than the ant, wanting to be at camp, not so striving, moving, camping contentment. (BLS.)

Set 4.   A lot of sensation in my body—sense of movement—not being content, malcontent—grief around being malcontent, remembering content. (BLS.)

Set 5.   Mostly in this blissful dance with my mother. Her holding me up and kissing me, almost Disney-like—content. It's enough to be loved. (BLS.)

Set 6.   That's it. It's just about this contentment and being loved, panning back to being on the lawn, back at church camp. I wasn't content, haven't been content, wandering around looking for it. Seeing my brother hold me up, drinking that in. At Breitenbush [where she had gone for therapy], don't feel like eating. That's what I'm developing, original content. (BLS.)

Set 7.   I'm just with my mother. In bliss, with my mother. It's comforting, profound, simple. Heart cavity, chest, being completely opened, drinking it in.

And what does that say about you?

I am loved.

With most clients, I would have formally installed this PC. Because her imagery was so profound and she had already done a lot of therapeutic work, I decided to see where her processing would go on its own. She immediately connected with recent and future events. (BLS.)

Set 8.   Now I'm seeing last summer on the couch [where she had been immobilized]. (BLS.)

Set 9.   I went back to being assaulted, trying to make the situation come out to my advantage, how I've spent the last 5 years trying in the worst sense. (BLS.)

Set 10.   I'm just running and running and running, to a police station. (BLS.)

Set 11.   It's like I'm playing everything over and doing it differently. (BLS.)

Set 12.   I haven't known how to be the "thou" instead of "it." I've been thinking more about the group of people I work with instead of the product. Was in the office of the guy who is the new director. How would I interview?

Imagine doing it. (BLS.)

Set 13.   I'd want to do all the research about the job, then focus on "How do I feel about the people?" I know I can work anywhere. There's mind changing going on. (BLS.)

Set 14.   This is going to change my life! I know what my work is and I'm going to find a place where I'm working with people of like mind. It's not about the right credentials. It's about the people and I'm in a very safe place to do that, not needing to run anymore. (BLS.)

Set 15.   I was in Sun Valley and Mom would pat me. Then after Virginia married Dad, waking up and crying for Mommy. She'd come in and pat me on my stomach. (BLS.)

Set 16.   Death is such a limiting concept. It's the presence that matters, not the form. It grows. (BLS.)

Set 17.   Just a baby sleeping on her tummy. (BLS.)

Let's go back and review the time from your conception to your mom's death to see if there's anything else. (BLS.)

Set 18.   Going through a little thing about not being a boy. Trying to take care of Dad to give him a boy. (BLS.)

Set 19.   Mostly I'm in this place where I'm really relaxed, like being in an alpha state. (BLS.)

Set 20.   No worries, no stress. I'm sleeping. Mom and Dad are taking care of things. (BLS.)

Set 21.   Thank God that mess has finally quieted down.

As you reflect back on that time now, what thoughts come to mind?

I'm safe and loved. (BLS.)

I'm going to add some thoughts that came to my mind. Just let whatever fits sink in and whatever doesn't, fall away while you focus on the time from your conception to your mom's death. While tapping her knees, I said, *I'm safe. I'm loved. I'm loveable. I'm capable. I'm trustworthy.* When I stopped tapping, I asked if any or all of them fit.

They all fit.

And how true do they feel, from 1, totally false, to 7, totally true?

Seven!

And while you focus on that time and those positive statements, is there any distress left in your body?

No, it still feels like an alpha state.

If we'd had more time, I would have added more sets to see if they would go to a "7+." Instead I suggested that she notice any changes in her eating or sleeping, letting her know that we might need to target them directly at some point. She drove home, 2 hours away, without difficulty. We had five 3-hour sessions, and one the following year after she'd obtained a teaching position at a university. Five years later, she continues to do well.

As you can see from this transcript, Jenny progressed naturally through the stages of Responsibility, Safety, and Choices, then connected the past with present and future events, so I didn't need to provide much structure. The following explanations show what to do if the client's processing doesn't proceed naturally, and how to ensure that all channels are cleared.

METHOD

(Part of an overall treatment plan for Complex PTSD)

Phase One: History and Assessment
- Obtain complete trauma/neglect history
- Both big "T" trauma, little "t" traumas, and repetitive traumas
- Pervasive environments/schema (including relationships)
- Current symptoms and circumstances
- Assess degree of dissociation and suicidal ideation/intent

Phase Two: Preparation/Safety Measures (See Chapter 17)
- Provide extensive information regarding what to expect during treatment
- Create a container to hold what is unresolved until it can be safely reprocessed
- Access a Safe State instead of Safe Place
- Reset/Reinstall Innate Emotional Resources/Clear Basic Circuitry
- Teach "Emotional First Aid" methods

Phases Three through Eight: Target trauma/neglect and schema chronologically
- Target experiences before age 3 using the Early Trauma Protocol
  - focus on manageable time periods, beginning before birth and continuing through age 3
  - target known (recalled or learned from others) trauma directly
  - target life-threatening events
- continue to target past trauma/neglect in the safest and most efficient way, given the level of dissociation, typically via the Standard Protocol
- target remaining symptoms and current distress (Present)
- create Future Templates

HOW THE EARLY TRAUMA
PROTOCOL WORKS

Fosha (2000, 2003) identifies the following criteria necessary for a therapy informed by affective neuroscience and attachment studies (summarized here):

1. An ability to access emotion and harness its healing resources by engaging the relevant neurobiological processes, which, for early

trauma, is not language and logic, but the right hemisphere's language of images, sensations, impressions, and urges.

2. Promoting a felt sense of safety in the therapeutic relationship is essential, sharing in the hard emotional work.

3. A means to work directly with defensive responses (fight/flight) to gain experiential access to feared/unbearable emotional experiences.

4. Once the patient feels safe, and the impact of defenses is cleared, the therapy must have a means for not only accessing but processing strong emotions without being retraumatizing, so the experience can be integrated and coherence achieved.

Sandra Paulsen, in response to this material, stated, "The Early Trauma Processing Protocol meets Fosha's criteria and more, within a modification of the Standard Protocol of EMDR, the most efficient means for processing trauma" (O'Shea & Paulsen, 2007, Handout, pp. 2–3).

I want to emphasize that the Early Trauma Protocol is an extension of our wonderfully researched EMDR Standard Protocol (F. Shapiro, 2001). The missing parts of the Standard Protocol are simply implicit rather than explicit here. Although the Assessment Phase is not verbalized (we are accessing a time when information was stored physically rather than verbally in implicit rather than explicit memory), the clinician needs to continually monitor every aspect of experience: images, emotions, physical sensations, and thoughts/beliefs, to ensure that all are fully reprocessed, returning to the target time period as many times as necessary. With early trauma, asking the Assessment questions seems to prevent access to the material rather than facilitating it, as it does with later experiences.

Safety/containment methods are especially necessary when reprocessing very early trauma/neglect. The Preparation Methods described in the previous chapter were specifically developed to meet those needs.

All that appears necessary is to provide sufficient *focal attention* to access the neural networks containing information needing to be reprocessed. Joan Lovett's (1999) storytelling method teaches us that parents, caretakers, and therapists can stimulate reprocessing, even with infants. With young children, having someone tell the story, using her methodology, works very well. Simply directing attention to either an experience (e.g., birth, or time period, e.g., "before you were born") has been equally effective with clients of all ages. Because we now know that a mother's emotional state directly impacts the child during pregnancy, how to access and repair the time before birth is included, as well as birth itself, and the first 3 years.

Because early trauma/neglect appears to be stored in the body, "imaginative (rather than cognitive) interweaves" stimulate continued reprocessing. Although it often occurs spontaneously, some clients need specific permission to imagine fleeing, fighting back, or receiving protection in order to experience a sense of Safety. Imagining getting what was needed (attention, love, protection, etc.) from the adults who should have protected them or imaginary resources rather than from their "adult self" results in a much stronger sense that they *deserved* loving, protective care and results in markedly greater ability to be self-protective. Doidge (2007) explains how imaginary interweaves can change behavior.

PHASE ONE: HISTORY AND ASSESSMENT

Maureen Kitchur's (2005) Strategic Developmental Model's emphasis on attunement, engendering hope and use of the genogram for quickly obtaining a comprehensive history, provides an efficient way to identify targets while educating the client about the impact of their life events. My definition of trauma is: "threat we're not prepared to handle." Mapping out a treatment plan together significantly decreases the potential for the therapeutic process itself to become unpredictable, and potentially traumatic. The following questions are particularly relevant when targeting early time periods.

1. *What do you know about your mom's pregnancy with you?*
2. *What do you know about your birth?*
3. *What was your dad's life like during that time? Mom's life?*
4. *Were their any miscarriages/stillbirths/abortions in your family? When?*
5. *What was going on in your family when you were born?*
6. *Were you a wanted/planned-for baby?*

Because high levels of dissociation typically result from early trauma, the clinician needs to continually assess the degree of dissociation present, from a few "trauma closets" to dissociative identity disorder (DID). I prefer Gerry Puk's (1992–2008) clinical signs of dissociative disorders found in the Part 2 of the *EMDR Institute Training Manual*. Many formal assessment tools are also available (e.g., the

Dissociative Experiences Scale [DES; Bernstein & Putnam, 1989], Dissociative Disorders Interview Schedule [DDIS; Ross et al., 1989], and Structured Clinical Interview for *DSM-IV* Dissociative disorders [SCID-D; Steinberg, 1994]).

PHASE TWO: PREPARATION/
SAFETY MEASURES

In addition to the Preparation Methods described in the previous chapter, "Emotional First Aid" methods give clients some sense of power over their distress, but only if they are easy to use and work *with* their system. Imagination, BLS, and acupressure methods such as Gary Craig's Emotional Freedom Technique (Feinstein, Eden, & Craig, 2006), have been the most helpful of all the methods I've tried. They release distress rather than attempting to manage or control it.

PHASES THREE THROUGH EIGHT

Focusing on sequential time periods is the safest way to target early trauma. If nothing specific has been identified, it's easiest to start by simply directing the client's attention to *"the time before you were born."* The longest periods I've used are: before birth, birth, first year, second year, third year. Time periods need to be short enough to prevent the client from being overwhelmed by the amount of material needing to be reviewed. They can be biological (conception, first trimester/3 months, second trimester, etc.), a month at a time, or unspecified, for example, *allow your focus to go to the next distressing experience,* when there was ongoing trauma and neglect. If you know or suspect the pregnancy was unplanned, starting with a focus on *"the time of your conception"* may access the origin of such beliefs as "I'm not wanted" and "I'm not important." It took me years to believe we could simply direct attention there in order to gain access to whatever material still needed processing. I vividly recall my client's body moving back and forth while he said in amazement, "I'm the sperm and I don't want to go." We were finally able to clear his feeling of "not wanting to be here." When I finally targeted my own conception, I realized it was the origin of my strange conflict about being seen (I was conflicted about doing presentations), the resistance I'd tried for years to overcome by forcing myself to perform onstage with my dance classes.

It's important to start from a Resourced State, so begin by saying, *"Let everything that still needs to be reviewed go into your container and say* (the client's Safe State cue words). *Let me know when you're ready. . . . Now we'll review the time (e.g., "before you were born" or "of your birth" or "after you were born") to be sure that any trapped energy is released and conflicting information is cleared up. All you need to do is notice what happens, just like you're viewing a video. I'll check in with you in a few minutes."* Knee taps seem to work best when accessing early material that is stored in the body. Length of sets varies greatly, and is often much longer than needed for later trauma.

The following shows the processes that lead to assigning correct Responsibility, a feeling of Safety, and Choices for the Future. Each phase must be complete in order to clear the next phase. Ideally, you will be able to complete all phases within each basic time period (before birth, birth, first, second and third years). Frequently, a client's experiences will make time periods flow together, so it's important not to be rigid. Going back, whenever the end of a channel is reached, by rechecking *"from the time you first came into being"* or a similar phrase, will ensure that resolution is complete.

Review the experience in order to assign correct Responsibility:

• Focus on whatever amount of time is manageable. The greater the amount of trauma (including neglect), or intensity of symptoms, the smaller the bits of time need to be (e.g., *"before you were born; your conception; your first week"* or *"moving forward in time to the next distressing experience"*).

• Add BLS (typically knee taps) and be sure Responsibility is correctly assigned.

MARTHA

This client is an EMDR therapist who wanted to clear her own prenatal and birth trauma, in addition to learning this protocol. Her processing illustrates many responses that I typically get when targeting early trauma (e.g., thoughts, insights, as well as feelings, both physical and emotional, cartoon or fantasy images, sayings and sometimes the words from songs).

Let everything that still needs to be reviewed go into your Jeweled Box.

It's in.

Now say, "I am complete and completely connected." Then tell me when you're ready.

Ready.

We'll start with the time before you were born. Just let your focus go to the time prior to the time of your birth. (BLS.)

Set 1.   It feels empty, alone. (BLS.)
Set 2.   I'm scared. (BLS.)
Set 3.   They don't want me. (BLS.)
Set 4.   It's not me. They just didn't want to be pregnant because my dad might get shipped off to war and Mom was sick the whole time she was pregnant with my sister. (BLS.)
Set 5.   No wonder I've always hated war [tears]. It didn't just hurt the people who were involved in it. It hurt me. (BLS.)
Set 6.   And it still hurts me. It's affected my whole life. (BLS.)

Release distress in order to reach a feeling of Safety:
- If physical or emotional distress doesn't release spontaneously, use the Imaginative Interweave: *Imagine what you need(ed) or need(ed) to do* (depending on whether the client is speaking in present or past tense).
- Allows the client to escape from the trauma, fight back, get protection needs met.
- Go back, go back, go back over each time period until there's no distress, emotional or physical, left, ensuring Safety has been accessed.

Set 7.   Probably why I was so big when I was born. I didn't want to come out. (BLS.)
Set 8.   I just want to stay in there. It's dangerous outside. (BLS.)
Set 9.   It feels tight.

Imagine what you need to happen. (BLS.)

Set 10.   I feel like I need to burst out.

Imagine it happening. (BLS.)

Set 11.   I'm flying around the room like Peter Pan. (BLS.)
Set 12.   Now I'm just sitting on a counter just checking the place out. (BLS.)
Set 13.   It seems pretty weird there but feels good to be out. (BLS.)

Set 14.   Just aware of the cabinets and counters. It sort of looks like a white kitchen.

Relearn/Repair locks in Choices for the Future:
• If Imaginative Repair doesn't spontaneously occur, use the Imaginative Interweave: *"Imagine what would have happened, if everything could have been the way you needed it to be"* or *" Imagine getting all that you needed."*
• Go back, go back, go back until there are no more changes and everything needed was provided by caretakers.
• Suggest possibilities only if they don't occur spontaneously, for example:
"Was your birth easy?"

"Did you get picked up when you needed to be?"

"Did you get enough to eat? As often as you needed ?"

"Did you get what you needed from your dad?"

If the client is unable to imagine *what could have been,* books such as *The Miraculous World of Your Unborn Baby* (Bradford, 1998) and *Bonding* (Klaus, Kennell, & Klaus, 1995) or *Your Amazing Newborn* (Klaus, M., & Klaus, P., 1998) can provide the images and information they don't have.

• Complete Relearn/Repair and Installation after each time period if possible.

Imagine what would have happened if everything could have been the way you needed it to be. (BLS.)

Set 15.   My mom lying in the sun while my sister played, taking their "sun baths." Having grown up in Wyoming, she loved being in California. Wow, I never got this before. I bet my love of airplanes—I used to have my pilot's license—came from my father working at Lockheed. But this time he wasn't building bombers. (BLS.)

See if there's anything else you needed. (BLS.)

Set 16.   They're talking to me about how excited they are about having me. They're happy instead of worried all the time.

Anything else? (BLS.)

Set 17. I was born in the ocean, like the water birth I saw at a training. My mom loved the water. She taught swimming during college. It was fun and exciting to come out instead of just weird. And my dad was right there.

See if there's anything more. (BLS.)

Set 18. We went home to meet my sister and they were just happily taking care of me. I was being breast-fed instead of bottle whenever I was hungry instead of the 4-hour feeding schedule they had then. And being rocked and loved and played with.

Let's make sure you got everything you needed. (BLS.)

Set 19. They're all just enjoying each other.

Knowing the sequence, that is, what to expect, is important when you're doing any trauma reprocessing. With Early Trauma, it's critical. Without an explicit Assessment Phase, it's easy to feel completely lost. Early in her use of EMDR, Dr. Francine Shapiro found that we process information in a consistent way, just as our body responds to a cut or other physical injury with a predictable sequence of events. From those observations, she derived the Responsibility→Safety→Choices paradigm. When I took my Part 2 training in 1993, I was impressed with the clarity of her descriptions, having developed assignments for a group sexual abuse treatment program that had the same sequence, one I couldn't have articulated so clearly. Since then, I've observed four additional stages (O'Shea, 1998). If you keep the basic three clearly in mind during desensitization, however, going back to target until Choices have been fully imagined and always Reevaluating at the next session, you will typically achieve complete resolution.

INSTALLATION AND BODY SCAN

1. If the session was complete, ask, *"What positive thoughts come to mind as you focus on (the time period or experience reviewed)?"*
2. Add your own PCs when indicated by saying, *"I'm going to add some positive thoughts, just let whatever fits sink in and whatever*

doesn't, fall away." Proceed with Standard Installation and Body Scan.

So when you go back to focusing on the way it happened, what do you get?

That who I am today really was dictated by what happened. I wouldn't be the therapist I am, helping people with trauma, if I hadn't had that beginning. When life gives you lemons, make lemonade.

And what does that say about you?

Wow! I'm the sugar. When I'm added to my patient's lives, we make lemonade from their lemon experiences.

So how true does "I'm the sugar" feel on a scale of 1 to 7 with one completely false and 7 completely true, feel now?

We quickly completed the Installation and Body Scan. Like so many other clients with early trauma, this session followed many previous ones, during which she experienced a near-death experience (her mother told her "they couldn't get your heart beat for a while"), stopped breathing (which she did when in distress and was also associated with later trauma), felt trapped when stuck in the birth canal (the family story was she bent her mother's tailbone during birth), and feelings of terror with pressure on her throat. She doesn't know if she was born with the cord around her neck, but had experiences during the reprocessing that felt like it.

CLOSURE (CONTAIN AND RESOURCE)

Whether the session was complete or incomplete, say: *Let everything that still needs to be reviewed, go back into your (container) and, when it's all in say* (his or her Safe State cue words). *Let me know when you feel relaxed and aware, or if you're having trouble.* With consistent repetition, most clients are able to quickly contain what is left and return to a sense of safety. Some will require additional assistance at times.

REEVALUATION

Go back as many times as necessary until each time period is completely reprocessed. Then review the whole early period (0–3 years) to be sure all networks have been updated. With several clients, I needed to return to early trauma as many as 12 times.

Optional Targeting Sequences

If known traumas dominate the client's early memories, it's usually best to clear them, then target by time periods to be sure the first 3 years are clear. If there is awareness of life-threatening events, or they are indicated by beliefs such as "I'm going to die" or "I want to die," they need to be targeted as soon as the client feels safe with you and ready to do EMDR processing. Known early events can be directly targeted using the Standard Protocol, though the client may not be able to identify cognitions or comprehend SUD and VoC Scale ratings. If they are suspected, access can be gained via such statements as, *"Allow your focus to go back to the first time you could have died."* When that event has been cleared, *"Now let your attention go to the next life-threatening experience,"* until all life-threatening experiences throughout the client's life have been cleared. If a wish to die is still present, imagining dying works in the same way as other imaginative attempts to escape from the trauma. It is critical for the clinician to allow sufficient time for the client to explore that option and release the desire to die. Safety is of the utmost importance here. Targeting early life threat would optimally occur in a protective setting with sufficient time available to fully clear all sources of suicidal intent.

When Complex PTSD doesn't appear to be present, instead of beginning chronologically, the clinician can also "float back" to the earliest memory available. This usually requires repetition of the instruction: *Now just let your focus go to anything earlier,* until no more "memories" surface. Sometimes clients will realize they are recalling a very early, even "in utero" experience, or it is indicated by a description such as, "It just seems dark and I feel frightened." All that's necessary, then, is to say: *Just notice* and switch to tactile BLS. Because you've already identified a targeting sequence by floating back, when the early experience is resolved, your next target will be whatever is next, chronologically, in the sequence. I typically switch to auditory or visual BLS when we begin targeting experiences occurring after age 5 or 6.

CONTINUE TARGETING LATER TRAUMA/NEGLECT

Continue trauma reprocessing in the safest and most efficient way, given the level of dissociation. Sometimes the early trauma will connect directly and chronologically to later trauma, allowing it to reprocess very quickly. I typically follow Kitchur's (2005) Strategic

Developmental approach, targeting relationships as well as experiences, then any remaining symptoms. When there was a pervasive atmosphere of danger, an ego state approach will be most effective. If it was necessary for your client to separate the Self into distinct personalities, highly structured DID methodology will be required.

USING THE EARLY TRAUMA PROTOCOL WITH INFANTS AND CHILDREN

The same principles apply to reprocessing early trauma/neglect with young children. If parents or caretakers are available, they can tell the story of what happened to the child, using the format above and including their thoughts and feelings (Review) specifying who was responsible for every part of the experience, plus what they wish they could have done at the time (Imaginative Release), and what they wish would have happened differently (Relearn/Repair), while the clinician taps bilaterally on toes, ankles, knees, or shoulders. I suggest that parents monitor their own distress while writing the story. If the parent's' distress is above a SUDS of 5, we need to reprocess their memory before telling it to their child, because children will focus on their parents' distress rather than their own. Only children with significant dissociation seem to need to have the story told in a third-person format. Telling it directly to the child using "you" instead of another name, typically works well. After the Release section is told or read, something like the following, in age-appropriate language, needs to be added: *"Let's see if there's anything that still needs to be remembered in your mind or body. I'll add taps to help you learn from it, so you won't have to feel bad anymore."* Then, following the Relearn/Repair section, *"Let's be sure you got everything you needed. I'll tap to see if we forgot anything. See if any pictures come into your mind or your body feels anything."* Keep checking periodically (the younger the child, the shorter the sets need to be) until no more changes occur. If no one who knows the story is available, I simply use the adult protocol, adjusting my language to the child's developmental level and simply asking the child to *tell me if anything changes.*

CONCLUSION

The Early Trauma Protocol, including preparation measures, provides a way to access what appear to be existing neural templates from prenatal and peri-natal experience through the first 3 years of life, that have the potential to "Reconnect the Self" and allow the therapist to participate as a healthy attachment figure while supporting the development of self-trust. Controlled research will be necessary to validate its efficacy.

REFERENCES

Bernstein, E. M., & Putnam, F. W. (1989). Development, reliability and validity of a dissociation scale. *Journal of Nervous and Mental Disease, 174*, 727–733.

Bradford, N. (1998). *The miraculous world of your unborn baby.* Chicago: Contemporary Books.

Doidge, N. (2007). *The brain that changes itself.* New York: Penguin Books.

Feinstein, D., Eden, D., & Craig, G. (2006). *The healing power of EFT and energy psychology: Revolutionary methods for dramatic personal change.* London: Piatkus.

Fosha, D. (2000). *The transforming power of affect: A model of accelerated change.* New York: Basic Books.

Fosha, D. (2003). Dyadic regulation and experiential work with emotion and relatedness in trauma and disorganize attachment. In M. F. Solomon & D. J. Siegel (Eds.), *Healing trauma: Attachment, mind, body, and brain* (pp. 221–281). New York: Norton.

Kitchur, M. (2005). The strategic developmental model for EMDR. In R. Shapiro (Ed.), *EMDR solutions: Pathways to healing* (pp. 8–56). New York: Norton.

Klaus, M., Kennell, J., & Klaus, P. (1995). *Bonding: Building the foundations of secure attachment and independence.* New York: Perseus Books.

Klaus, M., & Klaus, P. (1998). *Your amazing newborn.* New York: Perseus Books.

Lovett, J. (1999). *Small wonders: Healing childhood trauma with EMDR.* New York: Free Press.

O'Shea, M. K., & Paulsen, S. L. (2007). *A protocol for increasing affect regulation and clearing early trauma.* Paper presented at EMDRIA Conference, Dallas, TX.

Paulsen, S. L. (1994). *Ego state disorders.* Paper presented at the Third Annual International Conference on EMDR, Sunnyvale, CA.

Paulsen, S. L. (2007). The act-as-if and architects approaches: Treating dissociative identity disorder with EMDR and ego-state therapy. In C. Forgash & M. Copeley (Eds.), *Healing the heart of trauma and dissociation with EMDR and ego state therapy* (pp. 141–179). New York: Springer.

Porges, S. W. (2001). The polyvagal theory: Phylogenetic substrates of a social nervous system. *International Journal of Psychophysiology, 42*, 123–146.

Porges, S. W. (2004). Neuroception: A subconscious system for detecting threats and safety. *Zero to Three, 32,* 19–24.

Puk, G. (1992–2008). Clinical signs of dissociative disorders. In F. Shapiro (Ed.), *EMDR part 2 training manual.* Watsonville, CA: EMDR Institute.

Ross, C., Heber, S., Norton, R., Anderson, D., Anderson, G., & Barchet, P. (1989). The Dissociative Disorders Interview Schedule: A structured interview. *Dissociation, 2*(3), 169–189.

Scaer, R. (2001). *The body bears the burden: Trauma dissociation and disease.* Binghamton, NY: Haworth Medical Press.

Scaer, R. (2005). *The trauma spectrum: Hidden wounds and human resiliency.* New York: Norton.

Schore, A. N. (2001). The effects of early relational trauma on right brain development, affect regulation, and infant mental health. *Infant Mental Health Journal, 22,* 201–269.

Shapiro, F. (2001). *Eye movement desensitization and reprocessing: Basic principles, protocols, and procedures* (2nd ed.). New York: Guilford Press.

Siegel, D. J. (1999). *The developing mind: Toward a neurobiology of interpersonal experience.* New York: Guilford Press.

Siegel, D. J. (2002).The developing mind and the resolution of trauma: Some ideas about information processing and an interpersonal neurobiology of psychotherapy. In F. Shapiro (Ed.), *EMDR as an integrative psychotherapy approach* (pp. 85–122). Washington, DC: American Psychological Association.

Steinberg, M. (1994). *The structured clinical interview for DSM-IV dissociative disorders—revised (SCID-D).* Washington, DC: American Psychiatric Press.

Tinker, R., & Wilson, S. (1999). *Through the eyes of a child.* New York: Norton.

Wildwind, L. (1993). *Treating chronic depression.* Paper presented at the EMDR Conference, San Jose, CA.

RECOMMENDED READINGS

Axness, M. (1998). *What is written on the heart—Primal issues in adoption* (Adoption Insight Series, Vol. II). Granada, CA: Marcy Wineman Axness.

Becker, M. (2000). *The use of EMDR to resolve neonatal trauma.* Paper presented at EMDRIA Conference, Toronto, Canada.

Bowlby, J. (1988). *A secure base: Parent-child attachment and healthy human development.* New York: Basic Books.

Chamberlain, D. B. (1998). *The mind of your newborn baby* (3rd ed.). Berkeley, CA: North Atlantic Books.

Chamberlain, D. B. (2003). Communicating with the mind of a prenate: Guidelines for parents and birth professionals. *Journal of Prenatal and Perinatal Psychology and Health, 18*(2), 95–108.

Doidge, N. (2007). *The brain that changes itself.* New York: Penguin Books.

Forgash, C., & Copeley, M. (Eds.). (2007). *Healing the heart of trauma and dissociation with EMDR and ego state therapy.* New York: Springer.

Fosha, D. (2003). Dyadic regulation and experiential work with emotion and relatedness in trauma and disorganize attachment. Originally published in M. F. Solomon & D. J. Siegel (Eds.), *Healing trauma: Attachment, mind, body, and brain* (pp. 221–281). New York: Norton. Web version posted on David Baldwin's Trauma Pages (http://www.trauma-pages.com/a/fosha-03.php) with permission of the author.

Lake, F. (1978). Treating psychosomatic disorders relating to birth trauma. *Journal of Psychosomatic Research, 22,* 227–238.

Lanius, U. (2005). EMDR processing with dissociative clients: Adjunctive use of opioid antagonists. In R. Shapiro (Ed.), *EMDR solutions: Pathways to healing* (pp. 121–146). New York: Norton.

Levine, P., & Kline, M. (2007). *Trauma through a child's eyes.* Berkeley, CA: North Atlantic Books.

Maret, S. M. (2007). *Frank Lake's prenatal personality theory.* 13th International Congress of the Association for Pre and Perinatal Psychology and Health, Los Angeles, CA, February 21–26, 2007.

Paulsen, S. L. (in press). *Looking through the eyes.*

van der Kolk, B. A., McFarlane, A., & Weisaeth, L. (Eds.). (1996). *Traumatic stress: The effects of overwhelming experience on mind body and society.* New York: Guilford Press.

Verney, T. (1981). *The secret life of the unborn child: How you can prepare your baby for a happy, healthy life.* New York: Dell.

Verney, T. (2007). *Effect of stress on the unborn.* Paper presented at the 2007 Pre and Perinatal Society Conference, Los Angeles, CA.

Watkins, J. G., & Watkins, H. H. (1997). *Ego-state theory and therapy.* New York: Norton.

Chapter 19

Toward an Embodied Self

Integrating EMDR with Somatic and Ego State Interventions

Sandra Paulsen and Ulrich Lanius

People with dissociative disorders are like actors trapped in a variety of roles. They have difficulty integrating their memories, their sense of identity and aspects of their consciousness into a continuous whole. They find many parts of their experience alien, as if belonging to someone else. They cannot remember or make sense of parts of their past.
—David Spiegel (2008) in *Coming Apart: Trauma and the Fragmentation of the Self*

Sensory memory has a special place in information processing. It is our protection against living in a fragmented present.
—Nelson Cowan (1997) in *Attention and Memory: An Integrated Framework*

DIFFERENTIAL RESPONSES TO TRAUMA

With a view toward the integration of the self, the present chapter provides theoretical rationales for the use of both body therapy and ego state interventions during the different phases of treatment. It focuses on how to effectively integrate different ego state and body therapy interventions during the different stages of trauma treatment, such as stabilization, trauma processing, and reconnection, and how to integrate their use to maximize the effectiveness of EMDR treatment. In the last section, we focus on guidelines and hands-on techniques drawing from those different modalities, with specific suggestions to provide opportunities for more robust and comprehensive treatment.

Clinicians and researchers report that people show different experiential, psychophysiological, and neurobiological responses to trauma. They hypothesize two subtypes of trauma response, one characterized predominantly by hyperarousal and the other primarily dissociative, each one representing unique pathways to chronic stress-related psychopathology (e.g., Lanius, Bluhm, & Lanius, 2007; Lanius, Bluhm, Lanius, & Pain, 2005; Lanius, Lanius, Fisher, & Ogden, 2006; van der Hart, Nijenhuis, & Steele, 2006; van der Kolk, 1987).

Specifically, we discuss the use of different body therapy interventions to increase body awareness and mindfulness, their use for the development of somatic resources, and their usefulness in maximizing the integration of traumatic memories and action tendencies. Furthermore, we present techniques to enhance accessing ego states and how to use them to resource the client and to enhance efficient EMDR processing. We give guidelines on how to gauge when to proceed with EMDR processing and when to resort to body therapy or ego state interventions alone. Moreover, strategies are provided on how to integrate these techniques with regard to the preparation targeting, as well as interweaves in conjunction with the eight-phase EMDR protocol.

DISSOCIATION AND PSYCHOTHERAPY— WHY DISSOCIATION MATTERS

Dissociative symptoms can occur in a wide variety of disorders that include dissociative disorders, posttraumatic stress disorder (PTSD), including the more complex posttraumatic presentations (e.g., complex PTSD; disorder of extreme stress not otherwise specified), somatoform disorders, personality disorders (e.g., borderline personality disorder), attachment disorders, and many others. When dissociation is a significant part of the clinical presentation, it often presents a barrier to effective treatment. It tends to interfere with clients' sense of their own body, their ability to experience emotion, and emotional regulation. Moreover, dissociation tends to result in unpredictable ego state shifts and the continuity of self.

Dissociation and EMDR—Early Experience
with Complex Trauma Cases

As early as 1992, Paulsen identified that EMDR had a tendency to associate material that had been dissociated in PTSD and dissociative disorders (Paulsen, 1992). In the case of dissociative disorders, EMDR tended to break through dissociative barriers, suggesting that EMDR may affect an underlying neurobiological mechanism of dissociation (Lanius, 2000). Others (Fine et al., 1995; Shapiro, 1995, 2001) subsequently introduced changes to EMDR training that included the emphasis of significant precautions with regard to the use of EMDR in individuals with significant dissociative symptoms, and requiring the screening all clients for the presence of an undiagnosed dissociative disorder prior to conducting EMDR (Paulsen, 1993a, 1993b, 1995a).

Given EMDR's tendency to associate material, it may increase connectivity in the brain by breaking through dissociative barriers. If there is limited traumatic material, Information Processing typically occurs rapidly, with clients experiencing rapid resolution of symptoms without overwhelming clients' ability to process unresolved traumatic experience.

On the other hand, if there is an overwhelming history of trauma, usually including early childhood trauma or significant attachment trauma, traumatic material is often too extensive to be integrated using the EMDR Standard Protocol. Accessing of one traumatic experience often results in accessing multiple other traumatic experiences with the result that the clients become overwhelmed, exhibiting profound hyperarousal, dissociation, or combinations thereof, that interfere with mindfulness and dual awareness to the point where effective Information Processing no longer occurs and clients become retraumatized.

Adapting EMDR to Working with Dissociative Symptoms

While the EMDR Standard Protocol includes a significant focus on the body, this can be insufficient for clients to continue effective processing in cases of significant depersonalization and derealization (Lanius, 2000). To facilitate EMDR processing in clients with dissociative symptoms, histories of attachment trauma, and low ego strength, many clinicians have adopted a variety of interventions that are variants of ego state and somatic interventions. Paulsen established the ACT-AS-IF phased approach to using EMDR with dissociative clients, and the

ARCHITECTS approach for phases of EMDR processing of complex trauma cases (Paulsen, 2007a, in press). Those approaches integrated ego state therapy within the phases of EMDR. This chapter extends that integrated approach to include somatic interventions.

Many clinicians recognize the utility of somatic interventions. Under increased levels of stress, brain areas involved in higher levels of Information Processing (e.g., cognitive and emotional processing) become increasingly less active, resulting in diminished information processing. Moreover, as emotional numbing and affect intolerance are integral parts of traumatic stress symptoms and one of the hallmarks of dissociation, this seems to be, in part, attributable to a disconnection from the body (e.g., depersonalization). By focusing on somatic tolerance prior to accessing emotion, we help our clients increase affect tolerance. Panksepp (2001a, 2001b) has cogently argued that affect is largely a subcortical process, a notion that is supported in neuroimaging research (Damasio et al., 2000).

Many of these procedures can be used during the stabilization phase, prior to proceeding with trauma-focused work, but many of them also work well in tandem with the EMDR Standard Protocol in a way that can be conceptualized as an interweave, in a different form than the familiar cognitive interweave.

The writers have been studying the combination of these methods with the EMDR Standard Protocol for several years. We have the highest regard for the robustness of the EMDR Standard Protocol and believe it should be used wherever possible. This chapter is intending to provide guidance for when and how to utilize ego state and somatic procedure while maintaining the integrity of the Standard Protocol.

Fractionating and Titrating: Association, Dissociation, and Pacing the Processing

EMDR, ego state therapy, and somatic therapy fit together like hand and glove. This is not the serendipitous combination of any few therapies for a hybrid or eclectic result. Rather, it is the skillful use of an associative procedure (EMDR) with two therapeutic procedures, one that works with dissociation (ego state therapy) and one that works with dissociation's foundational substrate (somatic therapy). Both approaches can be used to prepare for and regulate the pace of association during EMDR by *deliberately* utilizing dissociation to determine pace and titrate affective intensity. EMDR tends to process rapidly, so with straightforward processing in simple cases, the processing does not require the same level of regulation ability. EMDR processing in simple cases can be set on "cruise control," the Standard Protocol, because it resembles an open road suitable for driving at high speeds. In complex trauma cases it is necessary to have the ability to either accelerate or decelerate as needed because the road has precarious twists and turns in it.

An extended Preparation Phase is sometimes necessary in complex traumatic stress presentations and attachment-related syndromes, particularly when dealing with the sequelae of chronic early trauma. Clinical practice suggests that the adjunctive use of body therapy and ego state interventions can be useful, during stabilization and later on in increasing the treatment response to EMDR.

Traditional treatment of complex PTSD and dissociative disorders has usually included hypnoanalytic interventions during which abreaction is considered an important part of treatment beginning with Janet in the 1900s (van der Hart, Brown, & van der Kolk, 1989), Watkins in World War II (Paulsen & Watkins, 2005), and up to present time (e.g., Fine, 1993; Kluft, 1984; Phillips & Frederick, 1995). Many such approaches can be conceptualized as ego state interventions. To this day ego state interventions remain one of the mainstays in the treatment of dissociative symptoms, both during stabilization and during trauma processing.

More recently, in conjunction with those early approaches to the treatment of dissociative disorders, both EMDR and body therapies have been used by practitioners in the treatment of complex trauma and dissociative disorders. Moreover, treatment of trauma has moved from the notion of abreaction and exposure toward information processing, consistent with the concept of neural networks (e.g., Paulsen, 2001; Shapiro, 1995). Apart from EMDR, information processing as a concept is now also used by cognitive behavior therapists (e.g., Foa & Hears-Ikeda, 1996), as well as body therapists (Ogden & Minton, 2000). Within the field of dissociative disorders, van der Hart, Steele, Boon, and Brown (1993) have cogently argued that the notion of abreaction be replaced by one of synthesis. Rather than the focus being on discharge alone, information processing therapies focus on the processing of information, that is, synthesis during which unprocessed memory traces are integrated and processed, whereas abreaction per se does not necessarily result in processing of information.

Dissociation and the Nature of Traumatic Memory

While the experience of day-to-day, nontraumatic events are commonly integrated into consciousness without the sensory aspects of the event being registered separately (van der Kolk, McFarlane, & Weisaeth, 1996), traumatic memories seem to be different in nature (e.g., flashbacks lack such integration of experience). Traumatic memories appear to be timeless, predominantly nonverbal, imagery-based memories (van der Kolk & Fisler, 1995). Somatic memory is an essential element of traumatic memory—trauma memories, at least in part, are encoded at an implicit level (Brewin, Dalgleish, & Joseph, 1996).

Dissociation, in particular, results in an alteration in consciousness that disrupts the integration of information, resulting in clients' inability to integrate memories into the present context and to integrate the totality of what is happening into personal memory and identity. Thus these memories remain isolated from ordinary consciousness (e.g., van der Hart, van der Kolk, & Boon, 1998).

Information Processing and the Body

A crucial aspect of information processing and the integration of unprocessed memory traces is what Janet (1928) referred to as "Personification." Personification denotes relating synthesized material to one's general sense of self, which should become regularly adapted through synthetic actions, and to becoming consciously aware of the implications of a personal experience for one's whole life, giving one's history and sense of self a continuity (Nijenhuis, van der Hart, & Steele, 2004). At the same time, both experiencing and reaccessing overwhelming events commonly interferes with these integrative mental actions (e.g., Marmar, Weiss, & Metzler, 1998). Even in the presence of factual memory of an event, the traumatic experience has become disembodied, as these quotes by trauma survivors who experienced a dissociative response during script-driven imagery in a neuroimaging study illustrate (Lanius, et al., 2002):

- "I was outside my body looking down at myself."
- "I was looking down at my own body while I was back reliving the car accident."

In the absence of an embodied self, personification fails. The conscious awareness of the traumatic event will remain factual knowledge that does not seem to pertain to one's self. Unintegrated somatic memories related to the traumatic experience will continue to drive symptoms in their various forms. In other words, if the clients become disconnected from the somatic sense of their body—out-of-body experiences are one of the more common dissociative symptoms—and this state persists for any length of time, effective EMDR processing cannot occur.

Thus, for information processing and personification to occur, both dual awareness and an embodied self are essential. The client, in addition to focusing inside in order to process the information from the past, needs to be able to attend to the external stimuli presented by the clinician. This dual attention provides context to the memory and constrains the client's reaction to it in most cases. The therapist often needs to remind clients in order to maintain the dual attention awareness, by saying, "It's not happening now," "it's old stuff." The dual focus and the "here and now" orientation aid in efficient information processing during EMDR treatment. In addition, the focus on the body, as part of the Standard Protocol, likely facilitates personification. The EMDR Standard Protocol maintains the dual focus in large part by means of Bilateral Stimulation (BLS) administered by the clinician, that at the same time stimulates an Orienting Response (also compare Barrowcliff, MacCulloch, Freeman, & MacCulloch, 2003). The client, by attending to the sensory input occurring in the present moment, becomes aware that the traumatic memory is just a memory, something that is not happening now, but is in the past.

Dual Focus and Body Mindfulness

In the case of complex trauma and severe dissociation, the EMDR Standard Protocol can show its limitations in a variety of ways. One is uncontrolled bridging into multiple traumatic events, reflecting the integrative nature of the EMDR procedure. This can lead to intense overwhelm with both hyperarousal and dissociation, resulting in a loss of dual focus and body mindfulness, thus blocking further information processing, frequently leading to destabilization of the client. Not only may this block further processing, but it may lead to the client being retraumatized, as well as in some cases triggering self-harming behavior. At the very least, it will lead to increased avoidance and reluctance on part of the client to proceed with further EMDR treatment.

It is the authors' opinion that maintaining dual focus and body mindfulness during EMDR processing is paramount for effective treatment. Clients need to experience themselves within their bodies for effective EMDR processing. In the case of the more complex posttraumatic presentations including dissociative disorders, using a combination of ego state interventions and somatic interventions—both in the Preparation/stabilization Phase, then later in conjunction with the EMDR Standard Protocol—dual focus and body mindfulness can be maximized, therefore assuring efficient information processing. It is essential that the dual focus be maintained by fractionating and titrating traumatic material to reduce both dissociation and hyperarousal through somatic and ego state interventions.

The Window of Tolerance

Ogden and Minton (2000) and Ogden, Minton, and Pain (2006) describe a modulation model that represents a visual representation of the biphasic response to trauma (van der Kolk, 1987), for example, hyperarousal and dissociation.

When individuals' arousal levels fall within the window of tolerance (see Figure 19.1), by definition they feel comfortable with their level of activation. This allows processing of somatic, perceptual, affective, and cognitive information. It is under those conditions that information processing is optimized.

Traumatized individuals, on the other hand, tend to exhibit both hyperarousal and dissociation (Lanius et al., 2005, 2006, 2007), resulting in dysregulated arousal. Hyperarousal frequently results in tension reduction behaviors and ultimate leads to increased dissociation and a freezing and numbing response. (In some clients with extensive trauma histories, when such trauma is accessed, hypoarousal may occur as a conditioned response rather than secondary to excessive hyperarousal.) At this point, large portions of the cerebral cortex shut down and no further processing of information occurs (see Figure 19.2).

The clinician can aid the clients in staying within their optimal level of arousal through both somatic and ego state interventions.

Effective information processing occurs only within the window of tolerance. At the upper end of the window, information processing breaks down, likely due to significant peritraumatic dissociation that co-occurs with the apparent hyperarousal. Once the adrenalin charge of the hyperarousal disappears, the client will commonly be hypoaroused, often with significant numbing and depersonalization that obviates effective EMDR treatment. Thus, in contrast to the Standard

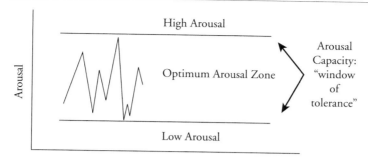

**Figure 19.1 Modulation Model: Optimum Arousal Zone
(from Ogden and Minton, 2000)**

Protocol, we suggest that in clients who tend to get stuck in significant hyperarousal or who flip from hyperarousal into depersonalization, the clinician work with the clients proactively to avoid as best as possible the extreme peaks of hyperarousal.

In clients who have a severe dissociative disorder, a switch commonly occurs at the point of extreme hyperarousal, with resulting unpredictable consequences for clinician and client. By keeping the client within the window of tolerance, uncontrolled switching can be reduced.

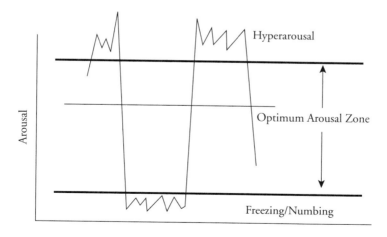

**Figure 19.2 The Modulation Model: The Bi-Phasic Response to Trauma
(from Ogden and Minton 2000).**

Ego State Interventions

Ego state interventions are based on the notion of a segmentation of the personality into different self-states or parts of the self, ranging from normal differentiation to a complete fragmentation of the self, dissociative identity disorder (DID). An ego state is defined as "an organized system of behavior and experience whose elements are bound together by some common principle, and which is separated from other such states by a boundary that is more or less permeable" (Watkins & Watkins, 1997; Watkins, 1986). Ego states may be organized to enhance adaptability in coping with specific events or problems and they can also be delineated by time dimensions, signifying the age at which formation occurred (child, adolescent or adult), affect, cognition, or bodily states, and so on.

In the authors' opinion, normal ego states reflect a functional self-system structure, in which information reflecting state dependent learning is grouped together for efficient retrieval. Ego state disorders, double binds, inner conflicts, or other unprocessed experience are held apart through relatively impermeable barriers, resulting in a range of symptoms.

A foundational premise of ego state therapy is that dissociated or disowned experience can be resolved by giving a voice to the perspective of that which has been disowned. Inner conflicts can be resolved by giving a voice to the sides of a conflict, so that each part's point of view can be explored and an overall perspective and consciousness of the poles of a conflict can bring resolution.

Federn (1952) introduced the term *ego state* and the notion of ego cathexis, where the subject ego state is executive, or, in Paulsen's terms (1992, 2007b, in press), "looking through the eyes." When an ego state is imbued with ego energy, it can articulate its perspective, including needs, burdens, and fears, thereby revealing cognitive errors or disorientation to person, place, or time.

To replace Federn's arduous language with plainer language, if ego state A is executive, or fully present in the room, it will use the language "I" in speaking of itself. If the same ego state is not executive, and rather is in the background as an object of discussion, it is in conscious mind but is not present in the room. Any other ego state, such as B, speaking of ego state A, will use third person pronouns "he, she, or it" because ego state A is experienced as "not me" and is "over there."

The device of shifting executive function (first person "I") to objective "he, she, or it" enables important insights and shifts to occur that might be harder to achieve if the ego state is only executive and in first person. For example, Cruella Mallificent may describe herself as a 21-year-old seductress with a cruel streak. When she is executive and interviewed by the therapist, she may seem haughty and imperious. When viewed as "that girl, she," Cruella is seen as "over there" by another part of the self that is executive for the moment. Suddenly, the newly executive part realizes that Cruella Mallificent appears in the mind's eye to be about 6 years old and is wearing high heels too big for her, a fur stole, and holding a cigarette holder.

The opposite is also true. As long as a part of the self is experienced as "not me" and "over there," the experience continues to be dissociated and cannot be processed to an adaptive resolution, whether with EMDR or any other method. When a therapist speaks directly to a pushed-away part, we add energy to that part, making it more salient, more in conscious mind, and more present in the room. When the part answers in the first person, "I," and is co-conscious or co-present with any other parts of self in a new way, the material begins to be owned and reassociated. Somatic experience is almost always in the first person (e.g., "I feel tingling"), although it can also represent dissociated (conversion) symptoms (e.g., "my hand is numb, and I don't know why," or even "her hand is tingling"). When clients describe a bodily symptom they doesn't understand, asking for an ego state that knows about that story may produce, in the mind's eye, specific information about the memory behind the symptom. Watkins and Watkins (1987) and Barabasz and Watkins (2005) described hypnotherapeutic procedures to enable ego and object cathexis as well as hypnotic abreactive procedures to use with ego states to detoxify memories. Others have contributed to this literature, emphasizing hypnotherapeutic procedures (e.g., Fine, 1993; Kluft, 1982). Paulsen (1995a, 1995b, 1996) published the first protocol integrating ego state therapy and EMDR (see also Watkins, 1994; Watkins & Paulsen, 2003, 2004). Lazrove and Fine (1996), Fine and Berkowitz (2001), Phillips (2007), Paulsen (2003, 2004a, 2004b), Lanius (2005), Forgash and Copeley (2007), Knipe (2007), and others have further developed those procedures. Watkins and Watkins conceptualized ego state therapy as a hypnoanalytic and hypnotherapeutic set of procedures, although recent writers utilize the procedures without formal trance induction (see Emmerson [2003], Paulsen [2007b]). The hypnosis tradition contributes a great deal to ego state therapy, including the use of the Dissociative Table procedure (Fraser,

1991, 2003; Paulsen, 1995b, 2007b, in press). Distancing maneuvers and fractionation procedures (e.g., Fine, 1993; Kluft, 1990) are especially useful for decelerating processing that is too intense. Paulsen (1995b, 2001, 2003, 2004b, 2007b, in press) has described the use of resources in the conference room to achieve distancing and accessing within the context of EMDR. Comparing EMDR and ego state methods of processing trauma are outside the scope of this paper, but have been considered by one of the authors and the father of ego state therapy (Paulsen & Watkins, 2003).

Phillips and Frederick (1995) published the first book on ego state therapy, which included a description of the application of ego state therapy to individuals outside of those who have a formal dissociative disorder. The founders of ego state therapy (Watkins & Watkins, 1997) laid out the psychoanalytic theoretical basis for and elements of ego state therapy, including adding or subtracting ego and object energy to activate or deactivate states.

The EMDR Standard Protocol

When we use the EMDR Standard Protocol, we work with sensorimotor, emotional, and cognitive aspects of information. These correlate with the three levels of brain architecture described by MacLean (1990): (a) The sensorimotor level of information processing (including sensation and programmed movement impulses) is initiated primarily by lower rear portions of the brain, (b) emotional processing by more intermediate limbic parts of the brain, and (c) cognitive processing by the frontal cortical upper parts of the brain. These three levels interact and affect each other simultaneously, functioning as a cohesive whole, with the degree of integration of each level of processing affecting the efficacy of other levels (e.g., Damasio, 1999; Schore, 1994, 2001, 2003).

The EMDR Standard Protocol integrates cognitive, emotional, and sensory information. Bottom-up processing focuses on sensory and sensorimotor processing. In individuals with significant dissociative symptoms accessing all levels of information processing simultaneously can be overwhelming and result in increased dissociation and decreased information processing.

The Nature of Traumatic Memories

Gazzaniga (1980) argued that memory is the result of a conglomerate of independently functioning mental systems that mainly reflect nonverbal processing systems in the brain. Memory is not a unitary process; rather, it is composed of multiple processes and systems (Tulving & Schachter, 1990). Memory of a specific event is not stored or processed in a single location in the brain but is distributed across a network of different brain areas.

Vivid remembering has been shown to activate areas of the somatosensory cortex (Wheeler, Peterson, & Buckner, 2000). When people recalled and reexperienced personal life episodes marked by sadness, happiness, anger, or fear, the process of feeling such emotions resulted in activation of the somatosensory cortex (Damasio et al., 2000).

Van der Kolk, McFarlane, and Weisaeth (1996) suggested that the experience of day-to-day, nontraumatic events is integrated into consciousness without the sensory aspects of the event being registered separately. Flashbacks, on the other hand, lack such integration of experience. Indeed, they have been described as timeless, predominantly nonverbal, imagery-based memories (Brewin et al., 1996; Lanius et al., 2004; van der Kolk & Fisler, 1995), lending support to the notion that the failure to integrate traumatic memories into the present context accounts for their ongoing disturbing nature (Lanius et al., 2005), as well as their timeless, predominantly nonverbal, imagery-based memories (van der Kolk & Fisler, 1995). Brewin et al. (1996) specifically referred to somatic memory—trauma memories that are at least in part encoded at the implicit, unconscious, level.

Selves and the Body

While it is common for trauma survivors to experience a fragmented sense of self, and in many cases multiple selves, there is ultimately only one body. The fragmentation of self at some level is cortical, even though it may relate to separate reptilian brain or animal defensive responses (Panksepp, 2001b). Within the lower brain structures the brain is unified; thus working with the body is ultimately integrative.

Due to the integrative nature of working on a body level, many very dissociative clients are phobic of experiencing themselves in their bodies, so it is challenging to work toward somatic awareness with them. At the same time, proceeding to EMDR and trauma-focused treatment without somatic awareness is likely to result in poor treatment outcomes.

Somatic awareness also increases the likelihood of accessing somatic memory. Traumatic memory tends to be nonverbal in nature, more likely accessed. For a lasting treatment effect, working with the somatic traces of traumatic memory is essential. The somatic memories that are responsible for a multitude of traumatic stress syndromes also give us the opportunity to integrate, reevaluate, and reprocess the experience that brought them about in the first place. As Cowan (1997) suggested:

> Sensory memory has a special place in information processing. It is our protection against living in a fragmented present, dominated by our own arbitrary and abstract interpretations of the outside world on a moment-by-moment basis. We think about things at a finite pace, and sensory memory of these things allows the memory of these things to linger while we think about them. (pp. 49–50)

We then reprocess them and integrate them into our present day experience.

Affect and the Body—The Importance of Subcortical Processes

Whereas healthy adults are able to control their emotional drives through cognitive processes, in the process they may deprive themselves of their emotional needs. Higher levels of processing can often influence and direct lower levels.

In PTSD, the opposite is commonly the case: Sensory fragments can take on a life of their own and intrude at any moment, beyond cognitive control. In this case, lower levels of processing may influence and direct higher levels. Our understanding of these processes can be informed by research with split-brain patients, who outside the laboratory context still behave in a unified manner during everyday activities, despite the fact that the main transcortical bridge or corpus callosum, that is, the fibers that connect the two halves of the brain) has been bisected. In this case, information is conveyed through lower subcortical structures or what has been referred as the subcortical bridge (Austin, 1998).

Sensory Fragments and the Subcortical Bridge

Austin (1998) suggested that the sorts of messages transferred across the subcortical bridge for the most part are "unconscious or preconscious codes, nuances we can never attach a name to." Similarly, Gazzaniga, Holtzman, and Smylie (1987) suggested that information relayed from right to left hemisphere in this way tends to be noncognitive in nature. When these messages cross over from the left side to the right, they may engage a kind of "response readiness." In the left hemisphere this information may facilitate potential speech responses that are already well rehearsed and ready to be uttered. This is the basis for what is referred to as bottom-up processing (see below).

Dissociation and Sensory Stimulation in EMDR

Sensory stimulation as it is used in EMDR may have multiple effects that are relevant to dissociation. Christman, Garvey, Propper, and Phaneuf (2003) suggested that sensory stimulation improved episodic memory, as well as increasing interhemispheric connectivity (Christman & Propper, 2001; Christman et al., 2003). Similarly, Parker et al. (2008) suggested that eye movements resulted in increased retrieval of memory, including associative and contextual information. Interestingly enough, eye movements also appear to reduce false recognition (Parker & Dagnall, 2007).

Furthermore, 40 Hz oscillatory brain activity that has been related to information processing. It is reset by sensory stimulation (Joliot, Ribary, & Llinas, 1994). That is, 40 hz brain activity occurs during REM sleep and the alert waking state. It appears to be involved in the temporal conjunction of different sensory components into one global image, an event that is referred to as temporal cognitive binding. This notion bears remarkable resemblance to Adaptive Information Processing (AIP). As Llinas (2002) suggested with regard to temporal cognitive binding, "It is this temporally coherent event that binds, in the time domain, the fractured components of external and internal reality into a single construct—the self" (p. 126).

Thus, the sensory stimulation that is part of EMDR likely has direct effects on memory and the integration of experience, and consequently on the person's sense of self.

Polyvagal Theory and EMDR

EMDR may facilitate attentional orienting (Kuiken et al., 2001). Based on Sokolov's (1963) work, MacCulloch and Feldman (1996) suggested that an investigatory orienting response (Sokolov, Spinks, Lyytinen, & Naatanen, 2002) may be an explanation for the EMDR effect. Traditionally, with regard to the autonomic nervous system, a distinction has been made between the sympathetic nervous system and the parasympathetic nervous system. Sympathetic and parasympathetic divisions typically function in opposition to each other. But this opposition is complementary in nature, not antagonistic. For an analogy, one may think of the sympathetic division as the accelerator and the parasympathetic division as the brake. For instance, sympathetic arousal prepares the body for fight and flight. The parasympathetic nervous system is not only involved in calming and relaxation, but also in a dissociative response.

Porges (2001), above and beyond differentiating between the sympathetic and parasympathetic nervous system, suggested that the parasympathetic nervous system can be further divided into two different branches: the dorsal vagal nervous system and the ventral vagal nervous system. Porges suggested that the dorsal vagal system is activated if the fight-or-flight response fails. It activates in dissociated or numbed response, as well as being involved in freezing, surrendering, preparing for death. The ventral vagal nervous system, sometimes also referred to as the social engagement system, is associated with social communication, self-soothing, and calming and thus with self-regulation and emotional regulation. (See Chapter 1.)

Porges's polyvagal theory dovetails with the notion of an orienting response being in part responsible for the EMDR treatment effect. The authors think that the sensory stimulation that is part of the EMDR Standard Protocol commonly results in an investigatory orienting response, interest affect, and a social engagement response. The sensory stimulation utilized in EMDR is reminiscent of the sensory stimulation involved in child rearing (visual, kinesthetic, auditory), and it likely produces not only an orienting response but also social engagement.

Treatment Implications

Research suggests that sensory stimulation increases integration of sensory traces and memory. At the same time, sensory input may also stimulate social engagement. Social engagement, the myelinated ventral vagal response, results in increased self-regulation and calming, thus decreasing the likelihood of a dorsal vagal response. It also likely produces interest affect, as part of an investigatory orienting response, both of which likely counter an unmyelinated ventral vagal (distress) or dorsal vagal dissociative response, thus increasing the likelihood of efficient information processing. (In the next session, "ventral vagal state" refers to the myelinated ventral state of relaxed interest and capacity for social engagement.)

As noted above, the sensory stimulation in EMDR likely has a twofold effect. On one hand, it increases affective regulation, thus maintaining the client's staying within the window of tolerance; on the other hand, it appears to increase associative access to memories. In that sense, sensory stimulation has both an accelerative and a braking function at the same time.

With severely dissociative clients, the effect of sensory stimulation is to accelerate processing by accessing previously dissociated memory. This acceleration will likely overwhelm any braking regulatory effect and the client's ability to integrate the information. This requires titration through ego state and other interventions. It is the authors' view that in extreme cases sensory stimulation needs to be stopped completely to avoid the introduction of additional traumatic material. At the same time, it is important to maintain dual awareness under these circumstances. The therapist needs to maximize social engagement and thereby increase the client's awareness of the here and now. Staying present is paramount.

ELEMENTS OF SOMATIC THERAPY

Somatic interventions are distinguished from other psychotherapeutic interventions in that they are expressed in markedly slowed-down time, in order to give clients ample time to experience the felt sense of their bodies. In somatic therapy it is understood that to associate dissociated experience one directs attention to body sensation and regulates the pace of the work with intermittent use of resourcing as long as necessary (Stanley, 2005, 2006). The following categories are drawn largely from Stanley (2005, 2006) in her Somatic Experiencing (Levine, 1997) and Somatic Transformation workshops.

Breathing

The EMDR Standard Protocol involves the therapist encouraging the client to take a deep breath after a set. This enhances body mindfulness and reminds the client to use one of the primary regulatory mechanisms they have available: breathing. Research suggests that breathing not only has a regulatory effect on physiological activity in the body, but also in the brain.

Breathing, as used in Taoist and Buddhist practice, as part of relaxation training, and as an essential part of somatic interventions, appears to have a profound effect on amygdalar hippocampal functioning. Frysinger and Harper (1989) found that inspiration increased the rate of cell firing in the limbic system, and the amygdala in particular, whereas expiration led to a decrease in cell firing—the brain was quieting. It's our observation in clinical practice that Buddhist types of breathing, which focus on relaxation, tend to be more effective with hyperarousal states. Taoist breathing approaches, which focus on maintaining tension in the body through prolonged expiration (e.g., shouting during martial arts), seem to be more useful in clients who exhibit dissociative responses. Thus, quenching amygdala activation by means of breathing during the recall of traumatic memories may optimize information processing by, on one hand, increasing, and, on the other hand, decreasing, amygdala activity.

Many therapists use extended, extremely long sets with clients. As a result, the focus on breathing can get lost. A dorsal vagal or dissociative response often involves shallow breathing, or even stopping breathing. In this case the therapist may invoke a somatic interweave: alerting the clients to their relative lack of breathing or shallow breath, or else reminding the clients to breathe. A word of caution: Many clients have learned to reduce unwanted physiological sensation through the use of breath. Therefore, the therapist may want to instruct the clients not to do that, but rather to focus on the body sensation and at the same time breath into it, without trying to get rid of the sensation; just noticing it.

Somatic Empathy

Somatic empathy is a foundational element that underlies all other somatic interventions (Paulsen & Stanley, 2006). It involves the therapist attending as completely as possible to the client's somatic experience. This may involve asking about and attending to the client's self report of subject experience, or, in an experienced therapist, using intuition to perceive the client's felt somatic sense in the therapist's own bodily experience (Solomon, Watkins & Paulsen, 2004). Somatic empathy is expressed by the therapists' activation of his/her own ventral vagal state, with its experience of connection to self, other, and contextual resources. In that resourced state, the therapist simultaneously attends closely to the client's felt sense. The client's experience is the shared focus of client and therapist. Holding this ventral vagal state potentiates the client's capacity to tolerate sensation. The therapeutic alliance becomes the holding environment in which the client can emerge from dorsal vagal shutdown or resolve sympathetic arousal in the safety of a connection with the therapist's healing expectancies, which strengthen the client's own.

Boundaries

Boundaries are crucial to one's sense of self, to a sense of safety, and to effective treatment of trauma-related disorders. Boundaries frequently fail to become properly developed through attachment injury; they become invaded in trauma, and sometimes become excessively rigid in an effort to ward off further trauma. The development of a client's sense of a boundaried self is crucial to effective treatment of dissociative disorders.

Boundaries can be explored with simple exercises involving body mindfulness. Clients can explore their response to physical proximity by focusing on the body while varying distance between themselves and the therapist. The therapist may then ask the clients to stretch out their arms with their hands raised vertically and ask them to draw an imaginary boundary around themselves and ask the clients what happens in their body. In most clients this will result in a sense of increased strength, but there are others who occasionally move into further collapse, as they will experience a sense of isolation—these clients are more likely to want to merge with the therapist. In this case, gentle but firm boundaries on the part of the therapist are crucial. In the case of a client wanting to merge, prior to moving into trauma treatment, these issues need to be explored from an attachment perspective, gently building somatic tolerance by using body mindfulness in the process. Other clients, on setting a physical boundary, may go into an inhibitory shame response. Such a response is a cue to do more work with the underlying attachment issues, to build more tolerance for the act of setting a boundary.

Another simple boundary exercise is the use of a string or cord of sufficient length for clients to make a circle around themselves. Again, the therapist needs to explore how the clients' sense of somatic self changes.

All these exercises are useful to help clients with experiencing a so-matic sense of self prior to embarking on trauma-centered treatment using the EMDR Standard Protocol. However, in the case of looping or overwhelm, they can also be used during EMDR processing to keep clients within the window of tolerance. For instance, clients can put the string or cord around themselves while engaging in EMDR processing. If clients are at the edge of hyperarousal, the therapist may consider asking the clients to get up, stretch out their arms with the hands up-ward, and draw a boundary around themselves, an interweave that combines boundaries with intentional movement (see below).

Somatic Resourcing

Somatic resourcing evokes and strengthens clients' capacity to be in their own ventral vagal state. With somatic empathy as a basis, the therapist expresses a respectful curiosity about the experiences that the clients find life enhancing. The clients describe either external environ-ments or internal phenomena that bring them comfort or pleasure or safety or other desirable felt sense. The therapist joins the clients with empathic delight as the therapist observes positive felt sense in the clients, whether by smiles, twinkling eyes, relaxation, leaning forward, or other expressions of connectedness and engagement.

With nondissociative clients, the therapist can next inquire what the clients are noticing in the body. With highly dissociative clients, re-sourcing occurs first by limiting discussion to the phenomenon that evokes the ventral vagal response, without asking the clients to notice the body. Over time, repeated engagement of the ventral vagal nervous system will create a safe state for the client to begin to notice somatic sense. Resources can be anything, ranging from a walk on the beach, the sight of a starry night, the brown eyes of a horse, the coo of a baby, prayer, or satisfaction at making a delicious coleslaw. It is important is to have a full armamentarium of resources to strengthen the clients' ca-pacity to be in a ventral vagal state. Improved access to ventral vagal states means the clients will be able to tolerate negative affect and so-matic pain better than without this resourcing.

Intentional Movement

In cases of unremitting hyperarousal, and even more so in cases of dor-sal vagal shutdown, the use of a movement interweave can reestablish a defensive response and bring the client back into the window of tolerance. In this case the therapist can ask clients to get up and move around. This tends to be profoundly resourcing to clients and usually brings them back to being present in their bodies.

Somatic Tracking

Damasio (1994) states: "The background body sense is continuous, though one hardly notices it, since it represents not a specific part of anything g in the body, but rather an overall state of most everything in it" (p.152). Ogden et al. (2006) find that "the capacity to sense and describe sensation and to uncouple it from trauma-related emotions and cognitions enhance the possibility of client's reintegrating the somatic experience of their trauma, in order to establish new meanings and understandings of their past" (p. 17).

Somatic tracking is another foundational element of somatic work. It refers to the therapist's inquiring, moment to moment, in a very relaxed and slow fashion, about the client's felt sense. Sometimes this involves asking what clients are noticing in their body, and where, in one moment and then the next. Sometimes tracking involves the therapist noticing something that clients may not yet have noticed, such as a clenching, or movement of an extremity, or a facial flushing.

The client is invited to report not the names of emotions, or interpretations, or cognitive reports, but the primitive and raw data of the felt sense of the body, namely descriptions of body sensations: pressure, warmth, tightness, heaviness, aching, and so on. If the client reports the name of an emotion, or a thought or image, the therapist then invites the client to report the somatic experience underlying that emotion or thought (such as tears, flushing, jaw clench) rather than the names of emotions or the thoughts themselves. Intuitive clinicians may pick up the sensory experience in their own body, without visually observing signs of it, and may wonder aloud if that felt sense is the client's experience as well.

Tracking refers also to therapist's ability to closely notice and follow the moment-to-moment process of clients' nonverbal behavior. These may be as subtle as pupil dilation, small sighs, or a pulse in neck. Tracking may result in awareness of a fidgeting of the extremities, which tends to indicate thwarted fight-or-flight responses and leads to other interventions. Ogden et al. (2006) suggest that by helping the clients slow down and become mindful observers of their orienting and attentional responses, their awareness their awareness of how and why they focus their attention is increased. When the therapist and clients are quietly tracking the clients' felt sense from moment to moment, clients are less likely to have their attention distracted. As clients come to focus on tracking their own bodily process, with curiosity, there is an increased capacity to tolerate affect, and one could say, an increased mindfulness skill, an internal stance of a nonjudgmental observing, wonder, and acceptance.

The pacing of tracking is somewhat similar to what clinicians do in EMDR therapy when we say, "Just notice it" or "Go with that," but with a difference. In EMDR all channels are equal (cognitive, affective, bodily). The only time a therapist would deliberately shift the client's attention to the somatic channel over other channels would be (a) if the client engages in excessive intellectualization and needs to be drawn to the body because there is a kind of looping occurring in which the Subjective Units of Disturbance (SUD) and Validity of Cognition (VOC) are not resolving, a kind of "circling the airport" loop, or (b) if the EMDR is stuck, a kind of "broken record" looping (Paulsen, 2007a). In somatic work, body sensation is considered to have primacy and is the foundational channel. Typical tracking queries might be *"What are you noticing in your body in this moment . . . (long pause) . . . and in this moment?"* For clients who are not highly dissociative, one asks specifically, *"Where exactly is that sensation of heaviness?"* whereas with a highly dissociative client, the therapist is quite content if the client can report "heaviness" or "aching." To draw a client away from conversation and to bodily sensation, a therapist may ask, *"What's happening in your body as we talk?"* and then *"What are you noticing in THIS moment?"*

A therapist may draw attention to something observed, such as fidgeting feet, or drumming fingers, or tension in the jaw, and invite the client to just notice those sensations with curiosity, and without speech, for some moments. If the client's attention returns to cognition, typically the therapist will gently redirect attention to the body. Tracking can be conducted with or without what EMDR practitioners call a "target." In order to train a client to track, it is wise to begin tracking without a target. There is an understanding that if traumatic material is ready, it will be held in the body and tracking will soon find the body sensations associated with the trauma.

Discharging

In somatic therapy, bodily held disturbance is understood to be observable by clinician and client, to the degree the client has learned to notice, as small discharges of energy. Evidence of spontaneous discharging of pent-up or thwarted sympathetic arousal includes: the fluttering of eyes, twitching, ticking, lip quivering, overt shaking, and more. The intervention involves inviting the client to merely notice the discharging sensation, without intervening in it bodily.

During EMDR processing, the therapist may make a somatic interweave by asking the client to notice what the body wants to do, just allowing it to happen. This may range from the body moving through shaking, twitching, limbs moving, the client enacting a variety of defensive responses, and so on. It is important that this occurs mindfully within the therapeutic relationship.

As a result of tracking, arousal or disturbance is accessed and begins to spontaneously discharge. Over time, clients become increasingly comfortable with noticing and allowing the natural process of discharging.

Spontaneous Oscillations

In the course of many somatic interventions, the therapist may observe the client engaging in a spontaneous rhythmic movement, whether a healing pulse, a rocking, or even spontaneous BLS behaviors (Stanley, 2007). In somatic therapy, it is understood that spontaneous oscillations are evidence of the body recalibrating itself, and coming into a new coherency, spontaneously (Siegel, 1999). The client is more likely to allow spontaneous oscillations if there have been prior experiences of deliberately evoked oscillations. Deliberate oscillations, described below, may prime the client to notice and allow spontaneous ones. In short, oscillation is understood as being on a continuum from deliberate and evoked to spontaneous (Stanley, 2007).

Evoked Oscillations

A primary assumption in somatic therapy is that the client's attention to disturbing material should be punctuated with repeated return to a more resourced sense of self. The therapist will ask the client to "pendulate" back and forth between the felt sense of a resource and the felt sense of a disturbance (e.g., focus on the trauma on one hand and the resourced state on the other, just going back and forth). This helps the client to stay in the window of tolerance between hyperarousal (sympathetic arousal flooding) and hypoarousal (dorsal vagal shutdown).

Moving back and forth between the painful and the resourced states titrates the intensity so the adroit clinician can keep the client in an optimal range where efficient information processing occurs. This can be considered "titration," but this pendulating is also an evoked oscillation, which will potentially catalyze the body's innate and spontaneous oscillations (Stanley, 2007).

When using the EMDR Standard Protocol with individuals who have significant ego strength and are sufficiently resourced, clients will often spontaneously access resourced self states and spontaneously process to an adaptive resolution. Clients who have ego state disorders may have limited resources to begin. When planning EMDR processing, the therapist resources clients before processing begins, or, if the processing gets stuck (loops), the therapist actively aids clients in accessing these resourced states by introducing a cognitive or somatic interweave during trauma processing. EMDR Standard Protocol differs from somatic therapy in this regard. In the latter, the therapist deliberately and rhythmically moves the client's attention between traumatic material and resource material, in order to prevent overwhelm or stuck processing. In the former, the therapist metaphorically stays off the track and allows the processing to proceed down the trauma track, only providing an intervention if the train is stuck.

Somatic Micromovements

An important somatic intervention is initiation of micromovements to release trapped sympathetic arousal. Sympathetic arousal is assumed to be present when the therapist observes fidgeting of the client's extremities. The therapist invites the client to notice what that extremity wants to do, what urge there may be behind the fidgeting. If the client does not know, the therapist may invite hypothesis testing about a particular urge. If, for example, the client has a clenched fist, but denies an urge to punch, the therapist may gently invite the client to test the hypothesis that there is a thwarted wish to punch, by allowing a very slow punching movement. A sudden, dramatic movement (instead of a very slow one) would release nothing and would only represent acting out. This is because a gradual attenuated movement is needed to release a thwarted sympathetic arousal impulse. The term *micromovements* describes these almost comically slow movements.

The therapist may offer physical resistance if appropriate for a given client and the therapeutic relationship. In the prior example, while the client is engaging in very slow punching movement, the therapists may extend their hand for the client to slowly "punch" or push against. The point of the resistance is not to engage in a contest, but to give the client the felt sense of punching successfully while making contact with resistance. Often clients will approach the task gingerly, so the therapists must shepherd the action to completion. For example, if the client is engaging in micromovement to express a thwarted urge to push away someone who violated the client's bodily boundaries, the client will often only push away a short distance, as if there is not much of a right to one's own space and body. The therapist may gently invite the client to continue, with language like, *"How would it be to continue that, that's right, fully extending the arms, that's it, all the way."* An energy-sensitive clinician will often notice waves of energy being released from the client in the final inches of the pushing away, as the arms are fully extended. Theoretically, the action activates the client's sympathetic nervous system, allowing release of the thwarted impulse. Clients commonly wish to express the motion rapidly, but again, this accomplishes nothing, and *"easy does it," "slower still"* are common therapeutic utterances. If the client is frightened or unable to engage in micromovements, the intervention is likely premature, and more resourcing and tracking experience is needed before doing them. Grounding will help restabilize a client who is not able to complete micromovements.

INTEGRATING SOMATIC AND EGO STATE THERAPIES INTO EMDR TREATMENT

The goal of EMDR therapy is to catalyze unprocessed experience that had a maladaptive learning outcome, and process it to an adaptive resolution using the brain's innate information processing system and healing tendency. Complete treatment of the disturbance being targeted is accomplished within a Three-Pronged Protocol that addresses the Past, Present and Future. The term *processed* is used to distinguish the work from talk therapy, and to describe the metabolizing or digesting of disturbing experiences so that it can be stored appropriately in the brain, retaining useful learning and meaning, and discarding that which is not useful. Often emotions, beliefs, and body sensations that have been frozen in the brain are discarded as a result of processing. The result of EMDR therapy is that the emotions and beliefs that are adaptive and healthy will remain, and will lead to adaptive and healthy behaviors and experiences. This processing occurs in a systematic manner that follows eight discrete steps, namely: (a) Client History and Treatment Planning, (b) Preparation, to include resourcing as needed, (c) Assessment of the EMDR target, (d) Desensitization using BLS, (e) Installation of the Positive Cognition (PC), (f) Body Scan where appropriate, (g) Closure of incomplete sessions, preparation for session to end, and (h) Reevaluation of the target at the subsequent session.

Because of the robustness of the EMDR protocol, the authors maintain its integrity while integrating ego state and somatic procedures (Paulsen, 2007a; Paulsen & Stanley, 2006; Paulsen & Watkins, 2005). The following will expand the definition of each EMDR phase and, for each phase, give examples of using ego state and/or somatic interventions.

History and Treatment Planning Phase

The initial step is for the therapist to take a thorough history of the client along with the presenting problem(s), and from those develop a treatment plan. This typically involves one or more specific EMDR targets that represent specific traumatic memories or disturbing experiences that prototypically represent recurring problem experiences. The therapist interviews to obtain additional present day triggers that evoke the disturbance, and identifies future desired experiences skills or performances.

In individuals with significant dissociative symptoms, attempting to take a detailed history prior to establishing therapeutic rapport with the clients and their parts will lead to unnecessary triggering and interfere with therapeutic progress. A detailed trauma history may be overwhelming during early stages of treatment or inaccessible because of amnestic barriers. Regardless, prior to initiating trauma-focused treatment, it is worth taking the time to gather an adequate history and formulate a treatment plan that starts with assuring or developing resources needed for processing traumatic material.

Depending on the severity of the client's dissociation, it may be useful to delay taking a detailed trauma history during the initial sessions before sufficient rapport is developed, as this may result in the client accessing traumatic material that is potentially overwhelming or accessing ego states that are not ready to be present in the therapy room or in conscious mind.

Behavioral signs indicative of dissociative symptoms include but are not limited to staring into space, trailing off, and impaired attention. Trancing behaviors such as repetitive rocking or leg bouncing, self-destructive behaviors that are often performed in an automated fashion (e.g., digging nails into skin), alterations in speech patterns, sophistication of level of language, postural changes, personality changes, changes in behavior such as suddenly wanting to leave the session, changing the topic, becoming aggressive, and childlike behavior are all suggestive of a dissociative disorder. Further, multiple previous diagnoses, Schneiderian first rank symptoms (such as "voices" and "thought insertion") (Kluft, 1987), evidence of seizure-like symptoms (Lanius & Lanius, 2000) and soft neurological symptoms (Gurvits et al., 2000), and significant headache activity are also potentially suggestive of a dissociative disorder.

Clients who exhibit any of the following will usually require more extended stabilization prior to proceeding with trauma-focussed treatment with the EMDR Standard Protocol. They show signs of:

- Being easily flooded with overwhelming feelings.
- Having the inability to experience positive emotions.
- Being unable to identify feelings and/or body sensations.
- Being actively suicidal/homicidal.
- Having poor impulse control.
- Abusing substances.
- Having significant dissociative symptoms.
- Having an unstable therapeutic alliance.
- Going through a current life crisis.

It is the therapist's responsibility to ensure clients are sufficiently stabilized prior to proceeding with the EMDR Standard Protocol. In clients who do not have internal resources or ego strengths, and who cannot identify emotions or body sensations, the use of the full protocol can produce feelings of failure, frustration, and regression.

In addition to administering psychometric measures such as the Dissociative Experiences Scale (DES)—some very dissociative clients present with spuriously low scores—a number of screening questions to evaluate for the possibility of dissociative symptoms can be a useful part of assessment:

- *Do people ever tell you that you have said things that you cannot remember?* (losing time)

- *Do any parts of your body ever go numb?* (somatoform dissociation)
- *Do you ever have any out-of-body experiences, like looking at yourself from the top of the ceiling?* (depersonalization)

Comprehensive assessment for dissociation via interviewing has been discussed elsewhere (Loewenstein, 1991; Ross et al., 1989; Steinberg, 1994a, 1994b, 1995).

From an ego state point of view, an essential area to assess is the presence or absence of a dissociative disorder, the type of dissociative disorder if one is present, the degree of both positive and negative affect tolerance, whether containment skills are present, and degree of identification with any perpetrator/aggressor. Kluft's (1994) Dimensions of Therapeutic Movement indicate that the dissociative clients with the best therapy outcome will be those who can establish a good rapport with the therapist, tolerate access to the system, have some degree of acceptance that there is a dissociative condition, tolerate the necessary and painful work, and comport themselves with the therapeutic structure and rules. These dimensions can be evaluated in the Assessment Phase with careful introduction of ego state procedures. With a dissociative client, the results of these questions may quickly indicate that all phases of therapy will be necessarily protracted to ensure safety. Shapiro (1995, 2001) includes the results of a Dissociative Disorder Task Force Report identifying red flags contraindicating proceeding with EMDR with clients early in the treatment of a dissociative disorder (Fine et al., 1995, 2001; Paulsen, 1995b, 2007a).

From a somatic therapy point of view, the therapist wants to get a sense of the clients' relationship with their body. Are clients able to be present in their body or do they dissociate when they try to be present in their body? Do clients disavow their body? What is the clients' capacity for body mindfulness? To what extent are clients able to tolerate body sensation? Can the clients tolerate both positive and negative affect?

Preparation

In this phase, it's important to establish a trusting relationship between therapist and client and to ensure that the client has sufficient inner resources and ego strength to do the necessary, often painful, work. This phase includes an informed consent process for how EMDR works and what the client may experience during and following EMDR treatment. Self-soothing techniques may be taught here to manage any between-session disturbance that emerges.

All phased approaches to treatment of dissociative disorders describe an extensive period of containment and stabilization before dealing with traumatic material (Kluft, 1982; Phillips & Frederick, 1995; Putnam, 1989). During that phase, the client's ego strength and internal resources are strengthened. Strategies for ego strengthening have been elaborated by Torem (1990), Phillips and Frederick (1995), and many others. Among EMDR practitioners, specific ego strengthening and Resource Development procedures have been put forward as well, (e.g., Korn & Leeds, 2002; Leeds & Shapiro, 2000; Paulsen & Golston, 2005; Twombly, 2005; Twombly & Schwartz, 2007). Paulsen and Golston emphasized a range of procedures including: attending to environmental factors that are destabilizing; introducing resourcing imagery including a nurturing or spiritual resource (Paulsen 1992, 1995b); orienting ego states to present person, place, and time; intervening with the ego states with the "highest ranking authority" (Frankel & O'Hearn, 1996); intervening with introjected perpetrators (Paulsen, 2004a, 2004b, 2007b, in press; Putnam, 1989; Watkins & Watkins, 1997); building grounding skills; and utilizing the Dissociative Table to identify and intervene in self-destructive dynamics (Fraser, 2003; Paulsen, 1995b, 2007b, in press). The "Paulsen Two-Step" (J. Golston, personal communication, 2006) is an important skill to help the client establish reliable abilities to both (a) contain the behavior, affect, sensation, and knowledge of cognitive elements (BASK) of a memory, and (b) contain or "tuck in" egotized parts of self (Paulsen, 2003, 2007b, in press).

The focus of treatment will be on skill building, especially self-soothing exercises, awareness of ego states, and somatic awareness. A series of collaborative experiments is often useful in increasing rapport.

If severe dissociation is present, using the Safe Place exercise in conjunction with BLS may result in the client bridging into traumatic material—the underlying assumption is that the BLS increases neural connectivity and thus is integrative. Therefore, during the initial session using a modified Safe Place Protocol without BLS may be useful. Alternatively, using the Safe Place exercise in conjunction with a Butterfly Hug (cross-lateral stimulation), appears to reduce the likelihood of bridging into traumatic material. The underlying theory is that cross-lateral stimulation is unusual and confusing to the brain, thus likely resulting in an increased orienting response. Regardless, the inability to do a Safe Place exercise should be considered as being of diagnostic significance with regard to possible dissociative symptoms or positive affect intolerance.

Many clients who are unable to benefit from the Safe Place exercise will be able to benefit from other forms of guided imagery. One of the procedures particularly useful is the "light stream" exercise that is taught as a closure exercise in the EMDR Institute trainings. It involves focusing on a distressing body sensation—mildly to moderately distressing is definitely preferable when using the exercise for the first time—and giving the sensation a shape, color, texture, and so on. The client is then asked to focus a healing light on the distressing shape. For most clients that will result in its disappearance. The "light stream" exercise is ingenious in that it encourages body awareness, while at the same time giving the client strategies to contain overwhelming sensations.

It has been the authors' experience that a modicum of body awareness is essential for a successful treatment outcome. Furthermore, increased body mindfulness, as well as somatic interweaves, appear to be associated with better treatment outcomes in clients with dissociative symptoms. Body awareness and somatic tolerance can be considered an essential precursor to affect tolerance. At this point, clients should know that body awareness is essential for a successful treatment.

A number of strategies increase body mindfulness. The authors commonly suggest to clients who have any issues with body mindfulness that they attend a yoga, tai chi, Pilates, or similar class. In some cases, martial arts training may be beneficial. At the same time therapists need to warn clients, especially those with severely impaired body mindfulness, that any of these may initially feel overwhelming. Generally, Pilates seems to be easier tolerated than yoga. With yoga in particular, it should be stressed that focus be on the more basic practices of yoga that focus on body mindfulness, rather than the more advanced practices that focus on spirituality, as the latter emphasize a loss of self—something that is contraindicated in dissociative disorders. Movement therapies can be beneficial and may often be less triggering and at the same time aid in reestablishing a defensive response.

Whether or not there is residual distress present at the end of the "light stream" exercise, this is a logical place for the next visualization/containment exercise: building a container where the clients can leave their distressing material until they choose to access it.

In clients who are able to give a history without major gaps suggestive of significant amnesia, or dissociative clients with good ego strength, the next step is the first ego state intervention (see below), an exercise to increase empathy for the self, particularly the child self, at the same time using a resourcing/imaginal nurturing intervention (O'Shea & Paulsen, 2007; Wildwind, 1992). It is important to describe the exercise to the clients and solicit their consent prior to asking them to engage in the exercise. In some cases, even listening to the content of the exercise will produce sufficient abreaction in the clients that the clients and therapist may collaboratively decide to postpone this exercise. However, a client who is unable to tolerate an ego state exercise to increase compassion for a child state is clearly unready to move forward with the EMDR Standard Protocol.

Exercise to increase compassion for a hurt child ego state: The following exercise is often very effective as a self-soothing method if combined with the Butterfly Hug. You may add this when you introduce the exercise to the client. If this is the case, demonstrate Butterfly Hug to client and say:

Cross your arms and tap with your hands on your shoulders.

Now I would like you to take just a moment and think about your adult self and then think about that little girl/boy within you that was hurt. (Use language appropriate to the client and their situation.)

If it's okay with you, imagine reaching out to that little girl/boy, holding him/her by the hand.

If it's okay, imagine holding on your lap that little boy/girl within you that got hurt.

Just imagine holding, hugging, soothing, comforting, and caressing him/her. (Repeat as necessary.)

Does that feel okay? (Make sure client feels comfortable with exercise.)

Just imagine holding, hugging, soothing, comforting, and caressing him/her. (Repeat as necessary).

Let him/her know that he/she is safe now.

(If appropriate) *Let him/her know that the adult within you is able to keep him/her safe now.*

(If appropriate) *Whatever happened then is not happening anymore.*

Just imagine holding, hugging, soothing, comforting, and caressing him/her. (Repeat as necessary.)

You can then use this exercise either as an interweave during trauma processing or specifically setting up the EMDR Standard Protocol with the adult holding the child. If this exercise evokes resistance or overt dissociation, do ego state interventions to identify which ego states are involved in preventing compassion for the hurt child ego state. Once identified, the concerns of resistant ego states can be addressed. A prominent example is that ego states that represent attachments to the client's perpetrator may be unable to imagine "looking through the eyes" (Paulsen, 2007a) of the child, rather than the eyes of the perpetrator. The more dissociative a client is, the more likely complex ego state interventions will be necessary before affect tolerance and compassion for the self can be tolerated. It is the authors' opinion that relationships between internal states engage the ventral vagal (or social engagement) nervous system, though the relationships are within a single person.

Inability to do the Safe Place exercise is also diagnostic. Sliding into trauma or being unable to do the Safe Place exercise or Resource Installation Protocol is a potential indicator of dissociative symptoms, as are significant difficulty, inability, or unwillingness to use self-stabilization techniques, including working with child ego states with compassion, as described above.

In the case of highly dissociative clients who have limited ego strength, limited emotional resources, or who live in threatening life circumstances, the Preparation Phase may take months or years.

When identifying ego states, it is useful to also identify how the client's sense of somatic self changes as they access different parts of the self. The therapist may ask the client, *When you focus on your adult self, what happens in your body? When you focus on the little girl within, what do you get in your body now?* For some clients, this can be achieved in this early phase; for others it will come much later, after more resourcing and ego state interventions have been conducted.

Somatic interventions in this phase might begin with enhancing therapeutic rapport with the use of somatic empathy, described earlier. This tactic, in the context of an authentic caring relationship with the therapist, may begin to remediate some of the injury associated with attachment failures, and failure to achieve the intersubjective developmental milestones (Trevarthen, 1993). For many dissociative clients, in this phase ego state work will be conducted as described in tactical integrationism, behind an amnesia barrier (Fine, 1993). This barrier spares the front part of the self from the painful work, leaving that state free to "do life." These front parts are also called apparently normal personalities (ANP) (Nijenhuis et al., 2004, and Chapter 15 in this book) in the structural theory of dissociation and contrast with emotional personalities (EPs), which may typically be found behind the amnesia barrier in DID. Working directly to detoxify trauma held by EPs is contraindicated in this phase.

Somatic resourcing may be introduced in this phase to strengthen the client and the client's specific ability to tolerate the felt sense of positive resources in the body. For dissociative clients, somatic resourcing will begin by referring only to the resources in general, with shared delight in those resources' positive attributes, to the degree the client can tolerate positive affect. For highly dissociative clients, the therapist waits to add queries about the specific felt sense in the body, while attending to the general resources. Grounding exercises are an important element for highly dissociative clients, ranging from pushing one's heels into the floor or counting red objects in the room to feeling the rain on one's face, which the authors (from Seattle and Vancouver, British Colombia) refer to as "the Northwest Special."

During the preparatory phase, it's relevant to include somatic resourcing with other kinds of resources. Resource Development can, on one hand, be construed as an ego state intervention, accessing positive self-states. From a somatic perspective, this can be viewed as embodying an experience of positive affect. From either vantage point, the development of resources prior to trauma processing is crucial with dissociative clients. It allows these positive resource states to be used later as interweaves when looping occurs during trauma processing including the use of evoked oscillation (also called pendulating) between trauma and resource, thus increasing the client's capacity to work through material that would otherwise be overwhelming.

Assessment Phase

In this phase of EMDR, the therapist helps the clients to articulate the elements of the target that EMDR will address. This begins with a picture that represents the most disturbing aspect of the memory, the words that best reflect the clients' present maladaptive belief about themselves, such as, "I'm a failure" or "I'm worthless." Then the therapist helps the clients articulate the words that reflect what the clients would rather believe about themselves, such as "I can be successful" or "I'm valuable." Another example of a Negative Cognition (NC) is, "I'm in danger" and a PC might be "I'm safe now," when the danger is actually passed. Next the therapist asks how true the desired PC feels on the VOC Scale, namely, a scale from 1 to 7, where 1 is completely false

and 7 is completely true. This rates the belief viscerally, not intellectually. The therapist next helps the clients identify the emotions associated with the disturbing experience and the body sensations that are
present in present time, when thinking about the disturbing memory.
The clients are asked the (SUD) level, namely, how disturbing the experience is now from 0 to 10, where 0 is completely neutral and 10 is
the most intense disturbance imagined. These questions tend to activate all the information channels associated with the neural network
hypothesized to hold the unprocessed disturbing experience. That activation will be important in the next phase, which for most clients will
begin with activating or "lighting up the net," a reference to the neural
network. For nondissociative clients, this phase may take one session
or less.

While nondissociative clients can usually proceed right through the
EMDR Standard Protocol, most dissociative clients need lengthy
preparations before they begin to target trauma. While in some cases
the issue is accessing parts of the self that hold traumatic material, in
many cases it is about how to titrate the intensity of the traumatic material to the point where the clients can remain present with it without
becoming stuck in either a hyperaroused or dissociative state. The task
is less "How do we step on the accelerator?" and more "Where is the
brake?" Fine (1993) described the use of fractionation procedures to
titrate affective intensity. See also Kluft (1990a, 1990b, 1990c). The long
hypnosis history offers many distancing maneuvers to assist with this
task. A client might imagine his trauma on a small screen, in black and
white, with the sound turned off. Francine Shapiro's (1995, 2001) train
metaphor, watching the traumatic incident go by the train window, is a
distancing maneuver. Beginning to practice these devices in the context of preparing for eventual trauma work can enhance the clients'
confidence in having the internal resources and armamentarium of
tools needed to tolerate difficult painful work. Once safely and successfully navigated, a dissociative client will be able to engage in
EMDR preparation for subsequent targets.

Beginning to instruct clients about PCs and NCs, and enabling internal discussion of those cognitions in the conference room, may take
considerable lengths of time. Clients may simultaneously believe such
mutually exclusive beliefs as "I am completely helpless" and "It's all
my fault," with the beliefs held by ego states with different functions.
Some of this work can be conducted cognitive-behaviorally in the conference room; some of it will not resolve until the trauma is detoxified

in subsequent phases. In some cases this will reveal double binds in which the client's own interest is at odds with the client's loyalty to a perpetrator. In working with dissociative clients, much of the art involves untangling blocking beliefs that would interfere with trauma processing, most especially identification with the aggressor, manifest as interference from introjected perpetrator ego states. Frankel has advocated working with the highest-ranking internal authorities first, before working with child/victim parts of self (Frankel & O'Hearn, 1996). This strategy has direct impact on EMDR preparations, because any application of the Standard Protocol on behalf of a child part of self would, for many clients, result in significant looping (stuck processing). Getting the introjects on board first is critical to planning a successful trauma processing with EMDR. This may be accomplished by orienting the introject (or other resistant ego states) to present person (the client's body), place (the town the client lives in and the therapist's office), and time (the present year). This may take a single session or much, much longer.

Watkins & Paulsen (2003) described the challenge, in planning trauma processing, in terms of (a) the capacity of the processor (strength of resources) and (b) the volume of traumatic material to be processed. For many dissociative clients, even though the capacity of the processor was increased in the containment and stabilization work of the Preparation Phase, it will still be necessary to titrate affective intensity by fractionating the volume of traumatic material to be processed at any one time. Paulsen (2007a, 2007b, in press) has described the combination of fractionation methods in EMDR in the ARCHITECTS approach to structuring EMDR in a dissociative client. In summary, the task is to break targets down into small, manageable pieces, either by alter personality, time segment, or BASK channel.

For dissociative clients it is often impossible, not to mention inadvisable, to work up all the channels as in the Standard Protocol. If one did, it would produce flooding, as described above. Another problem is that many times the executive ego state during the processing is a child state. A child state can no more articulate an NC and PC than a true young child could. Once the memory has been appropriately fractionated, and the selected ego state is present and executive ("looking through the eyes"), no more workup is needed. To fully work it up, with all steps of the Assessment Phase, would undo the containment steps and fractionation done in preparation for the processing.

In one sense, this appears to fly in the face of the Standard Protocol, which requires activation of the channels. In another sense, it complies with the Standard Protocol because the designated material to be processed is already activated.

In highly complex trauma cases, elaborate procedures may be necessary to fractionate the work and resource the client. Paulsen (2007a) described a case in which preparation included sending a group of introjects on a hypnotically suggested Norwegian cruise, battening down child parts not involved in the particular memory in a Norwegian stave church, and sending some apparently normal personalities for a walk in a Norwegian woods. At the same time, various powerful nurturing and resourcing ego states were deputized to resource the "star" of the EMDR process by standing by her, or even blending with her.

In somatic work, the intention is not to fully "light up the net" that holds unworked traumatic experience but rather to circumnavigate it, or "nibble around the edges" using pendulation or evoked oscillation procedures. The standard EMDR procedure already includes the somatic channel of experience, so in most clients, this phase requires no additional somatic interventions. If, during the Assessment Phase of EMDR, a client is revealed to not have the capacity to experience sensation in the body, it would be a contraindication to proceed until soma tolerance has been enhanced with a return to the Preparation Phase. For many dissociative individuals, somatic processing of trauma may proceed before EMDR may proceed. Evoked oscillations between disturbing material and resource material can begin to strengthen the client's capacity to tolerate disturbance. It also tends to increase confidence that disturbing material can be mastered because the disturbance decreases with each evoked oscillation.

During this phase, the therapist will overtly track, from moment to moment, those observable signs in the client's body of resource or disturbance. This may include gently commenting on observed flushing, relaxing or smiling, in the case of a resource, or clenching, twitching, or fidgeting, in the case of a disturbance. When tracking of sensation from moment to moment is intolerable, the work of detoxifying trauma is not ready to proceed. In contrast to EMDR, the noticing and tracking of client somatic experience alternates with resource states until the client is much more able to tolerate extended feelings of disturbance without dissociation.

During this phase, spontaneous oscillations may begin to be observed as the client grows increasingly comfortable turning attention

inward, observing and tolerating affect. Quite naturally and spontaneously, this attention to soma evokes subtle oscillations such as rocking side to side, forward and backward, or other rhythmic pulsations.
The therapist in this phase teaches the client to notice and leave time
and space for the spontaneous oscillations to complete. As these occur,
the client's capacity for and tolerance of affect and soma tend to increase.

Trauma Processing

For dissociative clients, the therapist and client will have already established the fraction of trauma that will be desensitized in any given
EMDR session. It will not be possible to process to a SUD of 0 and VOC
of 7, as it is with a nondissociative client. A rule in conducting EMDR
with a dissociative client is that the best-laid plans will go up in smoke,
unknown alters will emerge, the story will shift, and so forth (Fine &
Berkowitz, 2001; Paulsen, 2007a). Containment imagery will help keep
the parts of the memory NOT being worked on apart from that which
is being worked on). Distancing maneuvers such as a rheostat/dimmer
switch, projection screen, library of memories, and numerous other devices from the hypnosis tradition (Hammond, 1990) are very useful for
keeping the processing in the optimal mid-range (Ogden & Minton,
2000). The ego state interweaves described for nondissociatives in this
phase are completely necessary for dissociative clients as well. Sometimes looping in EMDR is the result of an angry or shameful part
pushed out of awareness. The processing can resume when that part is
given a voice, its viewpoint is understood, and it has accessed appropriate resources.

Targeting is probably the most difficult issue for clients who experience dissociative symptoms, as it directly relates to choosing which
neural networks will be activated, and to what extent those networks
become stimulated. In most simple cases, the authors find that, unless
there is an overwhelming recent traumatic event that needs to be addressed immediately, targeting in developmental sequence (e.g.,
Kitchur, 2005) aids the overall treatment by addressing developmental
issues that may have predisposed clients toward developing certain
types of self-limiting beliefs. Addressing attachment issues and earlier
traumatic experiences prior to the most recent traumatic experience
avoids accessing earlier trauma to the point where the clients flood and
are overwhelmed by the cumulative effects of their entire trauma his-

tory. This approach can be extended to addressing mental constructs representing prenatal and perinatal experiences (e.g., Becker, 2000; O'Shea, 2002). In many cases, proceeding in this way is a gentle way to introduce clients to EMDR and it will often result in a surprising amount of symptom resolution.

In the more severe dissociative disorders, targeting in developmental sequence can be problematic, especially in cases where the clients' primary and most severe traumatic experience occurred in their relationship with a primary attachment figure. In these cases, the authors prefer to work with the clients' parts to negotiate which aspects of the clients' traumatic experience can be targeted first. This can occur within the context of a dissociative table, a conference table of several ego states (Fraser, 1991, 2003). The introduction of adult resources (e.g., a wise self) is often productive in this context (Paulsen, 1995b). It's useful to give specific suggestions to the clients to stay with a certain aspect of a traumatic experience and to give the stop sign when bridging into additional traumatic material. Moreover, instructions to the clients to let the therapist know when they are losing connection with their body allows the therapist to assess if the clients are able to maintain a modicum of body awareness.

With regard to sensory stimulation, ego states exhibit a range of responses, which can differ markedly within a single client. It is the authors' experience that taps or auditory tones seem to be less stimulating, whereas Eye Movements (EMs) may be more activating as they stimulate more areas of the brain.

Taps or auditory stimulation, then, may be more appropriate for highly dissociative clients. Bilateral recordings with music may facilitate processing in individuals, possibly by accessing resourced states as the BLS is being embedded in pieces of music that are soothing to the client. Hand taps seem to work extremely well in many cases, but it is critical to make sure that the client in toto is comfortable with touch, lest the touch be experienced as a boundary violation or traumatic reenactment. Touch, unless it is specifically triggering to the client, is usually profoundly grounding. Touch is a primary reinforcer (Francis et al., 1999) and the quality of touch is related to extent of orbitofrontal cortex activation (Francis et al., 1999). Therapeutic touch, if appropriately exercised, may provide a relief from profound shame, as clients with a history of sexual abuse will often literally experience themselves as "untouchable." It provides the client with a learning experience that touch does not have to be sexual. At the same time touch can trigger problematic countertransference for therapists. One must be aware of ethical issues including scope of practice in one's licensing jurisdiction. If in doubt at all about the use of touch, do not use it, or seek consultation.

The length of sets can be used to titrate material. Short sets will result in limited new material being introduced during each set. On the other hand, if the client is able to remain present, sometimes extremely long sets are required due to the extensive traumatic material accessed by the client. When using very long sets, it is important that the therapist looks out for a collapsed posture that might indicate dissociation and the activation of the dorsal vagal nervous system, or dorsal vagal shutdown. It is also important to remind the client to breathe (also see above section on breath). Generally, we recommend that therapists use nonverbal cues to gauge the length of set (e.g., changes in EM, facial tension, body posture, breathing rate, facial color, swallowing, etc.). In addition, therapist may want to check with the clients, whether they are able to remain present, in addition to negotiating not only a stop sign but also a continue sign, so that both acceleration and braking cues are available wordlessly.

In the Standard Protocol with nondissociative clients, the neural network will have been activated in Phase Three. Phase Four proceeds by processing the experience using EMs, or other forms of BLS such as tactile or auditory stimulation. Clients have a range of responses, from little contemplation with lots of body sensation and affect, to little body sensation and affect and lots of cognition, to many other variations. Sometimes the associations spontaneously move to other experiences that are thematically related. The therapist returns the client's attention to the original target when any one channel appears clear. Processing continues until the target is associated with 0 or 1 disturbance on the SUD Scale, and 6 or 7 disturbance on the VOC Scale. The processing may complete in a single session or may need to be continued across multiple sessions. Even in nondissociative clients, ego state interweaves can be useful when processing "loops" or gets stuck. In the event of looping, an ego state interweave might sound like this: *"I'd like whatever part of the self comes up next to come into the conference room* (mind's eye) *at this time. And,* (client's name), *what, if anything, do you see?"* Whatever ego state is evident in the conference room is then interviewed regarding its concern. If it feels weak, resources are provided hypnotically or by ego state resources. If it identifies with the aggressor, the therapist orients the client to person, place, and time. If the part is worried about dying, a current and better job description is found. These ego state interweaves are extremely useful even for nondissociative individuals. Once the looping is resolved with an ego state interweave, the Standard Protocol resumes with BLS. No further ego state maneuvers are indicated in order to preserve the fidelity to the Standard Protocol, unless there is additional looping.

With dissociative clients, prior to conducting EMDR on a specific target, the therapist asks the client to bring all the parts together who have concerns about or involvement with the subject being targeted (e.g., in the conference room, around the table, or around in the healing circle). The therapist then solicits feedback from the parts about what aspect of the issue is ready to be worked on today, as well as which part or parts will be involved in working on this issue. If the issue relates to childhood trauma, it is wise to have an older part of the self hold, contain, witness, listen to, and support the traumatized child self. In cases of severe adult trauma, an a priori decision to "tuck away child parts" may be made together with the client.

Given that the majority of clients who dissociate have some difficulty being mindful of their body when accessing trauma, or mobilizing reptilian brain–based defensive response, it is appropriate to draw upon the gamut of somatic interventions and interweaves in order to facilitate ongoing EMDR processing and to deepen the treatment effect. In some cases, "bottom-up processing" may be appropriate. *Bottom-up processing* is a term used in sensorimotor psychotherapy, a somatic (body) clinical approach to facilitate processing of unassimilated sensorimotor reactions to trauma (Ogden & Minton, 2000). Bottom-up processing is related to somatic tracking. Whereas somatic tracking may occur within the preparatory phase or during stabilization, bottom-up processing is utilized in conjunction with trauma processing. Clients who exhibit significant dissociative responses often benefit from focusing on somatic sensations alone. This appears to reduce dissociation and aid information processing. Lanius (2000) adapted the work of Ogden and Minton (2000) with regard to bottom-up processing to EMDR, finding it useful in reducing dissociative symptoms.

The goal in the bottom-up approach is to target physical sensations, whereas the EMDR Standard Protocol integrates all levels of processing. Focusing on physical sensations alone, or alternatively, modifying the EMDR Standard Protocol, so that neither traumatic events, associated cognitions, nor emotions are initially targeted, is based on the notion that all unprocessed traumatic experience is to some extent pre-verbal (e.g., speechless terror) or precorticosensory in nature. Overall, bottom-up processing is considered foundational to emotional and cognitive processing. It includes not only overall body processing, but also fixed action patterns seen in active defenses (e.g., the startle reflex and the fight, flight, or freeze response), changes in breathing and muscular tonicity, and autonomic nervous system activation. The focus on physical sensation and sensorimotor responses alone was adapted to be used in conjunction with BLS as part of a comprehensive treatment approach in individuals with complex PTSD and dissociative symptoms.

For bottom-up processing, the EMDR Standard Protocol is adapted to aid clients to stay in touch with their bodies and develop body mindfulness. The Standard Protocol is inverted, and sensory, emotional, and cognitive aspects of traumatic experience are processed consecutively rather than together.

A decision to utilize the bottom-up processing protocol can be made a priori in conjunction with the client. Alternatively, the therapist may want to switch to somatic processing when clients are abreacting to a point where they are at risk of losing mindfulness and a sense of their body.

The idea is to slow down the material by staying at the sensory level. In this way, the information coming in is titrated and intense abreactions decreased by slowing down the spontaneous integration of affect, cognition, and sensory experience that usually occurs in EMDR. The voice of the therapist is used in an active manner (Active Stance) to engage and ground the client during the processing.

The Bottom-Up Processing Protocol lends itself to targeting the relationships with primary attachment figures, and to processing the client's somatic response even in the absence of specific images or verbal memories.

Prior to the client processing material, the therapist actively encourages the client to focus only on body sensations, not on emotions or thought or cognitions. The client is further instructed to blank out any material other than sensations. If such material comes up during processing, the therapist actively encourages the client to "drop the content" and return to focus on sensory experience alone. This type of processing helps fractionate the traumatic material by separating somatosensory from cognitive and affective processing.

Bottom-up processing may be insufficient for the complete resolution of the trauma, but it develops the body mindfulness necessary for affective and cognitive processing. Consequently, when the client is able to access the traumatic experience in its entirety, the Standard Protocol is used to complete processing, if necessary.

Thus, bottom-up processing may facilitate the integration of traumatic material through the subcortical bridge. This is one mechanism by which bottom-up processing may aid in transforming traumatic memories that are experienced as sensory fragments into a coherent narrative.

Moreover, as this process necessarily occurs slowly, bottom-up processing may avoid excessive emotional arousal or hyperarousal that interferes with the integration of information. With a pronounced focus on the body, it likely facilitates the experience of emotion. Without a sense of the body and sensory perceptions, it will be difficult to experience feelings. It further reduces the likelihood of dissociative responses through the pervasive focus on the body: Clients are encouraged to track even minimal physiological sensations in their body and therefore continue to be mindful of the present.

Somatic interweaves in this phase can be useful for stuck processing. Clients tending to intellectualize (not just normal cognitive processing, but pervasive preference for cognitive left-brain analysis without reduction in disturbance level during EMDR processing) may need to be encouraged to focus on the somatic channel to jump-start processing.

Somatic micromovements can resolve EMDR looping quite dramatically. Often in this phase, as indicated above, anger, or other thwarted sympathetic arousal response, is held apart, often because it is perceived as dangerous or shameful in some way. For some individuals, the gentle invitation to engage in a pushing away or other fulfillment of thwarted anger, or fleeing response as expressed in slow running movements, will enable attenuated discharge of the sympathetic arousal, and processing can resume. In some instances, the use of such micromovements will take the SUD to 0. F. Shapiro (personal communication, 2006) and O'Shea & Paulsen (2007), report that the same results can be achieved with an imaginal interweave in which the client imagines engaging in the fight-or-flight response. The first author finds that that is true, but that the somatic movements discharge significant and palpable releases of energy.

Somatic therapy prescribes pendulating between disturbance and resource states. This is specifically contraindicated within the EMDR Standard Protocol and is not recommended here for nondissociative clients. For dissociative clients, for whom processing is fractionated anyway, ensuring resourced ego states are still present, and ending with a resourced ego state makes sense and is necessary. See "Closure," below.

In cases in which the client is about to dissociate or already has dissociated to a point where significant derealization or depersonalization interferes with further EMDR processing, it can be useful to shift from EMDR processing with BLS to purely somatic work. That is, while EMDR, through sensory stimulation, provides the context of the here and now (the brake), it also increases access to memory (the accelerator). By replacing the sensory stimulation with somatic attunement and empathy to aid the client in remaining present, we are often able to slow the process down, aiding the client in titrating and working through an aspect of a traumatic memory without introducing new information. This can be combined with resourcing or grounding interweaves (e.g., focusing on the senses—smell, taste, sound, touch, vision). In some cases, getting the client to focus on micromovements in the body in the absence of BLS is sufficient to produce an orienting response, and thus a return to ongoing information processing.

Installation Phase

For a client who is not highly dissociative, once the SUD is 0 or 1 and the VOC is about 6, the therapist "installs" the desired PC, if it is still relevant to the client, with a few sets of BLS. The installation continues as long as the benefit is continuing to generalize across related domains and into the future. Any shortcomings in the desired cognition as originally articulated will become clear by this phase, and the PC can be adjusted here.

For dissociative clients, the Installation Phase will sometimes need to be omitted because the EMDR is fractionated. That is, one has to "quit while behind." Containment of the parts of the memory not yet to be processed, and the parts of the self not directly involved in the day's EMDR, can quickly become unraveled by trying to do an installation before its time. The therapist may be tempted to try to follow the Standard Protocol's requirement of an installation, but unless the therapy is far along, the attempt to prematurely install a PC in a dissociative client will only activate whole parts of self whose purpose is the opposite of the desired PC. In the place of an installation, a closure should be emphasized, to be described below.

Body Scan Phase

In the EMDR Standard Protocol, after the PC has been installed successfully, the therapist will check the work by asking the client to check the original target and see if there is any residual disturbance in the body. Any residual disturbance suggests that either there is a little left to process for this target, or the two may be at the juncture of a link to another related target that will best be targeted separately.

Note that within the Standard Protocol, if processing doesn't complete as measured by a SUD of 0 and VOC of 7, the Body Scan is omitted, as it would activate the next link in the memory chain and defeat the purpose of closure. For dissociative clients, a Body Scan at the end of a fractionated EMDR session is contraindicated for the same reason as for nondissociative clients. A Body Scan would bring forward the next alter or ego state in the process, when there is not enough time to accommodate the processing for that state.

Closure Phase

At the end of any EMDR session it is necessary to close down the process for transitioning to everyday life. If it is an incomplete EMDR session, it will be necessary to find a means to close down the session. This may involve resources or a form of self-soothing. The client is instructed what to expect if the processing continues, such as colorful dreams, or new thoughts, which should be recorded in a journal. For nondissociative clients, closure can proceed as per the Standard Protocol. To the degree that deep work has occurred, especially if ego state interweaves were employed, the "Paulsen Two-step" (Paulsen & Golston, 2005) closure method is useful: first containing the behavior, affect, sensation, cognition, imagery, and so on, of the memory, and second, distancing the emotional ego states from conscious mind ("tucking in" ego states). Paulsen often uses vault or container imagery for the first step, and "tucking in on fluffy white clouds that sail away deep inside" for the ego states (Paulsen, 2007b, in press). Checking to ensure the conference room is empty before the client departs is often wise, lest a child or protective part become executive. A child part can be reassured, and a protector can be appreciated and invited to catch some shut-eye in the ranger station/lookout tower on the horizon, where there are binoculars to keep an eye on things.

For dissociative clients, the same two closure steps are employed as for nondissociative clients when ego state methods are used. For dissociative clients, however, the closure method will involve not only tucking in the "star" of the EMDR, but also undoing any special hypnotic procedures that were employed to fractionate the EMDR session. Final agreements with salient child and adult ego states about handling continuing processing between sessions is important. The closure steps should never be omitted for dissociative clients, in order to secure safe transit home after the session and relative comfort during the week.

In somatic work, a lengthy session, with eyes closed, attending to somatic sensation is very deep work indeed. Therefore, it is often wise to save time at the end to begin to distance from the felt sense of the work by engaging in "meaning making." Stanley (2006) describes such queries: *"As we prepare to wrap up, what strikes you about the work we've done today?"* or *"What do you want to remember about this work today?"* Engaging the left hemisphere in this fashion prepares the client to end the session. Rather than trying to maximize processing to the end of the session, it makes sense to stop processing when there is an experience of triumph or mastery, thus ending processing when accessing a resourced start.

Reevaluation Phase

At the beginning of the subsequent sessions, the therapist checks the present SUD and VOC levels associated with the processed target to ensure that gains have maintained or increased. This sometimes identifies the next piece of experience to be processed. This is also a logical point to refer back to the original treatment plan to identify the next priority. For nondissociative clients, the usual EMDR procedure applies. With dissociative clients, the client and therapist will collaborate, and the therapist will rely on clinical judgment to determine whether, in a given session, the next fraction of a memory should be addressed with EMDR. Sometimes the client is best served by having time between EMDR sessions to synthesize the work and consolidate gains. Processing continues on a very deep level for weeks after profound EMDR sessions for highly dissociative clients. If it is advisable to continue processing the next fraction of a memory, the same preparatory steps for resourcing the client imaginally and titrating the volume to be processed should be repeated as in the prior EMDR work. Often aspects and fragments of a memory can be accessed somatically only, as for instance is the case with bottom-up processing.

Past, Present, and Future: The Three Prongs

Processing is not complete in EMDR until the targeted experience has been cleared in terms of past memories, present triggers, and future performance. Past, Present, and Future are the three prongs of EMDR treatment, and resolution of many symptom constellations require all three to be processed. Past, Present, and Future need to be integrated not only cognitively, but also affectively and somatically. Ultimately, clients being able to be present in their body in the here and now, and anticipating the future, will result in a coherent and integrated sense of self.

CONCLUSIONS

This chapter has described core elements of ego state and somatic therapies. It has given examples of how those therapies may be integrated into EMDR processing, including complex trauma cases. The list is not comprehensive, but begins to describe the range of options for accelerating or decelerating processing, whether it is EMDR processing or the process of therapy itself. The window of tolerance notion guides the decision of whether acceleration or deceleration is indicated at any given point in therapy or EMDR; pacing is always germane with complex cases. Understanding the role of the sympathetic nervous system in acceleration and the parasympathetic dorsal vagal nervous system in deceleration further informs our awareness of therapeutic pacing requirements. Finally, awareness of the parasympathetic ventral vagal nervous system for social engagement guides our understanding of resourcing, whether the resourcing be that of the engagement of the therapeutic relationship, engagement of the client's internal resourced states, or the relationship engagement between the client's states. To summarize the chapter in a sentence, ventral vagal connectedness between and within people is the name of the game to enhance association and integration.

REFERENCES

Austin, J. H. (1998). *Zen and the brain.* Cambridge, MA: MIT Press.
Barabasz, A. F., & Watkins, J. G. (2005). *Hypnotherapeutic techniques* (2nd ed.). New York: Brunner-Routledge.

Barrowcliff, A. L., Gray, N. S., MacCulloch, S., Freeman, T. C.A., & MacCulloch, M. J. (2003). Horizontal rhythmical eye-movements consistently diminish the arousal provoked by auditory stimuli. *British Journal of Clinical Psychology, 42*, 289–302.

Becker, M. J. (2000). *The use of EMDR to resolve neonatal trauma.* EMDRIA Conference, Toronto, Canada.

Brewin, C. R., Dalgleish, T., & Joseph S. (1996). A dual representation theory of post traumatic stress disorder. *Psychological Review, 103*, 670–686.

Christman, S. D., & Propper, R. E. (2001). Superior episodic memory is associated with interhemispheric processing. *Neuropsychology, 15*, 607–616.

Christman, S. D., Garvey, K. J., Propper, R. E., & Phaneuf, K. A. (2003). Bilateral eye movements enhance the retrieval of episodic memories. *Neuropsychology, 17*, 221–229.

Cowan, N. (1997). *Attention and memory: An integrated framework.* New York: Oxford University Press.

Damasio, A. R. (1994). *Descartes' error: Emotion, reason, and the human brain.* New York: Putnam.

Damasio, A. R. (1999). How the brain creates the mind. *Scientific American, 281*(6), 112–117.

Damasio A. R., Grabowski, T. J., Bechara, A., Damasio, H., Ponto, L. L., Parvizi, J., et al. (2000). Subcortical and cortical brain activity during the feeling of self-generated emotions. *Nature Neuroscience, 3*, 1049–1056.

Emmerson, G. J. (2003). *Ego state therapy.* Carmarthen, UK: Crown House.

Federn, P. (1952). *Ego psychology and the psychoses* (E. Weiss, Trans.). New York: Basic Books.

Fine, C., & Berkowitz, A. S. (2001). The wreathing protocol: The imbrication of hypnosis and EMDR in the treatment of dissociative identity disorder and other dissociative responses. *American Journal of Clinical Hypnosis, 43*(3–4), 275–290.

Fine, C., Paulsen, S., Rouanzoin, C., Luber, M., Puk, G., & Young, W. (1995). A general guide to the use of EMDR in the dissociative disorders: A task force report. In F. Shapiro (Ed.), *Eye movement desensitization and reproccessing: Basic principles, practices, and procedures.* New York: Guilford Press.

Fine, C., Paulsen, S., Rouanzoin, C., Luber, M., Puk, G., & Young, W. (2001). A general guide to the use of EMDR in the dissociative disorders: A task force report. In F. Shapiro (Ed.), *Eye movement desensitization and reprocessing: Basic principles, practices, and procedures* (2nd ed., pp. 441–445). New York: Guilford Press.

Fine, C. G. (1993). A tactical integrationist perspective on the treatment of multiple personality disorder. In R. P. Kluft & C. G. Fine (Eds.), *Clinical perspectives on multiple personality disorder.* Washington, DC: American Psychiatric Press.

Foa, E., & Hears-Ikeda, D. (1996). Emotional dissociation in response to trauma: An information-processing approach. In L. Michelson & W. J. Ray (Eds.), *Handbook of dissociation: Theoretical, empirical, and clinical perspectives* (pp. 207–224). New York: Springer.

Forgash, C., & Copeley, M. (Eds.). (2007). *Healing the heart of trauma with EMDR and ego state therapy*. New York: Springer.

Francis, S., Rolls, E. T., Bowtell, R., McGlone, F., O'Doherty, J., Browning, A., et al. (1999). The representation of pleasant touch in the brain and its relationship with taste and olfactory areas. *Neuroreport, 10*, 453–459.

Frankel, A. S., & O'Hearn, T. C. (1996). Similarities in responses to extreme and unremitting stress: Cultures of communities under siege. *Psychotherapy, 33*(3), 485–502.

Fraser, G. A. (1991). The dissociative table technique: A strategy for working with ego states in dissociative disorder and ego-state therapy. *Dissociation, 4*, 205–213.

Fraser, G. A. (2003). Fraser's "dissociative table technique" revisited, revised: A strategy for working with ego states in dissociative disorders and ego state therapy. *Dissociation, 4*(4), 205–213.

Frysinger, R., & Harper, R. (1989). Cardiac and respiratory correlations with unit discharge in human amygdala and hippocampus. *Electroencephalography and Clinical Neurophysiology, 72*, 463–470.

Gazzaniga, M. (1980). The role of language for conscious experience: Observations from split-brain man. In H. Kornhuber & L. Deecke (Vol. Eds.), *Progress in brain research: Vol. 54. Motivation, motor and sensory processes of the brain* (pp. 689–696). Amsterdam: Elsevier/North Holland.

Gazzaniga, M. S., Holtzman, J. D., & Smylie, C. S. (1987). Speech without conscious awareness. *Neurology, 37*(4), 682–685.

Gurvits, T. V., Gilbertson, M. W., Lasko, N. B., Tarhan, A. S., Simeon, D., Macklin, M. L., et al. (2000). Neurologic soft signs in chronic posttraumatic stress disorder. *Archives of General Psychiatry, 57*, 181–186.

Herman, J. (1992). *Trauma and recovery: The aftermath of violence from domestic abuse to political terror*. New York: HarperCollins.

Janet, P. (1928). *L'évolution de la mémoire et de la notion du temps*. Paris: A Chahine.

Joliot, M., Ribary, U., & Llinas, R. (1994). Human oscillatory brain activity near 40 Hz coexists with cognitive temporal binding. *Proceedings of the National Academy of Sciences USA, 22*, 11748–11751.

Kitchur, M. (2005). The Strategic Developmental Model for EMDR. In R. Shapiro (Ed.), *EMDR solutions: Pathways to healing* (pp. 8–56). New York: Norton.

Kluft, R. P. (1982). Varieties of hypnotic interventions in the treatment of multiple personality. *American Journal of Clinical Hypnosis, 24*, 230–240.

Kluft, R. P. (1984). Treatment of multiple personality disorder: A study of 33 cases. *Psychiatric Clinics of North America, 7*, 9–29.

Kluft, R. P. (1987). First rank symptoms as a diagnostic clue to multiple personality disorder. *American Journal of Psychiatry, 144,* 293–298.

Kluft, R. P. (1990a). An abreactive technique. In D. C. Hammond (Ed.), *Handbook of hypnotic suggestions and metaphors* (pp. 526–527). New York: Norton.

Kluft, R. P. (1990b). A vigorous abreactive technique. In D. C. Hammond (Ed.), *Handbook of hypnotic suggestions and metaphors* (p. 527). New York: Norton.

Kluft, R. P. (1990c). The fractionated abreaction technique. In D. C. Hammond (Ed.), *Handbook of hypnotic suggestions and metaphors* (pp. 527–528). New York: Norton.

Kluft, R. P. (1994). Clinical observations on the use of the dimensions of therapeutic movement instrument (DTMI). *Dissociation, 7,* 272–283.

Knipe, J. (2007). Loving eyes: Procedures to therapeutically reverse dissociative processes while preserving emotional safety. In C. Forgash & M. Copeley (Eds.), *Healing the heart of trauma with EMDR and ego state therapy* (pp. 181–226). New York: Springer.

Korn, D., & Leeds, A. (2002). Preliminary evidence of efficacy for EMDR resource development and installation in the stabilization phase of treatment of complex posttraumatic stress disorder. *Journal of Clinical Psychology, 58*(12), 1465–1487.

Kuiken, D., Bears, M., Miall, D., & Smith, L. (2001). Eye movement desensitization reprocessing facilitates attentional orienting. *Imagination, Cognition and Personality, 21,* 3–20.

Lanius, R. A., Bluhm, R., & Lanius, U. F. (2007). PTSD symptom provocation and neuroimaging: Heterogeneity of response. In E. Vermetten, M. Dorahy, & D. Spiegel (Eds.), *Traumatic dissociation: Neurobiology and treatment.* Washington, DC: American Psychiatric Press.

Lanius, R. A., Bluhm, R., Lanius, U. F., & Pain, C. (2005). Neuroimaging of hyperarousal and dissociation in PTSD: Heterogeneity of response to symptom provocation. *Journal of Psychiatric Research, 40,* 709–729.

Lanius, R. A., Lanius, U. F., Fisher, J., & Ogden, P. (2006). Psychological trauma and the brain: Towards a neurobiological treatment model. In P. Ogden, K. Minton, & C. Pain (Eds.), *Trauma and the body: A sensorimotor approach to psychotherapy.* New York: Norton.

Lanius, R. A., Williamson, P. C., Boksman, K., Densmore, M., Gupta, M., Neufeld, R. W., et al. (2002). Brain activation during script-driven imagery induced dissociative responses in PTSD: A functional magnetic resonance imaging investigation. *Biological Psychiatry, 52,* 305–311.

Lanius, R. A., Williamson, P. C., Densmore, M., Boksman, K., Neufeld, R. W., Gati, J. S., et al. (2004). The nature of traumatic memories: A 4-T fMRI functional connectivity analysis. *American Journal of Psychiatry, 161,* 36–44.

Lanius, U. F. (2000, April 7–8). *Dissociative processes and EMDR—staying con-*

nected. Presentation at the North West Regional EMDR Conference, Vancouver, BC.

Lanius, U. F. (2005, April 8–9). *Dissociative processes and EMDR—staying connected.* Full-day Pre-Conference Workshop at the Third Annual Conference of the EMDR Association of UK and Ireland: EMDR and the Demystifying of Complex Trauma and PTSD: Future Directions, University of Ulster, Jordanstown (Belfast), Northern Ireland.

Lanius, U. F., & Lanius, R. A. (2000, March 16–19). *Posttraumatic stress disorder, dissociation, and complex partial seizure-like symptoms.* Poster presented at the Third World Conference for Traumatic Stress Studies, Melbourne, Australia.

Lazrove, S., & Fine, C. G. (1996). The use of EMDR in patients with dissociative identity disorder. *Dissociation, 9,* 289–299.

Leeds, A., & Shapiro, F. (2000). EMDR and resource installation: Principles and procedures for enhancing current functioning and resolving traumatic experiences. In J. Carlson & L. Sperry (Eds.), *Brief therapy strategies with individuals and couples* (pp. 469–534). Phoenix, AZ: Zeig, Tucker, & Theisen.

Levine, P. A. (1997). *Waking the tiger: Healing trauma.* Berkeley, CA: North Atlantic Books.

Llinas, R. R. (2002). *I of the vortex: From neurons to self.* Cambridge, MA: MIT Press.

Loewenstein, R. J. (1991). An office mental status examination for complex chronic dissociative symptoms and multiple personality disorder. In R. J. Loewenstein (Ed.), *Psychiatric clinics of North America: Multiple personality disorder* (pp. 567–604). Philadelphia: W. B. Saunders.

MacLean, P. D. (1990). *The triune brain in evolution: Role in paleocerebral functions.* New York: Plenum Press.

Marmar, C. R., Weiss, D. S., & Metzler, T. J. (1998). Peritraumatic dissociation and posttraumatic stress disorder. In J. D. Bremner & C. R. Marmar (Eds.), *Trauma, memory, and dissociation* (pp. 229–252). Washington, DC: American Psychiatric Press.

Nijenhuis, E. R. S., van der Hart, O., & Steele, K. (2004, January). Trauma-related structural dissociation of the personality. Retrieved from http://www.trauma-pages.com/a/nijenhuis-2004.php

O'Shea, K. (2002). EMDR Institute Level II specialty presentation.

O'Shea, K., & Paulsen, S. L. (September 30, 2007). *A protocol for increasing affect regulation and clearing early trauma.* Workshop presented at the EMDRIA Conference, Dallas, TX.

Ogden, P., & Minton, K. (2000). Sensorimotor psychotherapy: One method for processing traumatic memory. *Traumatology, 6*(3), 3.

Ogden, P., Minton, K., & Pain, C. (Eds.). (2006). *Trauma and the body: A sensorimotor approach to psychotherapy.* New York: Norton.

Panksepp, J. (2001a). Neuro-affective processes and the brain substrates of emotion: Emerging perspectives and dilemmas. In A. Kazniak (Ed.), *Emotion, qualia, and consciousness* (pp. 160–180). Singapore: World Scientific.

Panksepp, J. (2001b). On the subcortical sources of basic human emotions and the primacy of emotional-affective (action-perception) processes in human consciousness. *Evolution and Cognition, 7,* 134–140.

Parker, A., & Dagnall, N. (2007). Effects of bilateral eye movements on gist based false recognition in the DRM paradigm. *Brain & Cognition, 63,* 221–225.

Parker, A., Relph, S., & Dagnall, N. (2008). Effects of bilateral eye movements on the retrieval of item, associative, and contextual information. *Neuropsychology, 22,* 136–145.

Paulsen, S. L. (1992). *Dissociative disorder specialty training.* EMDR Workshop, Part II, Honolulu, HI.

Paulsen, S. L. (1993a). *EMDR: A conceptualization within BASK theory of dissociation.* Paper presented at the Tenth International Conference of the International Society for the Study of Multiple Personality and Dissociation (ISSMPD), Chicago.

Paulsen, S. L. (1993b). *EMDR: Its use in the dissociative disorders.* Paper presented at the Tenth International Conference on ISSMPD, Chicago.

Paulsen, S. L. (1995a). *The use of EMDR with ego state disorders.* Paper presented at the Amsterdam EMDR Level II Training, Amsterdam, Holland.

Paulsen, S. L. (1995b). Eye movement desensitization and reprocessing: Its cautious use in the dissociative disorders. *Dissociation, 8,* 32–44.

Paulsen, S. L. (1996). *Working strategically with a self-system in EMDR.* Paper presented at the Fourth Annual International Conference on EMDR, Denver, CO.

Paulsen, S. L. (2001). EMDR. In R. Corsini (Ed.), *Handbook of innovative psychotherapies* (2nd ed., pp. 230–241). New York: Wiley.

Paulsen, S. L. (2003). *Interweaving EMDR and ego state therapy to energize disowned aspects of self.* Workshop at EMDRIA Conference, Denver, CO.

Paulsen, S. L. (2004a). *Softening the perpetrator introject.* International Society for the Study of Dissociation (ISSD) International Conference. New Orleans, LA.

Paulsen, S. L. (2004b). *Ego state therapy and EMDR: Activating, modifying and containing dissociated neural nets.* Invited Masters Series Lecture, EMDRIA Conference, Montreal, Canada.

Paulsen, S. L. (2007a). *Integrating somatic interventions and EMDR: Keeping it AIP "legal."* Workshop presented at the EMDRIA Annual Conference, Dallas, TX.

Paulsen, S. L. (2007b). Treating dissociative identity disorder with EMDR, ego state therapy, and adjunct approaches. In C. Forgash & M. Copeley (Eds.), *Healing the heart of trauma with EMDR and ego state therapy* (pp. 141–179). New York: Springer.

Paulsen, S. L. (in press). *Looking through the eyes of trauma and dissociation: An illustrated guide for EMDR therapists and clients.*

Paulsen, S. L., & Golston, J. C. (2005). *Taming the storm: 43 secrets of successful stabilization.* EMDRIA Conference, Seattle, WA.

Paulsen, S. L., & Stanley, S. A. (2006). *Giving the body a voice: How EMDR, ego state therapy, somatic experiencing and indigenous healing methods can cure somatic dissociation.* International Society for the Study of Dissociation, Fall Conference, Toronto, Canada.

Paulsen, S. L., & Watkins, J. G. (2003). *Comparing ego state therapy and EMDR techniques.* Workshop at the ISSD 20th Annual Conference, Chicago.

Paulsen, S. L., & Watkins, J. G. (2005). *Best techniques from the armamentarium of hypnoanalytic, EMDR, somatic psychotherapy and cognitive behavioral methods.* ISSD Fall Conference, Toronto, Canada.

Parker, A., & Dagnall, N. (2007). Effects of bilateral eye movements on gist based false recognition in the DRM paradigm. *Brain and Cognition, 63,* 221–225.

Phillips, M. (2007). Combining hypnosis with EMDR and ego state therapy for ego strengthening. In C. Forgash & M. Copeley (Eds.), *Healing the heart of trauma with EMDR and ego state therapy* (pp. 91–120). New York: Springer.

Phillips, M., & Frederick, C. (1995). *Healing the divided self.* New York: Norton.

Porges, S. W. (2001). The polyvagal theory: Phylogenetic substrates of a social nervous system. *International Journal of Psychophysiology, 42,* 123–146.

Putnam, F. W. (1989). *Diagnosis and Treatment of Multiple Personality Disorder.* New York: Guilford Press.

Ross, C. A., Heber, S., Norton, G. R., Anderson, D., Anderson, G., & Barchet, P. (1989). The dissociative disorders interview schedule: A structured interview. *Dissociation, 2*(3), 169–189.

Schore, A. (1994). *Affect regulation and the origin of the self: The neurobiology of emotional development.* Hillsdale, NJ: Erlbaum.

Schore, A. N. (2001). The effects of early relational trauma on right brain development, affect regulation, and infant mental health. *Infant Mental Health Journal, 22,* 201–269.

Schore, A. N. (2003). *Affect dysregulation and disorders of the self.* New York: Norton.

Shapiro, F. (1995). *Eye movement desensitization and reprocessing: Basic principles, protocols, and procedures.* New York: Guilford Press.

Shapiro, F. (2001). *Eye movement desensitization and reprocessing: Basic principles, protocols, and procedures* (2nd ed.). New York: Guilford Press.

Siegel, D. J. (1999). *The developing mind: How relationships and the brain interact to shape who we are.* New York: Guilford Press.

Sokolov, E. N. (1963). *Perception and the conditioned reflex.* New York: McMillan.

Sokolov, E. N., Spinks, J. A., Lyytinen H., & Naatanen, R. (2002). *The orienting response in information processing.* Hillsdale, NJ: Erlbaum.

Solomon, R., Watkins, J. G., & Paulsen, S. L. (2004). *Therapeutic self.* EMDRIA Annual Conference, Montreal, Canada.

Spiegel, D. (2008). *Coming Apart: Trauma and the Fragmentation of the Self. Cerebrum,* The Dana Foundation, accessed from http://www.dana.org/news/cerebrum/detail.aspx?id=11122

Stanley, S. (2005). *Somatic experiencing workshop: Year I.* Foundation for Human Enrichment, Colorado. Workshop conducted in Bainbridge Island, WA.

Stanley, S. (2006). *Somatic transformation training: Year II.* Institute for Somatic Transformation. Bainbridge Island, WA.

Steinberg, M. (1994a). *Interviewer's guide to the structured clinical interview for DSM-IV dissociative disorders* (Rev. ed.). Washington, DC: American Psychiatric Press.

Steinberg, M. (1994b). *Structured clinical interview for DSM-IV dissociative disorders* (Rev. ed.). Washington, DC: American Psychiatric Press.

Steinberg, M. (1995). *Handbook for the association assessment of dissociation: A clinical guide.* Washington, DC: American Psychiatric Press.

Torem, M. S. (1990). Modified ego-strengthening for MPD. In D. C. Hammond (Ed.), *Handbook of hypnotic suggestions and metaphors* (p. 343). New York: Norton.

Trevarthen, C. (1993). The self born in intersubjectivity: An infant communicating. In U. Neisser (Ed.), *The perceived self: Ecological and interpersonal sources of self-knowledge* (pp. 121–173). New York: Cambridge University Press.

Tulving, E., & Schacter, D. L. (1990). Priming and human memory systems. *Science, 247,* 301–306.

Twombly, J. H. (2005). EMDR for clients with dissociative identity disorder, DDNOS and ego states. In R. Shapiro (Ed.), *EMDR solutions: Pathways to healing* (pp. 88–120). New York: Norton.

Twombly, J. H., & Schwartz, R. C. (2007). The integration of the internal family systems model and EMDR. In C. Forgash & M. Copeley (Eds.), *Healing the heart of trauma with EMDR and ego state therapy* (pp. 295–312). New York: Springer.

van der Hart, O., Brown, P., & van der Kolk, B. A. (1989). Pierre Janet's psychological treatment of post-traumatic stress. *Journal of Traumatic Stress, 2*(4), 379–395.

van der Hart, O., Nijenhuis, E., & Steele, K. (2006). *The haunted self: Structural dissociation and the treatment of chronic traumatization.* New York: Norton.

van der Hart, O., Steele, K., Boon, S., & Brown, P. (1993). The treatment of traumatic memories: Synthesis, realization, and integration. *Dissociation, 6,* 162–180. Available at http://www.trauma-pages.com/vdhart-93.htm

van der Hart, O., Van der Kolk, B. A., & Boon, S. (1998). Treatment of dissociative disorders. In J. D. Bremner & C. R. Marmar (Eds.), *Trauma, memory, and dissociation* (pp. 253–283). Washington, DC: American Psychiatric Press.

van der Kolk, B. (1987). *Psychological trauma*. Washington, DC: American Psychiatric Press.

van der Kolk, B. A., & Fisler, R. (1995). Dissociation and the fragmentary nature of traumatic memories: Overview and exploratory study. *Journal of Traumatic Stress, 8*(4), 505–525.

van der Kolk, B. A., McFarlane, A., & Weisaeth, L. (Eds.). (1996). *Traumatic stress: The effects of overwhelming experience on mind, body, and society*. New York: Guilford Press.

Watkins, H. H. (1994). Ego-state theory and therapy. In R. Corsini (Ed.), *Encyclopedia of Psychology, Vol. 1* (pp. 469–470). New York: Wiley.

Watkins, J. G. (1986). *Hypnotherapeutic techniques: Clinical hypnosis, Vol. 1*. New York: Irvington.

Watkins, J. G., & Paulsen, S. L. (2003). *Ego state therapy: EMDR and hypnoanalytic techniques*. Workshop at the Society for Clinical and Experimental Hypnosis, Chicago.

Watkins, J. G., & Paulsen, S. L. (2004, March). Abreactions in EMDR and hypnoanalytic therapies. Workshop at the American Society for Clinical Hypnosis, Chicago, IL.

Watkins, J. G., & Watkins, H. H. (1997). *Ego-state theory and therapy*. New York: Norton.

Wheeler, M. E., Peterson, S. E., & Buckner, R. L. (2000). Memory's echo: vivid remembering reactivates sensory-specific cortex. *Proceedings of the National Academy of Sciences USA, 97*, 11125–11129.

Wildwind, L. (1992). Treating chronic depression. Paper presented at EMDR Conference, San Jose, CA.

Chapter 20

Direct Targeting of Intrusive Images:

A Tale of Three Soldiers

Elizabeth Massiah

IN A STATE OF AGITATION, ZACH ASKED ME, "DON'T YOU SEE THE CHILD'S hand sticking out of the mass grave? Don't you see the teddy bear a few inches away? It's right over there by the desk? Can't you smell it?" What can one do when the client tells you that intrusive images are not just in his head, but also in his sight—constantly?

Grant was amazed that I could not see the bodies stacked like cordwood that he sees most days. Sometimes the images are inside his head, sometimes on the wall or floor or in dreams. He could not tolerate even a few seconds of the traumatic material from the events without dissociating or going to his Safe Place.

Penelope sees her attacker's face on every man who comes within reaching distance. She sees dead bodies in every small space. And if she is alone, the face image will float around her in the air, unattached to anything, giving her no rest, no escape. Sometimes when driving she sees the images as an advertising billboard that travels parallel to her car, just within her field of vision.

Each client will be presented individually; however, to protect privacy and confidentiality, each person represents an amalgam of actual experiences. Some of the events are recent, some are many years in the past.

I use a modified EMDR protocol to rapidly and effectively work directly with dissociated memory images. Although many experts in the trauma field write about these intrusive manifestations, they have written little about how to work with them directly to provide relief from the intrusive manifestations. Van der Kolk, van der Hart, and Marmar (1996) included these images and hallucinations in their description of dissociation.

PROTOCOL FOR INTRUSIVE IMAGES

1. Install a Safe Place, a safe feeling, and a sense of being grounded in this room. Teach body awareness. Practice until mastered.
2. Directly target the intrusive images.
3. Develop the Negative Cognition (NC), the Positive Cognition (PC), and the Validity of Cognition (VoC) Scale.
4. Get the Subjective Units of Disturbance Scale (SUDS) score. Do not ask for emotions or body sensations at this time, if the client will flood emotionally.
5. Start Eye Movements (EMs).
6. If the images don't lessen with the EMs, help the client construct a fantasy that changes the image, either through transformation or disposal.
7. Continue EMs until the SUDS is much lower and VoC much higher.
8. Avoid Body Scans, and install the PC.
9. When the imagery is under control (possibly several sessions), proceed with therapy, including targeting the original trauma with the full Assessment Phase, including emotions and body sensations, when possible.

Targeting these "unreal or imaginary" experiences rather than the actual traumatic events is not usual practice, but the level of distress evident in these clients demanded action. Validating the illusions as an accurate reflection of the traumatic experience enhanced trust development. When we de-energized the frightful emotions connected to the illusion, life improved immediately for the client.

It's hard to achieve and maintain stability in multiply traumatized individuals. EMDR can be used as described here, to assist with these destabilizing symptoms. Gelinas (2003) provided a detailed discussion of using EMDR in treating trauma and working in a phase-oriented manner to support stability.

When working with severely, frequently traumatized women and men, the work of stabilizing can be daunting—indeed, this is often the most difficult work for both therapist and client. Usually the traumatizing events are not approached directly until stabilizing skills are well and truly in place. Working directly with the image, in all its details until the negative emotional charge is satisfactorily diminished, starts the healing, resulting directly in more hope. This encourages stability. And without hope, nothing will change.

To have the images validated and worked with directly was very important for the clients I describe. They experienced not being judged or seen as "crazy" by the therapist.

In each instance, this work began within the first four sessions. In these cases, the images were traumatic in and of themselves—these images are dissociated memory fragments, complete with the somatosensory data of the actual experience. Scaer wrote that "confusion between past and current events is the defining feature of dissociation" (2008, p. 3). This dissociated state continues, and is more pronounced, when a specific or general trigger is present. Although it serves as a protective device at the time of trauma, it is difficult to manage in treatment. Scaer (2008) described the impact on treatment as

> that confused, distracted state in your patient that prevents you from breaking through the fog into any semblance of meaningful contact. It's the patient "leaving the room," losing contact with you when you've barely touched on the traumatic material, or when an obtuse reference to some supposedly benign topic causes a short circuit to a traumatic cue in their memory. (p. 2)

Although many experienced clinicians are attentive to issues of dissociation in trauma, in my experience many are not. Dissociation is frequently not assessed or dealt with effectively in trauma treatment, as noted by Gelinas (2003) and Scaer (2008). For some clients, the very notion of deliberately approaching the trauma story is too frightening, so intensely so that the approach itself, preceding the memory, produces emotional flooding: hence the avoidance that is so characteristic of post traumatic stress disorder (PTSD). Yet these clients were not avoiding. Just the opposite—they could not escape the images.

Zach and Grant described the sights as constant companions, always visible, just varying in degree of clarity. Sometimes the images moved in and out of their heads, depending on stress levels and unknown triggers. These phantoms or images were not flashbacks. They were apart, without the client "in" the experience portrayed.

ZACH

Zach, who had asked me if I saw the child's arm and teddy bear pro-truding from the floor in my office, could not recall any nightmares or flashbacks that involved this image. He said that it was as if images from the videotape of traumatic events that runs unstoppably in his head jumped out of his head and were in his sight all the time. He de-scribed them as clearly as he could describe the carpet from which he saw them protrude.

We were in our third session. He was sleeping poorly and seldom felt rested. We had good results using the scent from various essential oils as grounding tools, as well as working on breathing, using the grounding technique of naming 5, 4, 3, 2, 1 items he could see, hear, or feel. We had developed a Safe Place that he could access easily, having reinforced it by anchoring it to a light touch on his hand. He could readily access his sense or place of safety and used it often.

In this particular session, he was agitated and quite shaky. He kept staring at a spot on the carpet, then looking away. At first, I did not catch the significance of this. He stared relentlessly several times, and with each look he became increasingly agitated, tearful, and seemingly less present.

The usual grounding and Safe Place techniques did not seem to reach him in this dissociated state.

Liz: *I am going to put some of this oil on your hand, for you to smell.*
Zach: It smells nice . . . she's still there.
Liz: *Zach, look at me—what color is my hair?*
Zach: (Hesitating, struggling to speak.) It's mostly gray.
Liz: *As I touch your hand, think about your Safe Place—and follow my fin-gers.*

I asked him to follow my fingers for six passes of my fingers. We had used sets of 7 or 8 EMs when installing and accessing affect toler-ance resources. He was familiar with this process. Just doing this, as I asked him to try to follow my own deep breathing, started him settling and his breathing slowed slightly.

Zach: I can't get there, she won't go away.

He continued to glance back at the spot on the floor. Since I had no context for the image he described, I asked him simply to tell me what was important for me to know about the image.

Zach: It's not right . . . they buried her alive and she died before she could dig herself out. Her teddy bear is rotten. It smells of death and hatred. (He gagged a little as he reported the smell.) Their bloody faces are in the background now.
Liz: *Whose faces?*
Zach: The four who died.

Zach had served on many Canadian military tours of duty that took him to many countries. Knowing his history, I realized that the girl was likely from an earlier trauma and the four from a more recent incident.

Liz: *What number would you give it?*
Zach: It's a 10+ . . . and I can't stop shaking.
Liz: *Follow my fingers.*

We did 22 Eye Movements (EMs). He shook vigorously, mostly in his arms and one leg. I encouraged him to not try to stop the shakes as they are a normal body reaction. As I did the EMs, he began to talk about the wish that he could have buried her. Since obviously that was out of his control at the time of the event and could not be done now, I was not sure how to proceed.

Liz: *This may not make sense, but what if we buried her image here today, the way you want?*
Zach: I'm not sure how.

Neither was I, but I began with Body Scanning and my cognitive interweaves of possible ways to "bury" her in the image. We experimented with altering the images. When he would make a change that was to his satisfaction, we used short sets of EMs, 8–12 passes, to anchor the change.

Over the next half hour or so, he worked with the image, adding soil gently to the protruding hand, covering the teddy bear as well. He had to decide on how warm the soil would be, what texture. Then he was concerned that it would not be dug up by animals or blown away, so he added grasses. He insisted on types and heights of grasses she would have liked. At each detail, we would use EMs as well as scaling the result. He had started with a SUDS of 10, and slowly it descended, eventually reaching a 2. We would add the Body Scan and use EMs to reduce it as much as he could—sometimes to no sensation, sometimes to a low level.

Liz: *What's happening to the image of the girl?*
Zach: She's almost buried and I am not so upset. I'm at 2 and that fits for me.

Next, he thought of flowers: Zach loves to garden. He took a few moments to figure out what to plant. Then he remembered some flowers grown in the child's village and added these to the image. He thought they would grow well without a lot of care. Again, we did the EMs. At no time did I try to dissuade him that the image was not real to him, although he had some concerns.

Liz: *It seems to me that the image is an important part of your story. It would be disrespectful to not honor it as real, since it reflects a real experience.*
Zach: Your working with me to change the picture gives me hope and courage for the rest of the images.

This process took the better part of an hour and a half, and Zach became very tired. The NC was starting to change to "I did what I could"; the SUDS went to a 2. Not much of a shift, but a start. Then he commented that the rest of the image was still awful, but that he felt calmer now that the little girl was properly respected.

As Zach left the office he looked at the spot on the floor and smiled a little. In subsequent sessions we have checked on how the little girl is, and even when other things have been added to the image, her grave has stayed intact. That in and of itself has been a huge source of hope for him (and for me).

In earlier sessions, Zach and I had talked about dissociation and had gone through several grounding techniques. Francine Shapiro (2001) provided a list of suggested ways to ground someone. We had used them all—thoroughly and successfully, we thought. Yet despite engaging all his senses, all of his real or imagined resources, the image still remained. Since Zach so clearly saw the image, the notion of working with the image as a target seemed reasonable to me. He was reexperiencing one traumatic event, and my goal was to get that reexperiencing to be tolerable and for him to have the experience of changing it himself.

The beauty of EMDR for me as a therapist is that I don't have to know the details. I don't really have to lead. I just have to work for safety and let the client lead. This empowers the client—and the therapist: By embracing the "image" as though it were "real," Zach is empowered to tackle other trauma stories.

Also, the altered images have become a way to measure how he is doing. Once, some of the flowers started to die. He was unable to return fully to the original image, since the burial site was now intact, but he replanted the flowers, putting in a different type—and now when we check back, they are okay. He says the image is more of a felt sense now than a visual image.

GRANT

Grant has a lifelong trauma history. Sexually abused as a child, he worked hard to master several martial arts as an adolescent. He and his brother were out of the country doing advanced training in various arts when his brother was attacked. He died in Grant's arms. Then Grant, as an adult, had many more traumatic experiences, some military-related, some not.

In early sessions with Grant, we installed the resource of being beside the stream behind his childhood home. The stream was a place of joy and safety and fun for many years. We used short sets of EMs and added some anchoring techniques. He would bring up the image of himself playing by the stream, then let it fade away as much as he could and still be calm. Then he would bring it up strongly again. We repeated this several times.

When he had facility with this, I added anchoring, getting his permission to lightly touch his hand when the image was as strong and clear as he needed it to be. After a few repetitions of this, with me touching his hand, I got him to touch his own hand, bring up the image, then let it fade just as far as he needed. Once this process was well in place, we would use this to anchor him as we began to approach traumatic material.

Since trauma, by its nature, precludes the ability to limit the experience, installing checks and controls is an important part of the process. For many people, body sensations help them to signal the therapist. EMDR requires body awareness, whether noticing what is happening bodily in response to a certain memory or feeling, or the overall Body Scans. Both Zach and Grant had only minimal body sensation connection. Penelope, of the "billboards," had some; she could sense her feet. But Grant had almost no sense of body awareness. He had to learn awareness over time.

Grant required several sessions before he could notice differences in his body sensations. To work on this, I suggested he notice the differences in some of his shirts. He was confused. I had asked him to bring part of his uniform to our session.

Grant: They are just my clothes. What do you mean, how do they "feel" on my back?

Liz: *You are wearing a flannel shirt today—why did you choose that one?*

Grant: No reason, it was just there.

Liz: *Compared to some of your other shirts, is it more or less itchy on your back?*

Grant: I'm not sure why that matters.

Liz: *Humor me on this . . . how about in comparison to your uniform? Touch your shirt and your uniform jacket and see if they are the same.*

Grant: It is much different—softer . . . flannel is not itchy. My uniform is.

Liz: *Okay, so that is different than other shirts, so you have a preference. You can touch it and feel the fabric and know that it feels different on your back than your uniform.*

Grant: Never thought of that.

Liz: *Can you rate the comfort from 0 to 10? Ten is perfect.*

Grant: Oh, about a 7.

Liz: *Can you hold on to that sense of comfort for a moment, maybe touch your shirt? Follow my fingers . . .* (We did 8 sets of EMs.)

Grant: I remember my favorite sweats too—they are an 8.

Liz: *Follow my fingers . . .* (7 sets of EMs.) *What do you notice on your back right now?*

Grant: My left shoulder is sore.

Note that he still was not able to connect the soft feeling of the shirt to his body—but he was able to notice some sensation. We frequently repeated this installation process using EMs as well as the anchoring described above. I thought that Zach and Grant would have a hard time doing the Body Scan. And I was right.

Liz: *So, just scan your body and tell me what sensations you have.*
Grant: I don't notice my body—I can't do that.
Liz: *I could ask you to think about a time when you were doing karate, and we could scale the sensations and use the Eye Movements. But let's try some actual movements here.* (He stood up, as did I. I asked him to assume a favorite posture from his repertoire.)
Grant: I like this attack movement—it's alert and comfortable.

We worked with sensing the differences when he shifted his weight or moved his arms. He began to notice differences in his body as he moved.

Grant: My left leg seems different than the right; it seems more solid on the ground.
Liz: *Notice that, and follow my fingers.* (7 sets of EMs.)

Grant and I worked through several approaches to stabilization, body awareness, and affect tolerance. He became quite adept at using them—until we tried to approach any traumatic material.

One of Grant's preferred places of safety, that visibly allowed his body to relax and his breathing to slow, was to remember the lake behind his boyhood home. He could identify various sensations in his body when he was in his Safe Place.

Liz: *So are you well enough connected to the lake to notice body sensations, to try to process the traumatic incident we talked about last time? 0 to 10, how ready do you feel right now to do this?*
Grant: 7 or 8.
Liz: *What do you notice in your body as you think about doing this?*
Grant: My shoulder is stiff.
Liz: *Follow my fingers* (7 sets of EMs) *and pay attention to the sore shoulder.*
Grant: It's softened and is okay.
Liz: *Let's check with the anchoring.*

He touched his hand and reported feeling safe and calm.

Liz: *Can you bring up just enough of the story so that we can work with it? Let me know when you have it.*

Grant: It's awful—I can smell him. (Faster breathing, agitated moving, then slower breathing, relaxed body, soft flush on face, smile forming.)

Liz: *I am puzzled—you seemed to be in the incident, then within a few seconds you relaxed.*

Grant: The lake is so great, I love being there.

Grant was so hypervigilant that my moving my arm to pick up my tea or a pencil would elicit a strong startle response. I learned to describe every move before I made it, including details of how fast or slow, how narrow or wide the EMs would be.

Grant: (Speaking rapidly) I am too scared to not tell you right now what happened in . . . (Breathing rapidly, flushed face, hands holding his bowed head.)

Liz: *It isn't necessary.*

Grant: Stop, Liz . . . if I don't tell you now, I won't ever, and I have to tell someone. We were on patrol and went over a hill, and saw a man hanging from a tree. He was being disemboweled slowly. They were singing and dancing and playing with his intestines as they pulled them out of him. They saw us coming and ran away. We cut him down and he died at my feet.

Liz: *Thank you for telling me, for trusting me with that story. Do you realize you are breathing rapidly and are flushed?*

Grant: No, I thought I was pretty calm and it's just hot in here.

Liz: *Can you look at that plant in the corner for a moment or two? Good, please tell me what it looks like to you, describe it for me.*

Grant: I don't know what it is, just a plant. It is green, has large leaves.

Liz: *Remember that you noticed how quickly it was growing when you were last here.* (I'd wanted him to notice the living aspect.)

Grant: Yeah, I remember.

Liz: *That's right, now just let your breath be as slow going in as you can for now, and twice as slow to come out. Breathe as though in a karate session, or when holding your gun just as you pull the trigger.* (I used these examples because both were ingrained from training and I hoped it would be a way for him to learn to use existing abilities. I hoped they would initiate a change in his breathing, and it worked.)

Grant: I am afraid of what you think me for telling you this.

Liz: *It is an honor to hear your story . . . and I wish you had not had to experience it.*

His anxiety was beginning to generalize to therapy sessions, afraid of not being able to do what he so strongly wanted to do. He commented that he needed to find a way to not be buried alive under all the images, illusion, memories.

We worked on a variety of NCs—"I am helpless," "I am weak," "I am afraid," "I don't think I can do this." I hoped to challenge this supporting belief sufficiently that he could effectively install a VoC such as "I can tolerate this," "I am safe now," "I trust myself to do this work," but to no avail. He said that he did not think he could tolerate bringing the many images up in order to work with them, but he wanted to simply find a way to control them—and he decided he could do that by drowning them in his lake.

So we did.

First Grant had to figure out how to gather all the traumas up and see if he could do that. He decided he could create just the right container for each of the stories and their associated emotional connections. His trauma history began with sexual abuse by his father, and continued from there into many stories of danger, threat to life and limb, helpless exposure to violence, and the many acts of horror he had witnessed. Grant did not realize that the sorting inherent in this exercise also involved knowing the content of each story and rating it in his own manner.

Since he could not stay out of his safety resource for more than a few seconds, he decided to bring the trauma stories into the Safe Place in a controlled manner. When we agreed on this, his body posture changed to a more forceful pose, he reported feeling stronger in his body, his breathing slowed, and his face seemed more relaxed. A Body Scan showed calmness and openness.

Although this approach seemed contraindicated—bringing the trauma into the Safe Place deliberately—it was effective. Grant was adept at organizing, planning, and improvising. He considered how to get the incidents into containers without having to recall them in detail—he decided to transform them into gravel of various types and sizes and to truck them to the lake.

Each of these many steps was processed using EMs and a Body Scan. Whenever any anxiety or other sense appeared in his body, we used EMs to settle it out. Regularly he would comment on aspects of the river/lake and visibly soothe as he did so.

In the next session, Grant decided to imagine driving the truck to the lake himself, with a trusted friend, instead of alone. This friend had been with him at many of the traumatic events, so they both knew the details. This meant he could do so without discussion of the events. Grant actually had fun, laughing at times as he envisioned getting the truck stuck and then unstuck. He determined the details of the size of truck; he had the controls in his imaginary hand, and he was able to direct the unloading. There were some events that, even after Grant had placed them in concrete, lead-lined holders, would still produce agitation. Whenever tension appeared in his body, we used EMs and Body Scans again until it subsided.

Grant decided that these items just being in the lake wasn't enough, so he gave the lake an ocean-like bottom, with deep crevasses, dark places. He put sea creatures in charge of warning him if some of the containers came loose in any way: Octopuses and sharks were his favorites, although he also had some dolphins to inform him of the state of the containers. A few containers resurfaced and had to be resunk.

Sometimes Grant was willing to try to process the trauma in the ones that resurfaced, but within seconds he would simply engage in reburying the issue—be it hallucination, image, memory—and would stay in his Safe Place.

The sheer number of events meant that getting them into the water took 10 sessions. Other issues were processed in this time, and there was a lot of other work to do. Grant's sense of safety, empowerment, and hope increased over time. At the end of each session we would check the NC and the VoC and they slowly moved.

Grant liked the idea of being in charge of his own rate of change and of how deeply each container needed to be buried. At times when he would get stuck on part of this process, I would interject a suggestion. Once he was satisfied, we installed the "burial" with short sets of EMs (8–10).

Eventually, after at least 10 sessions in which this was the primary activity, Grant decided the task was done. The SUDS was at 2 and staying there. The VOC was at 6 and staying there. He liked these numbers, insisting that many of the events were too horrific to ever be at 0. That was the manageable place for them to be at that time.

PENELOPE

Avoidance is enormously strong in trauma, for good reason. Some might think that this approach to the work of mending traumatic narratives is joining in with the avoidance shown by clients. Instead, the approach validates the person's experience without question or judgment. Penelope, the woman who saw the "billboards" of rotting bodies, could not chance any processing and left after three sessions. We had made a good connection, and I hope she returns to do the work.

This indirect approach allows clients to have a sense of control and empowerment. It provides a wide range of resources for clients to use in order to manage intrusive illusions, hallucinations, and images. It provides respect and credibility to the clients and to their lived experience. It allows some processing of otherwise intolerable material.

ZACH

Before treatment, Zach could not go up to bed unless he walked with his arms outstretched and his back touching the wall—so he could be sure where the floating images of piles of bodies were and he would not be surprised by them. Using the approach of working with the images themselves, he was finally able to go up to bed without this upsetting image accompanying him. He was able to designate one place in his house for the image, and have it be only in that one place. Then we could negotiate times and issues of contact with the images, and eventually, using the Standard Protocol, we were able to dissipate the emotional charge of the images.

Working in this way has allowed a sense of accomplishment and of hopefulness to become firmly rooted in the client's lived experience. If at times of high stress the image becomes more powerful, since it has already been a target to be worked with, it simply gets worked on a bit more until it retires again. Sometimes the trauma resolves and the illusion is gone, not to return.

This is the desired outcome, but it does not always happen. Even when there is no traditional resolution, the progress has been significant, building more skill and creating willingness to confront the "actual" event.

Zach, who saw the rotting hand of the little girl, says he now gets only fleeting images of her grave, and that reminds him that things are better. He is not sure he wants it to disappear completely, since that might rekindle his sense of not having done enough. I suspect that we will be able to work more with that, using EMDR to take away the traumatic reaction. Grant has "stored" his traumas in a way that allows him to live with them, having sorted through them without losing his safety.

This work is constantly teaching me, making me agile on my therapeutic feet, forcing me to find ways to try to maintain fidelity to the protocols of EMDR and still meet the needs of these frightfully traumatized women and men.

REFERENCES

Gelinas, D. J. (2003). Integrating EMDR into phase oriented treatment for trauma. *Journal of Trauma and Dissociation, 4*(3), 91–135.

Scaer, R. (2008). The dissociation capsule. Retrieved May 5, 2008, from http://traumasoma.com/excerpt1.html

Shapiro, F. (2001). *Eye movement desensitizing and reprocessing: Basic principles, protocols, and procedures* (2nd ed.). New York: Guilford Press.

van der Kolk, B., van der Hart, O., & Marmar, C. R. (1996). Dissociation and information processing in posttraumatic stress disorder. In B. A. van der Kolk, A. C. McFarlane, & L. Weisaeth (Eds.), *Traumatic stress: The effects of overwhelming experiences on mind, body, and society* (pp. 303–327). New York: Guilford Press.

Chapter 21

Attachment, Affect Tolerance, and Avoidance Targets in Obsessive-Compulsive Personality Disorder

Robin Shapiro

OBSESSIVE-COMPULSIVE DISORDER (OCD) CLIENTS HAVE REPETITIVE nonsensical behaviors and obsessive thoughts, and know that they're not being rational. Obsessive-compulsive personality disorder (OCPD) clients are something else. They're obsessed with control. They are detail oriented, to the exclusion of the big picture. They may get involved with organizational details, the minutiae of tasks, or tasks that have very little to do with what most needs to be completed in their jobs, their studies, their homes, and in their lives. Their homes may be frighteningly organized, everything in plastic containers in alphabetical order, or, if housework is on the "avoid" list, completely out of control. Like OCD people, they may hoard money or stuff, even worthless stuff. Some OCPD folks are prone to angry outbursts when their environments, kids, partners, or coworkers don't go with the program. They may be superficially nice, even helpful, but they're not usually capable of deep intimacy. They are the nightmare managers (and sometimes employees) from hell, micromanaging everything. They often don't keep or rise very far in employment, though they may work half again as many hours as other employees. And according to them, nothing is ever right with anything. Expect them to display depression, anxiety, and either massive Pollyannish denial or massive criticism of everything, including you.

"L-A-W-F-I-R-M-S"

Use "LAWFIRMS" as the mnemonic for recounting the symptoms of OCPD (Wikipedia, 2008):

L—Loses point of activity (due to preoccupation with detail)

A—Ability to complete tasks is gone (compromised by perfectionism)

W—Worthless objects (unable to discard)

F—Friendships (and leisure activities) excluded (due to a preoccupation with work)

I—Inflexible, overconscientious (on ethics, values, or morality, not accounted for by religion or culture)

R—Reluctant to delegate (unless others submit to exact guidelines)

M—Miserly (toward self and others)

S—Stubbornness (and rigidity)

Avoidance of anxiety is their unconscious organizing principle. Here's how it works: If I need to get the big job done, and feel anxiety when I think about the big job, I'll bring my attention to this little task that's not so scary and do it perfectly, for hours. Working on the little task makes me feel better. (Dan Goleman's [1985] book *Vital Lies, Simple Truths* describes the biology of this phenomenon.) When I take my attention away from that which makes me anxious, the pharmacy in my brain gives me really good drugs, endorphins. (This is why procrastination and self-distraction are so popular.) If I don't work on the scary task, I'll feel better, instantly. If I keep doing any intricately complex avoidance behavior, my brain keeps giving me good endorphins. If I've been self-medicating since childhood, by focusing on unimportant tasks, instead of on my anxious or checked-out or angry or abusive or controlling or absent parents and my own loneliness, I'm going to build a big neural net of reflexive avoidance/distraction behavior.

In my opinion, here's the etiology: Caregivers, most often mothers, for some reason can't connect well with their kids. Nonconnecting moms, be they passive or screaming, are frightening to kids. If kids (especially kids wired for more anxiety) learn to distract themselves by focusing on little tasks, they can dissociate/self-medicate away the terror of being all alone and taking care of themselves. What they don't learn is the nondissociative self-soothing techniques that arise from the attachment dance of connection, backing off a bit, and reconnection. So the children's only self-regulation comes from distraction and dissociation. The more they do it that way, the wider and deeper the neural network they build to that behavior. It quickly becomes reflexive and the personality disorder takes root.

TREATING OCPD

People with OCPD don't often come to therapy. Good therapy is the opposite of avoidance and their pathology keeps them away. However, once in a while, someone gets "drug in" by their spouse, or employer, or forced to therapy by their own miserableness and the work begins. Work on four things:

1. Stay on Task in the Sessions

They will try to control the session and keep you focused on the unimportant details. Don't let it happen. Get more assertive than you usually are, or you and your client will unhappily spin both your wheels for months. To that end, make and keep a strong alliance. Show your compassion and your grit. When they change the subject to some small distress of the day or how awful someone or something is, say, *Oh that's so upsetting when that happens! Let's go back and get the underlying material, so this won't have to be so distressing later on.* These clients will want to co-opt you into their avoidance schemas. Don't do it! Do gently point it out, with humor: *Whoops! There we go again! That reflex to stay away from the distressing material is so strong, you had me going there with you. I'm not going to let it get me! Let's go back to task. Are you ready to feel bad, again?* I might write "It's good to feel bad" or "Anxiety is your best friend" on my big whiteboard (which is in their line of sight) as an aid to keeping on task.

Since I start most clients off with Maureen Kitchur's genogram-based intake (2005) with its predetermined list of "nosy, snoopy questions," I'm able to keep the initial sessions on task, and then share what I think much of the therapy will be. Pay particular attention, in your questions, to attachment issues. Ask, *What was your mom like when you were little? How did she respond to you when you were sad, bad, or angry? What was your dad like and how did he respond? Did you have other caregivers? What was going on in your family when you were little (traumas, changes, milieu)? What did you do when you felt bad, as a kid?*

2. Work on Affect Tolerance and Self-Soothing

Tell them, *We'll start with little feelings, like 1-pound hand weights, and work up to the heavier 20-pound feelings.* Teach them containerizing of emotions, mindfulness techniques, relaxation, and containing their own inner babies. April Steele's Imaginal Nurturing (2007) is wonderful for healing attachment deficits, or use other kinds of ego state work. Have them sit with distressing affect for a few moments while you do Bilateral Stimulation (BLS), then for longer and longer periods as their capacity builds. Praise incessantly, for each small gain in ability to tolerate themselves. These people are full of shame; praise for feeling or doing something authentic is priceless for them.

3. Use EMDR to Target the Early Childhood Relationship with the Caregivers

Imagine looking into your mother's eyes when you were an infant. What do you notice in your body right now, as you imagine your mom? (Kitchur, 2005). Clear whatever comes up. Go through all the ages until there's no distress. See Chapter 18 in this book for more early trauma techniques.

4. Finally, Target the Avoided Things

I adore Jim Knipe's Level of Urge to Avoid (2005, and Chapter 4 in this book), a protocol that targets the "inappropriate positive affect" inherent in avoidance. Knipe would ask these clients, *How good on a scale of 0 to 10 would it feel to completely avoid that big project by focusing on sorting out your sock drawer? 10 is the best feeling you could have, 0 is no good feeling. Where do you feel that feeling in your body? Think about sorting the sock drawer and feel that good feeling.* (BLS.)

Often the "inappropriate positive affect" (the endorphins) go down by itself and the clients are left with the somewhat appropriate feeling of dread about what they've been avoiding. Then target the dread about the project, clear it, and have them imagine doing the damn thing, step by small step, clearing any trauma about each step as you go. And then imagine what having it finished would feel like. Install the good feeling of "finishing." Congratulate yourselves. Then move on to the next task. If the inappropriate affect doesn't go down by itself, I use the Two-Hand Interweave (R. Shapiro, 2005): *In one hand, hold how good it will feel to continue avoiding the project. In the other, hold the consequences for not doing it.* (BLS.) Your clients are very likely to feel their discomfort. Target it with the Standard Protocol and clear it.

Mindy, a Composite Case

Mindy, 50, is intelligent, knowledgeable, pleasant to talk to, and completely stuck. She's depressed, angry, and isolated. Her adult children avoid her. Her house is a mess and full of too much stuff. She works longer hours than anyone else in her office, yet is often reprimanded for not finishing tasks. She has no close friends. Even though she does good things for other people, what she does often doesn't fit what they need. (When she's doing something to avoid thinking about something else, she may not notice the needs of the recipient.) She's trying therapy one more time, "even though it never does anything" and, by the way, because her boss gave her an ultimatum: "Go to therapy and fix your work problems, or lose your job."

The first tip-off was her negativity. Everyone at work was stupid. The way they ran the office was wrong. Her kids were ungrateful and not running their lives the right way. Therapy didn't work. And she never felt good. I zeroed in on the depressive symptoms. She was on an antidepressant. (It didn't work either.) She didn't really exercise. Overweight, her diet leaned heavily toward carbs and sugar, even though she "knew better." Her house was a mess, to the point that her kids didn't want to meet her there. "The office is run so badly, I have so much work, it's hard to get to the housework." I noted the characterlogical lack of responsibility for anything and thought about the enormous shame that must be sitting under that defense.

We started with Kitchur's Strategic Developmental Model (2005). I explained that we would do a thorough intake, then use EMDR to clear her traumas in developmental order. It was hard for us to stay on task with the genogram/intake, but I kept turning the conversation back to the task at hand. (She reminded me of a horse that keeps turning back toward the barn, when the rider has other plans.) My directiveness, with another kind of client, would be showing a lack of connection and empathy. With Mindy, I was keeping the therapy from being derailed into her pathology. When we started talking about her divorce, she used angry words, but looked hurt.

Her family was "nice." Good, midwestern people. Small town. No overt abuse. Mother was anxious, narcissistic in personality, and logistically overwhelmed by seven kids. "She should have never been a mother. She didn't like it very much." Mother would blow up, periodically, when things weren't perfect. She was highly critical. Otherwise, "she wasn't really available." Father, a pleasant, passive guy, worked long hours, out of the house. A middle child, Mindy kept a low profile and did her own thing, working on craft projects in every spare moment. She "mostly" did her school work. Had friends but no "best friends." Finished college (in 6 years). Got married. Had kids. ("I probably yelled too much.") Worked. Got divorced. Current life was both overbusy and empty. She socialized on occasion, did needlework, and worked 60 or more hours each week. Her goals, which I had to drag out of her: (a) Don't get fired; (b) Have less depression; (c) Have a cleaner/tidier house; (d) Do better self-care; (e). Make a better relationship with her kids; (f) Make better relationships with people at work.

She had no true Safe Place. The concept of a place where you "didn't have to do anything" was terrifying, and to be avoided. We settled for a "Healing Place" that was clean and tidy and full of craft materials. ("Well, I have to have something to *do!*") We made two containers, moderate-sized for anxiety and a bigger one for rage. I explained my theory of OCPD and how her brain had reflexively trained itself to avoid anxiety, and that if something threatened that avoidance, her brain reflexively went into "fight" mode. She liked the explanation, partly because it didn't blame her. I explained that our job was to let her feel more anxiety, and that when we were successful, she might want to run out of the room, or she might reflexively get mad, and we'd deal with either feeling. We would try to create *a balance of enough anxiety to do the job, but not too much. If it's too much, let me know, and we can use the container and the Healing Place to cool it down.*

We did a few sessions of her telling me about how horrible work and her kids and her ex-husband were. Each time she started to explain, I'd slow her down, have her notice the emotion and where it was in her body, and do a little BLS, with mechanical tappers, on noticing the feeling. Each time we did slightly longer sets. First 5 rounds, then 7, then 10. When she could sustain 25 round-trips, I declared her ready for EMDR. The next session, I had her imagine herself as an infant, looking up at her mother. She froze, looked away from me, and deftly changed the subject. Bingo! I said, *This is great. You are doing exactly the behavior you came here for. Let's go after it!* What could she say? I redirected her back to target and back to her body. She growled, "Don't tell me what to do!" *Cool! We've got the anger response. Where do you feel that?* She laughed and frowned. "In my jaw and in my arms and legs. I want to run away and I want to push you and it's terrible." *Great! Go with that.* (BLS.) She settled into the processing and settled down. *Now, back to that infant and that mom. Look up into her face and notice your body.* "I'm tense and I want to get away." *0 to 10, how tense? 7. Go with that.* (BLS.) We processed. She would pop out of her experience, periodically, but was able to be directed back and to bear the affect. The anxiety shifted to sadness. "She couldn't be with me. There were all those other kids. She was stressed. I didn't have a chance." *Go with that.* She stayed with the sadness, until she signaled that she'd had enough. We stuck the remaining sadness in a container and visited the Healing Place. There was more time and I ran through April Steele's (2007) Imaginal Nurturing scenario: *Now, as you hold that newborn, notice her warm weight in your arms as she feels your strong arms around her. Look into her beautiful eyes.* At the end of the session, I gave her an *Imaginal Nurturing* CD, telling her to listen to it once each day. We discussed the best ways that she could avoid listening to it, and the best times she could actually listen to it.

Therapy continued. She was often late, sometimes missing sessions. If she came too late for processing we'd discuss the avoidance reflex, and we'd process, with BLS only, any current distress, building up her affect tolerance. Slowly, we worked through the childhood injuries: being ignored; the hours spent alone; Mother yelling; harsh criticism; and underneath it all a yearning for connection with no place to go. She became able to heft the heavier emotions, terror and shame. We processed the shame of her criticism and yelling that helped drive away her husband and that have kept her children at a distance. We became able to laugh together at her brain's reflexive avoidance and to start looking at its cost to her current life. As she could tolerate the shame of what she was doing at work, she began to take responsibility for the messes she'd created. We were ready for Step 4, clearing avoidance.

We started with a list of what she typically avoids and a list of favorite avoidance activities. She avoided anything that made her anxious: completion of big work projects (by doing them herself or delegating them), balancing her checkbook ("It's too scary to find out what I really owe"), cleaning certain areas of her house ("I just don't think about them"), cleaning up some misunderstandings and conflicts with her children and friends ("I don't know how it will go"), exercise and other self-care ("It will make me think how out of shape I am and then I'll feel hopeless"). She had many avoidance strategies: needle-point, reworking and rewriting insignificant parts of projects, cross-word puzzles and computer games, baking and eating exquisite desserts, overorganizing parts of her house, canceling social engage-ments to stay at work or to stay home and do avoidance activities.

Okay, Mindy. I want you to imagine planning to walk six blocks up and six blocks back on the trail by your house. She tensed. *What avoidance activ-ity would you rather do?* "Crossword puzzles and eating those chocolate decadence brownies I made." *How good would it feel to do a crossword puzzle and eat great brownies instead of walking? 10 is the best possible feel-ing. 0 is no feeling.* "An 8." *Where do you feel that good feeling?* "My chest and my shoulders." *Go with that.* (BLS.) "It feels even better, a 9." When it got to a 10, we went with Plan B, a Two-Hand Interweave: *In one hand, hold a crossword puzzle and two brownies and that great feeling that goes with them. In the other, hold the consequences of avoiding exercise.* She frowned. "It's starting to not feel so good." *Hah! Go with that.* (BLS.) "I'm thinking about how fat I am." *Keep going!* (BLS.) She moved into shame and hopelessness. "I'm in such bad shape, I'll never be okay. . . . I'm such an idiot to let myself get this fat." We kept going and the in-sight appeared. "No wonder I avoid exercise. Look at what goes with it." As the affect calmed, and the insight grew, we set up the Standard Protocol. *When you think about walking the trail, what are you saying to yourself about yourself?* Negative Cognition (NC): "I can't do it, I'll feel too bad." Positive Cognition (PC): "I can stand my feelings and I can walk." *Feeling?* "Anxiety and some shame." Subjective Units of Distur-bance (SUD): 7. *Body?* "Neck, throat, pit of stomach." As she processed, her brain took her to many other times that she had used food and other distractions to avoid tasks. Shame would alternate with insight. "I'm seeing how it (avoidance) really is a reflex. I'm not going to let it run me anymore." *Great! Keep going with that.* We eventually refocused on walking the trail. She said, "I can do it, if I'm willing to feel." *Are you?* "Yes!" *Go with that!* "Yes!" (BLS.) She saw herself walking the trail and noticing thoughts and emotions and enjoying the birds. We in-stalled, "I can do it and I can feel."

In subsequent sessions, we went after all her targets and all her avoidance strategies. Her reflexive resistance became weaker with each session. She began to get her house under control, and not just the overorganized parts. She began to tackle the work problems head-on. Our last targets were the interpersonal ones. When she finally had meaningful contact with her children, she apologized to each one for her angry outbursts and her choices of avoidance over intimacy. They were dumbfounded and deeply touched, but wary. She mended fences at work and began to participate in work-related social events. Our last target was how to use baking, crossword puzzles, and needlepoint mindfully and choicefully; as activities to enjoy, not as reflexive avoidance. She came back 2 years later, as she embarked on a new relationship, and her anxiety and avoidance arose again. A much briefer therapy allowed her to hang in (and hang out) with her new love.

CONCLUSION

I won't kid you. My example was an easiest-case scenario. These people need a long therapy and, since avoidance is their issue, they can bail early. A year is fast. Two years or more is quite possible. They've been reinforcing avoidance in themselves since babyhood and you and they have a lot of neural networks to rewire. And it's possible, with a good alliance and good attachment and affect work, for them to choose conscious recreation (vacations, breaks, movies) and relationships and getting their real work done, over reflexive busywork, blowups, inadequacy, and loneliness.

REFERENCES

Goleman, D. (1985). *Vital lies, simple truths*. New York: Simon & Schuster.

Kitchur, M. (2005). The strategic developmental model for EMDR. In R. Shapiro (Ed.), *EMDR solutions: Pathways to healing* (pp. 8–56). New York: Norton.

Knipe, J. (2005). Targeting positive affect to clear the pain of unrequited love, codependence, avoidance, and procrastination. In R. Shapiro (Ed.), *EMDR solutions: Pathways to healing* (pp. 189–212). New York: Norton.

Shapiro, R. (2005). The two-hand interweave. In R. Shapiro (Ed.), *EMDR solutions: Pathways to healing* (pp. 160–166). New York: Norton.

Steele, A. (2007). *Developing a secure self: An attachment-based approach to adult psychotherapy*. Gabriola, BC: Author. Order online at www.april-steele.ca

TREATING BODILY AND MEDICALLY BASED TRAUMA

Chapter 22

Clearing Medical Trauma
Robin Shapiro

MOST ILLNESSES ARE INCONVENIENT. SOME CAN KILL YOU. AND MANY that allow people to live can leave them in traumatized states. This chapter will address posttraumatic stress caused by medical conditons and medical interventions. The chapter can't be comprehensive: After reading it, I hope you will be alert to new targets and new ways to aim EMDR interventions at them and be able to generalize these targets to cover the gamut of medical trauma.

Even people with resilient nervous systems, who have good attachment, affect tolerance, calm temperaments, and few earlier traumas can develop posttraumatic stress disorder (PTSD) if they are the one in a thousand who wake up mid-surgery, paralyzed, unable to speak, in agonizing pain, and fully aware of the procedure. Others, with extensive trauma histories or poor affect tolerance or simply highly sensitive temperaments, can become traumatized by seemingly slight procedures. Don't assume that horrible experiences will create PTSD or that "piece of cake" procedures will leave clients unscathed. Find out what has been traumatic for your particular client. Medical trauma can link to historical trauma. Do a comprehensive intake of both medical and other distressing events before targeting a current distressing event.

Diagnoses may be traumatizing in themselves, especially ones that carry cultural baggage, such as cancer and AIDS (Sontag, 2001). Treatments may be harrowing and destructive to the point that some patients choose death over continuing to suffer the pain, side effects, or continuing trauma. Patients can suffer traumatic losses of mobility,

function, cognition, their regular appearance, and their closest relationships.

IN UTERO

According to Robert Scaer (2005), medical trauma can start before
birth:

> The ability of the fetus to process information from the major senses is
> relatively intact by the third trimester and very possibly much earlier. . . .
> (A)fter needling fetuses to obtain blood, Giannakoulopouos and his col-
> leagues (1994) were able to measure dramatic elevations of plasma corti-
> sol and endorphins that actually persisted after the traumatic event
> longer than one would expect in a child or adult. Cortisol and endorphin
> elevation provide compelling evidence that these infants experienced
> traumatic stress. Because the procedure involved needling the fetus, the
> only logical source of this chemical stress response would be the percep-
> tion of pain. . . . There is also evidence that the mother's stress levels
> have a direct and significant effect on the health and brain development
> of the fetus. . . . (E)xposure of the fetus to the stress-related hormones of
> the distressed mother is likely to alter the infant's adaptive capacity to
> further life stress. (pp. 106–107)

BIRTH

Birth can be traumatic, for both mother (see Chapter 23) and infant (see
Chapter 18). Luckily, birth trauma can be cleared. A young man came
in, complaining of being "stuck." He was intelligent, sensitive, passive,
and defeated, despite exemplary parents and few obvious traumas. He
had a useful advanced degree and, in a good economy, he was working a low-wage, low-skill job. We cleared his few known mild traumas
and then went fishing for other targets. I planned to ask him to scan inside as we searched through developmental stages for other trauma.
We didn't have to go very far. *Think about the day of your birth. You're
coming out to see your mother and your father. What do you notice inside, as
you imagine being born.* He smiled, saying, "They really want me!" And
then said, "I'm stuck. I can't move!" He looked agitated. Without time
for the Standard Protocol setup, I started the Bilateral Stimulation

(BLS). Then it was as if his body collapsed. (I imagine, now, that I was witnessing the switch from a hyperaroused ventral vagal state to a hypoarousal dorsal vagal state.) I kept saying, *Keep going. Stay with it*, though I had no idea what was happening. Suddenly, he screamed and grabbed his shoulder. While I peeled myself off the ceiling, he was howling, "It hurts! It hurts!" I urged him to continue, *Can you keep going?* (He nodded, eyes big.) *Go with it.* Two long rounds of BLS later, he was practically dancing in his chair, "I'm free. I'm free. I'm not stuck." *Go with that!* After installing "I'm free: I have choices," he called his mother to ask about his birth. He'd never been told that he'd been stuck in the birth canal and the doctor had snapped his clavicle in order to pull him through. Since then, his brain had been stuck in "stuck." The processing allowed his brain to know that he was free. We had one more session and a few follow-up phone calls. A month later, he had moved on from his "McJob" to an executive position in another company, committed to his girlfriend, and exchanged his depressed affect for excited engagement.

INFANCY

Childhood health issues bring many opportunities for trauma. Here is Scaer, again (2005), on premature infants being poked, stuck, and then socially isolated in intensive care units (ICUs):

> Chronically elevated levels of serum cortisol, instigated by the preemies' response to threatening and traumatizing sensory experiences, are likely to produce the same deficits in development of the hippocampus that we see in childhood and adult victims of trauma, resulting in long-term deficits in declarative memory mechanisms. (p. 109)

While most people don't "remember" these experiences, their bodies often do. If you know that your client had a premature birth, you can ask, *Think about being a tiny baby, all alone in a bright, noisy room, in pain. What do you notice in your body when you imagine that baby?* (Kitchur, 2005). Sometimes it's nothing. If so, go to the next target. If there's a body sensation, ask for a concurrent emotion, check for cognitions (sometimes there aren't any, sometimes there are), get a Subjective Units of Disturbance Scale (SUDS), and process it through. I've watched several extremely anxious people drop their shoulders and their anxieties with this simple intervention. Whether or not they had Positive Cognitions (PCs) at the setup, they ended up endorsing and installing variations of "It's over," "I'm safe," "I have control now."

All of my adult clients with fibromyalgia and some of them with anxiety disorders and odd dissociative phenomena, suffered from colic as infants. I've targeted the colic two ways: accidentally, through floating back: *When you focus on that sensation and feel that distress and feel that you're out of control, float back to the first time you felt that way.* Or, on purpose: *Think back to that colicky baby you were. Hurting, inconsolable, not able to notice people trying to connect to you. Nothing makes it feel better. It hurts. Where are you feeling that in your body? Go with that.* (BLS.) We keep targeting the colic feeling until it's gone. I've seen symptoms of fibromyalgia improve and, erratic, seemingly unexplainable fluctuations, from full panic to full shut-down dissociation, disappear after a few sessions. I can't promise that you'll cure all your clients who show these symptoms, but do target colic if it's in their histories.

A panicked client with a feeling of "something scary" by her face, and a sense of suffocation and helplessness, may be reexperiencing anesthesia or intubation, not (as many therapists first imagine, because we hear about it so often) oral sexual abuse. When doing the setup for these sensations, keep your mind open for *any* explanation. I've cleared clients' childhood experiences of choking for breath in oxygen tents, from intubations, while experiencing intense pain and while having croup (ask *Was it steamy?*). Often, we didn't know exactly what we were clearing until halfway through the session. Then, the other salient parts of memory arose as we continued the processing. Sometimes, with the clearing of early trauma, adult breathing problems disappeared. Other times, impairments continued with less concurrent anxiety.

ADOLESCENCE/SEXUAL HEALTH EXAMS

I don't work with many kids, but I have helped about 100 clients, women and men, clear the traumas of their first and subsequent "sexual health" exams. For many clients, their distress was secondary to prior experiences of sexual exploitation. Both teenage and adult clients abuse survivors may avoid these exams, or else abreact or dissociate during them. With abuse survivors, you must first clear the abuse incidents, then stressful previous examinations, and, if still needed, differentiate between an exam and abuse. *In one hand hold what your stepfather did to you. In the other, hold being in the doctor's office on the examination table. (BLS.) Which one can you leave? In which situation can you be in control? In which one are you older and stronger?* Then, if your client still holds anxiety about an upcoming examination, do a Future Template of him or her telling the doctor that abuse occurred, and that he or she must be apprised of every move and procedure that the doctor does. For some clients, that's not enough. I have accompanied two middle-aged, very dissociated clients to their first pap smears, making sure that adult parts stayed in the room, and debriefing the examinations after their appointments. As therapy, including EMDR processing, progressed, they were able to go by themselves.

For many, the exam itself held the trauma. First, the normally labile affect and increased social anxiety of any teen can complicate their reactions to illness and medical procedures. They worry about being found "weird." They may feel pathologically embarrassed. Pay special attention to the Negative Cognitions (NCs). You might hear, "I know I look weird, down there" or "I can't stand the embarrassment" or "It's weird that I felt so weird." People with social anxiety can be the most impacted. Their training says, "Don't show these parts." And they may worry more about being found "weird." Some families and cultures create more shame about "down there." EMDR can be helpful in clearing these traumas. So can simple facts about normal physiological variation. You may be the only one with whom they can talk about these things. Be cool!

AGING AND BODY IMAGE

Some people are terrified, shamed, and angered by the normal aging process. Each wrinkle or extra pound is a disaster. Any loss of function is a sign that they will become unlovable and useless. Groups prone to be most distressed by the normal aging process include people who earn their livings with their bodies (athletes, models, dancers, and entertainers), people, especially women, from some regions (Southern California, for one), and some upper- or upper-middle-class groups, people with social anxiety, and people with narcissistic personality disorder. It's helpful to dissect someone's distress about aging into cultural, temperamental, and characterlogical components, for discussion and treatment.

Here are some targets for the most distressed folks:

- NCs: "I'm ugly." "I'm worthless." "I'm unlovable."
- The onset of menopause: "I'm not a woman anymore."
- Erectile dysfunction: "I'm not a man anymore."
- Waning, in some, of sexual desire.
- Birthdays.
- Changing appearance.
- Lack of automatic sexual attention from others.
- Slight cognitive changes.

SURGERY

Surgeries bring their own set of traumas. First, in anticipation, abuse survivors often balk at having their sleeping bodies under the control of others. Surgeons can be famously unrelational and abrupt in calming fears. The surgery itself can yield trauma targets from the administration of anesthesia (especially ether, in the "old days") to waking up, disoriented or in pain, after surgery. One in a thousand patients wakes up during surgery. It's a horrible experience, as you will see below. And the aftermath of most surgery is pain, nausea, and temporary disability. Here are two stories:

Marina: Surgical Trauma

Marina was sent to me for "medical trauma." She was having multiple panic attacks, especially at night. She would wake up tearing her CPAP (continuous positive airway pressure) sleep apnea machine off her face, in a full-blown attack. She feared sleep, she was constantly anxious, and, after a productive life of work and mothering, could no longer drive, sleep, or function. She had good parents, a supportive husband and friends, and easy children. She had experienced trauma in six different surgeries, including a tonsillectomy as a child, a cesarean delivery with no anesthesia 17 years before, and a hysterectomy, 2 years ago, during which she woke up. As she spoke about the operations, she shook violently while tears streamed down her face. Luckily for both of us, after the usual preparations she was a perfect responder to EMDR trauma processing.

First surgery: She's 5. She's taken from her mother and wheeled into the emergency room. No one tells her what's going to happen. They hold her down and put a white thing close to her face and suddenly she can't breathe. She struggles. NC: "I'm going to die!" PC: "I survived. I'm okay." Validity of Cognition (VoC): 1 out of 7. Terror, in whole body, SUD 10. As she processes, she shakes violently. I tell her that it's a normal part of letting go of trauma, tell her to put the bilateral tappers under her legs and hold on to me. She stares into my eyes as I encourage her: *Stay with it. Keep going. Shake it through.* The panic/ SUD goes from a 10 to a 44 to a 3. Then she's 4 years old and her older brother is strangling her ("He liked to do that to see me struggle"). That clears and she goes to her phobia about using her CPAP nighttime breathing machine. The distress goes to a 0.5. We go back to the original anesthesia target; the SUD goes to 0. We install "I survived" and "I have control now." Marina looks like a different person.

At the next session, 2 weeks later, Marina reports that she "did great for 2 weeks. I slept with my CPAP. I feel much better. But for 2 days I've been anxious again." On inquiry, we find that two other surgeries were arising in her mind: the cesarean and the hysterectomy. First, the cesarean: "Everything was okay. They gave me a shot, but it didn't have time to take. I was so helpless! I couldn't handle the pain. It hurt so much I couldn't control my breathing." Again, she was shaking and sobbing as she spoke. She reported many NCs: "I'm helpless; I can't get away; I can't handle it; I'm dying; It will never end." We did one PC: "I survived." Panic, with an 8 SUD. She felt the echo of the pain in her body, but mostly her whole core was inflamed. She sobbed and shook during the processing, keeping a dual attention through the BLS, my voice, and intense eye contact. Before that surgery was fully processed, she jumped nodes to the hysterectomy (SUD 5), during which she had awoken. "I couldn't move." (People in surgery receive paralytics so that they can't move.) "I thought I was going to lose my mind." She renewed the shaking. Her arms appeared to want to move. I asked her what movement they wanted to do, and she slowly pushed up against my hands, as I had her focus on the sensations in her arms. Finally she said, "I can move!" She swatted my arms away more quickly and windmilled her arms. "It's over." "The pain is gone!" "I'm free." We checked these spontaneous PCs against each surgery. They were 100% true. The SUD was 0. We installed the cognitions.

Therapy continued for several months. We found more targets that had to do with breathing and helplessness: childhood allergies and undiagnosed asthma; being locked in a closet. We worked on skills to handle her underlying generalized anxiety, which had lessened after the trauma processing but still remained. Seven months into therapy, an ears, nose, and throat doctor told her that she had a deviated septum that predisposed her to breathing problems and that she needed surgery. I coached her in what to say to the surgeon and anesthesiologist about not wanting to wake up in surgery, and in getting sufficient pain medications. We cleared a small bit of anxiety before the surgery. She came through it wonderfully, with no residual trauma.

Heart Surgery

Anne, in her late 60s, had had an undiagnosed faulty heart valve. For many years, her condition caused periodic blackouts, chest pain, and trips to the emergency room. She had been told that it was "anxiety." When it was finally diagnosed, her doctors strongly suggested immediate surgery to replace the valve. During her surgery, her blood was shunted through a heart-lung machine ("the black box"), which kept it oxygenated, and her heart and lungs were stilled. Due to complications, the surgery went longer than usual. Anne, a writer, shares her journal with us:

> I was ill. Very ill. . . . My sternum was sawed open, ribs retracted, blood sent running through a nightmare of a black box; my heart was stopped, my lungs collapsed; the aortic valve was removed and replaced with a tissue valve from a cow. . . . Surgery was profoundly awful, aftereffects terrifying. After the surgery, I had the feeling that I'd lost everything in that black box—God, my husband, my son, myself—and I felt that I couldn't find any of us. Only the frightening black box. . . . I remember that when I was back in my room, I was aware enough to catch the nurse in medication errors, but I don't remember a whole lot else except that I would triangle myself, semi-sitting against the pillows because I was afraid to sleep. Sleep was terrifying, and I kept myself awake. Once at home in my own bed, I would have nightmares that I didn't remember and still didn't like to sleep. I was physically in much pain and very depressed.

At home, Anne had her first dissociative episode:

> I was asleep and I awakened to find myself levitating out of my bed and flying slowly through the bedroom door into my dining room and paus-

ing (midair) by the thermostat in the dining room. I couldn't get back into my body. I assumed a power position, became young, late thirties, at my most attractive, wearing a very fine royal blue knit wool suit with white blouse and trim, putting on my best power attitude and arguing very sensibly that I be allowed to go back into my body. I was out for a very long time. Somehow, I managed to call Robin around midnight; I'm not sure what phone I used. I was still out of body. Was I in bed? She talked me through it. I'm not sure what she did, but she got me back. This has never happened before or since.

When she called me that night, I used simple ego state therapy, and we invited the power-suited young woman back into the body, after pointing out to her that Anne was back in her (admittedly scarred and battered and much older) body and had survived the surgery, and that she no longer needed to argue for entrance. She "flew" back into the bedroom, and joined the body on the bed, the phone call ended, and Anne fell asleep.

Subsequent in-person sessions included using the Standard Protocol to clear the remaining sense of being stuck in the "black box." Anne said that she was somehow aware that her heart wasn't beating and that her lungs weren't breathing and that the power-suited woman was pleading for her body back. We also cleared her fear of fainting in public, and the instances when she had; the shame and helplessness of being told that her chronic illness was "all in your head" and her rage about being sick and misdiagnosed nearly to death. Anne regained her wits, her equanimity, and her strength. And she would rather die than undergo heart surgery again.

Cardiologists talk about "pump head," the condition of 42% of patients who have been on heart-lung machines who show permanent cognitive impairment (Fogoros, 2008). There is no sure explanation for the condition. I wonder how much "pump-head" is postsurgical PTSD. I wonder what percentage of cardiac patients could have their wits back after surgery if they received a psychological evaluation and, if needed, EMDR.

HEART ATTACKS

Heart attacks are obvious EMDR targets. They're scary, life-threatening, and leave people feeling helpless. Many heart attacks physically create fear and sometimes hostility, creating even more anxiety and loss of control. Good targets include the beginning of the event; other people's responses (or lack thereof); the subsequent treatment; the feeling of anxiety that may have accompanied it; the change of identity after the first attack (possible PCs: "I'm still a 'man.'" "I'm still alive." "I'm still me."); awareness of mortality; losses of function, roles, and sometimes friends; and worries about the next heart attack.

STROKES

There is anecdotal evidence that EMDR can promote healing and neural integration in stroke and other head-injury survivors (Flood, 1999). BLS, on its own, can often soothe the agitation present after recent strokes. Strokes may induce dissociation and arousal of old traumatic material. EMDR may be used to clear these distressing states, if the patient is able to participate. Flood (1999) reports that BLS may be used with people who are not yet verbal enough to do the entire protocol. Other targets include the trauma of the stroke itself and distress at losses of function.

CANCER

Cancer is one of the scariest words in the English language (Sontag, 2001). Every cancer is different and every cancer patient unique. Treatment can range from a 5-minute office procedure to years of surgery, radiation, and chemotherapy. Here are some ways that EMDR can be used to help people through the process, or to clear trauma after the treatment. Some of these methods can be adapted for other long, destructive illnesses.

Resources

Use Resource Installation (RDI) (Kiessling, 2005; Leeds, 1999) to get clients in touch with their strengths. You can start with *Think about a time when you overcame something hard. Got an image of it? What are you saying to yourself about that time? What feeling does it bring up? Where is that feeling in your body? Go with that.* (3 or 4 rounds of BLS.) *Now, can you bring this feeling and sense of strength into your current situation? Yes? Go with that. (BLS.)*

I use Roy Kiessling's (2005) "Conference Room of Resources" for people going through or about to go through a hard time. Here are Roy's words, with a little adaptation: *Imagine you're the head of a business, sitting at the head of a conference table. You can invite, one at a time, members you want to join the team. As you think about getting through this healing process, invite, one at a time, the skills and strengths you think will help you. What skill would walk in first?* You ask them what form or image represents each skill or strength (a lion for courage, Arnold Schwarzenegger for strength, etc.) and when you have a table full, ask them what it feels like to have the team. (Usually pretty good!) Ask them to remember a time, in the past, when these resources worked for them. When they've remembered, install it with BLS, and move on to the future. *Imagine your team getting you through this cancer treatment. When do you think they'll be most useful? . . . I want you to imagine calling them to order to get you through the surgery/the chemo/the radiation/losing your hair/when you're feeling low/the pain/being assertive with your doctor/ asking for help from friends, families, or coworkers and so on. Let's tap that in.* It's helpful to elicit people's worst fears while future-pacing "bringing in the troops" for support.

Targets

Some cancer treatments are relatively painless, in every way. Some are long and horrible. You can use EMDR to target:

- Loss of time, body mass, function, relationships, normal life, or, in some cases, body parts. Support and hasten the grief process by using EMDR on the cognitions and affect.
- Fear of pain. Coach your client to talk to doctors about setting up a good pain management system. When the system is in place, you can use a Future Template to have them imagine using the medications or morphine push or patch, as needed. Make sure they know that they need to take enough meds to stay ahead of the pain. Untreated and undertreated pain can become chronic.
- Actual pain. Almost any chronic pain will leave an electrical trace of itself in the brain, "hurting" long after the wound is healed. Use the Phantom Limb Pain protocol (Tinker & Wilson, 2005) to clear residual pain. Focus EMDR on the onset, course of the pain, and

losses associated with the pain. I've found that processing all but the most acute pain usually knocks it down a few notches, and sometimes more.

- Identity issues. *When you think of yourself without your breast/hair/ uterus/muscle /normal level of functions, what are you saying to yourself about yourself? What would you like to say? VoC? Emotions? SUD? Body sensation?*
- Guilt about needing what they need from caregivers. NCs: "I'm worthless (if I'm not contributing)." "I don't deserve care."
- Traumas that arise in treatment. The week after a successful lumpectomy, the surgeon, with no pain abatement methods and no warning, stuck a scalpel in Lori's breast to improve the drainage. Lori came in a week later, weeping, shaking, and still completely traumatized. While we processed the event, she again felt a sharp stab in her breast. Then it cleared. Her affect went from helpless/ hopeless to rage. As we continued to process, the client imagined many ways she could use a scalpel on the surgeon. The rage cleared. We imagined her real-life recourse. Her complaint, one of many examples of his brutality, got him fired from his HMO. Many traumas are less obvious, but people don't need to live with them. Move them as they arise. Remember that recent events may need to be processed more than once (F. Shapiro, 2001).
- Nausea. Some of the newer chemotherapies don't cause nausea. Many still do. I've used EMDR with people currently undergoing chemo and for people with "phantom nausea" long after the chemo is out of their systems.

  o Current Chemo. First, make sure that the client is taking every possible antinausea drug. Most oncologists are aware of the drugs. If your clients aren't assertive about symptoms, the on-cologist may not know that they need more of a medication, or a different one. With some chemo, food becomes an "alien sub-stance" no longer satisfying or fun or even edible. I use the Two-Hand Interweave (Shapiro, 2005): *Hold your former sense of food as tasty and enjoyable in one hand. In the other hand, hold your current awareness of food as a somewhat disgusting fuel that you need to take in order to survive. Got it? Go with that.* (BLS.) Find out the re-sponse. Sometimes it's grief at acknowledging what's happen-ing to their sense of food. Sometimes it's anger. Keep going with whatever the response is, until the client can hold food as fuel, then problem solve the best way to get innocuous food, especially protein, into them as often as necessary. Protein shakes or something else they can drink may be the best solution. I counsel chemo patients to avoid their favorite foods until the nausea passes, so they won't develop reflexive antipathies to foods they like.

o "Phantom Nausea." When a mammal eats something that makes it vomit, its brain creates nausea at the sight or aroma of the substance. Sometimes, after chemotherapy is long out of the body, a brain will continue to signal that a certain food is bad and will make you sick. In these cases, use the Standard Protocol to clear chemo-induced incidents of nausea and vomiting. It's gross, and it often works. The target is the food: *Think about pizza. See it, smell that cheesy aroma. What are you saying about yourself?* "Yuck! I can't eat it." *What would you like to be able to say?* "I love pizza and I want to eat it." *When you're looking at the pizza, what do you feel?* "Disgust" And so on. Sometimes their brains need a boost from the Two-Hand Interweave: *In one hand, hold the times when your body was full of chemo. The cells were sloughing off your stomach, and you were vomiting all the time. In the other hand, hold your chemo-free body and its healthy stomach. When I start tapping, start moving those hands farther apart, until we convince your brain that it doesn't have to protect you from food anymore. Ready? Go.* (BLS.) You may have to go rounds with different foods, first with the Standard Protocol, later adding in the Two-Hand Interweave.

- Fear of death. Let clients talk about death. Find out where else, if anyplace, they can talk about it. I never force people to talk about death. I let them know that it's an allowable topic. When they're ready, they bring it up. EMDR is not always necessary. I use EMDR when people feel inordinate guilt ("I'm abandoning my children/wife/parents"), fear of the process of dying, or fear of being dead. Sometimes they simply feel the grief of the thought of leaving this life. People with attachment issues often fear being alone. The Standard Protocol works wonderfully with these targets. You may have to modify the use of EMDR for a client who is weak or exhausted with shorter sets or simple tapping when the affect arises.
- Reentry. As people heal, they may have the energy to feel the traumas of their ordeal. Clean up any targets that arise. Then keep your

eyes open for other residuals. Some people hold unrealistic expectations of taking on their old full loads too quickly. Some people treat themselves too gingerly. In either case, I use the Two-Hand Interweave: *In one hand, hold the sick, sodden guy in that hospital bed, who couldn't do anything.* (BLS.) *In the other hand, hold the strong guy you were before you got sick.* (BLS.) *Notice the man you are now, with your right now capabilities and limits.* (BLS.) *What do you feel about where you're at right now?* (BLS.)

- Fear of relapse. Since cancer can return, it's unrealistic to go for a PC of "I'll always be healthy." You can, however, go for, "I'm healthy now." "I'm cancer-free." "I'm taking good care of myself." "I can handle whatever happens." "It's over and I survived." When the cancer (or at least this round) is over, make sure that the whole body knows it: *Bring that awareness of health and vitality into every cell.* (BLS.) *Does your whole body know that you're well now? Does any part need an extra dose of that knowing?*

SEXUALLY TRANSMITTED DISEASES

Except for AIDS, which can kill you, herpes is the worst. Warts come in a close third. All are permanent. You can give them all to your beloved. And if you are a person of integrity, you must speak about your health status to any potential sexual partner. Herpes, AIDS, and venereal warts targets can include a sense of rage and betrayal if it was transmitted by a trusted partner; shame for being tainted; or dread at passing on disease or having "the conversation." As with any sexually transmitted disease (STD), if your clients knowingly had unsafe sex, they will most likely (and most appropriately) feel stupid about it. The cognitions will reflect that. The NC may range from "I'm the scum of the earth" to "I'm an idiot" to "I'm tainted for life." The PCs may state, "I'm a good person who made a mistake." "I have a virus and I'm not going to pass it on." "I acted like an idiot, and I learned from it."

Other STDs are curable. You can take drugs, clear the infection, and then clear out the distress about having them, creating the PCs, "It's over," "I'm healed," and "I'll be safe from now on." You can use the Future Template to help clients avoid occasions of transmission: *You're at the bar. You want to go home with someone. How are you going to make sure that you stay safe? Can you stay safe if you get drunk? What's your limit? Are you prepared to have "the talk" and to use condoms, no matter what? Good. I'm turning on the tappers, and I want you to walk through the whole evening from going out to going home and what happens after. Pretend s/he wants to have unsafe sex, and imagine holding your ground. Your life may be at stake.* (BLS.) You can see the variety of issues that must be addressed. If your client is a drug or alcohol abuser, has poor impulse control, or is extremely codependent, you must tackle these underlying issues in the service of sexual safety (R. Shapiro, 1984–1986).

The viral infections, warts, AIDS, and herpes are another thing. First, they make you sick. People with AIDS may or may not respond well to the drug cocktails. There are always side effects, even in the best cases. Even now, AIDS or its treatments can make some sufferers permanently miserable, or kill them swiftly. Herpes carriers may be asymptomatic, or may suffer periodic "attacks" that involve pain and flulike symptoms. Either way, they may infect other people. Some women have herpes "attacks" with every menses. Warts can be the precursor to cervical cancer, though they may not show obvious symptoms, especially in men. EMDR treatment targets can include distress about the diagnosis, the treatment (or lack thereof), the symptoms, and the current health status. And if the sufferers are responsible people who want to date, they must be able to discuss their statuses. These discussions may lead to outright rejection from potential dates or mates, and can be devastating. Here is one way to tackle the issue:

- Target their first awareness of the infection. You may not clear to a 0 SUD, especially with AIDS, and especially if the client is symptomatic. Get the SUD as low as you can. Include room for grief, shame, or anger about the change in viral status.
- Do a survey about how others have responded to their status. Target any rejections—sexual, social, or familial. If the client hasn't told anyone, note their fears, and target *What if you told this or that person?* Cognitions are important. So is culture. Discussions of STDs are commonplace in the gay male community and in certain subpopulations of the heterosexual community. Minority cultures, some religious communities, and some regions or smaller towns may have strict sexual mores that may complicate both the shame issues and future discussions for an STD sufferer. Acknowledge the social pressures. *What's it like carrying this secret to church/in your town/in your family?* Go after any cognitions. *When you think about being at church and think about having herpes, what are you saying to yourself about yourself? What would you like to be saying? What feeling*

goes with . . . and so on. All religions contain the concept of grace and forgiveness, which can be incorporated into PCs. Some churches, families, and communities may not embrace grace or forgiveness. Be sure to acknowledge real concerns and never push people to be "out" to anybody, when it's not safe.

- Make a list of their biggest fears about being rejected. Target the list: *Imagine you're on the fourth date with a sweet guy and things are starting to heat up. You bring up the issue and he says, "I'm sorry. I really like you, but I really don't want to deal with that." And it's over. What does that say about you?* And so on.

- Then go after the present and the future. *What if you met someone today? Down the road, what if you meet someone?* It's much scarier when they have a particular person in mind.

- The worst-case scenario is if they've been sexual with someone (safely, or especially not safely) and must come clean. They need to expect to deal with the others' feelings of betrayal and anger. They may lose the relationship over the issue. Process through all the "ifs" with your clients. One useful cognition: "I'm doing the right thing now, even if she dumps me."

- The last step is having them practice telling a particular person. Clear the distress over telling. You may not reach a 0 SUD, but you will probably get close to a 7 on cognitions like "I'm a good person, doing the right thing."

- Be around to pick up the pieces, or celebrate, after the disclosure. Despite the best preparations, romantic rejection can be devastating. Help them clear grief, shame, and fears of future rejection. Don't expect a 0 SUD, but try for it. Do expect to clear much of the distress.

ILLNESS-RELATED RELATIONAL TRAUMA

Some trauma arises from others' real or imagined responses. Birth defects, chronic illness, or anything that sets a child apart (or an adult, for that matter) may create shame. If an inborn problem, accident, or chronic illness makes for many hospital visits, target the shame of difference or falling behind the class or being unable to participate in normal activities (sports/hikes/drama club).

There are rules about not being sick. You'll hear, "I'm letting down my family/my team/my clients by being sick." "I'm supposed to be the mom, not the patient." Kids might believe, "I'm bad because I'm making everyone upset." You can target all of these beliefs and their concurrent distress. Sometimes the trauma of injury, illness, or a medical procedure is secondary to the caregiver's response. You may target *that scared look on your father's face when he saw the blood.* Or, *the sound of your mother's crying at the diagnosis.* Or you may target the lack of response of a dysfunctional parent. I've heard, "We weren't allowed to be sick. Our parents were too busy/self-involved/dysfunctional." You can target that through the cognition: *Picture that little boy you were, limping on a broken foot, with nobody noticing. With that in mind, what are you telling yourself about yourself? . . . There's no one there? Well, that was true back then. What does that say about you? . . . You're not lovable? And you're not important? What would you like to believe now about yourself? You're worth taking care of? How true does that feel, 1 to 7?* And on to the rest of the Standard Protocol. You may find that your adult clients improve self-care and are better about accepting care from others when these early relational traumas are cleared.

Significant trauma may occur when significant others aren't up to the caregiving task. When husbands or best friends disappear, shortly after a catastrophic diagnosis, it can be more traumatic than the illness itself. Best friends, spouses, family, and life partners are not always the ones who can "show up" for physical and emotional support (R. Shapiro & Herival, 2006). Help your client find the people in their lives who can appear, and use EMDR to help them move through their disappointment, anger, and grief about the ones who can't.

It may not rise to the level of trauma, but the constant advice-giving of nearly every acquaintance can severely irritate most sick people. I've used the Future Template to help people find ways to stop the litany of "you must try this, that, and the other." First, we set up the worst incidence and clear it. NCs can run from "I'm an idiot (because they're telling me things everyone knows)" to "I'm evil (for wanting to kill this nice person)." PCs run from "I'm intelligent" to "I'm justified (for wanting to kill that clueless person)." After clearing the worst case, we move on to *What would you want to say if it started happening right now?* Clients come up with variations on "Thank you so much for trying to help, but I can't take in any more cures right now. Let's talk about something else or I'm going to think that you think I'm stupid."

Other relational trauma occurs during health care. Most medical providers are pressed for time. An impatient provider may inadvertently or even purposely shame patients for their responses, pain, or lack of progress. Sick people can project godlike or parentlike attributes on their doctors. If God, Mommy, or Daddy doesn't look you in the eye, believe your symptoms, return your calls, or treat you gently, it can have a significant impact on your esteem. A client, the innocent victim of a police beating, was roughly treated in the hospital, adding to his trauma. His treatment by the nurses was the second-largest trauma target of his therapy. An HIV-positive friend, in a central California hospital, was hospitalized for a medical procedure. The nurses put a sign on his door—"Homosexual Male"—and treated him as a "sub-human specimen." It was one of the most traumatic occurrences of his long and horrible illness. More subtle mistreatment by professionals, including broken promises, surprisingly painful procedures, and any perceived breach of trust, can bring on PTSD and may be targeted.

SECONDARY TRAUMATIZATION IN FAMILY, FRIENDS, AND HEALTH CARE PROFESSIONALS

Imagine the moment when his first seizure began. Right now, as you see it, what are you telling yourself about yourself. "I'm helpless." *What would you like to say?* "I can do things and I did things then." *How true does that feel, 1 to 7?* "2." *The feeling?* "Total panic and it's a 10." *Where in your body?* "Everywhere, except my hands and legs are limp, because I don't know what to do."

Obvious targets include the dramatic experiences of others' seizures, strokes, heart attacks, and accidents. There are many other possible EMDR targets including:

- Seeing the person in the hospital, immobilized and full of tubes.
- Seeing someone after the acute weight loss or other drastic physical change after surgery or a chronic illness.
- Witnessing someone in extreme pain.
- The daily grind of absolute responsibility to a chronically ill person.
- Resentment of the ill person for the change in roles, the trauma, the amount of care they need, the endlessness of the task. The NCs: "I'm bad because I resent her/was impatient/got mad/feel like running."

- Helplessly, watching a parent, a child, a friend, a patient, or a beloved decline, physically or mentally.
- The cognition, "I'm not enough."
- The loss of friends, activities, and self-care opportunities during a prolonged medical crisis.
- Dealing with unhelpful (or worse) health care professionals, systems, or insurance companies.
- Having to make life or death decisions about another person's care.
- Fear of the future life without the person.
- Dealing with end-of-life decisions and wondering if the right decision was made.
- Loss of the caretaker identity when the patient heals or dies.

Health care professionals and other caregivers are not immune to trauma. Whether it's a dramatic death in an emergency room or operating room, the slow wasting away of a longtime patient, or the cumulative effect of many suffering patients, professional caregivers can experience grief, trauma, and the worry of not having done enough. In the last years, there's been a "speed-up" in most health care institutions. Doctors, nurses, and others are expected to see more patients and often sicker patients, with no loss of efficiency. Crowded systems may not have the beds or the specialty services for good care. The staff suffers anxiety and sometimes trauma for the squeeze of having to do more without appropriate time, tools, and facilities. Medical settings can worsen the anxiety by blaming the staff for specific problems caused by system-wide deficiencies.

Professionals with preexisting shame, anxiety, or trauma issues suffer the most. Clear the old issues first, then tackle the professional trauma. Normalize the affects of grief and anxiety (even though "professionals" aren't supposed to have these feelings). Point out the system defects that may have contributed to problems. An important PC is "I do the best I can."

REFERENCES

Flood, B. (1999). *Stroke induced dissociative states and traumatic memory recall.* Paper presented at the EMDRIA Conference, Las Vegas, NV.

Fogoros, R. (2008). Pump head—cognitive impairment after bypass surgery.

About.com: Heart Disease. Retrieved March 15, 2008, from http://heartdis ease.about.com/cs/bypasssurgery/a/pumphead.htm

Giannakoulopoulos, X., Fisk, N., Glover, V., Kouris, P., & Sepulveda, W. (1994). Fetal plasma cortisol and B-endorphins response to intrauterine needling. *Lancet, 344,* 77–81.

Kiessling, R. (2005). Integrating resource development strategies into your EMDR. In R. Shapiro (Ed.), *EMDR solutions: Pathways to healing* (pp. 57–87). New York: Norton.

Kitchur, M. (2005). The strategic developmental model for EMDR. In R. Shapiro (Ed.), *EMDR solutions: Pathways to healing* (pp. 8–56). New York: Norton.

Leeds, A. (1999). *Strengthening the self: Creating successful treatment outcomes for adult survivors of abuse and neglect.* Workshop, Seattle, WA.

Scaer, R. (2005). *The trauma spectrum: Hidden wounds and human resiliency.* New York: Norton.

Shapiro, F. (2001). *Eye movement desensitization and reprocessing: Basic principles, protocols, and procedures.* New York: Guilford Press.

Shapiro, R. (1984–1986). *Psychosocial issues with HIV and STDs.* Trainings through AIDS/Mental Health Network, Seattle, WA.

Shapiro, R. (2005). The two-hand interweave. In R. Shapiro (Ed.), *EMDR solutions: Pathways to healing* (pp. 160–166). New York: Norton.

Shapiro, R., & Herival, M. (2006). Increasing resources and supports to improve adherence to treatments. In W. T. O'Donohue & E. R. Levensky (Eds.), *Promoting treatment adherence: A practical handbook for health care providers* (pp. 119–134). Thousand Oaks, CA: Sage.

Sontag, S. (2001). *Illness as metaphor and AIDS and its metaphors.* New York: Picador.

Tinker, R., & Wilson, S. (2005). The phantom limb pain protocol. In R. Shapiro (Ed.), *EMDR solutions: Pathways to healing* (pp. 147–159). New York: Norton.

Chapter 23

Treating Birth-Related Posttraumatic Stress

Katherine Davis

INTRODUCTION

Troubling symptoms of anxiety and depression in postpartum women are most frequently diagnosed and treated as postpartum depression (PPD) ("Shades of Baby Blues," 2004). In the not so distant past, those same symptoms might have been completely ignored. Trauma is one cause for PPD symptoms, and recent literature mentions trauma-focused psychotherapy, including EMDR, as an effective treatment for these problems (Kendall-Tackett, 2005). I hope that awareness of trauma will soon become widespread among the primary caregivers of new mothers and result in trauma-specific treatment. In my own clinical experience, a trauma history, triggered by or associated with pregnancy and birth, warrants therapy that is specific for trauma, when either PPD or posttraumatic stress disorder (PTSD) is suspected. With trauma treatment a woman may improve her symptoms of depression and anxiety to the degree that she no longer has either diagnosis.

Before outlining an EMDR treatment protocol, consider this case example of a birth-related trauma disorder.

THE CASE

Rela, a 32-year-old woman, was referred by her obstetrician for treatment of PPD and obsessive-compulsive disorder. The birth of her nor-

mal 7-pound baby boy, Benjamin, 3 months before, had precipitated a
period of reduced sleep, low energy, and obsessive worry "24/7" for
the mother. Referral information from the obstetrician: labor that was
10 hours and tolerable, an infant with no distress during labor or in the
neonatal period, and mother with no distress immediately postpartum. Her doctor had suggested antidepressants, but Rela worried
about that, too. She was breast-feeding and thought, despite reassur-
ances, that the medication might impact the baby. She decided that before taking the medication and stopping breast-feeding she would "try
therapy." Neither she nor the referring physician had much hope that
this would help.

History: Rela is the second child of two girls in a family torn by a
rancorous divorce that occurred when Rela was 10 and her sister 12.
The mother left the household with her boyfriend, whom she later
married. The father was granted custody of his two children with visitation to the mother.

The new husband was physically abusive to both the mother and
the girls, prompting the court to change to short, supervised visitation
for the mother, partially based on Rela's testimony. A family therapist
who saw Rela at the time described her as a resilient child, with
friends, who kept her grades at a superior level and talked about her
situation in a matter-of-fact but emotionally appropriate way. Rela was
sad about not seeing her mom very often, but is quoted, "But she's a
grown-up, and she could leave. Maybe she will." Improvement in the
family prompted termination from therapy when Rela was 11.

Rela continued to excel in school, earning an advanced degree, after
which she married. She remained close to her father and her sister and
was in steady contact with her mother. Her difficulty getting pregnant
resulted in years of infertility treatment. An incurable but treatable genetic disorder made pregnancy difficult. The one prior pregnancy concluded with a difficult, painful, and premature delivery of a 4-pound
girl. This child was expected to live, but died 6 days after her birth.
With her whole family in attendance, Rela was able to hold her daughter in her last moments.

She and her husband grieved this loss for 1 year before attempting
another pregnancy. The result was the birth of Benjamin. Rela recovered quickly from this birth. She had good support from her husband
and close family members, although she was unable to let anyone but
her husband care for Benjamin. Rela reports, "Everything is great now
and still I'm anxious and sad all the time. I just can't explain it."

Presenting symptoms included: intrusive thoughts, nightmares, depressed mood, increased anxiety, irritability, and hypervigilance. Energy was low, libido had not returned to predelivery levels, and appetite remained low.

Other issues impacted Rela's adjustment: The end of her maternity leave was approaching. The financial necessity of returning to work and leaving Benjamin with a babysitter terrified her. She also learned that her medical problem was worse, making it very dangerous to attempt another pregnancy. Her husband, previously in favor of another child, absolutely refused to consider it.

Identified risk factors included: early trauma (family divorce, loss of regular contact with mother), infertility, life-threatening physical illness (genetic disorder), previous traumatic and painful birth, and the death of an infant.

Treatment: The first three sessions were spent on history taking, an explanation of the psychobiology of trauma, description of EMDR, and teaching of stabilization methods. The husband was included in one of these sessions, in order to assess his strengths and any problems, and to solicit his cooperation in his wife's treatment plan. The next session established targets for processing. Starting with the most difficult aspect of her current situation, Rela spontaneously went to the death of Sara. Earlier events in her life (divorce and loss of contact with her mother), though surveyed by the therapist, did not seem to connect for Rela. The touchstone event was holding Sara in her arms and "seeing the life go out of her," with a Subjective Units of Disturbance (SUD) of 10. Other targets in this dominant cluster were: 5 months of worry and illness during the pregnancy, with a SUD of 9; extreme birth pain, SUD 7; funeral of Sara, SUD 7; previous fertility problem, SUD 5; decision to have no more children, SUD 5. Current targets were: worry about Benjamin, SUD 5; difficulty having others care for Benjamin, SUD 5. Future challenges: allowing Benjamin to do "normal" kid things, which might result in injury (jungle gyms, going to school), SUD 5; seeing friends have a second child, SUD 5.

Processing touchstone and other past events in chronological order took three sessions, after which Rela reported a marked decrease in worry and increased sleep and appetite. Present issues required two processing sessions, and a problem-solving joint session with her husband, resulting in Rela taking three more (unpaid) months of leave from work.

Rela seemed to bask in the renewed bonding with her child during this time. "I did not realize that every time I saw Benjamin smiling, growing, and just being, I thought of Sara who would never do those things. I felt disloyal when I enjoyed him." Scanning future issues revealed they were neutralized without processing. At the end of treatment Rela did not have the diagnosis of PPD with obsessive-compulsive components or the diagnosis of PTSD. It seems likely that the original diagnosis was incorrect, and she had suffered from chronic PTSD related to the birth of Benjamin and death of Sara.

DISCUSSION

It's important to identify trauma as a contributor of postpartum psychological problems. Medication (antidepressants) and supportive psychotherapy are the most often suggested therapy for PPD (Misiri & Kendrick, 2007). Antidepressants do not take full effect for a month and do not offer permanent improvement in trauma disorders (van der Kolk et al., 2007). Many women with either PPD or trauma disorders will fear the effects of medication on their nursing babies. Such women will either cease breast-feeding to take the medication or refuse treatment. Indeed, there are no long-term studies of the effects of medication on nursing infants, although some antidepressants are considered safer than others (Misiri & Kendrick, 2007).

Refusing treatment and ceasing breast-feeding represent less than optimal outcomes for these problems. The newborn period is critical for bonding between mother and baby, making it more likely that a child will enter the next developmental stages without deficits. The mother's untreated psychological symptoms threaten this bond. The baby's physical health is enhanced by breast-feeding, and other care that the baby receives may be subpar if the mother is anxious or depressed. Other unanticipated negative results in children, such as increased incidence of anxiety disorders and attention deficit/hyperactivity disorder (ADHD), and secondary problems in mothers, such as substance abuse and marital problems, have been reported when mothers remain untreated ("Maternal Depression," 2006).

Uncompromised, timely bonding between mother and newborn is vital. EMDR can effectively treat PTSD or posttraumatic stress syndrome (PTSS) in as few as 3 processing sessions. More complicated cases may take up to 12 sessions, with reduction in distress as the therapy progresses. You may increase the frequency of sessions to more than 1 a week to hasten the improvement. Treatment can be segmented to treat the most important issues first with a return to active processing after the newborn phase. When trauma plays a role in a more profound depression, a mother can be supported with medication while the trauma is treated. Medication can be reduced or terminated as improvement warrants.

Postpartum trauma disorders can result from several kinds of perinatal experiences, including:

- Those that are actually or perceived to be life threatening for infant or mother, including normal medical procedures that are not part of the normal experience of nonmedical people.
- Behavior by medical personnel that mother perceives as callous or demeaning.
- "Normal" behavior by mother that later embarrasses or shames her because it conflicts with her self-concept.
- Problematic outcomes such as damage to mother or infant or extreme labor pains.
- Memories of past traumatic events that are triggered by the birth event.

These experiences often have several things in common. They can occur suddenly, are dangerous (or are perceived to be) or overwhelm the normal coping skills of the woman. PTSD incidence may increase because birth itself can be life threatening. It happens so infrequently, and with such unpredictable variations, in the life of a woman that there is no opportunity to "master" the experience.

Other risk factors can increase the incidence of birth-related trauma disorder. Previous trauma of any kind can make people more vulnerable to retraumatization (Breslau, Chilcoat, Kessler, & Davis, 1991). Any difficulty in previous pregnancies, births, or infertility issues may increase the chance that the woman will develop a trauma disorder. Problematic birthing experiences related by significant others may precondition a woman to develop postpartum psychological issues. In one family all females had delivery "horror" stories to tell.

Normal medical procedures are not necessarily experienced as normal by nonmedical people. Something as simple as an intravenous line can be frightening. When pre-birth education includes such possibilities, the suddenness and perceived danger will be reduced and thus may not overwhelm the mother's coping capacity.

Not all eventualities can be planned. In one event the attachment of a fetal monitor to the mother's abdomen convinced her that she and her baby were in mortal danger. The pace of the birth made it difficult for her to absorb the information that it was only a precaution in case the fetus began to have distress. After delivery this mother became hypervigilant about her own and her baby's health. She was anxious and depressed and complained of frequent dreams in which she or her baby was about to die. After careful screening and preparation (described below), EMDR processing sessions cleared the symptoms in two sessions. Her first NC was "We are both going to die." Her second was "I cannot protect my baby." Although she was aware that these were not "true" statements, they "felt" true and compelled the postpartum symptoms.

Behavior by medical personnel can have a profound impact on the mother. In one instance the baby was stillborn, as anticipated. Caregivers had managed the pre-birth and birth experience very sensitively, giving the mother and father time with the baby's body. When it was time for the mother to leave, however, an attendant took the infant and (in the mother's words) "plopped" the little body on the scale, making a noise. That sound was engraved in the mother's mind and hampered her subsequent grieving process. As she accessed memories of her daughter, the sound would intrude. It took one processing session for this symptom to disappear, allowing normal grieving to proceed.

Shame as a result of normal behavior in a delivery usually has to do with conflict between the self-identity of the mother and the meaning she assigns the behavior. Some examples might include: "I am not a real woman" (because I had a caesarean delivery, or because I screamed in pain). "I am a bad mother" (because I objected when the "slimy" newborn was put on my bare chest). "I endangered, or damaged my baby" (because I took anesthetics).

The case examples mentioned above were each effectively treated with EMDR in three to five sessions. Take care to address other earlier learning that may be the touchstone event for these experiences. The touchstone event for the mother "screaming in pain" was witnessing a crying child in hospital, age 4, being told he was not a "real soldier" because he was crying. Other examples of needing to "be perfect" abounded in this woman's life. The clinician may choose to address these, or delay therapy until after the neonatal period, if symptoms can be reduced to tolerable levels.

Problematic outcomes, such as damage to the mother or infant or very painful labor, can be metabolized as traumatic and produce symptoms that interfere with functioning. Very often helplessness, loss of control, and an expectation of perfect performance are present in these situations. There may be a desire to get pregnant again soon, as a way to "redo" the experience and get it right this time.

Past traumatic events can increase the chance that the mother will develop a trauma disorder (Breslau et al., 1991). In this category the clinician should look for other births, other medical experiences, or times of heightened pain or illness. (See Chapter 22.) These past events may represent dysfunctionally held information and therefore may be capable of being triggered by similar sensations, emotions, cognitions, sights, sounds, or thoughts, all of which can occur in delivery.

PROTOCOL

The process of treating posttrauma psychological issues with EMDR is fairly simple and usually follows the Standard Protocols. Depending on the timing of the trauma, or how well consolidated the memories are, the clinician may elect to use the recent event protocol. If there is a need to carefully circumscribe the processing to a particular target, contained processing (described briefly below) can be used. Some aspects of the protocols, however, will need special management. All eight phases of EMDR are employed in treating this population. Only the aspects of the protocols that should be especially emphasized in this population will be covered here.

History and Preparation (Phases One and Two): One to Three Sessions.

If there is an urgent need to reduce symptoms in the mother, these sessions can be done within the first week to 10 days. The clinician addresses information important to this population: postpartum issues and normal behavior of newborns. Assess the living environment for needed resources, care, and social/emotional support. Assess outstanding medical problems in the mother or baby. Some of these, such as peritoneal healing in the mother or infant colic, can cause great distress but may get short shrift from medical personnel. Support active problem solving of these or similar issues.

Do careful differential diagnosis. Any psychological problem can coincidentally make its first appearance during this time. Nonpsychotic depression occurs within 6 months postpartum and looks much like other depressive disorders. There may be disturbances in mood, sleep, appetite, and energy. It's important to assess the degree of disturbance, since there is an overlap of symptoms with the normal experiences of parents of newborns: fatigue and loss of sleep.

Psychotic postpartum depression may result in suicidal/homicidal behavior and is an indication for immediate psychiatric evaluation. Symptoms may include delusions and hallucinations with onset within weeks of the birth. EMDR treatment is not indicated for psychotic postpartum depression. However, a careful assessment should be done to rule out complex dissociative disorders, which sometimes mimic psychotic episodes, producing Schneiderian symptoms such as "hearing voices." In such events after stabilization of the situation, the clinician may choose to use eye movement desensitization (EMD) or contained processing. to reduce distress within a very circumscribed target. Screening devices can be helpful as differential diagnostic tools. The Beck Depression Inventory II is a 21-item self-report instrument, published by BDI (Beck, Ward, Mendelson, Mock, & Erbaugh, 1961). You can use two others that are designed for postpartum women. The Edinburgh Postnatal Depression Scale (EPDS) is a 10-item self-report questionnaire, available at www.GraniteScientific.com (Cox, Holder, & Sagovsky, 1987). The Postpartum Depression Screening Scale (PDSS) is a 35-item Likert scaled self-report instrument, available at www.wpspublish.com (Beck & Gable, n.d.). In addition, the Impact of Event Scale–Revised is useful to assess traumatic aspects of the event(s) (Weiss & Marmar, 1995). The Dissociative Experiences Scale (DES) and the Structured Clinical Interview for Dissociative Disorders (SCID-D) are useful to assess the level of dissociation (Carlson & Putnam, 1993; Steinberg, 1994).

Ruling out situations that may be inappropriate for EMDR and establishing targets in those that are appropriate for EMDR is an important aspect of the first contacts with the client. What brings the client into therapy at this time, and the story of the events in question, is the starting point. The clinician will be listening for or eliciting information about the meaning of the event(s) to the client, normal birth situations that are experienced as negative 'or abnormal, other episodes similar in any way to this one (examples: loss of control, extreme pain), any damage issues in the mother or child, events perceived as dangerous or life threatening, and other times when the mother has experienced a trauma disorder or depression.

The touchstone event may be a much earlier event in the mother's life, or it may be specific to the current birth. The clinician should be prepared for either eventuality. Many mothers are in such distress that they have limited patience for addressing earlier events. The clinician should carefully explain the significance of the earlier events (if such exist), and the likely enhanced success when addressing them. But the clinician can start with presently disturbing events and be prepared to process earlier ones if necessary. Sometimes when the pain of the present event is reduced, clients feel a greater trust in the therapist and EMDR. They can then address the touchstone event.

It is often necessary to "overinvite" the story of normal birth experience that parents may have metabolized as traumatic. To fail to do so imperils the therapy. Example: Mr. and Mrs. B. presented for marital counseling 7 months postpartum. The clinician appropriately asked for information about the pregnancy, delivery, and neonatal period. The couple responded with big smiles and statements indicating that there had been "some difficulties," but "everything turned out okay." The clinician failed to get the details of the "difficulties," which resulted in months of stalled therapy. Finally, the story unfolded and included morning sickness for 6 months, a high-speed 60-mile drive to the hospital as the mother hemorrhaged, a very painful delivery, a fetus in distress, a surgical repair of birth damage to the mother, and months of colic in the newborn. The father was present for all of these experiences and was also traumatized by them, impacting his decision to have no further children, a central issue in the couple treatment. One EMDR session for the father and three for the mother were required to neutralize these events for each. As a couple, they worked through the other adjustment issues in three sessions. Here is a possible script that could have elicited the story:

Couple: There were difficulties, but everything turned out great.
Therapist: *Tell me about the difficulties.*
Couple: Oh, just the usual, morning sickness and a rushed trip to the hospital.
Therapist: *Well, sometimes even these "normal" things can have a big impact.* (Therapist explains psychobiology of trauma.) *What were the absolutely worst aspects of each of these events for you . . . even if your medical helpers called them "normal"?*

The explanation of the psychobiology of trauma and what can be done about it can have the immediate effect of normalizing the reaction the client is experiencing. As one mother put it, "Oh, I thought I was going crazy." Symptoms that are explained as treatable become more tolerable until they can be neutralized or improved.

Assessment and Desensitization (Phases Three and Four): Up to 12 Sessions

These phases vary according to the protocol used, but no matter what protocol is used, never minimize the history taking and preparation. The recent event protocol will often be appropriate because the traumatic event has happened within 3 months or because the event is not consolidated. When there is a narrative memory of the event, but various aspects of the memory do not seem linked on an information processing level, the memory may not be consolidated. Sometimes the NC may change for different parts of the memory. Example: In the case of the couple mentioned earlier, the mother's NC for the ride to the hospital was "Both of us are going to die." The NC for the surgical repair was, "I am deficient; not a real woman." Sometimes the Standard Protocol can be used and enhanced by employing the fourth step of recent event protocol, visualizing the event start to finish with eyes closed, and then stopping to process any disturbance that arises. This has the effect of efficiently picking up aspects of the event that the client may be less able to spontaneously access.

Use the Standard Protocol for most situations, but especially when it is clear that the present symptoms are based on an old memory or situation. Example: Mrs. A presented with a traumatic response to a recent birth. She had planned to use no anesthetic, but had accepted some painkillers during the delivery. Her NC about this event, was "I can't do anything right."

Therapist: *When did you first learn that about yourself?*
Client: I always knew that
Therapist: *What is your earliest memory about that?*
Client: When I was three I tried to help my mother by hitting my baby sister on the back. I thought I was burping her. My mother said, "You can't do anything right."

When a client is especially concerned about one particular part of the memory a clinician can use EMD. Processing is held to the target in question in this protocol. "Go back to target and what do you get?" becomes, "Go back to target and what do you get about _____(the target with the NC)?" In this situation the SUD may not go to 0, but may go to a more tolerable level. The protocol is: return to target, repeat the NC, take a SUD with each set, and every 4–5 sets ask, "What is different?" unless the client spontaneously tells you what is different. When SUD does go to 0, proceed to Installation, using the most positive statement possible. If SUD does not go to 0, do not ask "What keeps it from being a 0?" Do not do a Body Scan (F. Shapiro, 2001).

Example: One mother was particularly stuck on the fact that she passed feces during the delivery. She was so embarrassed that it prevented her getting postpartum care from her doctor. Reducing her disturbance from a 10 to a 2 enabled her to get care. Later, in addition to processing this target to 0 SUD, she addressed other aspects of her experience with the Standard Protocol.

Installation, Body Scan, Closure (Phases Five, Six, and Seven)

There are no distinct differences in these phases for postpartum issues and other kinds of cases, except perhaps in the Body Scan. If a mother has had a difficult delivery, she may have somatic symptoms that are related to the repair of damage from the birth. Clinicians should not assume that this is the case, but should do Bilateral Stimulation (BLS) to see if the discomfort can be reduced. Often there is a feedback loop between physical symptoms and unprocessed traumatic material that keeps each alive. This may remit with BLS, or can be targeted in another session. When trauma material is the cause of the symptom, the mother may access material that cannot be reached in other ways, enhancing the overall therapeutic result. Example:

Client: I have a stinging sensation where my stitches are.

Therapist: *Just bring your attention to that area.* (BLS.)

Client: Oh, it went away. . . . I just remembered a fall on a seesaw when I was 7. My babysitter said she hoped I wouldn't have trouble having babies. I know it's silly, but I worried about that when I got pregnant.

Therapist: *Just notice.*

Client: It feels just fine. I'm not damaged. I had a healthy baby.

Reevaluation (Phase Eight)

This phase goes much like it does in other kinds of cases, with one exception. Because infants change so dramatically in their first months, a mother may have a great need to simply discuss the baby. Allow time for this before getting into the target material.

Hooking the mother up with other support and education opportunities may reduce the need for such care, but the therapist should be receptive to this kind of interchange, since it strengthens the bond between client and therapist and serves the "invisible client" (baby) as well, increasing the mother's confidence and improving care.

SUMMARY

Traumatic stress is an underappreciated cause for postpartum psychological problems. It is important to assess trauma components in differential diagnoses, including depression. Once psychotic depression has been ruled out, the clinician can decide how much supportive care (medication, basic resource provision, or supportive psychotherapy) is needed. Throughout the therapy, maintenance of the relationship between clinician and client and attention to the relationships among mother, father, and baby are important. EMDR can be an efficient, effective treatment of trauma related postpartum anxiety and depression.

REFERENCES

Beck, A., Ward, C., Mendelson, M., Mock, J., & Erbaugh, J. (1961). An inventory for measuring depression. *Archives of General Psychiatry, 4*, 561–571.

Beck, C., & Gable, R. (n.d.). Postpartum depression screening scale. Los Angeles: Western Psychological Services.

Breslau, N., Chilcoat, H., Kessler, R., & Davis, G. (1991). Previous trauma and vulnerability to PTSD. *American Journal of Psychiatry, 156*, 902–907.

Carlson, E. B., & Putnam, F. W. (1993). An update on the dissciative experience scale. *Dissociation, 6*, 16–27.

Cox, J., Holder, M., & Sagovsky, R. (1987). Detection of postnatal depression: Development of the 10 item Edinburgh Postnatal Depression Scale. *British Journal of Psychiatry, 150*, 782–786, accessed at www.granitescientific .com

Kendall-Tackett, K. A. (2005). *Depression in new mothers: Causes, consequences, and treatment alternatives.* Binghamton, NY: Haworth Press.

Maternal depression: Effects on parenting practices. (2006). *Child Health Alert, 24*, 1–3.

Misri, S., & Kendrick, K. (2007). Treatment of perinatal mood and anxiety disorders: A review. *Canadian Journal of Psychiatry, 52*(8), 492.

Shades of baby blues. (2004). *Nursing, 34*(12), 56.

Shapiro, F. (2001). *Eye movement desensitization and reprocessing: Basic principles, protocols, and procedures* (2nd ed.). New York: Guilford Press.

Steinberg, M. (1994). *SCID-D: Structured clinical interview for dissociative disorders.* Arlington, VA: American Psychiatric Publishing.

van der Kolk, B., Spinazzola, J., Blaustein, M., Hopper, J., Hopper, E., Korn, D., et al. (2007). A randomized clinical trial of EMDR, fluoxetine and pill placebo in the treatment of PTSD: Treatment effects and long-term maintenance. *Journal of Clinical Psychiatry, 68,* 37–46.

Weiss, D., & Marmar, C. (1995). The impact of event scale–revised. In J. Wilson & T. Keane (Eds.), *Assessing psychological trauma and PTSD: A handbook for practitioners,* Chap. 13. New York: Guilford Press.

Chapter 24

Treating Multiple Chemical Sensitivities with EMDR

Robin Shapiro

MULTIPLE CHEMICAL SENSITIVITY (MCS) IS "SUSCEPTIBILITY TO LOW LEVels of environmental toxins that according to classic toxology (studies) . . . should not occur" (Bell et al., 1997). The symptoms can include "burning, stinging eyes, wheezing, breathlessness, nausea, extreme fatigue/lethargy, headache/migraine/vertigo/dizziness, poor memory & concentration, runny nose, sore throat, cough, sinus problems, skin rashes and/or itching skin, sensitivity to light & noise, sleeping problems, digestive upset, muscle & joint pain" (MCS.org Web site) in response to minimal exposure to chemicals or allergens.

A quick perusal of the literature shows three opinions about MCS. Simplistically, people with MCS are sick, or disturbed, or their brains are doing it to them. If they're sick, it's the fault of toxins in the environment, and medical or naturopathic practitioners must teach them to avoid all noxious stimuli. Victims must lead small, protected lives, until, possibly, they can work up to a biological tolerance of their environments. If they're disturbed, it's a manifestation of somatoform disease, depression, or an anxiety disorder, which often accompanies the MCS diagnosis. Others, including me, say that MCS is, like phantom limb pain, a brain/body response to a once valid stimulus, to which the brain/body is still reacting. Bell et al. (1997) postulate that in time-dependent sensitization (TDS) intermittent exposure to noxious (even subclinically noxious) substances can create oversensitization in some individuals. Based on the "phantom-limb" hypothesis, I've successfully treated people with MCS.

In MCS, the brain/body treats benign substances as enemies. In response to one big dose of a toxin, or in response to smaller, time-separated exposure, the immune system rises to the attack and stays on red alert status long after the initial trigger is gone. Most of the MCS sufferers I know fit into the "highly sensitive people" (Aron, 1996) category: people who show more physiological and psychological arousal to external stimuli, and who were more susceptible to posttraumatic stress disorder (PTSD) and anxiety than others. Their bodies are often at a higher "rev": They seemed ready, at any time, to go into an unmyelinated ventral vagal (fight-or-flight) mode. My plan of attack has been fourfold:

TREATMENT PLAN

1. Use Maureen Kitchur's (2005) Strategic Developmental Model to find and clear early and subsequent trauma with special attention to Katie O'Shea's "life-threatening targets." (See Chapter 18.)
2. Use Resource Installation to build up a sense of strength, safety, and peacefulness.
3. Use EMDR's Standard Protocol on targets related to MCS responses, both sufferers' experiences of feeling ill in response to the environment and specific triggers.
4. Use the Two-Hand Interweave (R. Shapiro, 2005) to differentiate between things that the body should rise up and attack (viruses, bacteria, and protozoas) and substances that the body need not respond to: chemicals, allergens, and odors.

A ONE-SESSION CURE

Emma is an intelligent therapist in her 50s who has liver problems that make her more sensitive to true toxicity than other people. Nine months before, she had moved back into her remodeled office and was poisoned, over the course of a month, by the outgassing of the new carpet. She choked and coughed and her eyes watered. She thought she had a bad cold, which improved when she was not working (at home) and got worse when she returned to work (with the toxic carpet). The "cold" theory didn't fit two of her symptoms: Her heart raced and she couldn't sleep. When she identified the true culprit, she and her landlord did all the appropriate abatement activities, "baking" and "blow-ing" the carpet, and her office became safe again. However, by then Emma was responding in similar ways to other odors and chemicals, and became alarmed at the number of places and activities that she was starting to avoid: the hardware store, garden stores, and any place where women might be wearing perfume.

Nine months later, Emma explained to me, "I'm wearing masks to go into movie theaters. I got so activated at a public gathering the other night, I had to get up and leave." As she described it, her eyes started bulging and tearing and she began to choke. Seeing the reflexive re-sponse happening in front of me, I said, *Let's fix this.* In one long ses-sion, we used EMDR to clear the response. We had done work before and I knew she was well resourced, so we set up the Standard Protocol on her response of the night before. Negative Cognition (NC): "I'm not safe." Positive Cognition (PC): "I'm safe now." Validity of Cognition (VoC) 1. Panic. Subjective Units of Disturbance (SUD) 8. In throat, face, belly. We processed through the immediate situation. I took her back to working in the room with the carpet. The SUD went back to 6 and I asked her, *When you feel that panic in your throat, face, and belly, can you go back to the first time you had that feeling?* "I was 6, I had a tonsillec-tomy. After I went home, it ruptured. I just started spewing a lot of blood. My dad was really scared as he took me to the hospital." *Go with that.* (BLS.) She cleared through that experience and the nasty sixth-grade teacher came up: "He was dictatorial and narcissistic and always humiliated me. For some reason, he had it out for me in particular. I was afraid to go into the classroom every day." (Talk about a toxic en-vironment!) We cleared that target and several more came up, all in-volving health or fear. When those were completely cleared, we went back to imagining the toxic office and the other toxins. We did the Two-Hand Interweave: *In one hand, hold bacteria and viruses, the things your body needs to defend against. Got them? Good. And in the other hand hold the benign things that your body doesn't need to defend against: odors, chemicals, detergents, allergens. Got those? Okay. Which ones does your immune system need to attack? Right! Which does your immune system get to ignore? Right. Go with that!* (BLS.) She got it right away, and I saw her body straighten and open up. She took a deep breath, sighed, and relaxed, saying, "I am safe. I don't need to react to all that stuff. I'm okay."

It's 5 years later. When I called Emma to ask permission for this chapter, I got an update: "Unlike before, I can go to hardware stores and theaters and libraries. Sometimes I go into places that are truly toxic, and I leave, but they're few and far between. I know my liver makes me more susceptible and I don't want to develop that reflex again!"

10 SESSIONS

Lois, in her late 50s, smart, funny, responsive, another "highly sensitive person" (Aron, 1996), well married, with good kids, had had MCS symptoms for 5 years since moving into a moldy rental house for 3 weeks. Her entire family had gotten ill there, Lois the most. "I got neurological stuff, but they didn't." After moving out of that house, Lois found that she was sensitized to many chemicals, odors, and environments. She had intense physical responses. "My tongue breaks out in sores. My eyes turn red and weep. My heart rate and breathing increase and I feel panicky." In the first session, as I was using a permanent marker to draw her genogram, she began to react to the smell of it and started to show these responses. I shifted to a water-based highlighter and her reaction slowly subsided. She had two goals, to vanquish her chemical sensitivity and to stop having claustrophobia and panic at feeling restrained.

In the second session, we did the Resource Installations. First, she remembered and we installed a time that she had done well and was proud (Leeds, 1999). Then we installed her experience of imagining all the people who loved her connecting to her, one by one. Then her Safe Place, a high desert cabin with a containment field around it that brought a sense of safety and relief. Lastly, we installed Kiessling's (2005) Conference Room of Resources. "Humor" walked into her conference room in the embodiment of Groucho Marx. "Determination" was General Patton. "Trust" was Mother Teresa. "Intentionality" was Walt Disney. And "Willingness" pranced in as a race horse. We used Bilateral Stimulation (BLS) to install the sense of each strength, and to imagine them working together throughout the therapy process. Then we began a ritual we did in every session: *Lois, in one hand hold bacteria and viruses, the things your body needs to defend against. Got them? Good. And in the other hand hold the benign things that your body doesn't need to defend against: odors, chemicals, detergents. Got those? Okay. Which ones does your immune system need to attack? Right! Which does your immune system get to ignore? Right. Go with that!* (BLS.)

In session three, we went after the earliest memories. Target: looking at her depressed mother's face. NC: "I'm stuck." PC: "I'm free to move." 1–7 Fear SUD: 6. In shoulders. She moved from shame to fear and embarrassment. "I didn't do well and I felt different." Then she moved between shame and grief about who she was and how she was treated. A memory of being left on the beach by her mother at 3 years old, arose. Her SUD rose to 10. She shook and cried and cleared it completely, coming to calm and endorsing, "I'm free to move and I'm not alone," for installations.

In session four, Lois reported being "calm and more self-loving." We checked both the memory of her mom's depressed face and being left on the beach. No juice in either. At my recommendation, Lois had read *The Highly Sensitive Person* (Aron, 1996), felt it was a fit, and said that she learned about respecting her limits and providing more containment for herself. We targeted the "disconnect between my parents." Her mom had been angry and threw the dinner on the floor and Dad had a "cold reaction." NC: "I'm helpless." PC: "I can take care of myself now." Sadness. SUD 6, in her heart. Many memories of the dinner table: Kids would make fun of Mom. Dad would laugh. Mom would leave. The SUD rose to 10 as she recalled that she herself had been the target of cruel dinnertime teasing. As we continued, the SUDs cleared completely. We installed, "I can take care of myself now." And she endorsed, "Now I live in a safe and friendly house."

We moved to the next target: a sense, without a firm memory, of being held down. NC: "The world is not safe. I'm not safe." PC: "I'm safe now." VoC: 2, Panic. SUD 10. Whole body. Lois's eyes locked in one place, and while the tappers ran continually, I used David Grand's (2007) Brainspotting to catch the spot with a long pointer. As she stared at the spot and the BLS continued, she began to shake and blink continually. I asked, *Are you still there?* "Yes, I'm fine." With no memory of what happened, the distress shook out of her system and cleared to a 0 SUD. She endorsed, "I'm safe," and we installed it. When we were done she had a realization: "My mouth and teeth were hurting and I realized that I need to take bigger bites of life. Limitation isn't necessary. I need to take risks and just bite!" We installed that, too, and wondered about early feeding issues. We discussed the Platinum Rule as a new goal for her: "Fill your own cup first. Give away only what is left over."

In session five, we went back to the smothering feeling. We did the entire EMDR setup, used bilateral tappers, and "held the spot" where her eyes fixated with the pointer, with a memory of Mom smoking and sad. While Lois processed this image about her mother, she felt her own lungs burning. Years ago, her mother had drowned and visited after death, saying, "You could go instead of me." Now Lois told her, "No. I'm staying here." This time the sense of smothering cleared completely, not to return.

In session six, 3 weeks later, Lois reported being "much less reactive" to every odor and chemical stimulus. We cleared several targets: a brother jumping on her stomach, dropping things on her, and pushing her down a steep cliff. Each NC and PC was about survival. Each time the trauma cleared, and Lois endorsed and installed, "I survived. I'm fine." Her mind went to times she got too hungry or too cold and fainted. Again, we cleared it and went to the PCs "I woke up" and "I survived."

In session seven we went way back. Lois came in extremely depressed, "leaden" for the first time in her therapy. Her voice, stance, and simple language signaled an infantile state, with none of her usual lively connectedness. She said that she historically fell into this state between 4 and 7 p.m. (which was the time, as a baby, she was alone with her depressed mother). After a fruitless attempt at EMDR processing of the state, I asked Lois, *Is this your yucky feeling or your mother's?* "It's hers and it's about having to be with me!" *Do you want to clear it out?* "Yes!" *Then we'll perform a momectomy* (R. Shapiro, 2005). *Where did your mother put her feeling of overwhelm and "yuck" into you?* "It's in my chest." *What's it made of?* "Her self-hatred and boredom and hating her life and disgust." *What's it like?* "Gray and sticky and heavy." *I'm going to turn on the tappers.* (BLS.) *As I do, I want you to take both hands and pull that stuff out of you and keep pulling it out until it's all gone.* She pulled out handfuls for about 4 minutes, tossing them out the window. As she pulled, her mood became visibly lighter. *Is it completely gone?* "Not yet." *Then get the rest out.* A minute later. *Gone now? What would you like there instead?* "Acceptance and self-love." *Go with that.* (BLS.) Lois spontaneously imagined picking up the bereft baby and nursing it and connecting to it. The "leadenness" hasn't returned.

Session eight was about positive affect. "All my life I've gotten too excited and people would be mean to me to get me to stop." We used the Standard Protocol to clear school and family incidents, including her current family, of times when she had been ridiculed for being excited. We ended with, "It's safe to feel good, even if other people don't like it."

Three weeks later, Lois returned after attending a Pransky couples' workshop. (http://www.pandacc.com/marriage.html). She found the workshop "life changing" and learned about creating goodwill, safety, calm, and compassion for her feelings, and to stop focusing on problems. In the workshop, her husband worked on his tolerance for her exuberance. We installed the sense of calm, being, and knowing that she had connected to in the workshop.

In session 10 we went after the remaining MCS symptoms. Before we began that day, Lois said that her reactions were already "about 50% gone." We planned to go after the first incidence of MCS, and then subsequent ones, and then target individual triggers for MCS symptoms. It didn't happen that way. Her process overtook my plans and I intelligently got out of the way. This is what happened:

Lois had told me that in our weekly Two-Hand sessions, of germs vs. ignorable stimuli, she had imagined a male overactive gremlin at the "controls" of her immune system. He was anxious and spoiling for a fight. In this session, I asked her if we needed a team of qualities to help deal with him (Kiessling, 2005). "Great idea." She selected Compassion/walking in as Kwan Yin, Flexibility/an elastic being, Patience/a bonneted pioneer woman, Strength/a hermaphroditic gardener, Protectiveness/Annubis (Egyptian god), Humor/Daffy Duck, Adventurousness/Indiana Jones, and Power/Amman Ra (the Egyptian sun god). The Egyptian ibis-headed god Thoth embodied all these powers. As we were installing this team with BLS, Lois told me to be quiet and ask me to continue the tapping. Several minutes later she started to laugh and said that she had handled her immune system. In her reverie, Thoth had invited the gremlin to dinner with the rest of the team. They plied him with honey-barley wine until he fell asleep. (This is similar to an Egyptian myth about a murderous god that was tamed with honey-barley wine.) When the gremlin wakes, he can be put to use for appropriate targets, like germs, not chemicals.

We had three more sessions after the "drunk gremlin" incident, during which we cleared a few recent traumas and set the goal for her to infect her family with her inborn silliness. In a follow-up phone call, 1 year later, the MCS symptoms had not returned. Lois said, "I'm just a normal person, with much less anxiety. I'm off the Xanax. I'm off Lamictal. I have no allergies and I'm off allergy medications." When she gave permission for this chapter, Lois wanted you, the reader, to know that she credits our therapy with much of her healing and that she was also helped by 30 sessions of Nambudripad's Allergy Elimination Techniques (http://www.naet.com/), her Science of the Mind practice through her church, her connection with "Universal Intelligence," George Pransky's workshop, and that before treatment she had the right attitude, "I need help. I surrender and I'll be receptive to what You send me."

MCS is treatable. In my opinion, it's a brain/body reflex like phantom limb pain, that happens in people who are biologically susceptible and who are exposed to a large enough toxin "load" and enough trauma to start the reaction. I've successfully treated several people with MCS using EMDR's Standard Protocol, Resource Installation, and the Two-Hand Interweave. Most of them were "highly sensitive" or had concurrent anxiety issues. Many, but not all of them, had early unresolved medical trauma. No clients that I know of have relapsed.

REFERENCES

Aron, E. (1996). *The highly sensitive person.* New York: Broadway Books.

Bell, I. R., Rossi, J., 3rd, Gilbert, M. E., Kobal, G., Morrow, L. A., Newlin, D. B., et al. (1997, March). Testing the neural sensitization and kindling hypothesis for illness from low levels of environmental chemicals. *Environmental Health Perspective, 105*(Suppl. 2), 539–547. Retrieved April 5, 2008, from http://www.pubmedcentral.nih.gov/articlerender.fcgi?artid=1469815

Kiessling, R. (2005). Integrating resource development strategies into your EMDR practice. In R. Shapiro (Ed.), *EMDR solutions: Pathways to healing* (pp. 57–87). New York: Norton.

Kitchur, M. (2005). The strategic developmental model for EMDR. In R. Shapiro (Ed.), *EMDR solutions: Pathways to healing* (pp. 8–56). New York: Norton.

Leeds, A. (1999). *Strengthening the self: Creating successful treatment outcomes for adult survivors of abuse and neglect.* Workshop, Seattle, WA.

Multiple chemical sensitivity (n.d.). Retrieved April 5, 2008, from http://www.multiplechemicalsensitivity.org/

Shapiro, R. (2005). EMDR with cultural and generational introjects. In R. Shapiro (Ed.), *EMDR solutions: Pathways to healing* (pp. 228–240). New York: Norton.

Shapiro, R. (2005). The two-hand interweave. In R. Shapiro (Ed.), *EMDR solutions: Pathways to healing.* New York: Norton.

UNIT VI

MORE EMDR SOLUTIONS

Chapter 25

EMDR with Sex Offenders in Treatment

Ronald J. Ricci and Cheryl Clayton

Therapists working with sex offenders (SOs) are familiar with treatment-resistant clients. They also know clients who are initially engaged, yet stall at a later point in treatment. We find that these issues are not only related to the fact that clients are mandated to treatment against their will, but also to issues of unresolved trauma. Sex offenders by and large have greater than average histories of developmental adversity (Seghorn, Prentky, & Boucher, 1987). Resulting attachment issues create an inability to trust, to relate meaningfully, and to self-regulate. Understandably, they often fear and resist the treatment process. More important is our recognition that trauma effects not only impede treatment engagement but also are etiological to the sexual offending behavior itself.

A new movement in the SO field is consideration of treatment readiness and treatment responsivity (Andrews & Bonta, 1998; Marshall, Marshall, Fernandez, Malcolm, & Moulden, 2008). Similarly, the field has turned attention to etiological factors of the offending behavior in developing treatment targets and methods. The fairly recent Good Lives model (Ward & Brown, 2004), for example, contends that assisting clients in adaptively obtaining human goods is the key to improving function and thus reducing reoffense risk. Trauma practitioners readily recognize that trauma sequelae, be it big "T" or little "t" trauma, can interfere with healthy acquisition of these basic human needs. The Self-Regulation model (Ward & Hudson, 2000) posits that developmental adversity can instill implicit beliefs that shape future behavior. We have found that to be true in our work (Ricci & Clayton,

2008). In SOs these beliefs often support offending. Their restructure is a core focus of SO treatment. Childhood sexual abuse and other developmental adversity can result in internal cueing that hampers effective self-regulation, sometimes inexplicably (see Ricci, Clayton, & Shapiro, 2006, for a complete discussion).

Given these contemporary ideas, the field is poised to incorporate trauma resolution into a comprehensive sex offender treatment model. EMDR offers an effective and efficient means of resolving trauma as well as restructuring long-held implicit beliefs stemming from the trauma.

EMDR practice with sex offenders follows the basic eight-phase treatment model, as it would with any client presenting trauma symptoms. In preparation for work with this special client population, EMDR clinicians should familiarize themselves with SO-specific treatment concepts. There are many facets of working with SOs that may be counterintuitive for clinicians working in more traditional mental health fields (e.g., limits of confidentiality, collaboration with probation/parole officers, the function of cognitive distortions). The potential philosophical and procedural differences between the two models must be recognized, acknowledged, and addressed as treatment progresses. The second primary difference, somewhat related, is the close coordination required with the primary SO clinician in developing treatment targets and to manage the potential philosophical differences between the two treatment modalities. Once these preparatory measures are established, the adjunctive EMDR treatment can begin.

We draw on several case examples in an effort to illustrate typical referrals as well as potential problems one might encounter in coordinating EMDR with standard SO treatment. We relate the situations to the phase of the Standard Protocol of EMDR treatment in which we encountered them.

EMDR PROTOCOL PHASES ONE
AND TWO—HISTORY TAKING
AND PREPARATION

Identifying trauma targets can look different with SOs than it does with other trauma clients. We find that many SOs have experienced trauma (often sexual abuse) at an age similar to that of the victims they sexually offend. We theorize that the offense-related "thinking knots" originate with these early traumas and compound over time in an apparent hedge against cognitive dissonance. We found that information processing with EMDR helps unravel these knots (Ricci & Clayton, 2008). We also found that resolving this trauma with EMDR reduces offense related sexual arousal (Ricci, Clayton, & Shapiro, 2006), one of the strongest predictors of sexual reoffense (Hanson & Bussiere, 1998). While some clients will be referred with trauma targets already identified, many will not. In those cases, the SO treatment provider is an excellent source of offense-specific information that can guide EMDR target identification.

The following two case examples illustrate typical referrals and the nature of some of the initial stages of collaboration in the referral process. Recall that by the time clients have been referred to EMDR treatment, they have been identified with issues suspected of impeding treatment engagement, and probably strongly linked to offending behaviors. The EMDR clinician can springboard from this previously completed work with additional history taking and preparation for treatment that facilitates trust and rapport building. While additional treatment targets will surface in the course of comprehensive EMDR work, much of the early phase work is already done.

Simon

Simon has two sexual abuse victims: a 16-year-old female and a 7-year-old female. Simon was sexually abused at age 6 and again at age 16. He has been engaged in sex offender treatment for 12 months. Despite good progress, his debilitating social anxiety remains, hampering full engagement in SO treatment. Simon has developed some degree of trust in his therapist's investment in helping him alleviate his emotional suffering. While working on his life history in his SO treatment, he has disclosed vague but distressing memories of sexual abuse. We hypothesized that these traumatic memories are at the core of his anxiety and instrumental in the etiology of his sexual offending. We identified other targets for trauma processing; the sexual abuse at age 6, however, is the earliest identified trauma memory. A referral was made to an EMDR provider. Simon was hesitant about engaging in trauma treatment, but agreed to do so based on his trusting feelings for his primary therapist. In this case, the basis of a therapeutic rapport is transferred with the client.

Victoria

Victoria has been involved in sex offense specific services for 18 months. Her primary therapist considers her to be fully engaged in treatment. Victoria struggles with an inability to intimately connect with family and peers despite targeted intervention. She recently identified intense rage toward her biological siblings. Victoria has identified rage as a contributing factor to her sexual offending. She names anger as the primary impediment to her ability to emotionally connect with others. Victoria offers convincing evidence that the rage goes back to early childhood, despite a lack of specific event memories. She recalls setting fires in fits of rage. She has provided a considerable amount of life history in her sex-offense-specific treatment and is referred to an EMDR clinician to address her issues with rage. The referring clinician was able to provide recent incidents that were used to "float back" to identify early trauma issues.

EMDR PROTOCOL PHASE THREE: ASSESSING THE LEVEL OF DISTRESS AND COMPONENTS OF THE TARGETED TRAUMA MEMORY

Oftentimes sexual offenders present to EMDR treatment reporting low Subjective Units of Disturbance Scale (SUDS) related to early trauma. While the referring clinician may classify an issue as problematic, clients may consciously acknowledge minimal distress related to it. At times, albeit more rarely, clients may even perceive their abuse history as beneficial. In these cases, the primary clinician plays an important role in encouraging and supporting the clients to proceed with the EMDR treatment.

Greg

Greg believed the years of brutal sexual abuse he experienced at the hands of caregivers made him a stronger person, independent and capable in the face of adversity. While he acknowledged that he had suffered years of emotional pain from memories of the abuse, Greg assigned a SUDS of 1 to that memory prior to processing.

Therapist: *I appreciate the strength you draw from what I perceive as misfortune. Let's go ahead and process that target anyway, just to see what ideas may be associated with it.* (Bilateral Stimulation [BLS].)

Greg: That time, I began to feel anger. I remember that feeling as a kid. But I haven't felt that in years related to this. (BLS.)

Therapist: *And that time?*

Greg: I started to feel sadness for my nephew (his nephew is not one of his victims). I don't know why. I haven't seen my nephew in years. And it doesn't make sense.

Therapist: *That's okay. Just go with that.* (BLS.) *And that time?*

Greg: Sadness. I felt sad for that kid that was me. (Crying.) I've never felt that before. I'm beginning to think maybe [the abuse] wasn't as . . . didn't help me. Hurt me. I feel hurt. And used. And I hate them. All of them.

This began the process of Greg being able to explore the complexities of his own abuse and eventually paved the way for clarity related to his sexual offending. In these cases the SUDS typically climbs as clients become consciously aware of their emotional pain, then eventually declines as the trauma is processed, similar to more conventional EMDR treatment.

Other clients see their childhood sexual experiences as neither harmful nor helpful, but as "not worth mentioning." While the SUDS may begin and remain relatively low, targeting these memories allows for the processing of problematic implicit beliefs that play a role in driving the offending behavior. This provides the client with insight and understanding that paves the way for deconstruction and reconstruction of distorted implicit beliefs.

Garth

Garth, for instance, was charged with possession of Internet child pornography. The sites he visited, pictures he captured, and online conversations he had were focused on incest, despite no apparent experience with that topic. Through disclosing his sexual development history in the course of SO treatment, he described a close relationship with a female cousin who used to come with her family to visit his family for several weeks each summer. He described theirs as a friendship, to include such seemingly benign things as campouts, sleepovers, and skinny-dipping. This relationship was selected as an EMDR target and Garth soon "discovered" the visceral feelings he held, and still holds, for this female cousin of his youth. This despite the fact he has not seen or heard from her in 40-plus years.

Therapist: *And what came up that time?*
Garth: An overwhelming sadness, deep in my chest. The kind I felt when my mother died. I mean it's that strong. (BLS.)
Therapist: *And that time?*
Garth: I feel stupid saying this, but it feels kind of like [my cousin] was my one true love. I mean I married my wife, who was my childhood sweetheart. I know I love her. I do. But even that, it seems now, was somehow about my cousin. It's strange. I'd never thought of any of this in this way before.

Shortly thereafter Garth began making etiological connections to the sexual ideas and fantasies that had developed over his lifetime, slowly and unnoticed, which culminated in his pursuit of incest involving pubescent females. Once he was able to identify the needs or "human goods" (Ward & Brown, 2004) that his offending was maladaptively trying to achieve, he was able to develop a meaningful nonoffending life plan that he could share with his wife whom he clearly greatly loved.

EMDR PROTOCOL PHASES FOUR THROUGH SIX: BILATERAL STIMULATION TO DESENSITIZE AND REPROCESS THE TRAUMATIC MEMORIES

Traditional SO treatment and the information processing paths typical in EMDR treatment are oftentimes incongruous. The Desensitization Phase of EMDR treatment is the one in which the client is most likely to demonstrate hesitancy and discomfort related to these differences. EMDR therapists recognize that processing often takes circuitous and arcane routes as the mind unravels beliefs that have been accumulated without the benefit of the "rational" or left orbitofrontal hemisphere of the brain. Cognitive stops along this route may be counter to the "teaching" in SO treatment, focused on cognitive restructuring. Close coordination with the referring clinician is necessary and essential in helping the client to negotiate this phase of the treatment.

Fred

In Phase Four of Fred's EMDR processing, he came to the idea that his sexual offending resulted from his having been molested by his older brother. He perceived a proscription from his treatment group to entertain these ideas, believing that such thoughts were considered "excuse making." Consequently, each time these beliefs would arise, he actively suppressed or altered them as he was taught in his CBT-RP (Cognitive Behavioral Therapy–Relapse Prevention) work. This belief was blocking the processing of the traumatic memories.

Therapist: *What came up that time?*
Fred: Things, thoughts that I know are wrong. Thoughts that are unhealthy. That my group would get on me for.

The EMDR therapist addressed this difficulty with his primary clinician, explaining the conceptual model of cognitive reprocessing outlined by EMDR protocol. They agreed that with careful monitoring she would give Fred "permission" to entertain whatever thoughts and feelings arose. The primary clinician discussed this with Fred prior to his next session.

Therapist: *What came up that time?*
Fred: That he imprinted me. By what he did to me.
Therapist: *Go with that.* (BLS.) *And that time?*
Fred: And that I imprinted my daughter. And that I hurt her, like he hurt me. I really hurt her. I can see now that she didn't want it, any more than I wanted it. I just wanted his attention. And the stuff he gave me. And so did she. I can see that now.

Similarly, participants in SO treatment are admonished against permitting unhealthy sexual fantasies. However, childhood trauma is sometimes replete with sexualized and exciting feelings that must be "unpacked" in order to clear up the irrational thinking that was created to buffer the realities.

Matthew

Matthew was molested during pubescence by an older teen he perceived as popular and attractive, traits with which Matthew naturally wished to be associated. During processing, Matthew bolted from his chair with alarm, reporting that he was having a "full-blown fantasy" about him (as an adult) having sex with a teenage male. It took a leap of faith on the part of the EMDR therapist to encourage him to go through with the "fantasy" with the hope that he would find resolution on the other side of it. The EMDR therapist was aware that teenage males were not Matthew's target population, but was apprehensive nonetheless. After only one eye set centered on this fantasy, Matthew was able to see clearly how he was "using" the teenage boy for sex, despite the fact he felt nothing for him, and was thereby able to see how his perpetrator had used him in a similar way. Once Matthew stopped "romanticizing" his childhood abuse, he was able to recognize the hurt and betrayal involved, and to recognize similar patterns in his own offending without distortion.

EMDR PROTOCOL PHASES SEVEN AND EIGHT: BODY SCAN AND FUTURE TEMPLATE

Phases Seven and Eight of EMDR protocol follow the route typical of other clients. Given the complexity and multideterminants of sexual offending behavior, we choose not to target the offending behavior itself for Future Templates. Installations are focused instead on healthy and adaptive coping with situations that may trigger problems in the future. Some examples are social anxiety, rejection or ridicule by others, feelings of inadequacy, perceived slights, and temptation to view pornography.

Carson

Carson was referred to EMDR treatment to address the childhood trauma of his mother's murder. He had organized his life around the trauma, continually rebelling against the legal system that he believed had let his mother (and him) down. A significant implicit belief he held was that the world was a dangerous place and that everyone, including the legal system, was out to get him. Naturally, he behaved in ways that tended to reinforce this belief, resulting in frequent involvement with the law. EMDR Standard Protocol cleared the trauma and Carson was able to accept responsibility for his actions and decisions. We installed Future Templates in which Carson practiced effective self-management in the face of perceived injustice. Carson envisioned such situations without need for retaliation. He then recognized how past beliefs and behaviors damaged relationships, thus increasing isolation as well as risk for continued problems.

REVISITING EMDR TREATMENT AS SEXUAL OFFENDER TREATMENT PROGRESSES

In some cases, despite what appears to be the offender's clarity related to his own abuse and offending, cognitive distortions or "thinking knots" persist. Stewart, for example, processed the sexual abuse he experienced at the hands of an older cousin to resolution, resulting in clarity about the dynamics of the relationship, and generalized the clarity in his own feelings and behaviors related to his child victims. Over the next year, however, group members detected a nagging and difficult-to-define issue that periodically arose during Stewart's treatment presentations. Despite lack of a clear "target," his primary therapist suggested another pass at EMDR (given the vast improvement she had witnessed from his last round of five sessions).

Stewart

Stewart: My SUDS (related to childhood sexual abuse by cousin) is still at 0.

Therapist: *What are the thoughts related to the memory?*

Stewart: That it wasn't my fault. That he was an asshole.

Therapist: *Then go with that. And that time?*

Stewart: For some reason I started thinking about my real father. I remember I used to hide in the cellar and watch my real father and mother having sex through the heating vent.

Therapist: *And what do you recall about that?*

Stewart: It was violent sex. He used to slap on her. Use things on her, like sanders and stuff. And she would scream. But you could tell she liked it. I masturbated to those screams in my head a thousand times. It was scary, but exciting, too.

Through processing these memories Stewart uncovered his feelings of sexual excitement that were mixed with feelings of abandonment. Stewart's abusive cousin was his best friend. Yet after a painful rape attempt, Stewart avoided him and therefore lost the relationship. The sexual violence was his primary memory of his mother before she left him in his grandmother's care to run off with a boyfriend. He never saw his mother again. His grandmother went on to sexually abuse Stewart as well, although he had never said that aloud, as he felt the disclosure betrayed the only person that cared for him in the world. Despite a lack of concrete formulations, Stewart's group members and therapist clearly recognized he had more unresolved issues that were barriers to reaching the level of insight necessary to develop a meaningful healthy life plan. Stewart graduated from SO treatment within months of having completed his last set of three EMDR treatment sessions.

Another indicator of the need for further EMDR processing is evidence of persistent poor decision-making, or "lapse" behavior. In SO treatment nomenclature, a lapse is a behavior that occurs as part of the offending behavioral cycle, and is indicative of movement toward a re-offense. For example, Michael had made considerable treatment progress and had benefited from EMDR related to resolving childhood abuse. Despite stellar and heartfelt treatment work, he periodically "lapsed" into poor decision-making regarding contact with teenage girls (his target population) or passive responses to situations that resulted in high-risk situations (e.g., family member insisting he supervise a young family member). The float-back technique was used to identify the sensation associated with his seeming inability to be assertive. During processing the following dialogue occurred:

Michael

Michael: It's like when my father used to make me follow him around, wouldn't let me out of his sight, but would yell at me for everything I did or tried to do that he asked me. (BLS.)

Therapist: *And that time?*

Michael: I feel a deep emptiness. Deep inside. It is saying I'm worthless. As good as nothing. (BLS.)

Therapist: *And now?*

Michael: I see that it became easier to just go along, not try, and not care either. It was the only hope that there wouldn't be punishment. That there wouldn't be ridicule. But I don't have to do that anymore. It doesn't make sense for my life now, as an adult. In fact, it's the exact thing that seems to make things worse instead of better.

ADDITIONAL CONSIDERATIONS

Another caveat related to EMDR treatment as adjunct to SO treatment is the pull toward thinking that EMDR might effect the "cure" for sexual offending. Recall that we view this trauma-informed treatment method as a means of enhancing, not replacing, standard SO treatment. While standard SO treatment has been shown to reduce recidivism (Hanson et al., 2002), denial of reoffense risk was determined to be a stable and acute dynamic risk factor (Hanson & Harris, 2000). It is important to help therapists and clients alike remain cognizant of empirically grounded concepts of SO treatment as a rehabilitation and not a "cure." Our experience with clients is that subsequent to EMDR their risk-awareness becomes clearer. It may be their ability to see the contributing factors more clearly—and not some inexplicable evil—that were and may again be at play in their offense cycle that helps them to accept reoffense as a possible, if not likely, risk. It is often therapists who promote the idea of the "historical problem" that need not be attended to in any meaningful way. This is more likely the therapists' desire to "fix," or a desire to remain strengths-based, than any realistic view.

Finally, and again somewhat related, is the hurdle of the skeptical and at times undermining (perhaps unintentionally) primary SO treatment provider. Most SO treatment providers are excellent at what they do. They are committed to what is often perceived as thankless and unpopular work—difficult work at best. Treatment providers become vested in their ideas and methods and tend to resist "newfangled" ideas that have no empirical support. The relapse prevention (RP) model, upon which most SO treatment providers base their treatment, was borrowed from the substance abuse field, with little beyond theoretical support that it might work (for a full discussion, see Marshall & Laws, 2003). One of the most comprehensive and well-designed longitudinal studies is Sex Offender Treatment Evaluation Project, which explored the effectiveness of intensive RP treatment on sexual reoffense. Those investigators concluded that their findings "generally do not support the efficacy of the RP model" (Marques, Wiederanders, Day, Nelson, & van Ommeren, 2005, p. 79). The field of SO treatment is in need of some fresh ideas to explore. Working to ensure the primary SO treatment provider is supportive of the trauma-based intervention is important to its success.

SUMMARY OF CONSIDERATIONS AND RECOMMENDATIONS

• Clinicians should familiarize themselves with SO-specific treatment before undertaking this treatment process. There are many facets of working with SOs that may be counterintuitive for clinicians working in more traditional mental health fields.

• Clinicians providing trauma resolution treatment to SOs should arrange to have close collateral contact with the primary treatment provider conducting SO-specific treatment. Philosophical differences between the two models must be recognized, acknowledged, and addressed as treatment progresses.

• Clinicians need to remain acutely aware of the legal and ethical considerations of working with this population. SO clients must be reminded that any admission of offenses not previously disclosed must be reported to the proper authorities. Furthermore, clinicians should make the SO client aware of the free and ongoing communication that will occur between the treatment and supervisory (probation/parole) teams.

• Clients should be screened carefully before engaging in this treatment intervention. Our clinical experience has shown that SOs with a history of psychosis are not appropriate for this treatment in an outpatient setting. Furthermore, safety plans and outside network support should be arranged before beginning this work with clients having histories of substance addiction or suicidal ideation or attempts.

• Clinical experience indicates that SOs often present themselves in a favorable light. Feedback from SO clients, including feedback about treatment results, should be received with caution. Objective and physiological measures (e.g., polygraph, penile plethysmograph) are important indicators of treatment progress and community safety. Any recommendations made to probation and parole and/or the legal system should be made by a qualified and/or certified SO treatment provider.

REFERENCES

Andrews, D. A., & Bonta, J. (1998). *The psychology of criminal conduct* (2nd ed.). Cincinnati, OH: Anderson.

Hanson, R. K., & Bussiere, M. T. (1998). Predicting relapse: A meta-analysis of sexual offender recidivism studies. *Journal of Consulting and Clinical Psychology, 66*(2), 348–362.

Hanson, R. K., Gordon, A., Harris, A. J. R., Marques, J. K., Murphy, W., Quinsey, V. L., et al. (2002). First report of the Collaborative Outcome Data Project on the effectiveness of psychological treatment for sexual offenders. *Sexual Abuse: A Journal of Research and Treatment, 14*(2), 169–194.

Hanson, R. K., & Harris, A. J. R. (2000). Where should we intervene? Dynamic predictors of sexual offense recidivism. *Criminal Justice and Behavior, 27,* 6–35.

Marques, J. K., Wiederanders, M., Day, D. M., Nelson, C., & van Ommeren, A. (2005). Effects of a relapse prevention program on sexual recidivism: Final results from California's sex offender treatment and evaluation project (SOTEP). *Sexual Abuse: A Journal of Research and Treatment, 17*(1), 79–107.

Marshall, L. E., Marshall, W. L., Fernandez, Y. M., Malcolm, P. B., & Moulden, H. M. (2008). The Rockwood preparatory program for sexual offenders: Description and preliminary appraisal. *Sexual Abuse: A Journal of Research and Treatment, 20*(1), 25–42.

Marshall, W. L., & Laws, D. R. (2003). A brief history of behavioral and cognitive behavioral approaches to sexual offender treatment: Part 2. The modern era. *Sexual Abuse: A Journal of Research and Treatment, 15*(2), 93–120.

Ricci, R. J., & Clayton, C. A. (2008). Trauma resolution treatment as an adjunct standard treatment for child molesters: A qualitative study. *Journal of EMDR Practice and Research, 2*(1), 41–50.

Ricci, R. J., Clayton, C. A., & Shapiro, F. (2006). Some effects of EMDR on previously abused child molesters: Theoretical reviews and preliminary findings. *Journal of Forensic Psychiatry and Psychology, 17*(4), 538–562.

Seghorn, T. K., Prentky, R. A., & Boucher, R. J. (1987). Childhood sexual abuse in the lives of sexually aggressive offenders. *Journal of American Child and Adolescent Psychiatry, 26*(2), 262–267.

Ward, T., & Brown, M. (2004). The good lives model and conceptual issues in offender rehabilitation. *Psychology, Crime and Law, 10*(3), 243–257.

Ward, T., & Hudson, S. M. (2000). A self-regulation model of relapse prevention. In D. R. Laws, S. M. Hudson, & T. Ward (Eds.), *Remaking relapse prevention with sex offenders: A sourcebook* (pp. 79–101). Thousand Oaks, CA: Sage.

Chapter 26

Using EMDR with Religious and Spiritually Attuned Clients

Martha S. Jacobi

As a client-centered therapy, EMDR is concerned with the whole person. The EMDR Standard Protocol, in its eight phases and three prongs, explicitly attends to clients' cognitive, emotional, physical, and social contexts. Implicitly, EMDR encompasses the religious and spiritual dimensions of life, including but not limited to those acknowledged by the client, and those of the surrounding cultures in which the client was raised and currently lives.

This chapter recognizes the importance of religious belief, practice, and spiritual experience to many clients being treated with EMDR. It seeks to offer guidance to EMDR therapists in identifying, assessing, and working directly with the religious and spiritual dimensions of our clients' lives. It is written from my perspective as a pastoral psychotherapist and theologian, both a clergyperson and a clinician.

HISTORY AND THEORY THROUGH A
RELIGIO-SPIRITUAL LENS

The world we human beings inhabit is a religious place. From the ziggurats, towers, and temples of ancient peoples, to today's synagogues, mosques, meeting halls, churches, shrines, and meditation rooms, human experience has included space and time dedicated to ritual action and, sometimes, the cultivation of transcendence. As Karen Armstrong wrote, "There is a case for arguing that *Homo sapiens* is also *Homo religiosus*. . . . Like art, religion has been an attempt to find meaning and value in life" (1993, p. xix). Armstrong also noted that while "religion can be abused . . . it seems to have been something that we have always done" (p. xix). Indeed, a religio-spiritual dimension still pervades human experience, even after the rise of scientific method, dualism, and the well-known rejections of religion made by numerous 20th-century thinkers, Freud among them.

ANOTHER LEGENDARY "FOUNDING STORY": A WALK THROUGH THE PSYCHIATRIC WARD

In 1920, Anton Boisen, a Presbyterian minister, had a psychotic episode that landed him in a psychiatric hospital, where he received the best treatment of his day (Boisen, 1960). He received spiritual support through the letters of a trusted clergy colleague and the insight of a former psychology professor, William Lowe Bryan, that "at the peak of a human crisis there is a turning toward feeling, toward reorganization, toward reconnection" (cited in Leas, n.d.). Happily, Boisen recovered.

Reflecting on his illness and recovery processes, Boisen became among the first to reintegrate religion and spiritual experience with the social and psychological sciences. He did so in his many books and articles and, in 1925, by developing an educational program for religious professionals, Clinical Pastoral Education, using case-study and action-reflection methodology (Boisen, 1945, 1960; Dykstra, 2005; Leas, n.d.). Boisen is credited with laying the foundation for the theory and praxis of pastoral theology, the caregiving aspect of ministry occurring in a contextual relationship with an individual or family.

A FORTUITOUS RECONNECTION

In the last two decades the social and psychological sciences have begun their own rapprochement with religion and spiritual experience. Indeed, both the American Psychological Association (2002) and the National Association of Social Workers (1999) now affirm the importance of clients' religious backgrounds as being of equal importance with ethnic, socioeconomic, and other cultural considerations.

Serendipitously, EMDR was discovered and developed in *this* time, in *this* milieu, and references to spirituality, transcendence, and issues of religious trauma are increasingly common in the EMDR literature (Botkin with Hogan, 2005; Dworkin, 2005; Grand, 1999; Kitchur, 2005; Lipke, 2000; Parnell, 1996, 1997; F. Shapiro, 2001; Silver & Rogers, 2002). Yet clinical colleagues and consultees tell me that they lack comfort and training in working with clients who want their religious commitments, alienations, and spiritual experiences included in their treatment. What follows is offered to increase your confidence in working with religious and spiritually attuned clients, even when their traditions differ from your own, and to provide you with specific strategies for integrating clients' spirituality into their treatment with EMDR.

CONTRIBUTIONS FROM PASTORAL THEOLOGY

A New Way of Listening

One of the distinct contributions of pastoral theology to the general field of psychotherapy is a particular way of listening that I have come to think of as "listening with a fourth ear."[1] If with Reik's "third ear" we listen in, with, between, and under the spoken and nonverbal "words" for the latent content of a client's communications, with the "fourth ear" we tune-in to the religious and spiritual dimension of the client and her/his story. Our fourth ear listens for religious and spiritual themes such as guilt, shame, sin, judgment, forgiveness (or lack thereof), justice, grace, wisdom, revelation, enlightenment, compassion, and hope. Our fourth ear listens for the client's interpretation of

---

1. Leonard Horwitz uses the metaphor of a "fourth ear" in reference to group therapy where, he asserts, the fourth ear attends to the common theme emerging from group members' contributions (L. Horwitz. [1991]. Evaluation of a group-centered approach. In S. Tuttman (Ed.), *Psychoanalytic group theory and therapy: Essays in honor of Saul Scheidlinger* (pp. 279–286). Madison, CT: International Universities Press.) Irene C. Brower's use of the phrase "4th ear" is limited to a plea for a general "sensitivity" to clients' spirituality as a parallel to that regarding culture and ethnicity in the social work profession. (Irene C. Brower. [1984]. The 4th ear of the spiritual-sensitive social worker [microform]. Ann Arbor, MI: University Microfilms International.) The use of the "fourth ear" in the present chapter is distinct from each of these and represents the author's integrative, pastoral psychotherapeutic perspective.

religio-spiritual experience: Is it positive, negative, neutral, or mixed? With our fourth ear we hear the degree to which a client's internal experience is or is not consistent and congruent with the stated beliefs of his/her faith tradition. And with our fourth ear we listen for the often unconscious, or minimized, influence of childhood religious experience on the client's religio-spiritual development, current life functioning, and internal structures of meaning.

Externally, the religio-spiritual beliefs that a client holds and articulates may or may not coincide with that client's functioning. Our fourth ear hears any areas of noncongruence and facilitates a particular attunement with the client that honors the client's beliefs and ambivalences.

Narrative and Meaning

A second distinct contribution of Anton Boisen and pastoral theology is the kernel of what has become narrative theology and psychotherapy, the process of listening through the client's life narrative (Leas, n.d.). Leas wrote, "For Boisen . . . the depth experiences in the struggles of [people's] mental and spiritual life, came from listening and telling story. . . . We make sense of life through the stories we tell." Our fourth ear, therefore, listens through the stories clients tell, through the narratives of their lives, as they offer intrinsically held meanings of religio-spiritual language and experience.

RELIGION, SPIRITUALITY, AND
THE EMDR THERAPIST

In order to listen well to others with the fourth ear, we need to listen through our own stories. This self-reflective process is familiar to therapists, but not always applied to the religio-spiritual dimensions of our own lives. So as you read the specific clinical strategies below, I invite and encourage you to reflect on your story as well, listening to yourself with your fourth ear. Listen to what may be external, ritual practice (commonly referred to as "religion") as well as a sense of internal "experience" (commonly referred to as "spirituality"). Listen for presence and absence; for immanence, unitive experience, and transcendence. Listen for times of expansiveness and times of emptiness. Let your fourth ear listen through your story . . .

CLINICAL STRATEGIES 1: HISTORY TAKING
AND PREPARATION

Religio-Spiritual Assessment

A client's religio-spiritual history will unfold throughout the course of treatment. In the History Taking phase, however, the therapist begins an assessment of the religio-spiritual issues relevant to the client, asking questions that are both direct and exploratory. Ambuel (2005), West (2000), and Fitchett (1993) each provide a model for spiritual assessment that may be useful to EMDR therapists. Extrapolating from their work, from the field of pastoral theology, and from nearly 30 years of pastoral ministry, I find there are three groups of questions that are particularly helpful in EMDR:

- *Were you raised in any particular religious or faith tradition? What was that? What was your family's involvement? Tell me about that . . .*
- *What is your involvement with that tradition today? How did that come to be?* and/or, *What kind of religious or spiritual path, if any, do you follow now? What practices, if any, do you keep? Tell me about that . . .*
- *Was your family's tradition common in the place where you grew up? What was that experience like for you then? What do you think of it now?* (The client's experience of being in a religious majority or minority may be of particular importance, even in locales that tolerate religious pluralism. If a client was raised in a locale where religious homogeneity is the norm, whether by law or by choice, this may be a "red flag" issue warranting further exploration and possibly trauma history assessment.)

Note that these are mostly open-ended questions, phrased to elicit the client's story and the nature and meaning of religion and spirituality within that story, and to do so in a relational context. These are also questions that can be followed up naturally, as relevant to a client's presenting issues and treatment needs. In this manner, the religio-spiritual assessment becomes foundational for a spiritually oriented, collaborative EMDR treatment process, facilitating a seamless and natural integration of the client's religio-spiritual resources and challenges into the Standard Protocol.

Consider the following vignettes. Karen, Leah, and Steve represent typical clients in my practice, but are composite creations for illustration. The religious and spiritual experiences attributed to them are those of actual clients and are shared with their permission. The clinical dialogues are reconstructions made in consultation with the clients. Note the weaving of direct and exploratory questions, and the therapist's use of fourth-ear listening.

Vignette #1: Karen

Karen, 27, came to therapy a year after her mother died. Her father had a chronic and debilitating illness. Karen's grief process had activated memories and anxiety related to childhood experiences of growing up in the presence of her father's illness and its chaotic effect on the family.

Therapist: *Were you raised in any particular religious or faith tradition?*
Karen: Yes. Catholic.
Therapist: *What was your family's involvement?*
Karen: We went to mass a lot, you know more than Christmas and Easter, but not every Sunday. I loved the rituals and traditions.
Therapist*:   Tell me about that . . .* (Therapist is eliciting specific history and the meaning of it to Karen.)

Karen told me her family prayed the rosary at home every night, and described sensory experiences during church services, especially sounds and smells: the choir singing, the sound of the organ, the smell of incense, and the quiet hush of midnight mass at Christmas. Karen said she loved the stories of the mystics, and as a child, she pretended to be a mystic when she played. Karen disclosed that when her parents were fighting she experienced Jesus coming to her in a cloud; in it, the noise of the fighting vanished and she would feel Jesus' arms holding her.

Therapist: *Was that helpful to you then?*
Karen: Oh yes. Sometimes I still do that—go into a cloud and imagine Jesus holding me—when I'm really upset. . . .
Therapist: (Notes to self the possibility of a dissociative—yet adaptive and positive to the client—use of spiritual experience and religious imagery.)

Vignette #2: Leah

Leah, 55, considers herself a native New Yorker despite her family's move to another state during her adolescent years. Leah returned to

New York in her adult years to work. Leah was not an eyewitness to the terrorist attacks of September 11, 2001, but was deeply distressed by them and began experiencing flashbacks of childhood trauma and a near-fatal accident in early adulthood.

Therapist: *Were you raised in any particular religious or faith tradition?*
Leah: Well, half of my family is Jewish.
Therapist: *Which half?* (Therapist is aware that this may matter for Leah's sense of self and identity, as well as religious affiliation.)
Leah: My father's—so they don't really consider me Jewish (Leah explains the role of maternity in Jewish self-definition.) But I grew up all around my father's family at holidays. (Leah discusses her positive experiences at Passover gatherings, as an example.)
Therapist: *And your mother?*
Leah: Christian, I guess, but we never went to church or anything. But we had a Christmas tree . . . and a menorah.
Therapist: *What was that like for you, observing two traditions?*
Leah: It was okay. They told us about their different backgrounds, but they weren't really observant, so it wasn't confusing at all.
Therapist: *What kind of religious or spiritual path, if any, do you follow these days?*
Leah: I'm a very spiritual person. During high school and college I became Mormon; there were a lot of Mormons around there. . . . (Leah describes her attraction to the Mormon faith and articulates well the sense of "substitute family" that it provided for her at a vulnerable time in her life). But I left that years ago. . . . (Leah discussed her reasons for leaving Mormonism, including her understanding of Mormon beliefs about marriage and her growing sense of alienation from the church as an aging single woman who is "unlucky at love—or maybe I'm doomed.") Today, I guess I'd consider myself Christian. Sometimes I go to the Community Church—that's how I got referred to you—but I'm not really happy there either (Leah explains why.) (Therapist uses fourth ear in listening to the mingling of religious and self-cognitions, the client's anxiety and trauma symptoms, and attachment and affiliative experiences, positive and negative.) So, I'm a mix. Did that answer your question?
Therapist: *Yes.* (Therapist's fourth ear also hears Leah's mingling of religious practice and affiliation with her self-understanding as a "spiritual person." Therapist follows up, exploring the referral and the client's thoughts and feelings about it.)

Vignette #3: Steve

Steve, 44, came to therapy for help in parenting his adolescent son who, among other behaviors that Steve found objectionable, wanted nothing to do with church, religion, or the Bible. Steve was angry with him and verbal altercations between them were escalating. Steve has just reported being raised in a "Bible-believing" church.

Therapist: *"Bible-believing . . . " Was your church affiliated with any larger group or was it independent?*

Steve: (States the name of a religious body in the United States.)

Therapist: (Being aware that Steve's church body is underrepresented in the locale in which he was raised,) *Was your childhood church experience common there, in those years?*

Steve: Yes. It still is. (Therapist is surprised, and notes to self that Steve understands himself as part of a religious majority in his home community, that this experience seems unitive and supportive for him, but not his son, for whom Steve's faith tradition is a religious minority where he now lives.) Everyone goes to church there on Sundays. And they read their Bibles. . . . (Steve speaks at length about the Bible, admitting that he doesn't read it as often as he "should" anymore.) (Therapist's fourth ear hears an incongruity and a confessional quality to the disclosure, and wonders how this relates to Steve's relationship with his son. Therapist tunes her fourth ear to listen for possible themes of guilt, shame, forgiveness, and lack of self-acceptance in Steve's story.)

Therapist: *So, what kind of religious or spiritual involvement do you have, now?*

Steve: (Sighs.) It's been difficult here, finding a church, because I'm very conservative in my beliefs. I admit, we don't go every Sunday here, but we did find a church that's okay. But my son just refuses to go at all. He needs to go; he needs to have a moral compass. So we spend a lot of Sunday mornings arguing about it.

Therapist: *Your church experience here is very different from back home.*

Steve: It sure is.

Karen, Leah, and Steve all have life stories with rich religious and spiritual dimensions. Their religio-spiritual narratives reveal resources, active cognitions both negative and positive, and challenges. We will return to their stories later in the chapter.

Incorporation of Spiritual Images, Themes, and Practices as Resources

In the religio-spiritual assessment, clients self-identify aspects of their traditions, practices, and experiences that they view as strengths and resources. If you are not familiar with your clients' traditions or practices, ask them to tell you about them. Clients are generally happy to share what they know with their therapists. This process helps clients to recognize sources of healing within themselves in fresh ways. It also reveals areas of experiential disconnect from formal belief systems, to be heard by the fourth ear for further exploration and/or processing.

Additionally, it can be helpful to educate yourself by reading about your clients' traditions. Many resources, in print and online, are available giving brief overviews of the beliefs, rituals, and practices of most world religions and spiritual traditions. A resource list is provided at the end of this chapter.

The Preparation phase of EMDR intentionally encourages clients to bring their religious and spiritual experiences into their therapy, in and as a positive and supporting frame. In the vignette of Karen, we strengthen her sensory experiences at Christmas Eve mass and her experiences of being "held by Jesus" with sets of Bilateral Stimulation (BLS). Such resources are particularly helpful for child ego-states, both during processing and between sessions.

Therapist: *Can you image yourself at Christmas Eve mass right now?*
Karen: Yes. (BLS)
Therapist*:   What are you noticing now?*
Karen: The smell of the candles and incense.
Therapist   *Go with that . . .* (BLS) *How is that now?*
Karen: It's like I'm there now—or it's here now. It's nice.
Therapist*:   And that sense of the cloud, and being held by Jesus . . . Can you imagine that now?*
Karen: Yes, it's so comforting, nice. (BLS)
Therapist*:   How do you experience that physically right now?*
Karen: I feel calm, all over.
Therapist*:   Just notice that . . .* (BLS)
Karen: Especially in my chest, my heart . . . on my arms . . . (BLS)
Therapist*:   And you can hear the sounds around you now?*
Karen: (Sounds surprised.) Yes.
Therapist*:   Just notice that. . . .* (BLS)

As with the enhancing of any client-perceived resource, keeping the sets of BLS short and focused aids in enlivening and enriching the spiritually based resource. Likewise, the extent to which any current maladaptive dissociative process may also be present for Karen "in the cloud, held by Jesus" will likely emerge as its felt sense is deepened and "in-corporated" in her body. If present, it can then be handled as any other maladaptive process would be. In fact, this is what happened with Karen and she learned to differentiate for herself when she was "escaping to Jesus" (maladaptive) and when she was "resting in Jesus" (adaptive).

Specific affect management and Resource Development techniques (Leeds, cited in F. Shapiro, 2001) with which EMDR therapists are already familiar can easily be adapted to integrate the religious imagery, language, and belief system of the client. Examples include:

- The "Light Stream" visualization (F. Shapiro, 2001) can be modified with imagery and language congruent to the client's belief system. *"Imagine there is a healing light coming from _____ (God, Jesus, the heavens, the Blessed Mother, the divine, Adonai, the Name, the Universe, your angel(s), etc.) . . . What color might you associate with that light?"*
- Breathing exercises and meditations can include the use of a mantra, word, prayer, phrase, or faith statement that carries a calming and positive sense for the client. *"Breathe in the breath of life; breathe out all that is life diminishing or takes life away." "Breathe in peace; breathe out worry."*
- A "mindfulness" approach to affect management can bring in a religious figure or spiritual guide as a relational resource (F. Shapiro, 2001) to observe and be "with" the client.
- As a variant of Kiessling's (2005) Conference Room of Resources, a "spiritual support team" can be called and gathered, their presence in the client's awareness enhanced with sets of BLS.
- What I call the "Spirituality Resource" is a variant of the Body Resource (Grand, 2003). The Spirituality Resource focuses around the client's physical, embodied, felt sense of the divine—God—light—Spirit—spirit—peace—spirituality—faith—hope—compassion—enlightenment—or whatever word-image is relevant to the client.

Therapist: *Where in your body do you feel that sense right now?*
Client: The crown of my head. (BLS.)

Associative imagery is then elicited and enhanced with BLS:

Therapist: *What color (sound, shape, texture, etc.) associates with that sense right now?*
Client: Yellow. (BLS.)

Where appropriate in all of these approaches, have the client identify his/her felt sense of the images, words, or guides in the body and then incorporate further with short sets of BLS.

It is simple and direct to ask clients what religious or spiritual images are helpful for them (F. Shapiro, 2001). During the religio-spiritual assessment your fourth ear may have tuned-in to a resource already in use by the client. Or, your familiarity with the traditions of your client's experiences may provide images to offer. For Leah, her Passover experience provided an actual, felt, and positive sense of belonging that became a helpful therapeutic reflection. For Steve, biblical phrases such as "Your word is a lamp to my feet . . . ,"[2] "The Lord is my shepherd . . . ,"[3] and "Train children in the right way . . . "[4] (New Revised Standard Version) were used with breathing meditations between sessions as he prepared to address the trauma of his own religious and spiritual dislocation, loss of community support for himself and his family, and his difficulties with his son. For Karen, participation in a Buddhist sangha (meditation group), which she began attending while in treatment, gave her a deep sense of peace and opportunity to integrate her in-session mindfulness and breathing meditations with her out-of-session expanding spirituality.

Intentionality, creativity, and therapist-client collaboration derived from fourth-ear listening are the hallmarks of deep and thorough preparation with religious and spiritually attuned clients. Such preparation feels natural and comfortable to the client. It is a process whereby clients come into a new and positive kinesthetic awareness of their external religious practices and internal spiritual experience. It is a process that equips them for EMDR's active processing phases, as well as for Closure. Between sessions, it gives clients new ways to use familiar strengths and resources.

---

2. Psalm 119:105.
3. Psalm 23:1.
4. Proverbs 22:6.

CLINICAL STRATEGIES 2: WORKING WITH RELIGIO-SPIRITUAL THEMES, ISSUES, AND EXPERIENCES DURING EMDR PROCESSING

We now consider some of the ways in which the active processing phases of EMDR encompass the religio-spiritual dimension of clients' lives. This dimension may or may not be explicitly referenced during these phases, by either you or your client. Nonetheless, because of the integrative work done in History Taking and Preparation, the religio-spiritual dimension of the client's life is now already "in the room" and on the EMDR "train" (F. Shapiro, 2001). Indeed, the therapeutic context and relationship will have become a "sacred space." And for religious and/or spiritually attuned clients, only when the therapeutic context and relationship become sacred space will there also be a truly safe place for processing the traumas, dislocations, and disorientations of their lives.

In the active processing phases, psychological, religious, and spiritual issues are often intertwined, and processing of targets in any of these domains appears to activate and bring healing through the associative channels related to each. When and as this happens, trust your client's inner healing wisdom and the EMDR process. It is a powerful combination!

Themes

In the active processing phases of EMDR the fourth ear listens for religio-spiritual themes manifesting (a) as cognitions, negative and positive; (b) in the emotional state of the client; and (c) in the client's somatic experiences. Keeping in mind the spiritual resources of the Preparation phase and the meaning of positive religio-spiritual experiences to the client, the therapist remains attuned and equipped to offer interweaves appropriate to the client's particular spirituality. Clients report experiencing such interweaves as being in a seamless flow with their processing and congruent with both their internal and external religio-spiritual contexts.

Case Example #1, Leah: The Therapeutic Context as Sacred, Safe Space— Spiritual Themes in Negative and Positive Cognitions

When Leah says, "I'm doomed," it turns out to be a pervasive Negative Cognition (NC). It is also a manifestation of a negative valence in

Leah's intrinsic, internal spirituality, congruent with her feelings of isolation, alienation, shame, and despair. At first Leah could not imagine any Positive Cognition (PC) for herself. Revisiting the Religio-Spiritual Assessment, exploring and listening through her story, led to the meaning of the NC, and an emergent PC:

Therapist: *When you say, "I'm doomed," what exactly does that mean to you?*
Leah: That nothing ever works out, that I'm a freak. I don't have a husband, I'll never have a husband, and I'll be a bitter and lonely old maid. (Scrunches her face.) I already am. I'll be alone forever.
Therapist: *Just hypothetically, if it were possible for you to experience some kind of genuine sense of belonging—without that feeling of conditional acceptance you've talked about—what do you think that might be like for you?*
Leah: Well, I don't think it's possible. But sure, it would be nice. I'd like it.
Therapist: *What might that possibility mean to you, if it could happen?*
Leah: That maybe there's still hope for me.
Therapist: *"Maybe there's still hope for me." Are those words that you might want to believe for yourself now?*
Leah: (Laughs.) Yes, of course!

Leah's Validity of Cognition (VOC) of 2 for the PC, "Maybe there's still hope for me," while low, surprised her, as did the small spark of hope she felt associated to it. Returning to her NC and emotional feelings, Leah said she still felt "desperate and anxious, but maybe not quite as much as before."

Case Example #2, Karen—Spiritual Interweave

Karen became stuck and began looping while processing a fight between her parents. Her NC: "It's my fault." PC: "It's not my fault; they both had big problems," with a VOC of 3. Karen reported emotions of guilt, sadness, and shame, felt in her heart, stomach, and head, and gave a rating of 7–8 on the Subjective Units of Disturbance Scale (SUDS). Here, the Spiritual Interweave begins as a variant of Kiessling's (2005) Resource Interweave.

Therapist: *Do you remember that image, that sense, of being held by Jesus, in the cloud?*

Karen: Yes.

Therapist: *Good. Can you bring up that experience now, and stay present with it, hearing the sounds around you?*

Karen: Yes.

Therapist: *Good.* (BLS) *If you were being held by Jesus right now, what might he be saying to you?*

Karen: He'd tell me I'm okay, that it *is* very sad, and that it's not my fault. (Cries.)

Therapist: *Go with that . . .* (BLS)

Karen: It wasn't my fault then, and it isn't my fault now, either.

Therapist: *Go with that . . .* (BLS)

The Spiritual Interweave brings the positive, intrinsic meaning of Karen's religious experience into her processing, thereby helping Karen move through a transformational arc from her NC to her PC. The Spiritual Interweave also gives Karen the beginnings of an emergent spiritual experience within her processing.

ISSUES

Targets and Blocking Beliefs

Sometimes a client will raise a religious issue as a presenting problem, or a religious issue emerges in the form of a blocking belief. Examples of such issues include:

- Fear of going to hell
- Inability to believe that God (or the divine, etc.) cares about the client
- Distress from having done something contrary to the doctrines of the client's faith tradition

With Boisen (1945) and the pastoral theological tradition, I view such spiritually oriented issues as existential crises, disorienting to the client. These issues often represent a conflict between the client's explicitly articulated and functionally operative religio-spiritual beliefs. Furthermore, they may be reflective of developmental gaps, attachment problems, and/or prior life trauma for which an earlier coping strategy—that happened to be religious—no longer works.

Steele (2004) noted the correlation of unitive religious traditions as expressions of the human need for connection, and the correlation of devotion to particular religious and spiritual figures as expressive of attachment needs. Therefore, when a presenting issue is religious in nature, the fourth ear listens carefully for areas of possible religio-spiritual disconnect or discrepancy in the client's story. The active processing phases of the Standard Protocol are then followed, in the spiritually safe, sacred space of the therapeutic relationship.

Proceed as you would with any other target or blocking belief. Trust your clients to provide what will be the most accurate psycho-spiritual-emotional language to express the issues at hand. Trust the EMDR process to help clients resolve any distress in the intersection of faith and life, and to emerge with a fresh perspective and frame for the religio-spiritual dimensions of their lives.

Religious Trauma

When some aspect of their religio-spiritual experience itself has wounded them, clients will present with religiously based trauma. Common precipitants are family problems, sexual orientation, and behaviors that become known to and are viewed negatively by others in the client's religious tradition, resulting in feelings of alienation, guilt, and shame. Not infrequently such persons become excluded from the organization's gatherings and/or its rituals and public expressions of piety (worship services or other sacred rites). Sexual abuse by the leadership of religious organizations, whether clergy, consecrated, or from the general membership, leaves layers of trauma, sometimes compounded by the manner in which the religious organization responds to the victim. As noted earlier, clients may experience trauma from being part of a religious minority in the locale in which they were raised or currently reside.

Less known, rarely acknowledged, but occurring frequently: Clients can experience trauma from interpersonal interactions common to all organizations, including those that are religious. Painful experiences include the organization's failure to provide support to an individual or family at a time of illness, death, or other crisis. Conversely, a client might experience the organization, its leaders, and/or fellow members as intrusive and violating of their emotional, physical, or financial boundaries. Religious trauma occurs for some upon learning that they have been removed from a membership roster, usually because of particular forms of nonparticipation. In these situations (usually not disclosed without an intentional religio-spiritual assessment in History Taking and beyond), clients typically present with anger, grief, and a wrenching sense of alienation. The fourth ear needs to listen to discern the degree to which these feelings may also extend to God, the divine, the universe—to whoever and whatever (Jenson, 1973) is the object of the client's ultimate concern (Tillich, 1957) or loyalty (Boisen, 1945).

In these cases, insofar as a client's religio-spiritual experience has filled developmental needs for attachment and intersubjective connection, there is significant potential for religious trauma to uncover and expose other, earlier life trauma. EMDR theory calls for locating the early-life touchstone(s) and processing from there. For many clients this standard approach is effective and healing.

For some clients, the presence of religious trauma reveals a complex web of interconnected and mutually reinforcing NCs and experiences, high SUDS levels, with PCs hard, if not impossible, for the client to identify. When this happens, processing, if the client gets that far, becomes mired in a knotted, looping chain among the various NCs and, in my experience, is impervious to the standard EMDR interventions and interweaves. Even an expansion of the concept of a blocking belief to a "blocking web of beliefs" may fail to untangle it.

What I observe is a time-transcendence of religious experience and trauma that confounds EMDR's linear, three-pronged (past, present, future) approach. In EMDR we work from the premise that "the past is present." With complex religious trauma, the tenses blur together, and associations tend to jump "horizontally" across channels and "time zones," thereby eluding resolution. If and when this happens, do not expect processing to be simple, "clean," or uncomplicated. But do remember, "It all connects." Processing strategies to consider include:

- Begin with the religious trauma, informed by your fourth-ear listening.
- Remain alert to developmental gaps, past trauma, and/or ego states that may be represented in the client's religious experience and/or trauma.
- Allow for non-time-sequential, parallel targets and processing to emerge concurrently or alternating with the original target.

- Develop comfort and clinical agility in moving among and between these processes, sometimes within the same session.
- Know that it may take time for SUDS levels to reach 0 across all the targets.

And most important:

- Trust your client's inner healing wisdom and the EMDR protocol as the knotted web begins to unravel and reweave itself into a new pattern of intrinsic spirituality and empowered religious choice.

To the best of my knowledge, EMDR has never "taken spirituality or faith away." On the contrary, EMDR tends to broaden clients' perspectives on religion, spirituality, and faith, and deepen their relationship with them (Jacobi, 2005; Parnell, 1996).

Traumatic "Loss of Faith"

Whatever its source, trauma disrupts systems of meaning. Pauline Boss (2006) wrote eloquently on the dynamics of meaning-loss, and the reader is referred to her work for an in-depth treatment of these dynamics.

For religious and spiritually attuned clients, this disruption of meaning potentially reaches to the core of their being and their faith, bringing forth a diversity of religio-spiritual "symptoms" including rage, despondency, a searching for meaning-in-suffering, and sometimes a rejection of their pretrauma religio-spiritual practice and/or beliefs. For some of these clients, loss of faith represents a trauma deeper and more painful than the event that precipitated it. For them, the therapist's unconditional acceptance is paramount. This is not a time for reassurance; it is, rather, a time for fourth-ear listening through the un-sense and the non-sense, through the disorientation and dislocations of the client's trauma and spiritual story. For the client, it is a time of experiential crisis, seemingly unending grief, and invisible loss, internally, and often externally, in the loss of a religio-spiritual community.

In the context of EMDR, traumatic spiritual disruption and loss of faith may present in the religio-spiritual assessment as a primary issue of concern. Or, it may appear within the "picture representing the worst part" (F. Shapiro, 2001) of the issue being addressed. However religio-spiritual trauma emerges, it is always the client's experience and needs to be honored as a part of who this client is, now. Sometimes the client will want to address loss of faith directly, sometimes not, and sometimes both. Again, trust the client's inner healing wisdom and the purposive nature of grief. And trust the EMDR process within the spiritually safe, sacred space of the therapeutic relationship. Remember, it is not the purpose of EMDR to "bring faith back the way it was before." Yet resolution of the precipitating trauma typically includes increased resilience for living in the present, "where healing, hope and life ultimately have the last word" (Jacobi, 2005, p. 3).

EXPERIENCES

In the case example of Karen earlier in the chapter, we saw a Spiritual Interweave disengage looping, restart processing, and initiate an emergent spiritual experience in the session. This is a common phenomenon. As Parnell (1996) observed, clients often experience a new sense of inner, intrinsic spirituality emerge as resolution of trauma occurs and the VOC moves to "7" during the Installation phase. This phenomenon sometimes happens even for clients who have not previously considered themselves religious or spiritually attuned, though they are likely to use different language and images to describe their experience. Finally, when the Body Scan feels clear to the client, returning to the Spirituality Resource, which may happen spontaneously, helps the client further integrate the EMDR-facilitated healing with the positive qualities and characteristics of her/his spirituality and its felt sense in the here and now:

Therapist: *As you bring up those words [the PC], and notice the calmness in your body, let the place in your body "come to you" where you experience [the Spirituality Resource], now . . .*
Client: Right here, in my heart.
Therapist: *Go with that . . .* (BLS) *What color (sound, shape, texture) associates with that now?*
Client: A light blue.
Therapist: *Go with that . . .* (BLS)

This is a powerful moment in the Closure phase. Time may seem to stand still, and immanence and transcendence to coalesce in a unitive experience for the client, yet one that remains grounded in the present.

Religious clients may describe the moment as feeling mystical, or deeply spiritual, and speak of their changed perspective on the old trauma using words such as liberation, freedom, or feeling alive again (or for the first time ever).

Awe-inspiring as such moments are, for client and often therapist alike, this chapter would be incomplete without addressing the spontaneous spiritual experiences that some clients have while processing. Clients themselves are often stunned by them, or say that "something weird is happening . . ." Clinicians are often trained to interpret such moments as pathological. And yet: (a) something happens; and (b) what happens usually has a health-promoting meaning to the client. Examples of experiences that clients have reported to me include:

- Feeling fully present and simultaneously, fully "one" with all that is;
- Having a felt sense of water washing away the distress and negative feelings associated with a trauma;
- Watching the words of the NC being carried away by angels;
- A sense of presence-in-the-room of someone who has died;
- A visitation of the Blessed Mother (Mary).

Each of these examples has a quality of mystical experience to it. What is important for the EMDR therapist to know is that these experiences are real to the clients, if not to us. I did not see or otherwise experience the Blessed Mother, but my client most certainly did. My role was to witness her experience, in the moment, and to help her identify its meaning for her.

There may be various neurophysiological explanations for these events, but in EMDR, the crucial issue is the meaning of the event to the client. Moreover, it is natural, even expectable, for religious images and/or spiritually understood experiences to emerge in the processing flow of a religious or spiritually attuned client. The presence of images and experiences alone is not inherently pathological. On the contrary, when the client's spiritually understood experience is received as presented and honored for what it is, the differentiating assessment of "meaning-to-client" readily appears.

When spontaneous spiritual experiences happen during processing, clients may initially appear to be dissociated. Visual tracking often stops, replaced by a fixed gaze, but not a blank stare. Clients may appear to be looking "at" something. Alternatively, clients may close their eyes and "go deeply inside," yet remain fully present and able to report "what's happening now." When this occurs, the appropriate therapeutic response is in the form of an interweave.

Case Example #1

Client: I'm watching these angels flying away with those words [the NC]-like typed letters, held by the angels . . .

Therapist: *Go with that . . .* (BLS)

Client: They're flying away . . . they're going . . . they're gone. . . . Wow, that was weird.

The "Meaning Interweave":

Therapist: *What does that experience mean to you now?*

Client: Those words are gone. They're not me. That's not who I am, or what I am. . . . Wow!

Therapist: *Go with that . . .* (BLS) *What's happening now?*

Client: Nothing. . . . It's calm.

Therapist: *Just notice that . . .* (BLS) *. . . And now?*

Client: Still calm.

The therapist then returns to target and checks the SUDS, returning to the Standard Protocol procedures from there.

Case Example #2

The client suddenly looked startled, and fixed her gaze "at" something I didn't see, her jaw dropping.

Therapist: *What's happening?*

Client: I don't know . . . (short gasp) . . . it's the Blessed Mother! (Client's voice has a hint of the accent of her grandparents' country of origin.) She's here—oh my gosh—I don't see her face, but she's here.

Therapist: (Maintains silent attentiveness, occasionally asking *"What's happening now?"* until the apparent vision has faded.)

Client: What was that? Did that really happen?

Therapist: *What do you think?*

Client: It was like—it was a visitation! Whoa!

The "Meaning Interweave":

Therapist: *What does it mean to you, right now?*
Client: That no matter what happens with [the issue], I'm not alone. I'm really not alone. Life can be hard and painful sometimes, but I can get through it.
Therapist: *Go with that . . .* (BLS) (Therapist notes the possibility of a spontaneously emerging PC, but first returns to target, to see what comes up, check SUDS, and proceeds accordingly.)

Should you start to feel anxious in the face of your clients' spiritual experiences:

- Breathe!
- Give yourself some BLS in the session, by tapping your toes or your feet while your clients are processing.
- Remember that your clients may be at least as surprised as you are by what is taking place.

Remember, also, that whatever it is that "happens" ultimately has done so from within your clients' inner wisdom and is in service of their deepest integrative healing.

SUMMARY

I encourage EMDR therapists to develop familiarity and comfort with their own religio-spiritual history and practice, and its current meaning to them; to cultivate a "fourth ear" for attunement to the explicit and implicit spiritual themes, issues, and experiences of their clients; and to utilize spiritually sensitive and creative interventions throughout the Standard Protocol.

RESOURCES

Dowd, E. T., & Nielsen, S. L. (Eds.). (2006). *The psychologies in religion: Working with the religious client.* New York: Springer.

Magida, A. J. (Ed.). (1996). *How to be a perfect stranger: A guide to etiquette in other people's religious ceremonies.* Woodstock, VT: Jewish Lights.

O'Donnell, K. (2007). *Inside world religions: An illustrated guide.* Minneapolis, MN: Fortress Press in cooperation with LionHudson, Oxford.

Pinkney, A. M., & Souweine, I. (2005). World religions. In M. Blanchard (Series Ed.), *Spark Charts.* New York: SparkNotes LLC, Barnes & Noble Publishing.

REFERENCES

Ambuel, B. (2005). *Taking a spiritual history. Fast Facts and Concepts #19* (2nd ed.). End-of-Life Palliative Education Resource Center. Retrieved April 2, 2008, from www.eperc.mcw.edu

American Psychological Association. (2002). *Ethical principles of psychologists and code of conduct.* Retrieved April 2, 2008, from http://www.apa.org/ethics/code2002.html

Armstrong, K. (1993). *A history of God.* New York: Ballantine Books.

Boisen, A. T. (1945). *Religion in crisis and custom: A sociological and psychological study.* New York: Harper & Brothers.

Boisen, A. T. (1960). *Out of the depths: An autobiographical study of mental disorder and religious experience.* New York: Harper & Brothers.

Boss, P. (2006). *Loss, trauma, and resilience: Therapeutic work with ambiguous loss.* New York: Norton.

Botkin, A. L., with Hogan, R. C. (2005). *Induced after death communication: A new therapy for healing grief and trauma.* Charlottesville, VA: Hampton Roads.

Dworkin, M. (2005). *EMDR and the relational imperative: The therapeutic relationship in EMDR treatment.* New York: Routledge.

Dykstra, R. C. (2006). Introduction. In R. C. Dykstra (Ed.), *Images of pastoral care: Classic readings* (pp. 1–21). St. Louis, MO: Chalice.

Fitchett, G. (1993). *Assessing spiritual needs: A guide for caregivers.* Minneapolis, MN: Augsburg Fortress.

Grand, D. (1999). *Defining and re-defining EMDR* (Rev. ed.). Bellmore, NY: BioLateral Books.

Grand, D. (2003). *Natural flow EMDR.* Workshop presented in New York, NY.

Jacobi, M. (2005). A therapist's reflections on the use of EMDR in providing services to people affected by 9/11/01. *Lutheran Counseling Center's mental health ministry outreach response in the aftermath of September 11, 2001: A research analysis and summary reports* (Section 10, pp. 1–3). Mineola, NY: Lutheran Counseling Center.

Jenson, R. W. (1973). *Story and promise.* Philadelphia: Fortress.

Kiessling, R. (2005). Integrating resource development strategies into your EMDR practice. In R. Shapiro (Ed.), *EMDR Solutions: Pathways to healing* (pp. 57–87). New York: Norton.

Kitchur, M. (2005). The strategic developmental model for EMDR. In R. Shapiro (Ed.), *EMDR solutions: Pathways to healing* (pp. 8–56). New York: Norton.

Leas, R. (n.d.). *The ACPE History Network presents the biography of Anton Theophilus Boisen.* Retrieved February 28, 2008, from http://www.acpe.edu/networks/boisen_bio.htm

Lipke, H. J. (2000). *EMDR and psychotherapy integration: Theoretical and clinical suggestions with focus on traumatic stress.* Boca Raton, FL: CRC Press.

National Association of Social Workers. (1999). *Code of ethics.* Retrieved April 2, 2008, from http://www.socialworkers.org/pubs/code/code.asp

New Revised Standard Version Bible. (1989). Division of Christian Education of the National Council of the Churches of Christ in the United States of America. In B. M. Metzger & R. E. Murphy (Eds.), *The new Oxford annotated Bible (1991).* New York: Oxford University Press.

Parnell, L. (1996). EMDR and spiritual unfoldment. *Journal of Transpersonal Psychology, 28*(2), 129–153. Retrieved April 21, 2008, from http://www.emdrinfo.com/pdfs/emdr-spiritual-unfolding.pdf

Parnell, L. (1997). *Transforming trauma: EMDR.* New York: Norton.

Shapiro, F. (2001). *Eye movement desensitization and reprocessing: Basic principles, protocols, and procedures* (2nd ed.). New York: Guilford Press.

Silver, S. M., & Rogers, S. (2002). *Light in the heart of darkness: EMDR and the treatment of war and terrorism survivors.* New York: Norton.

Steele, A. (2004). *Developing a secure self: An approach to working with attachment in adults for EMDR therapists* (2nd ed.). Gabriola Island, BC: Author.

Tillich, P. (1957). *Dynamics of faith.* New York: Harper Colophon Books.

West, W. (2000). *Psychotherapy and spirituality: Crossing the line between therapy and religion.* London: Sage.

EMDR Glossary

Adaptive Information Processing Model: the theoretical model of EMDR that refers to the innate tendency of the brain to process disturbing life experiences to an adaptive resolution.

Blocking Belief: a cognition that stops EMDR processing, for example, "I'll never get over this."

BLS: Dual Attention Stimulus, Bilateral Stimulation. As EMDR has responded to research, the name of the eye movement, tapping, and audio tones have changed at least three times. First we had "Eye Movements." Now Bilateral Stimulation or Dual Attention Stimulus best describes the effect of the eye movements or other stimulation that accompanies processing in EMDR.

Body Scan: Phase Six of the Standard Protocol, in which, after the bulk of the processing is complete, clients are asked to think about the disturbing event and notice their bodily sensations. Any sensations are targeted with BLS.

Desensitization: Phase Four of the Standard Protocol, in which BLS is used to process the distressing event.

Future Template: Inoculate against future distress. Imagine triggers. Imagine performing well. "What skills behaviors and information do I need for optimal functioning in the future?" The Future Template is part of EMDR's Three-Pronged Protocol, in which attention is brought to the Past, the Present, and the Future components of a particular processing target.

Looping: A form of blocked response in which the client is cycling through the same sensations, emotions, images, or thoughts, rather than processing them through to an adaptive resolution.

Negative Cognition (NC): The old, currently illogical, thought about self that is connected to a disturbing event.

Positive Cognition (PC): The currently true thought about self that clients strive for in EMDR processing. PCs are measured with the seven-point Validity of Cognition Scale (VOC).

Resource Development/Resource Installation (RDI): A Preparation Phase procedure of front-loading remembered or imaginary positive strengths, experiences, attributes, or (less often) external support. RDI is used for clients who cannot tolerate regular EMDR processing, and is not usually necessary for clients with good affect tolerance.

Safe Place/Calm Place/Healing Place: Introduced in the Preparation Phase, the imaginary Safe Place is used as a resting place during prolonged reprocessing, a method of reducing distress at the end of an incomplete session, and a self-care method between sessions.

Standard Protocol:
- *Phase One: Client History* includes client readiness, client safety factors, and dissociation screening.
- *Phase Two: Preparation* includes creating a bond with the client, setting expectations, creating a Safe Place, and testing the Eye Movements or Dual Attention Stimulus.
- *Phase Three: Assessment* includes selecting the picture or disturbing event, identifying the Negative Cognition (NC), developing a Positive Cognition (PC), rating the VOC (or VoC), naming the emotion, estimating the Subjective Units of Disturbance (SUD or SUDS), and identifying Body Sensations.
- *Phase Four: Desensitization* includes reprocessing the memory, using BLS.
- *Phase Five: Installing the Positive Cognition* is done while holding the memory in mind.

- *Phase Six: Body Scan* involves searching for any bodily disturbance.
- *Phase Seven: Closure* includes homework, expectations, and, if needed, bringing the client to a state of emotional equilibrium.
- *Phase Eight: Reevaluation* includes checking in at the next session to see if the client requires new processing for associated material.

SUD/SUDS: Subjective Units of Disturbance Scale, a 0–10 scale that measures the intensity of negative affect.

VOC: Validity of Cognition Scale, a subjective 1–7 scale that measures the believability of a suggested PC.

Index

Leeds, A., 22, 29, 103, 125, 139, 155, 169, 211, 298, 363, 424, 451
le Grange, D., 134
Lendl, J., 221, 231
Level of Urge to Avoid (LOUA), 55
Levine, P., 124, 223, 351
Lidov, C., 183
life issue, performance, 225–226
life vs. traumatic events, bulimia, 154–155
light regulation, depression, 26
Lightstone, J., 206
    treating binge-eating and bulimia, 204–216
Linehan, M., 126
Liotti, G., 51, 130
Lipke, H. J., 474
Lipton, B., 294
listening, pastoral theology, 474–475
Llinas, R., 349
Lock, J., 134
Loewenstein, R. J., 362
looping, 496
loss of faith trauma, 488–489
love, strength, 246
Lovell, C., 126
Lovett, J., 313, 322
Lynn, B., 292
Lyytinen, H., 349

McCreery, J., 15
MacCulloch, M. J., 341
MacCulloch, S., 341
McFarlane, A., 204, 290, 340, 347
McGee, J., 175
McKelvey, A. M., 242, 262
MacLean, P. D., 346
McManamy, J., 25
McShane, J., 110
Major Depression Inventory (MDI), assessment, 16–17
Malcolm, P. B., 459
mania, bipolar disorder, 43–45
marijuana, depression, 25–26
Marmar, C., 340, 390, 442
Marques, J. K., 470
Marshall, L. E., 459
Marshall, W. L., 459, 469
Massiah, E., 389
Maxfield, L., 185
Mayo Clinic staff, 11
meaning, needs inventory, 278
medically based trauma, 415–416
    adolescence/sexual health exams, 418–419

aging and body image, 419–420
birth, 416–417
cancer, 424–428
case study for surgical trauma, 420–422
heart attacks, 423–424
heart surgery, 422–423
illness-related relational trauma, 430–432
infancy, 417–418
in utero, 416
Resource Installation (RDI), 424–425
secondary trauma in family, friends, and health care professionals, 432–433
sexually transmitted diseases, 428–430
strokes, 424
surgery, 420–423
targets, 425–428
treating, 3–4
medical providers, depression, 26–27
medications, bipolar clients, 41–43
Mellody, P., 100
Menard, W., 166
Mendelson, M., 16, 442
MentorCoach, 263
Metzler, T. J., 340
micromovements, somatic therapy, 358–359
Miller, A., 91
Miller, W., 42
Minnesota Starvation Experiment, 111
Minton, K., 11, 91, 141, 208, 339, 342, 343, 371, 374
Misiri, S., 438
Mitchell, S., 243
Mock, J., 16, 442
moderate depression, case example, 28–33
modulation model, 143, 342, 343
mood disorders, relationships, 45–46
Motivational Interviewing techniques, bipolar disorder, 42
Moulden, H. M., 459
multiple chemical sensitivity (MCS), 448–449
    one-session cure, 449–451
    opinions, 448
    ten-sessions, 451–455
    treatment plan, 449
Murphy, P., 110
Murray, W. H., 271
myths, eating order, 159